Understanding Laboratory and Diagnostic Tests

D0022390

Understanding Laboratory and Diagnostic Tests

Delmar's Health Information Management Series

Marie A. Moisio, MA, RRA

Elmer W. Moisio, PhD, RN

DELMAR
CENGAGE Learning·

Australia • Brazil • Japan • Korea • Mexico • Singapore • Spain • United Kingdom • United States

DELMAR
CENGAGE Learning

Understanding Laboratory and Diagnostic Tests: Delmar's Health Information Management Series
Marie A. Moisio, Elmer W. Moisio

Publisher: Susan Simpfenderfer

Acquisitions Editor: Marlene Pratt

Developmental Editor: Jill Rembetski

Project Editor: William Trudell

Art and Design Coordinator: Carol D. Keohane

Production Coordinator: James Zayicek

Marketing Mangager: Darryl L. Caron

Cover Design: Brucie Rosch

© 1998 Delmar, Cengage Learning

ALL RIGHTS RESERVED. No part of this work covered by the copyright herein may be reproduced, transmitted, stored or used in any form or by any means graphic, electronic, or mechanical, including but not limited to photocopying, recording, scanning, digitizing, taping, Web distribution, information networks, or information storage and retrieval systems, except as permitted under Section 107 or 108 of the 1976 United States Copyright Act, without the prior written permission of the publisher.

For product information and technology assistance, contact us at
Cengage Learning Customer & Sales Support, 1-800-354-9706
For permission to use material from this text or product, submit all requests online at **www.cengage.com/permissions**
Further permissions questions can be emailed to
permissionrequest@cengage.com

Library of Congress Control Number: 97-13352

ISBN-13: 978-0-8273-7854-4

ISBN-10: 0-8273-7854-8

Delmar
Executive Woods
5 Maxwell Drive
Clifton Park, NY 12065
USA

Cengage Learning is a leading provider of customized learning solutions with office locations around the globe, including Singapore, the United Kingdom, Australia, Mexico, Brazil, and Japan. Locate your local office at **international.cengage.com/region**

Cengage Learning products are represented in Canada by Nelson Education, Ltd.

For your lifelong learning solutions, visit **www.cengage.com/delmar**

Visit our corporate website at **www.cengage.com**

Notice to the Reader
Publisher does not warrant or guarantee any of the products described herein or perform any independent analysis in connection with any of the product information contained herein. Publisher does not assume, and expressly disclaims, any obligation to obtain and include information other than that provided to it by the manufacturer. The reader is expressly warned to consider and adopt all safety precautions that might be indicated by the activities described herein and to avoid all potential hazards. By following the instructions contained herein, the reader willingly assumes all risks in connection with such instructions. The publisher makes no representations or warranties of any kind, including but not limited to, the warranties of fitness for particular purpose or merchantability, nor are any such representations implied with respect to the material set forth herein, and the publisher takes no responsibility with respect to such material. The publisher shall not be liable for any special, consequential, or exemplary damages resulting, in whole or part, from the readers' use of, or reliance upon, this material.

Printed in the United States of America
10 11 12 13 14   19 18 17 16 15

Contents

Preface

Understanding Laboratory and Diagnostic Tests is written and designed to meet the needs of allied health students and professionals who desire a basic understanding of clinical laboratory and diagnostic tests. This textbook presents information about commonly performed tests. The information includes the type of test, that is, blood chemistry, radiographic, urine; the body system, organ, or tissue involved in the test; the diagnostic significance of the test; the purpose or indications for the test; the risks, if any, associated with the test; and a *brief* description of how the test is performed.

The idea for this textbook is a result of the authors' experience teaching this type of material to students enrolled in various allied health educational programs. This first edition incorporates classroom handouts, lectures, study guides, and critical thinking exercises that have been developed by the authors and successfully used by students.

Understanding Laboratory and Diagnostic Tests has been carefully designed for use in educating personnel for health careers such as health information technology and management, medical coder, medical transcriptionist, health unit coordinator, and nursing. Information is presented using appropriate medical and health terminology so that students at all levels become familiar with the language of the health care environment.

The text is divided into two sections: Laboratory Tests and Diagnostic Tests. The organization of the text provides maximum flexibility for the instructor. Chapters can be presented in the order that best suits instructor preference and student need.

Understanding Laboratory and Diagnostic Tests includes several features that are designed to enhance teaching and learning. These features include:

- Learning objectives, which are intended to provide focus to the student
- Key terms, abbreviations, and acronyms that represent terminology that is particularly unique to the chapter
- Tables and figures that reinforce and summarize information about individual tests or groups of tests

- Chapter summaries that can be used for class discussion and review
- Chapter exercises that offer a variety of reinforcement activities
- Case studies that allow students to demonstrate critical thinking skills

In addition, appendixes such as the Alphabetical List of Tests and the List of Tests by System provide another way to locate information in the text. Glossaries of key terms, abbreviations, and acronyms are provided as quick references.

A comprehensive instructor's guide is available. The guide includes answers for all chapter exercises, quizzes for each chapter, and a sample teaching outline.

Acknowledgments

The authors would like to acknowledge the following consultants and reviewers:

Consultants

Donna Ayotte, BSN, R.N.
Radiological Nursing Supervisor
Marquette General Hospital
Marquette, Michigan

Jeannie Cottrell-Truax, R.T.(R), RVT, RDMS, RDCS
Director of Ultrasound
Marquette General Hospital
Marquette, Michigan

Kristine Gorsalitz, R.N.
Director of Nursing
Superior Endoscopy Center
Marquette, Michigan

John Howko, M.Ed., R.T.(R)
Director, School of Radiography
Marquette General Hospital
Marquette, Michigan

Andreas Koutouzos, CNMT, ARRT (N)
Director of Nuclear Medicine
Marquette General Hospital
Marquette, Michigan

Marsha E. Lucas, M.S., MT (ASCP)
Assistant Professor
Department of Clinical Laboratory Sciences
Northern Michigan University
Marquette, Michigan

Karin M. Stulz, M.A.E.
Instructor
Walker L. Cisler College of Business
Northern Michigan University
Marquette, Michigan

Reviewers

Paul Bell, MS, RRA, CTR
Assistant Professor
Health Information Management
School of Allied Health Sciences
East Carolina University
Greenville, NC

Sue Ellen Bice, MS, RRA
Health Services
Mohawk Valley Community College
Utica, NY

Suzanne Kuhl Davis
Medical Record Technology
Burlington County College
Pemberton, NJ

Shirley J. Higgin, Med, RRA
Allied Health
Spokane Community College
Spokane, WA

Margie Konik, RRA
Instructor
Health Information Technology
Chippewa Valley Technical College
Eau Claire, WI

Marjorie H. McNeil, MS, RRA
Assistant Professor
Health Information Management
School of Allied Health Sciences
Florida A & M University
Tallahassee, FL

Karen Melcher
Health Information Technology
Northeast Iowa Community College
Calmar, IA

Elaine Pont, CMA, CLT (NCA), CLA (ASCP)
Instructor
Morse School of Business
Hartford, CT

Connie Regener, MA, RRA
Business Science
Saddleback College
Mission Viejo, CA

Lou Ann Schraffenberger, RRA
Health Information Management
University of Illinois at Chicago
Chicago, IL

Jody Smith
Health Information Management
St. Louis University
St. Louis, MO

Introduction

Understanding Laboratory and Diagnostic Tests has been developed for allied health students who need a basic understanding of clinical laboratory and diagnostic tests. This "basic understanding" is defined as knowing the name of the test; what the test is used for; diseases, diagnoses, or disorders associated with the test; and the normal range or results of the test.

This textbook is different from other laboratory or diagnostic books because it *is* a textbook. Each chapter focuses on a category of laboratory or diagnostic tests, provides learning objectives, key terms, a discussion of commonly performed tests, and a variety of chapter exercises.

Understanding Laboratory and Diagnostic Tests is divided into Part I: Laboratory Tests, and Part II: Diagnostic Tests. The laboratory test section is organized according to clinical laboratory tests. These tests include various blood studies, urine and fecal tests, cerebrospinal fluid tests, other body fluid tests, and culture and sensitivity testing. The diagnostic section is organized according to test categories, such as ultrasound, nuclear medicine, radiography, endoscopy, and miscellaneous diagnostic tests.

Each chapter presents the following information about each test, as applicable:

- A description of the test, which includes the test name, why the test is performed, and a brief summary of how the test is performed
- The normal ranges for each test
- The variations from normal, which describe what happens when the specific test results fall outside the normal range
- Interfering circumstances, which are situations or conditions that interfere with accurate test results

The detail of each category of information will be determined by the complexity of the individual laboratory or diagnostic test.

This text was created as a result of the authors' experience teaching this type of material to students enrolled in various allied health educational programs. This first edition of *Understanding Laboratory and Diagnostic Tests* incorporates class handouts, lectures, and study guides that have been tested by actual students. Case studies are included at the end of the chapter to give students an opportunity to demonstrate a "working" knowledge of laboratory and diagnostic tests.

The tables, figures, and sample reports are included to reinforce material presented in the body of the text. You will note that some chapters have a review table early in the chapter, with more detailed information presented on subsequent pages. Lists of key words, abbreviations, and acronyms are provided to serve as a foundation to help you understand laboratory and diagnostic terminology.

Since test results are reported as metric measurements, some common metric terms are reviewed here. Gram is the metric term often used to denote mass or weight, meter is used to denote length, and liter indicates volume. There are a variety of prefixes that can be linked to gram, meter, and liter. Each metric prefix has a specific meaning. Metric prefixes commonly used in laboratory test results are kilo (1000), deci (.1), centi (.01), milli (.001), micro (.000001), and pico (.000000000001).

Combining a prefix with any one of the basic metric units identifies the amount, size, or weight of a given substance. For example, a kilogram (kg) is equal to 1000 (kilo) grams; a milligram (mg) is equal to .001 (one-thousandth) of a gram. Therefore, a substance that is measured in kilograms has more weight or mass than a substance measured in milligrams.

This same procedure can be applied to meter and liter. Since many substances found in the body are measured with prefixes such as milli, micro, and pico, it is apparent that we are indeed fortunate to have access to accurate laboratory results. A list of units of measurement and their meanings used in this text can be found on the inside front cover. It is worth a few minutes of your time to review those abbreviations.

Good luck as you begin your journey toward a better understanding of laboratory and diagnostic tests. The authors hope you learn as much from using this text as they did from writing it!

Laboratory Tests

Chapter 1

Blood Cell Tests

Key Terms, Abbreviations, and Acronyms

bands

basophilia

basophils, basos

complete blood count, CBC

differential white cell count, diff

eosinopenia

eosinophilia

eosinophils, eosinos

erythrocyte sedimentation rate, ESR, sed rate

hematocrit, Hct

hemoglobin, Hgb

hypochromic anemia

lymphocytopenia

lymphocytosis

lymphocytes, lymphs

mean corpuscular hemoglobin, MCH

mean corpuscular hemoglobin concentration, MCHC

mean corpuscular volume, MCV

mean platelet volume, MPV

monocytosis

monocytes, monos

neutropenia

neutrophilia

packed cell volume, PCV

platelet count

polymorphonuclear leukocytes, PMNs, polys

red blood cell count, RBC

red blood cell indices

segmented neutrophil, segs

stabs

white blood cell count, WBC

Learning Objectives

Upon completion of this chapter, the learner should be able to:

1. Identify the major components of blood and describe the the basic function of each component.
2. Compare the two types of blood collection procedures.
3. Identify and describe commonly performed blood cell tests.
4. Differentiate between red blood cell, white blood cell, and platelet tests.
5. Relate specific blood cell tests to appropriate diagnoses.

Introduction

A wide variety of blood tests are covered in this text, ranging from the basic blood cell tests that count and measure blood cell number and size, to the more complex and diagnostically significant blood chemistry tests in subsequent chapters. This chapter focuses on blood cell tests that identify variations in the number of blood cells, describes the function of certain blood cells, and identifies diagnoses related to variations in the number of blood cells. In addition, this chapter includes a brief review of blood composition and blood collection procedures.

Composition of Blood

The average adult has about 5 liters (5–6 quarts) of blood, which is divided into plasma and cells. Plasma, which accounts for about 3 liters, is the liquid portion of blood. The cells, which account for about 2 liters, are referred to as the formed elements or cellular component of blood.

Blood Cells

Blood cells are classified as erythrocytes (red blood cells), leukocytes (white blood cells), and thrombocytes, also called platelets. Each type of blood cell has specific functions. A brief description of the cell, its functions, and unique characteristics follows.

Erythrocytes. Erythrocytes are the most numerous cells, second in size, and easily identified by their unique biconcave disk shape. Red blood cells are formed in the red bone marrow, live about 120 days, and are removed from the blood stream by phagocytes, cells that are able to engulf and digest cellular debris. The spleen is the primary site of phagocytosis of aged red blood cells. The liver and bone marrow also play a role in removing or recycling red blood cells.

The main functions of erythrocytes are to carry oxygen to all parts of the body and to bring carbon dioxide to the lungs. The hemoglobin in the red blood cell is the carrier for oxygen and carbon dioxide. Therefore, in order for oxygen and carbon dioxide to move throughout the body, an adequate number of mature, functioning red blood cells must be available. The red blood cells must also contain the appropriate amount of hemoglobin. Additional red blood cell functions are discussed in relation to the laboratory tests covered in subsequent chapters.

Leukocytes. Leukocytes are the largest in size and represent the fewest number of blood cells. There are two major types of leukocytes: granulocytes and agranulocytes. Granulocytes, also called **polymorphonuclear leukocytes (PMNs)**, are the most numerous and have dark-staining granules in the cytoplasm. These cells are further classified as neutrophils, eosinophils, and basophils. Agranulocytes, also called mononuclear leukocytes, do not have dark-staining granules in the cytoplasm. Agranulocytes are further classified as lymphocytes or monocytes.

Leukocytes are chiefly responsible for fighting infection by identifying, engulfing, and destroying foreign organisms. They are active in the immune response by producing antibodies to foreign organisms. Additional information about the function of each type of leukocyte is discussed with the blood cell tests related to the specific type of leukocyte.

Thrombocytes. Thrombocytes, also called platelets, are essential for coagulation. Without an adequate number of functioning platelets, an individual would bleed to death. Additional information about the coagulation function of platelets is discussed in Chapter 4, Coagulation Studies. Figure 1-1 shows the various blood cells and emphasizes the difference in size and shape.

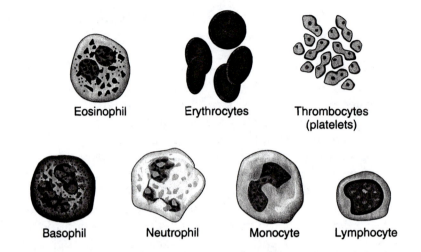

Figure 1-1.   Types of blood cells. Leukocytes include monocyte, lymphocyte, neutrophil, eosinophil, and basophil.

Plasma

Plasma, the fluid or liquid component of blood, is about 90% water. The remaining constituents of plasma include a variety of substances either dissolved or suspended in this watery medium: proteins; minerals such as calcium, potassium, and sodium; glucose; lipids; cholesterol; and waste products. Other components include antibodies, enzymes, and hormones.

The primary functions of plasma are to transport nutrients and other necessary chemicals to all body cells and to bring waste products to the body systems and organs that serve as waste disposal centers. The effects of variations in the level of plasma components are discussed in Chapters 2 and 3, Blood Chemistry Tests.

Blood Collection Procedures

There are two basic types of blood collection procedures: skin (dermal) puncture and venipuncture. Skin puncture is used to collect capillary blood. The puncture site for adults and children is usually the fingertip, and for infants the sites are the heel or the great toe. Venipuncture is necessary for most diagnostic tests. As the name implies, blood is withdrawn from a vein through the use of a needle and special collection tube or syringe.

Variations in the Number of Blood Cells

The blood cell tests in this chapter deal primarily with variations in the number of each type of blood cell. The results of these tests may not identify a specific disease, but they do provide valuable information about the patient's condition.

There are several general terms associated with the increase or decrease in the number of each type of blood cell. An overview of these terms is presented here. The diagnostic significance of this information is detailed in the discussion of each individual blood cell test.

Variations in the Number of Erythrocytes

Red blood cell disorders are classified as anemia, erythrocytosis, and erythremia. Anemia is defined as a reduction in the number of circulating red blood cells due to blood loss; a decreased production of red cells; an increased destruction of red blood cells; or a deficiency of hemoglobin. Erythrocytosis is defined as a slight increase in circulating red blood cells, while erythremia is an excessive increase in circulating red blood cells.

Variations in the number of circulating red blood cells can be caused by a variety of conditions. However, if the clinician suspects that there is a problem with the production of red blood cells, a bone marrow aspiration may be ordered. Bone marrow can be withdrawn from the posterior iliac crest, anterior iliac crest, and the sternum. Bone marrow aspiration is performed by a physician and requires written consent from the patient or the patient's legal representative.

Variations in the Number of Leukocytes

White blood cell disorders fall into one of two categories: leukocytosis, a slight increase in the number of white cells, or leukopenia (leukocytopenia), a decrease in the number of white cells. Since there are many types of white blood cells, the cell count of each specific type can indicate a variety of problems or diagnoses. Specific cell counts and their diagnostic significance are presented with each blood cell test.

Variations in the Number of Thrombocytes

Thrombocyte or platelet disorders are classified as thrombocytopenia, a decrease in the number of platelets, or thrombocytosis, a slight increase in the number of platelets. An excessive increase in the number of platelets is often referred to as **thrombocythemia**. Variations in the number of thrombocytes can be the result of bone marrow disorders. Thrombocytopenia is the most common cause of bleeding disorders. Thrombocytosis can be the result of a variety of conditions such as acute blood loss, following splenectomy, some anemias, and chronic diseases. Other causes of thrombocytosis are related to specific hematological disorders, such as autoimmune hemolytic anemia.

Variations in Blood Cell Structure and Function

Variations in the structure and function of blood cells may not only cause disease, but may also occur as a result of a disease process. In health, mature, functioning blood cells enter the bloodstream and are able to carry out the work of the blood. In disease, immature, poorly formed cells may be found in the blood and are often unable to carry out the work of the blood.

Blood Cell Tests

The blood cell tests presented in this chapter focus on cell number, size, or structure. Tests are presented by individual cell type and include diagnoses related to variations from normal.

Normal ranges of blood cell tests depend on a variety of factors including the age of the individual being tested and the individual laboratory standards where the tests are run. There are a variety of factors that may cause an abnormal test result. These factors are listed with the description of each test.

Complete Blood Count (CBC)

The **complete blood count (CBC)** is a laboratory test that identifies the number of red and white blood cells per cubic millimeter (mm^3) of blood. It is one of the most routinely performed blood tests and provides valuable information about the patient's state of health. The CBC measures and evaluates the cellular component of blood.

The tests included in the complete blood count are white blood cell tests, which include the white blood cell count and the differential white cell count; red blood cell tests, which include the red blood cell count, hematocrit, and hemoglobin count; red blood cell indices, which include the mean corpuscular volume, the mean corpuscular hemoglobin, and the mean corpuscular hemoglobin concentration; and the thrombocyte test, or platelet count. Figure 1-2 is a sample complete blood count report.

PATIENT NAME: Holly, Berry		
HEMATOLOGY I	NORMAL RANGE	RESULTS
Hemoglobin	12–16 g/dl	12.5
Hematocrit	37–47%	36.4
Erythrocytes	4.2–5.4	4.22
Leukocytes	5000–10000/mm3	7800/mm3
Neutrophils	55–70%	85% (H)*
Monocytes	2–8%	4%
Lymphocytes	20–40%	30%
Basophils	0.5–1%	0.7%
Eosinophils	1–4%	2%
Platelet Count	140,000–400,000	500,000 (H)*
MPV	2–4 m/diameter	1.3 m/diameter (L)*
ESR	0–20 mm/hr	10 mm/hr
*indicates abnormal: H = higher than normal and L = lower than normal.		

Figure 1-2.   Complete blood count report

White Blood Cell Tests

The **white blood cell count** and the **differential white blood cell count** identify the number and type of white blood cells present in the blood. Both tests provide useful diagnostic information.

White Blood Cell Count; Leukocyte Count (WBC)

The white blood cell count identifies the number of white blood cells in a specified volume of blood. The white cell count is then expressed as so many thousand white blood cells per cubic millimeter ($/mm^3$). Cell counting is usually accomplished by an automated cell counter, but can be done using a microscope with a special counting chamber.

Normal Range

Adults and Children	5000–10,000/mm^3
Children 2 years or younger	6200–17,000/mm^3
Newborns	9000–30,000/mm^3

Variations from Normal. An increase in the overall number of white blood cells is called leukocytosis. This is a very general term and can be the result of a wide variety of conditions such as infection, hemorrhage, trauma, malignancy, general hematologic problems, and leukemia. A decrease in the number of white blood cells is called leukopenia, and can occur for reasons that include viral infections, bone marrow disorders, spleen disorders, immune problems, AIDS, and nutritional deficiencies.

Interfering Circumstances. The white cell count is affected by the time of day (lower levels in the morning and a late afternoon peak), age, and gender. Smoking can cause up to a 30% increase in total white blood cells.

Differential White Blood Cell Count; Differential Leukocyte Count (diff)

The differential white blood cell count is used to identify the percentage of each type of white cell relative to the total number of leukocytes. The five types of leukocytes are neutrophils, eosinophils, basophils, monocytes, and lymphocytes. Each leukocyte has a unique function. Table 1-1 identifies each type of white cell and its function.

Since each of the white cells is unique, normal range and clinical implications of the increase or decrease in each type are presented individually.

Neutrophils

Neutrophils are the most numerous of the white cells and appear to be the body's first defense against bacterial infection and severe stress. During an

Table 1-1.   White Blood Cell Identification and Function

Cell	Function
Neutrophil	Combats bacterial infection (increase during stress)
Eosinophil	Prevents excessive spread of inflammation (responds to allergic disorders and parasitic infections)
Basophil	Responsible for allergy symptoms
Monocyte	Phagocytizes bacteria, viral material, and cellular debris
Lymphocyte	Combats acute viral and chronic bacterial infections; important role in the immune system

acute bacterial infection, neutrophils function as phagocytes. Neutrophils remain in the blood stream for approximately 7–10 hours.

Neutrophils are also known as segmented neutrophils (segs) or polymorphonuclear leukocytes (PMNs, polys). The names given to the neutrophils depend on the maturity of the cells and the appearance of the nucleus of the cells. Mature neutrophils are identified by their characteristic segmented or lobed nucleus and are called **segs**, or **segmented neutrophils**. Immature neutrophils are called **bands** or **stabs** because the nucleus is not segmented.

Normal Range (Adult)

Neutrophils   55–70% of all white cells

Variations from Normal. An increase in the number of circulating neutrophils is called **neutrophilia** and can be caused by various bacterial infections; inflammatory diseases such as rheumatic fever, rheumatoid arthritis, stress, tissue death or damage; and granulocytic leukemia. When reporting an increase in neutrophils, the terms "shift to the left" or "shift to the right" may be used. A shift to the left simply means that the increase in neutrophils is due to an increase in the number of immature neutrophils. A shift to the right, although rarely used, may indicate that abnormal or mature neutrophils predominate.

A decrease in the number of circulating neutrophils is called **neutropenia**, and can be caused by viral diseases and infections such as measles, mumps, rubella, hepatitis, and influenza. Bone marrow injury and anorexia nervosa can exhibit neutropenia.

Interfering Circumstances. Various treatments, such as radiation therapy and chemotherapy, carry the risk of decreasing neutrophils. Antibiotics, psychotropic medications, and some antidepressants can also play a role in neutropenia.

Lymphocytes (Lymphs)

Lymphocytes (lymphs) are an important part of the immune system and play an active role in combating acute viral and chronic bacterial infections. There are two types of lymphocytes, T cells and B cells. The differential count does not identify or enumerate the number of T and B cells.

Normal Range (Adult)

Lymphocytes   20–40% of all white cells

Variations from Normal. An increase in the number of lymphocytes is called **lymphocytosis** and is seen in a variety of diseases. Viral diseases such as rubella, measles, mumps, viral respiratory infections, atypical pneumonia, infectious hepatitis, and infectious mononucleosis exhibit lymphocytosis. Bacterial infections such as syphilis and pertussis can also cause lymphocytosis. Malignant causes of lymphocytosis are lymphocytic leukemia and lymphoma.

A decrease in lymphocytes is called **lymphocytopenia** and is seen primarily when the immune system is suppressed as in diseases such as AIDS and systemic lupus erythematosus.

Monocytes (Monos)

Monocytes (monos), although small in number, perform an important defense function in the body. These large cells are phagocytes and respond to bacteria in the same manner as neutrophils. Monocytes remain in circulation longer than neutrophils and phagocytize bacterial and cellular debris. Phagocytosis is the process of engulfing and destroying microorganisms and cellular debris. Monocytes also act as phagocytes in some chronic inflammatory diseases such as arthritis.

Normal Range

Monocytes   2–8% of all white cells

Variations from Normal. An increase in the number of monocytes is called **monocytosis** and is seen during infections such as tuberculosis and bacterial endocarditis. Diseases such as chronic ulcerative colitis, malaria, rheumatoid arthritis, and hemolytic anemia can exhibit an increase in the monocyte count. A decreased monocyte count is not usually identified with any specific disease processes.

Eosinophils and Basophils (Eosinos, Basos)

Eosinophils (eosinos) are minimally phagocytic, but play a role in the antigen-antibody response, in allergic reactions, in combating parasitic infections, and in the dissolution of blood clots. The main function of eosinophils seems to be to prevent the excessive spread of inflammation. **Basophils (basos)** play an important role in allergic reactions by releasing the histamine that is responsible for allergy symptoms.

Normal Range

Eosinophils	1–4% of all white cells
Basophils	0.5–1% of all white cells

Variations from Normal. An increase in eosinophils is called **eosinophilia** and is associated with allergy attacks, asthma, hay fever, and parasitic infections. Certain skin diseases, tuberculosis, Hodgkin's disease, and granulocytic leukemia result in an increase in eosinophils. A decrease in eosinophils is called **eosinopenia** and is associated with an increase in adrenal steroid production and acute bacterial or viral inflammation.

An increase in basophils is called **basophilia**, and is seen in myeloproliferative diseases such as polycythemia vera and chronic granulocytic leukemia. Chicken pox, small pox, chronic sinusitis, and ulcerative colitis may also be present with basophilia. Because the normal basophil count is small to begin with, a decrease in number may not be detected. However, prolonged steroid therapy, hormone imbalance, thyrotoxicosis, and severe allergic reactions often result in a basophil decrease.

Interfering Circumstances. As with other white blood cell counts, age, stress, time of day, and steroid therapy can interfere with eosinophil and basophil counts.

Red Blood Cell Tests

One of the major functions of erythrocytes is to carry oxygen to all parts of the body. In order to do this efficiently, there must be an adequate number of red blood cells and the red blood cells must contain an adequate supply of functioning hemoglobin. Erythrocyte tests include the **red blood cell count, hematocrit**, and **hemoglobin**. These tests are closely related and provide different ways to measure the adequacy of red blood cell production and function. Other common red blood cell tests include **red blood cell indices** and the **erythrocyte sedimentation rate**.

Red Blood Cell Count; Erythrocyte Count (RBC)

The red blood cell count identifies the number of red blood cells found in a cubic millimeter of blood (mm^3). The count is usually accomplished by an electronic or automated counting device.

Normal Range

Men	4.7–6.1 million/mm^3
Women	4.2–5.4 million/mm^3
Infants and Children	3.8–5.5 million/mm^3
Newborns	4.8–7.1 million/mm^3

Variations from Normal. A decrease in the number or function of red blood cells is called anemia. Factors that can cause anemia are decreased red blood cell production, increased red blood cell destruction, and blood loss. Certain diseases can also cause a decrease in red blood cells. Some of these diseases include Hodgkin's disease, leukemia, rheumatic fever, and diseases that affect the bone marrow where red blood cells are produced.

An increase in the number of red blood cells is called erythrocytosis, a slight increase, or erythremia, an excessive increase. Many factors can contribute to this increase, such as an overproduction of red blood cells or a decrease in the amount of blood plasma. Conditions such as dehydration, severe diarrhea, acute poisoning, and chronic lung disease can also cause an increase in the red blood cell count.

Interfering Circumstances. The results of the red blood cell count can be altered by several nondisease situations. These would include the posture or position of the patient when the blood was drawn, exercise, age, altitude, pregnancy, and various legal and illegal drugs.

Hematocrit (Hct); Packed Cell Volume (PCV)

The purpose of the hematocrit or **packed cell volume (PCV)** test is to determine the percentage of red blood cells in whole blood. The hematocrit is reported as a percentage because it is the proportion of red blood cells compared to the amount of plasma in whole blood.

The term "hematocrit" literally means to separate blood. A sample of blood is placed in a tube that contains an anticoagulant, which prevents clotting. The sample is mixed, and three distinct layers will separate out. Figure 1-3 shows these three layers.

The bottom layer represents the hematocrit value and is composed of red blood cells, approximately 45% of the total blood volume, with variations allowed for men and women. The middle layer is a thin, whitish layer called the buffy coat, approximately 1% of the blood volume, which is made

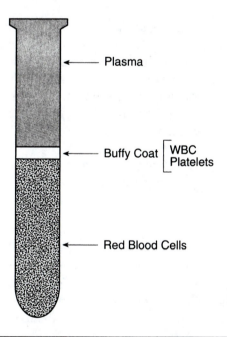

Figure 1-3.   The three layers of normal blood after settling in a tube.

up of white blood cells and platelets. The upper layer is the liquid plasma, which comprises the remainder of the total blood volume.

Normal Range

Men	42–52%
Women	37–47% (in pregnancy: >33%)
Children	30–42%
Newborns	44–64%

Variations from Normal. Since the hematocrit is the percentage of red blood cells in whole blood, a decrease in hematocrit values is an indication of some type of anemia. Therefore, anything that causes a decrease in the number of red blood cells will result in a decrease in the hematocrit. Blood loss, conditions where there is increased destruction of red blood cells, leukemia, and diseases that interfere with red blood cell production will exhibit a low hematocrit. It must also be noted that overhydration, or an increase in plasma volume for any reason, can result in a relative decreased hematocrit value.

An apparent increase in the hematocrit must be closely analyzed. Since the hematocrit is reported as a percentage of red blood cells to blood volume, any decrease in the volume of plasma would result in a mathematical increase in the hematocrit. Therefore, if the patient has lost blood plasma, the blood will be very concentrated and the hematocrit will be increased. When an increase in hematocrit is related to the increase in the actual number of red blood cells, erythrocytosis or polycythemia is the result.

Interfering Circumstances. Factors that can influence hematocrit results include age, pregnancy, gender, and living in high altitudes.

Hemoglobin (Hgb)

Hemoglobin is a protein-iron complex that is the main constituent of red blood cells. In fact, red blood cells contain approximately 90% hemoglobin. The primary functions of hemoglobin are to transport oxygen from the lungs to the cells and to carry carbon dioxide from the cells to the lungs to be expelled. The hemoglobin test is used to indirectly evaluate the oxygen-carrying capacity of the red blood cells. The hemoglobin count is also used to diagnose, evaluate, or assess the treatment of various types of anemia.

A normal red blood cell count does not automatically translate into a normal hemoglobin value. Abnormal production of any portion of hemoglobin could result in decreased levels of hemoglobin per red blood cells. Once a sample of blood is taken, the hemoglobin level is determined by automated electronic equipment. Generally, the hemoglobin value is approximately one-third of the hematocrit value. Therefore, a person with a 45% hematocrit would be expected to have approximately 15 grams of hemoglobin per deciliter of blood (15 g/dl).

Normal Range

Men	14–18 g/dl
Women	12–16 g/dl (in pregnancy: >11 g/dl)
Children	11–16 g/dl
Newborns	14–24 g/dl

Variations from Normal. Hemoglobin levels can exhibit temporary variations immediately after blood transfusions, hemorrhages, and burns. A decrease in the hemoglobin level can be found in various anemias. Other diseases and factors that result in a hemoglobin decrease include hyperthyroidism, cirrhosis of the liver, transfusions of incompatible blood, Hodgkin's disease, lymphoma, and reactions to various chemicals and drugs. Since iron is necessary for the production of hemoglobin, a decreased hemoglobin level may signal the need for blood iron tests. These tests are described in Chapter 3, Blood Chemistry Tests.

An increase in hemoglobin levels is found in any situation that results in an increased number of healthy red blood cells. Diseases associated with increased hemoglobin values are chronic obstructive pulmonary disease and congestive heart failure.

Interfering Circumstances. Factors that can affect hemoglobin results include pregnancy, altitude, age, gender, and excessive fluid intake. Various medications may cause an increase or decrease in hemoglobin levels.

Red Blood Cell Indices

The red blood cell indices are used to determine the size of the erythrocyte and the hemoglobin content of the red blood cells, and to identify specific types of anemia. The indices are not individual blood cell tests, but are the result of applying mathematical formulas to the hemoglobin value, hematocrit value, and red blood cell count. Each index has its own formula that is automatically computed as a part of the complete blood count.

Red blood cell indices include the **mean corpuscular volume**, which describes the average volume (size) of an individual red blood cell; the **mean corpuscular hemoglobin**, the average weight of the hemoglobin in an average red blood cell; and the **mean corpuscular hemoglobin concentration**, which is the average concentration or percentage of hemoglobin within each red blood cell.

Mean Corpuscular Volume (MCV)

The mean corpuscular volume describes the average size of an individual red blood cell in cubic microns (μm^3), and is calculated by multiplying the hematocrit percentage by 10, and then dividing that result by the red blood cell count. The size of red blood cells can have clinical significance in various types of anemia.

Normal Range

Adults and Children	80–95 μm^3
Newborns	96–108 μm^3

Variations from Normal. When there is a decrease in the mean corpuscular volume, the erythrocytes are microcytic, or smaller than normal. Microcytic red blood cells are seen in iron deficiency anemia, lead poisoning, and thalassemia.

An increase in the mean corpuscular volume indicates that the red blood cells are macrocytic, or larger than normal. Pernicious anemia is associated with macrocytic red blood cells.

When the mean corpuscular volume is within normal range, the red blood cells are normocytic, or of normal size. Aplastic, hemolytic, and temporary blood loss anemia are associated with red blood cells that are normal in size.

Mean Corpuscular Hemoglobin (MCH)

The mean corpuscular hemoglobin is the average weight of hemoglobin in an average red blood cell. This weight is calculated by multiplying the hemoglobin count by 10 and then dividing by the red blood cell count. The result is reported in picograms (pg). The mean corpuscular hemoglobin is adequate for diagnosing severely anemic patients, but is a non-specific result.

Normal Range

Adults and Children   27–31 pg
Newborns   32–38 pg

Variations from Normal. An increase in the mean corpuscular hemoglobin is seen in macrocytic anemia, while a decrease is associated with microcytic anemia.

Mean Corpuscular Hemoglobin Concentration (MCHC)

The mean corpuscular hemoglobin concentration measures the average concentration or percentage of hemoglobin within each red blood cell. The MCHC is calculated by dividing the hemoglobin value by the hematocrit value, and multiplying the result by 100. The mean corpuscular hemoglobin concentration is most valuable for classifying anemias.

Normal Range

Adults and Children   32–36%
Newborns   32–33%

Variations from Normal. A decrease in the mean corpuscular hemoglobin concentration indicates that the red blood cells contain less hemoglobin than normal and is classified as **hypochromic anemia**, which means the red blood cells lack color. Iron deficiency anemia is the most common type of hypochromic anemia.

An increase in the mean corpuscular hemoglobin concentration usually indicates **spherocytosis**. Spherocytosis is defined as an increase in the number of abnormal, spheric, red blood cells called spherocytes. Spherocytes have a smaller amount of membrane and a full complement of hemoglobin so the mean corpuscular hemoglobin concentration is elevated. Table 1-2 lists the classifications of anemia based on the red blood cell indices values.

Table 1-2.   Anemias and Associated Red Blood Cell Indices

Red Blood Cell Index	Iron Deficiency Anemia	Blood Loss Anemia	Pernicious Anemia
MCV	Decreased	Normal	Increased
MCH	Decreased	Normal	Variable
MCHC	Decreased	Normal	Variable
RBC size	Microcytic	Normocytic	Macrocytic
RBC color	Hypochromic	Normochromic	Not applicable

Erythrocyte Sedimentation Rate (ESR, Sed Rate)

The erythrocyte sedimentation rate is the rate at which red blood cells settle out of unclotted blood in an hour. The results are expressed as millimeters per hour (mm/hr). This is a nonspecific test because it does not identify any particular disease. In fact, the ESR can be normal in many disease processes.

The erythrocyte sedimentation rate is useful in determining the progress of inflammatory diseases, rheumatoid arthritis, rheumatic fever, and acute myocardial infarction. The speed at which the red blood cells fall to the bottom of the test tube corresponds to the degree of inflammation.

Normal Range

Men	<50 yrs	0–10 mm/hr
	>50 yrs	0–13 mm/hr
Women	<50 yrs	0–13 mm/hr
	>50 yrs	0–20 mm/hr
Children	0–10 mm/hr	

Variations from Normal. An increase in the sed rate is usually due to inflammation or tissue injury. When sed rates are greater than 100 mm/hr, likely causes, except in pregnancy, are infections, malignancies or collagen vascular diseases. A decrease in the sed rate is associated with polycythemia vera, sickle cell anemia, and a deficiency in the plasma protein fibrinogen.

Interfering Circumstances. Many factors can influence the erythrocyte sedimentation rate. Refrigerated blood samples, blood left standing for more than two hours before the test, menstruation, and pregnancy will cause a nonpathological increase in this test. Age and certain drug therapies may also cause variations in test results.

Platelet Count Tests

Platelets, also called thrombocytes, are the smallest cells in the blood. These cells do not have a nucleus, are round or oval, flattened, disk-shaped structures, and are necessary for coagulation. Some texts refer to platelets as fragments of cytoplasm.

Two tests that measure or count the number of platelets are the **platelet count**, which measures the number of platelets in the blood, and the **mean platelet volume (MPV)**, which provides information about platelet size. Platelet function tests are covered in Chapter 4, Coagulation Studies.

Platelet Count

A platelet count test often follows a decreased platelet count that was estimated from a peripheral blood smear. The platelet count is an important blood test because thrombocytopenia is the most common cause of bleeding diseases. This count is used to evaluate bleeding disorders due to liver disease, thrombocytopenia, and anticoagulant therapy. The test is also ordered for patients who have diseases associated with bone marrow problems, such as leukemia and aplastic anemia. The platelet count is expressed as the number of platelets per cubic millimeter (mm^3) of blood.

Normal Range

Platelets   150,000–400,000/mm^3

Variations from Normal. An abnormal increase in the number of platelets is called thrombocythemia or thrombocytosis. This increase is seen in diseases such as malignancies, early stages of chronic granulocytic leukemia, polycythemia vera, tuberculosis, chronic inflammatory disease, and chronic blood loss.

A decreased platelet count is known as thrombocytopenia and can result in significant bleeding problems. Diseases that decrease the platelet count include pernicious and aplastic anemias, and idiopathic thrombocytopenic purpura (ITP). A low platelet count is commonly seen in AIDS cases. Exposure to various chemicals and the toxic effects of many drugs can also lead to thrombocytopenia. Individuals who have serious platelet deficits often show signs or symptoms such as petechiae, bleeding from gums, nosebleeds, and gastrointestinal bleeding.

Interfering Circumstances. Platelet counts can show a normal increase at high altitudes, after strenuous exercise, and in the winter. A normal decrease occurs on the first day of an infant's life and before menstruation.

Mean Platelet Volume (MPV)

The mean platelet volume provides information about the relative size of platelets, which is calculated by a cell analyzer and compared to what is observed on a microscope slide. The diameter of the platelet is expressed in micrometers (μm). The MPV is a useful diagnostic tool for thrombocytopenic disorders.

The relative size of platelets varies with platelet production. When the overall platelet count drops, functioning bone marrow produces younger and larger platelets to compensate for the decreased number of platelets. This process results in an increased mean platelet volume. Lack of bone marrow function results in the decreased production of platelets, a diminished platelet size, and a decreased mean platelet volume.

Normal Range

Platelets   2–4 μm in diameter

Variations from Normal. An increase in the diameter of the platelets occurs in systemic lupus erythematosus, idiopathic thrombocytopenic purpura in remission, various anemias, myeloproliferative disorders, and a variety of chronic disease processes. A decrease in the size of platelets is associated with aplastic anemia, megaloblastic anemia, and hypersplenism.

Summary

- Blood is composed of plasma, the fluid portion of blood, and cells, which are the erythrocytes, leukocytes, and thrombocytes or platelets.

- Blood can be collected by way of skin puncture and venipuncture.
- The white blood cell count identifies the number of leukocytes in a cubic millimeter of blood.
- Five different types of leukocytes are measured in the differential white blood cell count.
- An increase in neutrophils can signify a variety of bacterial infections, stress, inflammatory diseases, or leukemia.
- An increase in lymphocytes is seen in many infectious diseases, acute viral and chronic bacterial diseases, lymphocytic leukemia, and lymphoma.
- Monocytes, the largest white blood cells, act as phagocytes for bacteria, viral material, and cellular debris.
- The main function of eosinophils appears to be to prevent the excessive spread of inflammation. These cells also respond to allergic disorders and parasitic infections.
- Basophils appear to be responsible for allergy symptoms.
- The red blood cell count identifies the number of erythrocytes in a cubic millimeter of blood.
- The hematocrit or packed cell volume identifies the percentage of red blood cells in the whole blood volume.
- The red blood cell count, hematocrit, and hemoglobin values are used to classify various anemias and evaluate anemia therapies.
- Red blood cell indices are mathematical calculations based on the red blood cell count, hematocrit, and hemoglobin values.
- Red blood cell indices include the mean corpuscular volume (MCV), the mean corpuscular hemoglobin (MCH), and the mean corpuscular hemoglobin concentration (MCHC), and are used to evaluate anemia.
- The mean corpuscular volume (MCV) describes the average volume (size) of an average red blood cell.
- The mean corpuscular hemoglobin (MCH) is the average weight of hemoglobin in each red blood cell.
- The mean corpuscular hemoglobin concentration (MCHC) identifies the percentage of hemoglobin in the red blood cells.
- The erythrocyte sedimentation rate (ESR, sed rate) measures how long it takes for red blood cells to settle out of unclotted blood.

- Factors that interfere with red blood cell tests include age, gender, pregnancy, and living at high altitudes.
- Platelets are the smallest cells in the blood and are necessary for coagulation.
- An increase in the number of platelets is called thrombocythemia or thrombocytosis.
- A decrease in the number of platelets is known as thrombocytopenia.
- Thrombocytopenia can result in significant bleeding problems.
- Platelet counts are helpful in evaluating and monitoring bleeding disorders.
- Aplastic anemia is associated with a decreased platelet count.

CHAPTER REVIEW

1. Identify the following blood cell tests:

a. Measures platelet size _____

b. Percentage of red blood cells in whole blood _____

c. Percentage of each type of white blood cell _____

d. Measures and evaluates the cellular component of blood _____

e. Percentage of hemoglobin within each red blood cell _____

f. Rate at which red blood cells settle out of unclotted blood _____

g. Average size of red blood cells _____

h. Measures the number of erythrocytes in blood _____

i. Important for assessing different anemias _____

j. Performed to evaluate bleeding disorders _____

2. Identify the white blood cells associated with the following:

   a. Combats bacterial infection by phagocytosis; increase during stress

   _____

   b. Combats acute viral and chronic bacterial infections; important part of the immune system

   _____

   c. Largest white blood cell; phagocyte in chronic inflammatory diseases; decreased levels not usually associated with disease

   _____

   d. Prevents excessive spread of inflammation; responds to allergic disorders; parasitic infections; dissolution of blood clots

   _____

   e. Responsible for allergy symptoms

   _____

3. Give an example of a disease associated with an *increase* and a *decrease* in the following blood cells or blood cell tests.

Test	Increase	Decrease
a. Leukocyte count	_____	_____
b. Lymphocytes	_____	_____
c. Eosinophils	_____	_____
d. Monocytes	_____	_____
e. Red blood cell count	_____	_____
f. Hemoglobin	_____	_____
g. Hematocrit	_____	_____
h. MCV	_____	_____
i. MCHC	_____	_____
j. Platelet count	_____	_____

Select the answer that best completes the following statements.

4. Blood loss anemia is associated with

   a. Macrocytic red blood cells   _____

   b. Normocytic red blood cells   _____

   c. Increased mean corpuscular hemoglobin _____

   d. Decreased red blood cell count   _____

5. Iron deficiency anemia is associated with

   a. Normocytic red blood cells   _____

   b. Normochromic red blood cells   _____

   c. Decreased mean corpuscular hemoglobin
      concentration   _____

   d. Increased mean corpuscular hemoglobin _____

6. Pernicious anemia is associated with

   a. Macrocytic red blood cells   _____

   b. Microcytic red blood cells   _____

   c. Decreased mean corpuscular hemoglobin
      concentration   _____

   d. Decreased mean corpuscular hemoglobin _____

7. List the four major components of blood and describe the function of each.

8. Compare the blood collection techniques of skin puncture and venipuncture. Under what circumstances would each procedure be used?

Case Studies

1. Jane Johnson is a 39-year-old female who saw her family physician because she was having unusually long and heavy menstrual periods and was fatigued. On reviewing her record you discover that the physician has documented the diagnosis of anemia without indicating a specific type. Identify the types of anemia discussed in the chapter. Discuss the blood tests that the physician could order to differentiate between the types of anemias. Describe the normal value range for each of the tests and the diagnostic significance of each test.

2. In the course of doing a routine physical exam on Leroy Brooks, a 48-year-old man, the physician has ordered a complete blood count. What blood tests are usually included in a complete blood count? Describe the components of blood being measured by the tests and the normal range for those components. Would the same normal range apply to Mr. Brooks if he were 8 years old? What possible value do these tests have for the physician in treating the patient?

3. Dr. Lewis, an oncologist, reviewed the blood test results of Jennifer Wallace, a 55-year-old cancer patient, and concluded that she is experiencing neutropenia. What is neutropenia? Identify the blood tests that could be used to identify neutropenia. Would you expect Ms. Wallace's test results to be higher or lower than the normal range? Discuss the possible conditions or illnesses that could cause neutropenia.

Challenge Activity

After reviewing the blood cell tests presented in this chapter, identify one or two diseases that are associated with an increase or decrease in several of the tests. Using the information you have gathered, write your own case study. Have another student analyze your case study and ask the student to add his or her comments.

Chapter 2

Blood Chemistry Tests (Part I)

Key Terms, Abbreviations, and Acronyms

bicarbonate, HCO_3^-

bilirubin

blood buffer system

blood urea nitrogen, BUN

calcium, Ca^+

Chem 12, Chem 24

chloride, Cl^-

cholesterol

C-peptide

creatinine

direct or conjugated bilirubin

fasting blood sugar test, FBS

glucagon

glucose tolerance test, GTT

high-density lipoprotein, HDL

indirect or unconjugated bilirubin

insulin

insulin-dependent diabetes
mellitus, IDDM

lipoprotein

low-density lipoprotein, LDL

lytes

magnesium, Mg^+

noninsulin-dependent diabetes
mellitus, NIDDM

phosphorus, P; phosphate, PO_4

postprandial blood sugar test,
PPBS, 2-hour PPBS

potassium, K^+

radioimmunoassay

SMAC 12

sodium, Na^+

standard oral glucose tolerance
test, SOGTT

total bilirubin

triglyceride

uric acid

very-low-density lipoprotein,
VLDL

Learning Objectives

Upon completion of this chapter, the learner should be able to:

1. Identify and define the blood chemistry tests presented in this chapter.
2. Organize blood chemistry tests according to defined categories.
3. Explain the effects of increased or decreased serum electrolyte levels.
4. Compare the diagnostic significance of various blood sugar and related tests.
5. Compare three types of lipoproteins and their influence on atherosclerotic diseases.
6. Assess the diagnostic importance of the metabolic end product tests in relation to liver and kidney function.

Introduction

Blood chemistry tests provide a means of measuring the blood levels of various body chemicals. The presence, absence, increase, or decrease in the levels of these chemicals are useful diagnostic tools. Few diseases exhibit an abnormality in a single chemistry test. Several blood chemistry tests must be performed in order to identify the abnormal patterns established for a particular disease. Modern clinical laboratories are equipped to conduct a variety of tests using a single blood sample.

All members of the health care industry quickly become familiar with abbreviations such as **SMAC 12, Chem 12, Chem 24**, and so forth. Each of these notations relates to an automated blood chemistry panel. SMAC 12 stands for Sequential Multiple Analyzer by Technicon, which is an automated method used to analyze twelve different chemical components of the blood. Chem 12 and Chem 24 also refer to automated blood testing methods used to analyze twelve and twenty-four different chemical components of the blood, respectively.

Automated blood chemistry test results are reported as chemistry profiles and contain test results as well as the range of normal for each test. Figure 2-1 is a sample chemistry profile. The profile contains the name of the test, the individual's test results, and the normal range. Abnormal results

MEMORIAL COMMUNITY HOSPITAL
Anytown, Michigan

CHEMISTRY PROFILE

RUN ON 11/21/—

WATSON, MARK   MR# 00-00-00   COLLECTED: 0800

			Normal Range
NA	136	mEq/L	(136–145)
K	6.4 (H)*	mEq/L	(3.5–5.5)
CL	103	mEq/L	(90–110)
BUN	24 (H)*	mg/dl	(10–20)
Creatinine	1.6 (H)*	mg/dl	(0.7–1.5)
Uric acid	9.5 (H)*	mg/dl	(2.1–8.5)
Calcium	7.5	mg/dl	(9.0–10.5)
Phosphorus	5.0 (H)*	mg/dl	(2.7–4.5)
Glucose	60 (L)*	mg/dl	(70–115)
Total Bili	0.1	mg/dl	(0.1–1.0)
Chol tot	150	mg/dl	(110–200)
Triglyceride	41	mg/dl	(40–160)

*indicates abnormal results: H = high and L = low.

Figure 2-1.   Sample blood chemistry profile

are highlighted. Test results are expressed as milliequivalent per liter (MEQ/L) and milligram per deciliter (MG/DL).

Many blood chemistry tests can be categorized under several broad headings. This chapter covers blood chemistry tests that measure electrolytes, blood sugars and glucose, lipids and lipoproteins, and metabolic end products. Chapter 3 addresses enzyme, hormone, and protein tests, as well as several thyroid function tests.

Electrolyte Tests

The term electrolyte refers to the positively (+) or negatively (–) charged particles called ions. Electrolytes are present in the body's extracellular fluid, fluid outside the cells that includes blood serum or plasma, and in the body's interstitial fluid, the fluid in the space between cells. Electrolytes are also found in the intracellular fluid, the fluid within the cell itself.

In blood chemistry studies, electrolytes generally refer to the four plasma ions: sodium, potassium, chloride, and bicarbonate. These plasma ions are also referred to as **lytes** and are the ones most commonly measured when electrolytes are ordered as a laboratory test. Three less commonly measured electrolytes include calcium, magnesium, and phosphate.

Plasma electrolytes are categorized as cations, the positively charged ions of sodium, potassium, calcium, and magnesium; and as anions, the negatively charged ions of chloride, bicarbonate, and phosphate. Negative and positive ions must be kept in balance for blood to remain neutral. Table 2-1 displays the names, chemical symbols, and some major functions of the seven electrolytes discussed in this chapter.

Sodium (Na+)

Sodium has the highest extracellular concentration of all electrolytes measured in the plasma and plays a primary role in controlling the distribution of body water between extracellular and intracellular fluid. Sodium is involved in the transmission of nerve impulses and helps heart muscle retain its ability to contract.

Because sodium is necessary for critical bodily functions, the body is able to maintain an overall base level of plasma sodium. In health the levels of sodium are kept within a very narrow range; in disease only slight changes in overall concentration are noted.

Normal Range

136–145 mEq/L

Variations from Normal. Hypernatremia, an increased plasma sodium level, is relatively uncommon. Hypernatremia is associated with dehydration and insufficient water intake, Conn's syndrome (the excessive secre-

Table 2-1.   Names, Chemical Symbols, and Functions of Electrolytes

Electrolyte	Symbol	Functions
Sodium	Na^+	Distribution of water between extracellular and intracellular fluid
		Nerve impulses
		Heart muscle contractibility
Potassium	K^+	Nerve conduction
		Muscle activity
		Cardiac muscle function
Calcium	Ca^+	Bones and teeth
		Muscular contraction
		Nerve impulses
		Coagulation Factor IV
Magnesium	Mg^+	Muscular contraction
		Carbohydrate metabolism
		Coagulation process
Chloride	Cl^-	Distribution of water between cells and plasma
		Acid/base balance
Bicarbonate	HCO_3^-	Maintenance of normal pH
		Transportation CO_2 from tissue to lungs
Phosphate	PO_4	Generation of bony tissue
Phosphorus	P	Glucose and fat metabolism
		Energy transfer and storage

tion of aldosterone), hyperadrenalism or Cushing's disease, diabetes insipidus, and coma.

Hyponatremia, a decreased sodium level, usually reflects an excess of body water. Conditions that may cause an actual reduction in plasma sodium include severe burns, severe diarrhea, severe nephritis, diabetes, cystic fibrosis, Addison's disease (partial or complete failure of adrenocortical function), malabsorption syndrome, and certain diuretic medications.

Interfering Circumstances. Recent trauma, surgery, or shock may cause increased sodium levels. Oral contraceptives, anabolic steroids, corticosteroids, and laxatives may be linked to increased sodium levels. Decreased levels may be caused by diuretics, vasopressin, and sodium intravenous (IV) fluids.

Potassium (K+)

About 90% of **potassium** is concentrated within the cells and the remainder is contained in blood and bone. Plasma potassium influences nerve conduction, muscle activity, and, most important, cardiac function. Minimal changes in plasma potassium levels can have profound and adverse affects on heart muscle. Since the kidneys do not reabsorb or conserve potassium, adequate dietary intake is necessary to prevent potassium deficiency.

Normal Range

Adult	3.5–5.0 mEq/L
Children	3.4–4.7 mEq/L
Infant	4.1–5.3 mEq/L

Variations from Normal. An increase in plasma potassium levels, hyperkalemia, is usually attributed to renal failure. Other common causes of hyperkalemia include acidosis, Addison's disease, internal hemorrhage, and massive tissue or cellular damage. Since 90% of potassium is contained within the cells, cell damage as in cases of burns, chemotherapy, and disseminated intravascular coagulation (DIC) results in the release of potassium into the blood.

Hypokalemia, a decrease in plasma potassium, is most often associated with loss of fluid from the gastrointestinal tract. Therefore, any disease process that causes diarrhea or severe vomiting has the potential for creating potassium deficiency. Other disorders associated with hypokalemia include malabsorption syndromes, hyperaldosteronism (increased secretion of aldosterone), Cushing's syndrome, and renal tubular acidosis.

Hypokalemia can cause serious cardiac problems such as premature ventricular contraction, paroxysmal atrial tachycardia, ventricular tachycardia, and ventricular fibrillation. Plasma potassium levels of 2.5 mEq/L or less, or 6.5 mEq/L or more can cause heart problems that lead to death.

Interfering Circumstances. Venipuncture, intravenous fluid administration, and certain medications can alter plasma potassium levels. The common practice of opening and closing the fist with a tourniquet in place prior to venipuncture may increase potassium levels. Intravenous fluid administration without adequate potassium supplements can lead to potassium depletion. Medications that may cause an increased potassium level include heparin, histamine, mannitol, and lithium. Drugs that may cause a decreased level are insulin, aspirin, cisplatin, and potassium wasting diuretics.

Dietary habits do not usually interfere with plasma potassium levels. A relatively well-balanced diet will provide an adequate supply of potassium. However, excessive licorice ingestion can cause a decrease in plasma potassium levels.

Calcium (Ca⁺)

Approximately 98% of all **calcium** is stored in bones and teeth. Calcium that is present in the bloodstream circulates in the ionized, or free state, and in a protein-bound form with albumin. It is the ionized form of calcium that is used in bodily processes such as muscular contraction, cardiac functioning, hormone secretion, cell division, and the transmission of nerve impulses. Ionized calcium is essential for blood coagulation.

Normal Range

Total plasma calcium	9.0–10.5 mg/dl
Free calcium	3.9–4.6 mg/dl

Variations from Normal. Hypercalcemia, increased plasma calcium, is associated with many diseases but is most clinically significant in its association with cancer. The most common cause of increased calcium in the blood is metastatic bone disease. Cancers of the lung, breast, thyroid, kidney, and testes are likely to metastasize to bone. Hodgkin's disease, multiple myeloma, and leukemia may also cause hypercalcemia. Other disorders or conditions associated with increased calcium levels are hyperparathyroidism, Paget's disease of bone, prolonged immobilization, and Addison's disease.

Since much of the plasma calcium is bound to albumin, decreased plasma calcium levels, hypocalcemia, can be related to a lowered plasma albumin level. Once this possibility has been eliminated, hypocalcemia can be indicative of hypoparathyroidism and renal failure. Vitamin D deficiencies and malabsorption associated with sprue, celiac disease, and pancreatic dysfunctions contribute to decreased plasma calcium levels. Since calcium is essential for clotting, any condition that decreases the amount of ionized calcium can subsequently lead to coagulation and hemostasis problems.

Interfering Circumstances. Certain dietary considerations can interfere with accurate plasma calcium test results. Vitamin D intoxication or excessive milk ingestion, defined as three quarts of milk per day, can cause an increase in plasma calcium.

Prescription and over-the-counter drugs such as heparin, magnesium salts, oral contraceptives, aspirin, and corticosteroids and excessive use of laxatives may cause a decrease in plasma calcium. Drugs that influence an increase of plasma calcium include lithium, vitamin D, thiazide diuretics, thyroid hormone, and hydralazine, an antihypertensive medication.

Magnesium (Mg⁺)

The bulk of **magnesium** is combined with calcium and phosphorus in the bones, with very small amounts present in the bloodstream. Magnesium is necessary for muscular contraction, carbohydrate metabolism, and protein synthesis. It is usually filtered by the kidney through the glomerulus, and reabsorbed into the bloodstream by the renal tubule. Magnesium levels can be used as an indicator of metabolic activity and renal function. Since magnesium is present in a variety of foods, a normal diet will maintain the body's magnesium supply.

Normal Range

1.6–3.0 mEq/L

Variations from Normal. An increase in plasma magnesium, hypermagnesemia, is usually caused by renal dysfunction or failure. Other diseases or syndromes associated with increased magnesium levels include hypothyroidism, Addison's disease, and dehydration. Excessive ingestion of magnesium via antacids, such as milk of magnesia, will also cause an increase in plasma magnesium.

Hypomagnesemia, decreased plasma magnesium, is usually due to some type of chronic dietary or intestinal absorption problem. Diseases such as ulcerative colitis, chronic alcoholism, chronic pancreatitis, and chronic diarrhea will exhibit decreased magnesium levels. Other situations that result in hypomagnesemia include toxemia of pregnancy, hyperthyroidism, hypoparathyroidism, cirrhosis of the liver, and excessive secretion of the hormone aldosterone.

Magnesium deficiencies can be corrected by the proper administration of magnesium sulfate. Early symptoms of magnesium deficit include muscle cramps, tremors, and insomnia. It should be noted that decreases in urinary magnesium may be detected before decreases in plasma magnesium. Low levels of calcium and potassium may mask the presence of hypomagnesemia.

Interfering Circumstances. A variety of medications can interfere with laboratory measurement of magnesium levels. Prolonged treatment involving lithium, magnesium products such as antacids and laxatives, and salicylate products such as aspirin will cause a false increase in plasma magnesium levels. This is particularly possible in the face of renal dysfunction. Administration of calcium gluconate, which is used to replenish the body's calcium reserves, can also interfere with testing methods and cause a false result that indicates a decreased magnesium level.

Chloride (Cl-)

Chloride, an important negatively charged electrolyte, is present in the extracellular spaces in combination with sodium and hydrogen. Chloride has two main bodily functions: to help control the distribution of water between the cells and blood plasma and to help maintain the acid-base balance in the body.

Normal Range

90–110 mEq/L

Variations from Normal. Variations in chloride levels must always be considered in relation to other electrolytes, particularly sodium and bicarbonate. An increase in plasma chloride will correspond to an *increase* in sodium levels or a *decrease* in plasma bicarbonate levels. Measuring chlorides can be helpful in diagnosing acid-base and water balance disorders.

Increases in plasma chloride levels are seen in dehydration, eclampsia, Cushing's syndrome, and anemia. Plasma chloride is decreased with severe vomiting, diarrhea, burns, and heat exhaustion. Other diseases and syndromes that result in chloride deficits include ulcerative colitis, Addison's disease, and diabetic acidosis.

Interfering Circumstances. Drugs that may cause an increase in chloride levels are androgens, cortisone preparations, estrogens, and nonsteroidal anti-inflammatory drugs. Decreased chloride levels can be associated with corticosteroids, hydrocortisone, and diuretics containing thiazide or mercury.

Bicarbonate (HCO_3^-)

Bicarbonate plays an important role in the **blood buffer system**, which helps maintain the normal blood pH of 7.4. Simply put, the blood buffer system is activated by a buildup of positively charged hydrogen ions in the body. When this buildup occurs, bicarbonate, a negatively charged ion, combines with the hydrogen to produce a weak acid, or buffer, called carbonic acid. After a series of chemical reactions, an equilibrium is established and pH levels are held within the normal range. Variations in bicarbonate concentrations will affect the pH levels in blood.

Bicarbonate also serves as a transport mechanism to move carbon dioxide (CO_2) from the body tissues to the lungs where it is exhaled. Carbon dioxide is a waste product and must be removed from the bloodstream.

Normal Range

22–26 mEq/L

Variations from Normal. Decreased bicarbonate concentrations results in acidosis, a blood pH of 7.35 or less. Acidosis is seen in renal failure, a variety of respiratory diseases in which the lungs retain carbon dioxide, and poorly controlled diabetes mellitus.

Increased bicarbonate concentrations results in alkalosis, a blood pH greater than 7.45. Alkalosis is associated with hyperventilation, excess intake or retention of bicarbonate, and loss of gastric acid due to vomiting or potassium depletion.

Phosphate (PO₄); Phosphorus (P)

About 85% of the body's **phosphorus** is found in bones and teeth and is combined with calcium. The rest of phosphorus is in the soft tissues. Phosphorus in the blood exists as **phosphate**, which is necessary for the generation of bony tissue; the metabolism of glucose, fats, and proteins; and the storage and transfer of energy. The range of normal for adult phosphate levels is significantly different than the range of normal for children. The difference is partially attributed to the increased level of growth hormone present in children until puberty.

Due to the relationship between calcium and phosphorus, blood phosphate concentration is closely linked to plasma calcium. Increased phosphorus levels are accompanied by a decrease in calcium and, conversely, decreased phosphorus levels are accompanied by an increase in calcium.

Normal Range

Adults	2.7–4.5 mg/dl
Children	4.5–5.5 mg/dl

Variations from Normal. Hyperphosphatemia, increased phosphorus level, is most commonly associated with kidney dysfunction as in renal insufficiency, severe nephritis, and renal failure. Hypoparathyroidism, increased growth hormone, vitamin D excess, bone tumors, and Addison's disease also demonstrate increased phosphate concentrations. In most of these situations, a decrease in plasma calcium is also present and diagnostically significant.

Hypophosphatemia, decreased phosphorus level, is associated with hyperparathyroidism, rickets in childhood, osteomalacia in adults, malabsorption syndromes, malnutrition, and an excessive amount of insulin in the body. Hypophosphatemia is accompanied by an increase in plasma calcium.

Interfering Circumstances. A false increase in phosphate follows the use of laxatives or enemas. Oral laxatives may increase phosphorus levels as much as 5 mg/dL within a few hours. Destruction of red blood cells will also cause hyperphosphatemia.

Blood Glucose and Related Blood Sugar Tests

Glucose, a simple sugar, is the main blood carbohydrate and a major source of energy for all cells. The **fasting blood sugar (FBS), postprandial blood sugar (PPBS)**, and the **glucose tolerance test (GTT)**, or **standard oral glucose tolerance test (SOGTT)**, are three of the most frequently performed blood sugar tests and are used to determine the level of glucose in the blood. Variations in blood glucose levels are broadly categorized as hyperglycemia, or increased blood sugar levels, and hypoglycemia, or decreased blood sugar levels.

Related blood sugar tests measure the body's ability to produce insulin and glucose. Insulin and glucose production can be monitored by measuring blood levels of **C-peptide**, the residue of insulin formation; **glucagon**, a hormone that stimulates the production of glucose; and **insulin**, the hormone responsible for glucose metabolism. Table 2-2 identifies each blood glucose test and related diagnostic applications.

Table 2-2.   Blood Glucose and Related Blood Sugar Tests

Test	Diagnostic Application
Fasting blood sugar (FBS)	Diabetes screening
Postprandial blood sugar (PPBS)	Confirms diabetes
Glucose tolerance test (GTT)	Rule out diabetes; confirm hypoglycemia
C-peptide	Secretory function of pancreatic beta cells; inappropriate insulin injection
Glucagon	Assess pancreatic conditions and disorders
Insulin	Diabetes; secretory function of pancreatic alpha cells

Fasting Blood Sugar (FBS)

The fasting blood sugar test measures the plasma level of glucose. Results are reported as the number of milligrams per deciliter (mg/dl) of blood. The test is performed to detect any disorder of glucose metabolism, primarily diabetes, and is also used to assess the management of diabetes. As the name implies, the client must refrain from eating approximately four to twelve hours prior to the test. If the client is an insulin-dependent diabetic, both food and insulin can be withheld until the blood specimen is drawn.

Normal Range

Adults	70–115 mg/dl
Children	60–110 mg/dl
Newborns	30–80 mg/dl

Variations from Normal. An increase in blood glucose, hyperglycemia, usually indicates diabetes. Myocardial infarction, meningitis, or encephalitis, all of which produce acute stress in bodily processes, may also cause an elevated blood glucose level. Other conditions associated with hyperglycemia include an increased secretion of glucocorticoids from the adrenal glands as seen in Cushing's disease, pituitary and pancreatic adenomas, pancreatitis, hyperthyroidism, and chronic illness or inactivity.

Hyperglycemia is sometimes seen during pregnancy and is called gestational diabetes. The condition is usually diagnosed during the latter half of the pregnancy and is caused by an increased secretion of the placental hormone lactogen. Lactogen can inhibit the action of insulin, thereby increasing the blood glucose level. Gestational diabetes presents a risk to the fetus and mother and must be closely monitored throughout the pregnancy.

Hypoglycemia, a decrease in blood glucose, is often caused by an overdose of insulin or skipping meals. Other causes of hypoglycemia include pancreatic islet cell malignancy, severe liver damage, hypothyroidism, cortisol deficiency, and pituitary hormone deficiency.

Interfering Circumstances. Many drugs can interfere with fasting blood sugar results. Steroids, particularly prednisone, and diuretics can significantly alter test results. Anesthesia, stress, and obesity may also affect blood glucose levels.

Postprandial Blood Sugar (PPBS); Two-Hour Postprandial Blood Sugar (2-hour PPBS)

While many practitioners use the fasting blood sugar test results as a primary screen for diabetes mellitus, the postprandial blood sugar test (PPBS) is often used to confirm the diagnosis. Prior to the test the client fasts overnight and then consumes a meal that contains approximately 100 grams of carbohydrates, or drinks a special 100-gram carbohydrate drink. Two hours after eating, a venous blood sample is drawn and analyzed. The purpose of the PPBS test is to assess the body's response to the ingestion of carbohydrates in a meal.

Like the fasting blood sugar test, the postprandial blood sugar test measures the plasma level of glucose. The value of the postprandial test is its ability to identify diabetic conditions that may not be clearly revealed by the fasting blood sugar test.

Normal Range

Age 50 or less	70–140 mg/dl
Age 50–60	70–150 mg/dl
Age 60+	70–160 mg/dl

Variations from Normal. A two-hour postprandial glucose level greater than 200 mg/dl is indicative of diabetes mellitus.

Interfering Circumstances. Diseases and conditions that affect the results of the fasting blood sugar test will also affect the postprandial blood sugar test. Smoking during the test period can cause an increased glucose level.

Glucose Tolerance Test (GTT); Standard Oral Glucose Tolerance Test (SOGTT)

The glucose tolerance test is a timed test of the glucose concentration in both the blood and urine. This test is used to confirm or rule out diabetes and is a definitive test for diagnosing hypoglycemia. After fasting overnight, the client is given a concentrated amount of glucose dissolved in a flavored, water-based drink. Blood and urine samples are collected over a three- to four-hour period.

In health, the insulin response is immediate and in sufficient quantity to tolerate the glucose load and to move the glucose from the blood to the cells of the body. There will be a minimal and temporary rise in plasma glucose levels within the first hour, with a return to normal levels in the second hour of testing.

Normal Range

Fasting	70–115 mg/dl
30 min	less than 200 mg/dl
1 hour	less than 200 mg/dl
2 hours	less than 140 mg/dl
3 hours	70–115 mg/dl
4 hours	70–115 mg/dl

Variations from Normal. Individuals who are diabetic or hypoglycemic will not be able to tolerate the glucose load administered during the glucose tolerance test. Diabetic clients will exhibit increased glucose levels that exceed 190 mg/dl at one hour; 165 mg/dl at two hours; or 145 mg/dl at three hours. Different types of diabetes can be identified by the glucose elevation at specific time intervals.

Type II or **noninsulin-dependent diabetes mellitus (NIDDM)**, which is characterized by a delay in the secretion of insulin or a decreased number of insulin receptor sites, displays an elevated glucose level until the two-hour point. Type I or **insulin-dependent diabetes mellitus (IDDM)**, which may be characterized by a lack of insulin or the absence of its secretion, displays an elevated glucose level throughout the test period. Gestational diabetes also displays an elevated glucose level throughout the test period.

The hypoglycemic individual will also have trouble handling the glucose load administered during the glucose tolerance test. The glucose load will trigger high insulin levels, which will in turn mobilize the glucose to leave the blood. Consequently the blood glucose level will drop below normal at two hours, and remain low for the remainder of the test period. Figure 2-2 is a graphic representation of plasma glucose levels and the possible disorders identified by the glucose tolerance test.

Interfering Circumstances. Circumstances surrounding the patient's lifestyle can interfere with test results. Smoking and exercise during the test period

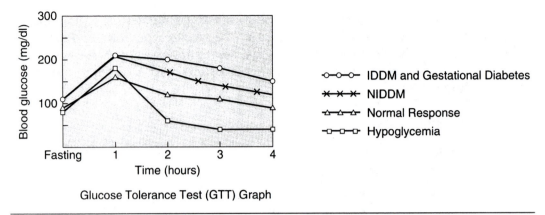

Glucose Tolerance Test (GTT) Graph

Figure 2-2.   Blood glucose levels associated with disorders identified by the glucose tolerance test.

can stimulate glucose levels. Prolonged inactivity and weight reduction di-
eting prior to testing can produce inaccurate results.

Specific drugs and medications will interfere with glucose tolerance.
These include insulin, large doses of aspirin, oral contraceptives, estrogens,
anti-inflammatory drugs, nicotine, lithium, and thiazide diuretics.

C-Peptide

C-peptide is formed in the islets of Langerhans, specifically the beta cells,
of the pancreas during insulin production. Since insulin and C-peptide are
secreted into the bloodstream in near equal amounts, measuring C-peptide
levels provides a reliable indication of blood insulin levels. The C-peptide
test is also used to assess the secretory function of the beta cells, and to
identify individuals who may be injecting insulin for nontherapeutic reasons. C-peptide levels are reported as nanogram per milliliter (ng/mL).

The C-peptide test is particularly helpful in measuring blood insulin
levels in diabetic patients who have developed insulin antibodies as a result of being treated with pork or bovine insulin. C-peptide is not affected
by the presence of insulin antibodies.

Normal Range

0.78–1.89 ng/mL

Variations from Normal. Increased C-peptide levels are associated with insulinoma, a benign tumor of the beta cells of the pancreas that causes the excessive secretion of insulin. Since most C-peptide is degraded in the kidney, renal failure results in elevated C-peptide levels.

Decreased C-peptide levels are associated with a radical pancreatectomy and diabetes mellitus. Fictitious hypoglycemia, hypoglycemia caused by secretive injection of insulin, can be identified via decreased levels of C-peptide.

Interfering Circumstances. Obesity and oral hypoglycemic medications or agents may alter C-peptide test results.

Glucagon

Glucagon, a hormone secreted by pancreatic alpha cells, assists in the maintenance of blood glucose levels. When blood glucose levels decrease, glucagon stimulates the conversion of glycogen into glucose, which results in an increase in blood glucose. Glycogen, the stored form of glucose, is found primarily in the liver. Measuring plasma glucagon levels assists in diagnosing pancreatic conditions and disorders. Glucagon levels are reported as picogram per milliliter (pg/mL).

Normal Range

50–200 pg/mL

Variations from Normal. Glucagon levels increase in the presence of acute pancreatitis, diabetes mellitus, severe diabetic ketoacidosis, and glucagonoma, a pancreatic alpha cell tumor. Since glucagon may be metabolized by the kidneys, chronic renal failure or kidney transplant rejection has the potential to cause increased glucagon levels. Decreased glucagon levels are associated with chronic pancreatitis, loss of pancreatic tissue, and idiopathic glucagon deficiency.

Interfering Circumstances. Lifestyle circumstances that may alter glucagon test results include prolonged fasting or moderate to heavy exercise. Therapeutic interventions that alter glucagon test results consist of radioactive scans within forty-eight hours of testing; drugs such as insulin and glucocorticoids that may increase glucagon levels; and drugs such as secretin and propranolol that may decrease glucagon levels.

Insulin

Insulin, a hormone secreted by pancreatic beta cells, regulates metabolism of carbohydrates and is responsible for maintaining a constant blood glucose level. Insulin lowers blood glucose levels by promoting the transport of glucose from the bloodstream into the cells. Insulin levels can be measured by **radioimmunoassay,** a technique that uses radioactive substances to determine the concentration of specific blood constituents. Insulin levels are reported as microunits per milliliter (µU/mL).

Normal Range

4–20 µU/mL

Variations from Normal. Diseases such as acromegaly, Cushing's syndrome, and insulinoma (a benign tumor of the insulin secreting cells of the pancreas) are associated with an increased level of insulin. Decreased insulin levels are seen primarily in diabetes.

Interfering Circumstances. Food intake and obesity may cause false increases in insulin levels. Recent administration of radioisotopes may affect test results, as will use of oral contraceptives. Other drugs that may cause increased insulin levels include corticosteroids and levodopa.

Lipid Profile

Lipids are fat substances that provide energy to the body; are necessary for the production of steroid hormones and bile acids; and have a role in creating cell membranes. Two dominant lipids are **cholesterol** and **triglyceride.** Cholesterol and triglycerides are transported in the bloodstream by **lipoproteins,** which are complex molecules consisting of plasma proteins and lipids. Lipoproteins are categorized as **high-density lipoproteins (HDL),** cholesterol-rich plasma proteins; **very-low-density lipoproteins (VLDL),** triglyceride-rich plasma proteins; and **low-density lipoproteins (LDL)**, the cholesterol-rich product of very-low-density lipoprotein breakdown.

A lipid profile includes measuring plasma levels of cholesterol, triglycerides, HDLs, LDLs, and VLDLs. The purpose of the lipid profile is to detect disorders of lipid metabolism and to assess the risk of atherosclerosis, arteriosclerotic heart disease (ASHD), and peripheral vascular disease. Table 2-3 identifies each lipid test and related diagnostic applications.

Table 2-3.   Lipid Profile Tests

Test	*Diagnostic Application*
Cholesterol	Atherosclerosis; coronary artery disease
High-density lipoprotein (HDL)	"Protective" for atherosclerosis
Very-low-density lipoprotein (VLDL)	Major source of cholesterol-rich low-density lipoproteins
Low-density lipoprotein (LDL)	Deposits cholesterol into the peripheral tissue; ASHD; atherosclerosis; peripheral vascular disease
Triglyceride	Coronary and vascular disease; fat metabolism

Cholesterol

One of the most tested lipids in the body, cholesterol is sometimes only associated with arteriosclerotic vascular disease. Cholesterol, however, is an important component of the body and is necessary for the production of bile acids, steroids, and cellular membranes. In addition, cholesterol plays a role in maintaining the skin's resistance to water-soluble substances and prevents excess evaporation of water from the body.

About 75% of cholesterol is transported in the bloodstream via low-density lipoproteins, and the remaining 25% is bound to high-density lipoproteins. In the past, blood cholesterol was reported only as total cholesterol. Current laboratory practices include the measurement of high-density lipoproteins, low-density lipoproteins, and very-low-density lipoproteins.

Normal Ranges. Normal ranges will vary with age, diet, and geographic location. Since there are many variables that affect plasma cholesterol levels, most references give a desirable range based primarily on age. Under most circumstances, an upper limit of 200 mg/dl or less is desirable.

Adult/elderly	less than 200 mg/dl
Children	120–200 mg/dl
Infant	70–175 mg/dl
Newborn	53–135 mg/dl

Variations from Normal. High levels of cholesterol are associated with atherosclerosis and an increased risk of coronary artery disease. Other diseases linked to elevated cholesterol include uncontrolled diabetes, obesity, and hypothyroidism. Type II familial hypercholesterolemia is an inherited disorder characterized by high levels of plasma cholesterol and early evidence of atherosclerosis. Hyperlipidemia type IIA is another name for type II familial hypercholesterolemia.

Decreased levels of cholesterol occur when cholesterol is not absorbed from the gastrointestinal tract as in malabsorption syndromes, liver disease, hyperthyroidism, anemia, and sepsis. Other conditions associated with decreased cholesterol include pernicious anemia, hemolytic jaundice, severe infections, and terminal stages of debilitating diseases such as cancer.

Interfering Circumstances. Pregnancy and removal of the ovaries will cause elevated cholesterol results. Drugs that cause an increased cholesterol level include adrenocorticotropic hormone, anabolic steroids, oral contraceptives, Dilantin, diuretics, and vitamin D. Decreased cholesterol levels are associated with drugs like allopurinol, androgens, erythromycin, Mevacor, niacin, and nitrates.

High-Density Lipoprotein (HDL)

High-density lipoproteins (HDL) are plasma proteins that function as carriers of plasma cholesterol. Measuring the cholesterol contained in the HDL molecule is predictive of the individual's risk for coronary artery disease. It is believed that the HDL molecule carries cholesterol from the peripheral tissues of the body to the liver, where the cholesterol is converted into bile acids and eventually excreted. Cholesterol that is part of the high-density lipoprotein molecule will not be deposited in blood vessel walls. Because of this, HDL is sometimes referred to as the "good" cholesterol and is believed to have a protective effect on the circulatory system.

Normal Range

Men   >45 mg/dl
Women   >55 mg/dl

Variations from Normal. Some variations in high-density lipoprotein levels are based on gender and age. Increases in HDL levels are not often seen as problematic. However, since the liver is responsible for the metabolism of HDL, a nontherapeutic elevation of HDL levels can signify liver disease. Most individuals are more concerned about low HDL levels.

Decreased availability of high-density lipoproteins may leave more cholesterol free to be deposited in the peripheral tissue of the body. Low levels of HDLs increase the risk of ASHD.

Interfering Circumstances. Lifestyle factors that influence HDL levels include smoking and alcohol ingestion, which decreases HDLs. Exercise can raise HDL levels. Drugs that may cause a lipoprotein increase are aspirin, oral contraceptives, steroids, and sulfonamides.

Very-Low-Density Lipoprotein (VLDL); Low-Density Lipoprotein (LDL)

Very-low-density lipoproteins (VLDLs) are plasma proteins composed primarily of triglycerides and small amounts of cholesterol. The VLDLs transport triglycerides from the liver to the peripheral tissue. The breakdown of VLDLs is a major source of low-density lipoproteins (LDLs), which are cholesterol-rich plasma proteins. Increased levels of very-low-density lipoprotein is accompanied by increased levels of low-density lipoproteins. Very-low-density lipoproteins are associated with atherosclerosis, but not to the same degree as low-density lipoproteins.

Low-density lipoprotein, a primary transporter of cholesterol, delivers and deposits the cholesterol into the peripheral tissues. Because of this function, LDLs are sometimes referred to as "bad" cholesterol and are associated with atherosclerosis, ASHD, and peripheral vascular disease.

The VLDL and LDL levels are mathematical calculations that utilize the total cholesterol, triglyceride, and HDL values. The VLDL is usually expressed as a percentage of the total blood cholesterol. The LDL is determined by subtracting the HDL minus one-fifth of the triglyceride level from the total cholesterol. The VLDL and LDL levels can be calculated manually or as part of an automated lipid profile test.

Normal Range

Low-density lipoprotein	60–180 mg/dl
Very-low-density lipoprotein	25–50% of total cholesterol level

Variations from Normal. Elevated LDL levels increase the individual's risk for ASHD and peripheral vascular disease. Other diseases associated with increased LDLs include type IIA familial hyperlipidemia, multiple myeloma, hypothyroidism, kidney and liver syndromes, and diabetes.

Increased VLDL levels are primarily caused by type IV hyperlipidemia, a common form of increased lipoproteins that is sometimes familial. Type IV hyperlipidemia is also called endogenous hypertriglyceridemia. Other diseases associated with elevated VLDLs include alcoholism, obesity, diabetes mellitus, chronic renal disease, and pancreatitis. A diet rich in fatty foods and animal fats may also elevate LDL and VLDL levels. Malnutrition and malabsorption syndromes will result in decreased LDL and VLDL levels.

Interfering Circumstances. Very-low-density lipoprotein and low-density lipoprotein results can be altered by binge eating. Drugs that increase lipoprotein levels include oral contraceptives, estrogen, progestin, and steroids.

Triglyceride

Triglycerides, the main form of stored fat in humans, are an important source of energy. Triglycerides exists in the bloodstream and are transported throughout the body by VLDLs and LDLs. Excess plasma triglycerides are stored in the body's adipose tissue.

Measurement of triglyceride levels is part of the lipid profile. The triglyceride test is used to evaluate the individual's risk of coronary and vascular disease, and to identify atherosclerosis. The test can also provide information about the body's ability to metabolize fat.

Normal Range. Variations in triglyceride ranges are affected by gender, age, and diet.

Men   40–190 mg/dl
Women   35–160 mg/dl
Children   30–100 mg/dl

Variations from Normal. Elevated triglyceride levels increase the individual's risk of atherosclerosis, ASHD, and peripheral vascular disease. Other clinical conditions associated with increased triglycerides include all types of hyperlipidemia, poorly controlled diabetes, pancreatitis, kidney syndromes, and toxemia. Individuals with a history of myocardial infarction may show increased triglycerides for up to one year postinfarction. A high-carbohydrate diet may contribute to high triglyceride levels.

Decreased triglyceride values are seldom seen as a clinical problem. Genetic defects and chronic problems of malnutrition and malabsorption syndrome will exhibit decreased triglyceride levels. Other diseases associated with low triglycerides are chronic obstructive pulmonary disease, brain infarction, and hyperthyroidism.

Interfering Circumstances. A temporary increase in triglycerides can be triggered by alcohol consumption and a pretest meal high in fats. Pregnancy, oral contraceptives, and estrogen are also associated with elevated values. Drugs that may decrease triglyceride levels include ascorbic acid, the anti-tumor enzyme asparaginase, and lipid-lowering agents such as clofibrate.

Metabolic Tests

The metabolic processes of the body result in the production and elimination of a variety of waste products known as metabolic end products. Frequently performed metabolic end product tests include **bilirubin**, a waste product of hemolysis; **blood urea nitrogen (BUN)**, a test that measures plasma urea, the nitrogenous waste product of protein metabolism; **creatinine**, the waste product formed in the muscles; and **uric acid**, a waste product derived from the breakdown of nucleic acids. Analyzing plasma bilirubin and blood urea nitrogen levels provides the clinician with valuable information about liver function. Blood urea nitrogen, creatinine, and uric acid plasma levels assist in diagnosing kidney problems. Table 2-4 identifies each metabolic end product test and related diagnostic applications.

Table 2-4.   Metabolic End Products Tests

Test	Diagnostic Application
Bilirubin	Destruction of RBCs; liver dysfunction
Blood urea nitrogen (BUN)	Liver and kidney functions
Creatinine	Kidney excretory function; decreased muscle mass
Uric acid	Diagnostic for gout

Bilirubin

Bilirubin is a waste product resulting from the lysis of red blood cells and the release of hemoglobin. The heme (iron) portion of the hemoglobin molecule is converted into the bile pigment bilirubin. Bilirubin is a yellow pigment. An abnormally increased blood concentration creates a jaundiced discoloration of the skin, whites of the eyes, and mucous membranes.

Bilirubin is eliminated from the body through a complex process involving the liver. There are two main forms of bilirubin: **indirect or unconjugated bilirubin**, which is transported to the liver as a bilirubin-albumin complex and converted to **direct or conjugated bilirubin** that is eventually excreted in feces and urine. Liver malfunction can inhibit this process. Consequently bilirubin will not be converted to excretable products and will accumulate in the blood.

Bilirubin testing can include measuring the levels of indirect bilirubin, direct bilirubin, and **total bilirubin**, the sum of direct and indirect bilirubin.

Normal Range

Total bilirubin	0.2–1.0 mg/dl
Indirect bilirubin	0.1–0.7 mg/dl
Direct bilirubin	0.1–0.3 mg/dl
Newborn total bilirubin	1–12 mg/dl

Variations from Normal. Elevated indirect bilirubin is usually associated with increased destruction of red blood cells, destruction of hemoglobin as seen in hemolytic anemias, pernicious anemia, sickle cell anemia, transfusion reactions, and hemolytic disease of newborns.

Abnormally elevated indirect bilirubin concentrations may also indicate liver dysfunction in that the liver is unable to convert indirect bilirubin to direct bilirubin. Hepatic diseases associated with elevated indirect bilirubin include hepatitis, cirrhosis, and extensive liver tumors.

An increase in direct bilirubin levels usually indicates an inability to excrete bilirubin. Gallstones, tumors, bile duct obstruction, and cancer of the pancreatic head can cause increases in direct bilirubin.

Interfering Circumstances. Improper handling of the blood sample can alter test results. Exposure of the specimen to sunlight or high-intensity artificial light at room temperature will decrease bilirubin concentration. Shaking the blood specimen and the presence of air bubbles may also decrease bilirubin levels.

Drugs that cause increased bilirubin include allopurinol, anabolic steroids, ascorbic acid, diabinese, codeine, steroids, diuretics, and oral contraceptives. Drugs associated with decreased levels are barbiturates, caffeine, penicillin, and high doses of salicylates.

Blood Urea Nitrogen (BUN)

The BUN test measures the amount of urea nitrogen in the blood. Urea, the end product of protein metabolism, contains nitrogen, is formed in the liver, carried via the blood to the kidneys, filtered in the glomerulus, and subsequently excreted. Blood urea nitrogen is directly related to the metabolic function of the liver and the excretory functions of the kidneys. This test is used as a gross indicator of glomerular ability to filter urea from the blood.

While nearly all kidney diseases cause inadequate urea excretion and a subsequent rise in BUN, other conditions will affect BUN levels as well. Kidney function is more accurately assessed using the BUN in conjunction with creatinine test results.

Normal Range

Adult   10–20 mg/dl
Child   5–18 mg/dl

Variations from Normal. Azotemia, increased BUN levels, is usually caused by inadequate excretion due to kidney diseases such as glomerulonephritis, pyelonephritis, and acute tubular necrosis. Other causes of azotemia are urinary obstruction, excessive amounts of protein intake and metabolism, dehydration, myocardial infarction, and chronic gout. Decreased BUN levels are seen in liver failure, overhydration via excessive intravenous fluids, malnutrition, impaired absorption, and pregnancy.

Interfering Circumstances. Dietary habits and age can affect BUN levels. Low-protein, high-carbohydrate diets can decrease blood urea nitrogen, and a high-protein diet will increase BUN. Inefficient concentration of the urine can cause increased BUN levels in the elderly. Drugs that may cause increased BUN levels are cephalosporins, cisplatin, aspirin, tetracyclines, and thiazide diuretics. Streptomycin may cause a decreased BUN.

Creatinine

Creatinine is a waste product of creatine phosphate, a substance used in skeletal muscle contraction. Production of both creatine phosphate and creatinine is a function of muscle mass and is not affected by diet, age, gender, or exercise. Since creatinine is excreted solely by the kidney, plasma creatinine levels provide diagnostically significant information about kidney excretory function.

Although the plasma creatinine test is a more sensitive indicator of kidney disease than the BUN, both are used to diagnose impaired kidney function. These tests are important components of renal function studies.

Normal Range

Adult   0.7–1.5 mg/dl
Children   0.3–0.7 mg/dl

Variations from Normal. Increased plasma creatinine levels are directly associated with kidney malfunction. However, about 50% of kidney function must be lost before creatinine levels rise. Renal conditions like glomerulonephritis, pyelonephritis, acute tubular necrosis, and urinary tract obstruction will cause increased creatinine levels. Diseases that affect kidney function or that increase muscle mass are also associated with elevated plasma creatinine. Examples of these diseases include diabetes, conditions that impair renal blood flow, acromegaly, and gigantism.

Decreased creatinine levels are associated with decreased muscle mass. Muscle depletion or wasting is seen in severe debilitation, starvation, and muscular dystrophy.

Interfering Circumstances. Since creatinine is not affected by diet, exercise, or hormones, the major interfering circumstances are drugs or medications. Creatinine values may be increased by chemotherapeutic agents such as cisplatin, and drugs that are toxic to the kidneys such as cephalosporins.

Uric Acid

Uric acid is a product that is formed by the breakdown of nucleic acids. Most uric acid is excreted by the kidneys and some is excreted by the gastrointestinal tract. The main purpose of the uric acid test is to diagnose gout, a condition in which uric acid settles in tissues and joints, particularly joints of the big toe. The uric acid test is also used to monitor the treatment of gout.

Normal Range

Men	2.1–8.5 mg/dl
Women	2.0–6.6 mg/dl
Children	2.5–5.5 mg/dl

Variations from Normal. Hyperuricemia, increased uric acid in the blood, is a result of excessive production of uric acid. Overproduction of uric acid is caused by excessive cell destruction and the subsequent breakdown of nucleic acids; excessive cell production and destruction as seen in leukemia; and inefficient excretion of uric acid, as in kidney failure. Conditions associated with hyperuricemia are lymphomas, metastatic cancer, starvation, multiple myeloma, lead poisoning, and many other chronic and systemic diseases.

Decreased uric acid levels are seen in Wilson's disease, a rare inherited disorder of copper metabolism. Fanconi's syndrome, a group of disorders that include renal tubule dysfunction, the presence of glucose and phosphate in the urine, and bicarbonate wasting, exhibits decreased uric acid levels in the blood.

Interfering Circumstances. Although stress may cause an increase in uric acid levels, drugs such as ascorbic acid, low-dose aspirin, caffeine, cisplatin, diuretics, and Aldomet are more commonly associated with hyperuricemia. Decreased uric acid levels may be caused by drugs such as high-dose aspirin, Imuran, corticosteroids, estrogens, and warfarin.

Summary

- Blood chemistry tests provide a means of measuring various chemical components of the blood. Variations in plasma levels of these chemical compounds provide the clinician with valuable diagnostic information.
- Blood chemistry tests can be categorized under the following headings: electrolytes, blood sugars and glucose, lipids and lipoproteins, metabolic end products, enzymes, hormones, and protein tests.
- Plasma electrolytes include sodium, potassium, calcium, magnesium, chloride, bicarbonate, and phosphate.
- The most commonly measured electrolytes are sodium potassium, chloride, and bicarbonate.
- Variations in one or more electrolytes can be caused by a wide variety of diseases from dehydration to metastatic bone disease. Conversely, variations in one or more electrolytes may also cause problems that include decreased contractility of heart muscle and water retention.
- Blood glucose and related blood sugar tests are used to assess the production and metabolism of glucose, the maintenance of blood glucose levels, and the production of insulin.
- The fasting blood sugar, postprandial blood sugar, and glucose tolerance test measure blood glucose levels.
- C-peptide, glucagon, and insulin level tests monitor the production of insulin and glucagon.
- Diseases associated with variations in blood glucose and insulin range from diabetes mellitus to pancreatic cell tumors.
- A lipid profile includes measuring plasma levels of cholesterol, triglycerides, high-density lipoproteins, very-low-density lipoproteins, and low-density lipoproteins.

- Variations in plasma lipid levels are predictive of atherosclerosis, arteriosclerotic heart disease, coronary artery disease, and peripheral vascular disease.
- Metabolic end product tests include bilirubin, blood urea nitrogen, creatinine, and uric acid.
- Bilirubin and blood urea nitrogen are diagnostically significant for liver diseases and disorders.
- Blood urea nitrogen, creatinine, and uric acid are performed in order to diagnose kidney problems.

CHAPTER REVIEW

1. Identify the following blood chemistry tests:

a. Measures plasma ions of sodium, potassium, chloride, and bicarbonate _____

b. Primary screen for diabetes mellitus _____

c. Definitive test for hypoglycemia _____

d. Highly reliable test for confirming diabetes mellitus diagnosis _____

e. Measures ability of liver to convert glycogen to glucose _____

f. Measures blood insulin levels in the face of insulin antibodies _____

g. Most commonly ordered lipid test _____

h. Identifies familial type IV hyperlipidemia _____

i. Identifies type IIA familial hyperlipidemia _____

j. Provides information about the body's ability to metabolize fat _____

k. Identifies hemolysis, liver dysfunction, bile duct obstruction, and related diseases

_____

l. Measures metabolic function of the liver and excretory function of the kidneys

_____

m. Sensitive indicator of renal disease

_____

n. Diagnostic for gout

_____

2. Organize these blood tests according to the following categories:

a. Blood glucose and related test

_____

b. Electrolyte tests

_____

c. Lipid profile

_____

d. Metabolic end product tests

_____

Bicarbonate

Bilirubin

Blood urea nitrogen

Calcium

Chloride

Cholesterol

C-peptide

Creatinine

Fasting blood sugar

Glucagon

Glucose tolerance test

High-density lipoprotein

Insulin

Low-density lipoprotein

Magnesium

Phosphate

Postprandial blood sugar

Potassium

Sodium

Triglyceride

Uric Acid

Very-low-density lipoprotein

3. Identify a disease that is related to an increase and decrease of each plasma electrolyte.

Electrolyte	Increase	Decrease
a. Sodium	_____	_____
b. Potassium	_____	_____

c. Calcium   _____   _____

d. Magnesium   _____   _____

e. Chloride   _____   _____

f. Bicarbonate   _____   _____

g. Phosphate   _____   _____

4. Briefly discuss the metabolic end product tests according to the following questions:

    a. Which tests are performed to identify renal problems? Why?

    b. What are some of the renal disorders identified by increased and decreased test levels?

    c. Which tests are used to assess liver function? Why?

    d. What types of liver dysfunction are identified by these tests? What are some of the specific liver diseases or disorders identified by increased and decreased test levels?

Case Studies

1. Elsie Elliason, a 70-year-old woman, was admitted to the emergency room of the hospital with severe vomiting and diarrhea. She has been experiencing these symptoms for the past several days. The ER physician suspects that she is experiencing hypokalemia. What electrolyte test would the physician order to confirm hypokalemia and what might the result be? Why is this particular electrolyte important to normal body function? What impact did Ms. Elliason's physical symptoms have on the electrolyte?

2. Dr. Rice, an internist, ordered an FBS on Alfred Holms, a 54-year-old male diabetic. According to the patient record, the FBS was 250 mg/dl. Does this test result indicate hypoglycemia or hyperglycemia? What is the difference? Could this be a form of gestational diabetes? Discuss whether Dr. Rice would order a PPBS and a GTT and what value they would serve.

3. Crystal Hampton is a 60-year-old female with a diagnosis of type IV hyperlipidemia. In reviewing her record, you discover that the physician has ordered a lipid profile. What is a lipid profile and what specific substances does it measure? Project what the results might be in Mrs. Hampton's case? One of the fats being measured is called "good cholesterol," what is the medical term for "good cholesterol" and what is the function of this type of cholesterol? How would the test results differ if this were a male patient?

Challenge Activity

Describe the blood chemistry tests, and the results of those tests, that would be associated with each diagnostic statement in the following list. Is there any one test that specifically identifies each disease? Which, if any, of these diseases have similar blood chemistry test results?

Cushing's disease (hyperadrenalism)
Hypoglycemia
Pancreatitis

Chapter 3

Blood Chemistry Tests (Part II)

Key Terms, Abbreviations, and Acronyms

acid phosphatase

adrenocorticotrophic hormone, ACTH

alanine aminotransferase, ALT

alkaline phosphatase, ALP, alk phos

antidiuretic hormone, ADH

aspartate aminotransferase, AST

calcitonin

cortisol

creatine kinase, CK

creatine phosphokinase, CPK

ferritin

gastrin

growth hormone, GH

human chorionic gonadotropin, HCG

isoenzyme

lactic acid dehydrogenase, LD, LDH

lipase

prostate-specific antigen, PSA

prostatic acid phosphatase, PAP

serum glutamic oxaloacetic transaminase, SGOT

serum glutamic pyruvic transaminase, SGPT

somatotropic hormone, STH

syndrome of inappropriate ADH secretion, SIADH

testosterone

thyroid stimulating hormone, TSH

thyroxine, T4

total iron-binding capacity, TIBC

transferrin

transferrin saturation

triiodothyronine, T3

Learning Objectives

Upon completion of this chapter, the learner should be able to:

1. Identify and define commonly performed enzyme, hormone, thyroid, and iron tests.
2. Categorize blood enzyme tests according to disease processes or diagnoses.
3. Link the creatine kinase and lactic acid dehydrogenase isoenzymes with specific tissues and organs.
4. Explain the effects of increased and/or decreased serum hormone levels.
5. Compare the diagnostic significance of each thyroid function test.
6. Discuss serum iron tests as they relate to various anemias.

Introduction

This chapter continues the discussion of blood chemistry tests and includes enzyme, hormone, thyroid function, and iron tests. Identifying the presence, absence, and increase or decrease of these specific chemicals can provide practitioners with diagnostically significant information about organ function and health. Many of these tests are organ and disease specific.

Enzyme Tests

Enzymes are proteins produced by living cells that influence the chemical reactions of an organism. Most enzymes are produced in small quantities, and their action takes place within the cells. Digestive enzymes are produced in larger quantities and are active in the digestive tract. Enzymes are present in the bloodstream in relatively small quantities.

Since enzymes are predominantly found within the cells, increases in enzyme blood levels are usually indicative of cell death or destruction. Enzymes can be linked to specific disease processes that affect specific organs.

For example, creatine kinase (CK), aspartate aminotransferase (AST), and lactic acid dehydrogenase (LDH) are enzymes that are associated with cardiac function and disease, specifically myocardial infarction. Figure 3-1 displays blood levels of these enzymes in the days following myocardial infarction.

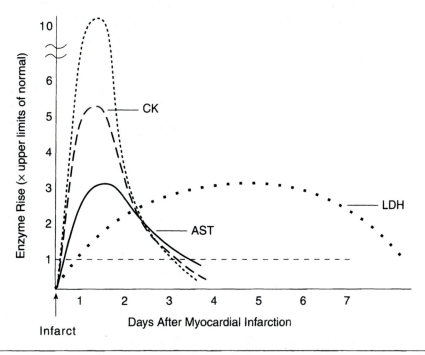

Figure 3-1. Cardiac enzyme levels during the post–myocardial infarction period

Although prostate-specific antigen is *not* an enzyme, it is presented with acid phosphatase since both are used to identify diseases of the prostate. Liver problems can be diagnosed via alkaline phosphatase (ALP, alk phos) and alanine transaminase (ALT) serum levels.

While blood enzyme levels provide valuable diagnostic information, clinicians do not routinely rely on one or two laboratory tests. Increases or decreases in serum enzyme levels must be evaluated in context with other appropriate diagnostic studies. Frequently ordered enzyme tests are discussed individually.

Acid Phosphatase, Prostatic Acid Phosphatase (PAP)

The enzyme **acid phosphatase** is present in various tissues, including bone, liver, kidneys, spleen, and red blood cells. Since the highest concentration of acid phosphatase, also known as **prostatic acid phosphatase (PAP)**, is in the prostate gland, the diagnostic significance of acid phosphatase levels relates to that gland. Acid phosphatase levels are used to diagnose and stage cancer of the prostate, especially when the disease has metastasized to the bone.

Acid phosphatase levels are used to monitor the effectiveness of prostate cancer treatments. Successful surgical intervention or treatment by estrogen therapy results in decreased acid phosphatase levels. Elevated acid phosphatase levels after treatment can indicate metastasis and a poor prognosis.

A high concentration of acid phosphatase is also present in seminal fluid, which is a component of semen. In cases of suspected rape, vaginal secretions may be tested for acid phosphatase.

Normal Range

Adults   0.11–0.60 U/L

Variations from Normal. A significant elevation of acid phosphatase usually indicates metastatic cancer of the prostate. Moderate increases of acid phosphatase levels are associated with carcinoma in situ of the prostate, Paget's disease, multiple myeloma, renal impairment, and any malignancy that has metastasized to the bone.

Interfering Circumstances. Palpation, biopsy, or cystoscopy of the prostate may cause high acid phosphatase levels. For this reason, rectal and prostate examination should be withheld for two to three days before acid phosphatase levels are measured.

Drugs such as androgens in females and clofibrate in both men and women may increase acid phosphatase levels. Alcohol, fluorides, oxalates, and phosphates may decrease acid phosphatase levels.

Prostate-Specific Antigen (PSA)

Prostate specific antigen (PSA) is a protein found in normal prostate cells of all males. Identifying variations in the serum levels of this antigen is the most effective way to diagnose prostate cancer, identify tumor recurrence, and monitor the response to therapy for prostate carcinoma. The prostate-specific antigen and the prostatic acid phosphatase tests are used to identify and monitor tumors of the prostate.

Normal Range

Men   <4 ng/mL

Variations from Normal. Caution must be used when interpreting PSA results. While increases in PSA levels occur in 80% of patients exhibiting prostate cancer, the degree of increase may represent very different diagnoses. Prostate cancer, benign prostatic hypertrophy, and prostatitis can display increased prostate-specific antigen results.

Based on the normal range cited above, an increase in serum PSA levels of 4.0–8.0 ng/mL may indicate benign prostatic hypertrophy or possible cancer of the prostate. Elevations in excess of 8.0 ng/mL are highly suggestive of malignancy. As with any diagnostic tool, PSA test results must be used in conjunction with other clinical information, such as PAP results, digital rectal exam, and biopsy of suspicious tissue. Surgery, radiation, or hormone therapy that successfully treats the prostate tumor will result in a significant reduction in serum PSA levels. After therapy and an initial decrease in PSA levels, a subsequent and significant PSA increase indicates a recurrence of the prostate cancer.

Interfering Circumstances. Palpation or biopsy of the prostrate or a recent rectal examination may cause a temporary increase in PSA levels.

Alanine Aminotransferase (ALT); Serum Glutamic Pyruvic Transaminase (SGPT)

Alanine aminotransferase (ALT), also known as **serum glutamic pyruvic transaminase (SGPT)**, is an enzyme that behaves as a catalyst in various bodily functions. This enzyme is found predominantly in liver cells, with lower concentrations present in the heart, muscle, and kidney. Since ALT is so closely associated with the liver, variations in serum levels are used to diagnose liver disease and to monitor treatments for hepatitis or other liver disorders.

Normal Range

Adults	5–35 U/L
Elderly	May be higher than adult
Infant/Newborn:	May be twice as high as adult

Variations from Normal. Increased alanine aminotransferase levels are almost always associated with some type of liver dysfunction. When liver cells are destroyed, ALT is released into the bloodstream. Moderate to high ALT increases indicate hepatocellular disease. Mild elevations can indicate cirrhosis of the liver, metastatic liver tumor, and jaundice caused by obstructive or other liver disease. In addition to various disease processes, drugs that are toxic to the liver can also trigger an increased ALT.

While alanine aminotransferase is primarily associated with the liver and its disorders, there are other organs and diseases associated with this enzyme. Muscular dystrophy, severe muscular trauma, myocardial infarction, and renal failure will also display increased ALT levels.

Interfering Circumstances. Many drugs can cause increased ALT levels, including acetaminophen, allopurinol, ampicillin, cephalosporin, codeine, oral contraceptives, salicylates, tetracyclines, and verapamil. All clinical personnel should be aware of patient medications that may affect this test result.

Alkaline Phosphatase (ALP; alk phos)

Alkaline phosphatase (ALP) is an enzyme found in the liver, bone, and epithelium of all bile ducts. It is also present in the intestinal mucosa and placenta. Levels of this enzyme are used to identify liver and bone disorders, although other diseases can display an increase or decrease in alkaline phosphatase.

Normal ranges are affected somewhat by sex, and most definitely by age. Since alkaline phosphatase levels are affected by new bone formation and/or growth, high bone-growth periods, from birth through adolescence, would account for the higher normal ranges for those age groups.

Normal Range

Adult	17–142 U/L
Children 0–12 yr	145–530 U/L

Males 12–14 yr	200–495 U/L
14–16 yr	130–525 U/L
16–20 yr	65–260 U/L
Females 12–14 yr	104–420 U/L
14–16 yr	70–230 U/L
16–20 yr	50–130 U/L

Variations from Normal. Increased alkaline phosphatase levels are associated with the following bone diseases: Paget's disease, osteomalacia, metastatic bone tumors, rickets, and sarcomas arising from bone. Healing fractures also display elevated ALP levels, as do bone growth and pregnancy.

Liver diseases associated with increased ALP levels include obstruction of biliary ducts and obstructive jaundice, hepatitis, liver cancer, cirrhosis, and infectious mononucleosis. In order to confirm liver-related diseases, elevated alkaline phosphatase levels must be correlated with other liver function tests.

Ulcerative colitis, hyperparathyroidism, pulmonary and myocardial infarctions, and cancer of the lung or pancreas exhibit increased alkaline phosphatase levels. Decreased ALP levels are seen in malnutrition, hypothyroidism, and severe anemias.

Interfering Circumstances. A variety of drugs can produce mild to moderate elevations or decreases in alkaline phosphatase levels. Allopurinol, antibiotics, methyldopa, tetracyclines, and oral contraceptives may increase test results. Decreased levels can be caused by cyanides, fluorides, oxalates, and zinc salts.

In addition to drugs, the condition of the blood specimen also affects test results. The alkaline phosphatase level increases at room temperature and the level decreases in anticoagulated blood.

Aspartate Aminotransferase (AST); Serum Glutamic Oxaloacetic Transaminase (SGOT)

Aspartate aminotransferase (AST), also known as **serum glutamic-oxaloacetic transaminase (SGOT)**, is an enzyme found in tissues and cells where there is high metabolic activity. Very high concentrations are present in heart muscle, liver cells, and skeletal muscle cells. Lesser but noteworthy concentrations are also in the kidneys, pancreas, brain, spleen, and lungs. Aspartate aminotransferase is released into the bloodstream by virtue of cell injury or death. The AST enzyme is one of the substances tested in the cardiac enzyme series. Diseases that affect liver cells also affect AST levels.

Normal Range

12–35 U/mL

Variations from Normal. Increases in AST/SGOT levels are most often associated with myocardial infarction and various liver diseases. In myocardial infarction, the level may increase from 4 to 10 times the normal amount, while liver disease may display levels of 10 to 100 times the normal range. Acute and chronic hepatitis, primary or metastatic liver cancer, alcoholic hepatitis, and Reye's syndrome produce increased AST levels.

Other diseases associated with elevated AST include acute pancreatitis, trichinosis, gangrene, progressive muscular dystrophy, brain necrosis, and cerebral infarction. Decreased AST levels are seen in beriberi, diabetic ketoacidosis, and pregnancy.

Interfering Circumstances. Drugs that may cause an increase in aspartate aminotransferase are antihypertensive medications, cholinergic agents, warfarin, erythromycin, and oral contraceptives. Exercise may also cause increase test results.

Creatine Kinase (CK); Creatine Phosphokinase (CPK)

Creatine kinase (CK), also called **creatine phosphokinase (CPK)**, is an enzyme that is found primarily in heart and skeletal muscles, and to a lesser extent in the brain. It is the main cardiac enzyme studied in patients with heart disease. Creatine kinase can be divided into three chemically distinct forms called **isoenzymes:** CK-BB (CK$_1$), CK-MB (CK$_2$), and CK-MM (CK$_3$). The isoenzymes are associated with specific organs, organ damage, and diagnoses. CK-BB is linked to brain tissue and the gastrointestinal and genitourinary tracts; CK-MB is primarily associated with cardiac muscle and cardiac cells; and CK-MM is predominant in skeletal muscle. Measuring total CK levels and identifying specific isoenzyme levels provide the clinician with valuable diagnostic information about heart, skeletal muscle, and central nervous system disorders.

Normal Range

Total CPK/CK Levels

Men	6–11 yr	58–185 U/L
	12–18 yr	35–185 U/L
	19+ yr	25–135 U/L
Women	6–7 yr	50–145 U/L
	8–14 yr	35–145 U/L
	15–18 yr	20–100 U/L
	19+ yr	15–130 U/L
Newborn		68–580 U/L

Variations from Normal. Increases in total CK levels are usually indicative of myocardial infarction, and can also be associated with skeletal muscle disease and brain injury or trauma. In order to identify the specific organ or disease process involved, CK isoenzyme levels must be measured.

The CK-MB isoenzyme is most directly related to myocardial cellular damage. The degree of increased CK-MB levels assists the physician in determining the degree of myocardial infarction and in timing the onset of the infarction. Higher CK-MB levels usually indicate that significant infarction has already occurred. Specific diseases associated with elevated CK-MB include myocardial infarction, cardiac ischemia, and myocarditis.

An increase in CK-BB levels is associated with pulmonary infarction, brain injury, cerebrovascular accident, Reye's syndrome, and intestinal ischemia. CK-MM increases are linked to muscular dystrophy, recent convulsions, electromyography, crush injuries, and polymyositis, an inflammation of several muscles.

Interfering Circumstances. Medications that may cause increased CK levels include aspirin, ampicillin, anticoagulants, and morphine. Intramuscular injections, recent surgery, and strenuous exercise may also increase CK levels. Decreased levels may be associated with early pregnancy.

Lactic Acid Dehydrogenase (LD, LDH)

Lactic acid dehydrogenase (LDH) is an enzyme found in many body tissues such as the heart, liver, kidneys, skeletal muscle, brain, and lungs. Since LDH levels peak within three to four days after myocardial infarction, increased serum levels provide valuable information for a delayed diagnosis of myocardial infarction.

Lactic acid dehydrogenase has five organ-specific isoenzymes: LDH-1 originates from heart tissue and red blood cells; LDH-2 originates from heart tissue, kidneys, and the brain; LDH-3 is primarily associated with the brain, skeletal muscles, liver, and lungs; LDH-4 is found in the liver, brain, and skeletal muscles; LDH-5 comes from the skeletal muscle and liver.

Normal Range. Variations in reported values are common. Check with the laboratory for agency-specific normal ranges.

Total LDH	0.4–1.7 mol/L

Isoenzymes	*% of Total*
LDH-1	17–27%
LDH-2	28–38%
LDH-3	19–27%
LDH-4	8–16%
LDH-5	6–16%

Variations from Normal. An increase in the lactic dehydrogenase level is usually associated with myocardial infarction. Other conditions that cause increased LDH levels include pulmonary infarction, hemolytic anemias, liver and kidney diseases, and malignant neoplasms. Because LDH is found in many tissues and organs, LDH isoenzyme levels provide diagnostic information about specific organs or tissue.

An increase in the isoenzyme LDH-1 is a sensitive and distinctive indicator of myocardial infarction, and is also seen in red blood cell hemolysis, cerebrovascular accident, and muscular dystrophy. Increased LDH-2 levels also indicate myocardial infarction, cerebrovascular accident, muscular dystrophy, and lymphoproliferative disorders. Pulmonary infarction, renal necrosis, acute pancreatitis, and malignant lymphoma are associated with LDH-3 increases. LDH-4 increases can be caused by hepatitis, renal necrosis, acute glomerulonephritis, and infectious mononucleosis. Elevated LDH-5 levels are found in liver trauma, muscular dystrophy, and skeletal muscle trauma. Figure 3-2 displays the patterns of LDH isoenzymes associated with myocardial infarction, pulmonary infarction, and liver disease.

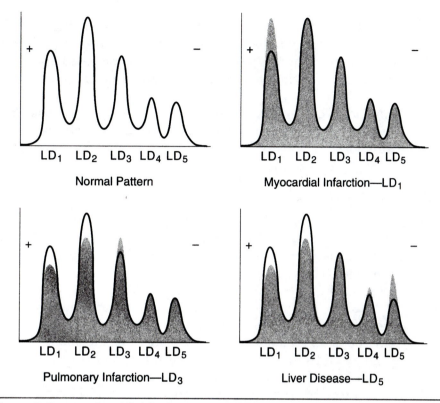

Figure 3-2.   Lactic acid dehydrogenase isoenzyme levels associated with specific diagnoses.

Interfering Circumstances. Strenuous physical activity and hemolysis of blood may cause an increase in LDH levels. Drugs such as aspirin, narcotics, anesthetics, and alcohol may also increase LDH levels, while ascorbic acid may result in decreased levels.

Lipase

Lipase, an enzyme produced and secreted by the pancreas, assists in the breakdown of triglycerides. Serum lipase levels provide specific diagnostic information about the pancreas.

Normal Range. Normal values vary depending on method used.

Variations from Normal. Increased lipase levels indicate pancreatic damage as seen in acute pancreatitis, pancreatic cancer, and chronic relapsing pancreatitis. Other diseases associated with increased lipase levels include cholecystitis, peritonitis, and severe renal disease.

Interfering Circumstances. Drugs that may increase lipase levels include codeine, morphine, and meperidine. Decreased levels can be caused by calcium ions.

Hormone Tests

Hormones are specialized chemical substances that are produced and secreted by endocrine cells and tissue, circulate in the blood, and affect the metabolic activity of specific "target" cells and organs. Hormones are often referred to as chemical "messengers."

Healthy endocrine glands provide a constant source of hormones that are only secreted when needed to maintain homeostasis, a stable internal environment. Metabolic rate, blood pressure, metabolism of all nutrients, primary and secondary sex characteristics, and regulation of serum electrolytes are all affected by increases and decreases in hormone levels.

Measuring hormone levels provides the clinician with information related to the specific gland responsible for the production and secretion of the hormone. In addition, increased or decreased hormone levels affect the function of target cells and organs.

Antidiuretic Hormone (ADH)

Antidiuretic hormone (ADH) is manufactured by the hypothalamus, secreted by the posterior lobe of the pituitary gland, and controls the amount of water reabsorbed by the kidneys. An increase in serum osmotic pressure or a decrease in blood volume triggers ADH release. Circulating ADH targets kidney cells and more water is reabsorbed, thereby increasing blood volume. Antidiuretic hormone is also known as vasopressin because it causes constriction of arterioles, which in turn raises blood pressure.

Normal Range

1–5 pg/mL

Variations from Normal. Increased serum levels of antidiuretic hormone give rise to **syndrome of inappropriate ADH secretion (SIADH)**, a condition marked by inappropriately high levels of ADH secretion. The high levels of antidiuretic hormone cause an excess amount of water to be reabsorbed by the kidneys, which in turn affects the body's fluid and electrolyte balance. Alterations of individual electrolytes can affect neurologic, cardiac, and metabolic functions.

Diseases related to SIADH include cancer of the lung, thymus, pancreas, and urologic tract. Lymphomas, leukemia, several pulmonary diseases, and brain tumors can also exhibit SIADH.

Inadequate or decreased secretion of antidiuretic hormone is seen in diabetes insipidus. It must be noted that diabetes insipidus can also be caused by the kidney's inability to respond to ADH stimulation. Trauma, tumor, and inflammation of the brain, or surgical removal of the pituitary gland, cause insufficient ADH secretion.

Interfering Circumstances. Dehydration, decreased blood volume, and stress may cause increased antidiuretic hormone levels. Drugs related to increased levels include acetaminophen, barbiturates, estrogen, nicotine, some diuretics, and tricyclic antidepressants.

Overhydration and increased blood volume may cause decreased ADH levels. Drugs related to decreased levels include alcohol, morphine antagonists, and phenytoin.

Human Chorionic Gonadotropin (HCG)

Human chorionic gonadotropin (HCG) is a hormone that appears in the blood and urine of pregnant women as early as ten days after conception. HCG is one of several hormones produced by the placenta. Blood-level measurement of this hormone has long been used to confirm pregnancy. The presence of HCG does not necessarily indicate a normal pregnancy. HCG levels can be used to diagnose a variety of reproductive-related pathologies.

Normal Range

Routine pregnancy tests	None
Pregnant	8–10 days 5–40 IU/L
	Levels vary throughout remainder of pregnancy

Males	<2.5 IU/L
Nonpregnant females	<5.0 IU/L
Postmenopausal females	<9.0 IU/L

Variations from Normal. Increases in human chorionic gonadotropin not related to normal pregnancy are associated with ectopic pregnancy and hydatidiform mole of the uterus. Certain uterine, testicular, and ovarian cancers also exhibit increased HCG levels. Once pregnancy has been established, threatened abortion, incomplete abortion, and intrauterine fetal death are marked by an inappropriate decrease in human chorionic gonadotropin.

Interfering Circumstances. Conditions that may interfere with tests results include lipemia, hemolysis, and ingestion of drugs such as anticonvulsants, hypnotics, and tranquilizers.

Cortisol

Cortisol is the most abundant glucocorticoid hormone secreted by the adrenal cortex. Glucocorticoid hormones play an important role in maintaining blood glucose levels, metabolizing food, and functioning as anti-inflammatory agents. Cortisol stimulates the liver to produce glucose, inhibits the effect of insulin, and decreases the rate at which cells use glucose. Measuring blood cortisol levels is the best way to evaluate adrenal activity. Under normal circumstances cortisol secretion is higher in the morning and lower in late afternoon and early evening.

Normal Range

| 8:00 A.M. | 6–28 g/dl |
| 4:00 P.M. | 2–12 g/dl |

Variations from Normal. Consistently elevated cortisol levels are found in patients with Cushing's syndrome and those individuals under the stress of trauma or surgery. Other conditions associated with an increased cortisol level include hyperthyroidism, adrenal adenoma, and an overproduction of **adrenocorticotropic hormone (ACTH)**. Decreased levels are seen in Addison's disease, hypopituitarism, hypothyroidism, hepatitis, and cirrhosis.

Interfering Circumstances.

Pregnancy, recent isotope scans, and physical and emotional stress can cause increased cortisol levels. Caffeine and smoking cause elevated cortisol levels. Estrogen, oral contraceptives, and aldactone may also elevate cortisol levels. Decreased levels are associated with drugs such as prednisone, androgens, and phenytoin.

Gastrin

Gastrin is a hormone produced and secreted by specialized cells in the stomach. During normal gastric activity, gastrin stimulates the secretion of gastric acid, which aids in digestion and maintenance of the pH environment in the stomach. Gastrin levels can help differentiate patients who have regular peptic ulcer disease from those who may have other conditions. Individuals with regular peptic ulcer disease exhibit normal gastrin levels.

Normal Range

Adult

16–60-yr-old male	<100 pg/mL
16–60-yr-old female	<75 pg/mL
Over 60 yr	<100 pg/mL

Variations from Normal. Gastrin levels in excess of 1000 pg/mL are a reliable indicator of Zollinger-Ellison syndrome, a gastrin-producing pancreatic tumor. Highly increased gastrin levels can be supportive of diagnoses such as hyperplasia of the G-cells of the stomach, gastric cancer, or pernicious anemia. Individuals who carry these diagnoses may also present with aggressive peptic ulcer disease.

Interfering Circumstances. Peptic ulcer surgery, gastroscopy, and insulin-dependent diabetes may produce a falsely elevated gastrin result. Antacids, cimetidine, ranitidine, and omeprazole may also cause an increase in serum gastrin levels. Serum gastrin concentration may increase fivefold after drinking 3 cups of coffee.

Growth Hormone (GH); Somatotropin; Somatotropic Hormone (STH)

Growth hormone (GH), also known as somatotropin and **somatotropic hormone (STH),** is released by the anterior lobe of the pituitary gland and is essential to all parts of the body that are associated with growth. This hormone affects the growth rate of children and adolescents, increases tissue mass, and stimulates cell division. Somatotropin is essential for the maintenance of the epiphyseal disk, the area where bone growth occurs, of long bones. Throughout life, growth hormone also plays a role in increasing protein synthesis, breakdown of fats, and blood glucose levels. Growth hormone tests are used to confirm over- or underactive pituitary disease, and to identify growth problems during all stages of life.

Normal Range

Adults and Children	<10 ng/mL
Newborns	10–40 ng/mL

Variations from Normal. Overproduction or increased levels of growth hormone can lead to gigantism in children or acromegaly in adults. Gigantism, characterized by abnormally large body proportions and abnormal sexual development, is usually attributed to hypersecretion of growth hormone during childhood. Acromegaly, characterized by enlargement, thickening, and elongation of facial and extremity bones, is the result of hypersecretion of growth hormone in adults. Increased growth hormone levels are also associated with hypoglycemia and anorexia nervosa.

Decreased growth hormone levels during childhood can result in the premature closure of epiphyseal disks, which in turn causes a cessation of growth known as dwarfism. Other conditions related to decreased growth hormone levels are pituitary insufficiency, hyperglycemia, and failure to thrive.

Interfering Circumstances. Stress, exercise, and low blood glucose levels may cause increased growth hormone levels. Many drugs such as amphetamines, estrogens, glucagon, histamine, and insulin may also increase GH levels. Decreased levels are seen in obese patients and individuals who use corticosteroid medications.

Testosterone

Testosterone, a male hormone, is responsible for sperm production and development of male secondary sex characteristics. Small amounts of testosterone are secreted by the ovaries and adrenal glands in women. Testosterone measurements assist in the assessment of various testicular conditions, pituitary function, and ovarian tumors or virilism in women.

Normal Range

Adult Males	300–1200 ng/dl
Adult Women	30–95 ng/dl
Adolescent Males	75–400 ng/dl
Adolescent Females	20–64 ng/dl

Variations from Normal. Increased testosterone levels in males can be caused by adrenal hyperplasia and adrenocortical or testicular tumors. Young men with an excess of this hormone may display precocious puberty and sexual behavior. Ovarian and adrenocortical tumors, adrenocortical hyperplasia, and polycystic ovaries may cause elevated testosterone levels in females. Excessive amounts of testosterone usually lead to the masculinization of females as evidenced in hirsutism, cessation of menstrual periods, and development of other male secondary sex characteristics.

Decreased testosterone levels in males are associated with cryptorchidism, hypogonadism (a deficiency in the secretory function of the testes) and Klinefelter's syndrome.

Interfering Circumstances. Drugs that may increase testosterone levels include anticonvulsants, barbiturates, estrogens, and oral contraceptives. Decreased testosterone levels are associated with alcohol, steroids, digoxin, and androgens.

Thyroid Function Tests

Since thyroid hormones affect most cells of the body, a functioning thyroid gland is essential to health. Thyroid function is controlled by the action of thyroid stimulating hormone (TSH), which is a hormone secreted by the anterior lobe of the pituitary gland. TSH stimulates the thyroid to produce and secrete the thyroid hormones thyroxine, triiodothyronine, and calcitonin.

Assessment of thyroid function can be accomplished by measuring serum thyroid hormone levels and TSH levels. Clinical implications of increases or decreases of these substances are discussed individually.

Thyroxine (T4)

Thyroxine (T4) is the most abundant thyroid hormone secreted by thyroid follicular cells. Thyroxine increases the body's metabolic rate, sensitizes the cardiovascular system in order to increase cardiac output, stimulates cellular differentiation, affects the maturation of the skeletal and central nervous systems, and is involved in other physiological processes.

Measuring thyroxine levels provides a reliable test of thyroid function, assists in ruling out hypothyroidism and hyperthyroidism, and is useful in the evaluation of thyroid hormone replacement therapy.

Normal Range

>10 yr   4–11 g/dl

Variations from Normal. Increased thyroxine levels are associated with various conditions known as hyperthyroid states. Hyperthyroid states can be caused by overactive thyroid nodules and/or thyroid tumors, which are diseases in and of themselves. These conditions, which usually result in an elevated thyroxine secretion, contribute to other disease processes. Specific diseases include thyrotoxicosis, Graves' disease, which is characterized by an enlarged thyroid and exophthalmos; Plummer's disease, also called toxic nodular goiter; and acute thyroiditis.

Decreased thyroxine levels are associated with various conditions known as hypothyroid states. Since thyroxine is necessary for many bodily functions, manifestation of thyroxine deficiencies may be evidenced in many systems. Patients may appear sluggish, thick-tongued, and may take on a "greasy" appearance. In the most severe form of hypothyroidism, myxedema, there is pronounced swelling of the hands, face, feet, and periorbital tissue. Left untreated, hypothyroidism can lead to coma and death.

Interfering Circumstances. Iodinated contrast studies, pregnancy, and drugs such as estrogens, heroin, methadone, and oral contraceptives may cause elevated thyroxine levels. Decreased levels are associated with anabolic steroids, lithium, and antithyroid drugs.

Triiodothyronine (T3)

Triiodothyronine (T3) is another hormone secreted by the follicular cells of the thyroid gland and appears to have the same functions as thyroxine. Although triiodothyronine accounts for a very small percentage of thyroid hormone secretions, it is very concentrated and highly potent. As with thyroxine, triiodothyronine plays an important part in many cellular and metabolic processes. The serum T3 test is an important part of the thyroid function laboratory tests.

Normal Range

110–230 ng/dl

Variations from Normal. Increased triiodothyronine levels are associated with hyperthyroidism, T3 thyrotoxicosis, thyroiditis, and thyroid tumor. Decreased levels are seen in hypothyroidism, starvation, and chronic illnesses.

Interfering Circumstances. Iodinated contrast studies, pregnancy, and drugs such as estrogens, heroin, methadone, and oral contraceptives may cause elevated triiodothyronine levels. Decreased levels are associated with anabolic steroids, lithium, and antithyroid drugs.

Calcitonin

Calcitonin, the hormone secreted by the parafollicular cells of the thyroid gland, functions to lower blood calcium levels. As serum calcium levels increase, calcitonin secretion also increases and the hormone encourages the movement of calcium from blood to the bones. Calcitonin also inhibits calcium reabsorption by the kidneys. The serum calcitonin test is used to evaluate individuals with suspected medullary carcinoma of the thyroid gland.

Normal Range

<50 pg/mL

Variations from Normal. Increased calcitonin levels are indicative of medullary carcinoma of the thyroid. Other diseases associated with increased calcitonin include oat cell carcinoma of the lung; breast and pancreatic cancers; thyroiditis; and pernicious anemia. Decreased calcitonin levels may not be diagnostically significant.

Interfering Circumstances. Drugs that may cause increased calcitonin levels include calcium, epinephrine, glucagon, and oral contraceptives.

Thyroid Stimulating hormone (TSH)

Thyroid stimulating hormone (TSH) is secreted by the anterior lobe of the pituitary gland and, as the name implies, stimulates the thyroid gland to produce and secrete thyroxine (T4) and triiodothyronine (T3). Measuring TSH levels is the most sensitive test for identifying and differentiating primary and secondary hypothyroidism.

Primary hypothyroidism is a result of thyroid gland malfunction or disease. In secondary hypothyroidism, the thyroid gland is unable to secrete adequate levels of T3 and T4 due to the failure of the pituitary gland or hypothalamus to secrete appropriate amounts of thyroid-related hormones.

Normal Range

1–4 U/mL

Variations from Normal. Increased TSH levels are indicative of primary hypothyroidism, thyroiditis, and lack of thyroid growth or development. Decreased TSH levels are associated with secondary hypothyroidism, hyperthyroidism, and pituitary dysfunction.

Interfering Circumstances. Drugs that may increase TSH levels include antithyroid medications and lithium. Decreased levels may be seen with aspirin, heparin, and steroid use.

Iron Tests

Iron is necessary for the production of hemoglobin and is an essential element in living cells. Over 90% of the body's iron is present as a component of hemoglobin and in the storage form **ferritin**. Iron is transported throughout the body via **transferrin**, a trace protein found in the blood.

Measuring blood levels of iron itself has limited diagnostic value, except in the case of iron poisoning. Therefore, in order to obtain diagnostically significant information, serum iron levels are measured in relation to transferrin, total iron-binding capacity, and ferritin levels. Serum tests that measure transferrin, iron, and total iron-binding capacity are used to evaluate and differentiate diagnoses of anemia. The ferritin test is used to measure available iron stores.

Ferritin

Ferritin, the storage form of iron, is formed in the intestine and stored in the liver, spleen, and bone marrow. Eventually, the iron is incorporated into hemoglobin. Serum levels of ferritin provide a good indication of the available iron stores in the body.

Normal Range

Men	12–300 ng/mL
Women	10–150 ng/mL
Newborn	25–200 ng/mL
1-month-old	200–600 ng/mL
2–5 months	50–200 ng/mL
6 months–15 yr	7–142 ng/mL

Variations from Normal. Anemic conditions associated with increased ferritin levels are megaloblastic anemia and hemolytic anemia. Iron storage disorders such as hemochromatosis and hemosiderosis cause high ferritin levels. Diseases such as alcoholic and/or inflammatory liver disease, metastatic cancer, breast cancer, and Hodgkin's disease also show an elevated ferritin level. Decreased ferritin levels are seen in iron deficiency anemia, severe protein deficiency, and in patients undergoing hemodialysis.

Interfering Circumstances.

Ferritin test results can be elevated if the patient has recently received a blood transfusion or eaten a meal high in iron. Various iron preparations may also cause an increased ferritin level. Menstruating women may exhibit decreased ferritin levels.

Transferrin Test; Total Iron-Binding Capacity (TIBC)

Since iron itself is highly toxic, iron present in the blood is bound to transferrin, a serum protein that transports iron. Under normal circumstances, there is much more transferrin available than is needed for iron transport, and only 30–40% of available transferrin is bound to iron. Measuring serum iron levels is accomplished by quantifying the amount of iron in a particular blood sample after the iron is freed from transferrin.

Total iron-binding capacity (TIBC) is an indirect measure of serum transferrin. The blood sample is exposed to enough excess iron so that all the transferrin can combine with the added iron. Once the serum iron level and TIBC have been identified, the **transferrin saturation,** the percentage of transferrin bound to iron, can be calculated by dividing the serum iron level by the TIBC.

Normal Range

Iron	60–190 µg/dl
TIBC	250–420 µg/dl
Transferrin	200–400 µg/dl
Transferrin Saturation	30–40%

Variations from Normal. Various anemias are associated with increases and/or decreases in serum iron, transferrin, transferrin saturation, and TIBC. Serum iron levels increase with hemolytic anemias, especially thalassemia, while decreased serum iron levels are associated with iron deficiency anemia. Transferrin increases in iron deficiency anemia and decreases in microcytic anemias caused by chronic disease. Transferrin saturation levels increase in aplastic anemia and thalassemia. Decreased transferrin saturation levels are associated with iron deficiency anemias. Elevated TIBC levels are found in iron deficiency anemia. Decreased TIBC levels are seen with hemolytic anemia, pernicious anemia, and sickle cell anemia. Table 3-1 presents

Table 3-1.   Serum Iron Tests Associated with Various Diagnoses of Anemia

Iron Test	Increased Serum Levels	Decreased Serum Levels
Serum iron	Hemolytic anemia thalassemia	Iron-deficiency anemia
Transferrin	Iron-deficiency anemia	Microcytic anemia
Transferrin saturation	Aplastic anemia thalassemia	Iron-deficiency anemia
TIBC	Iron-deficiency anemia	Hemolytic anemia, pernicious anemia, sickle cell anemia

each iron test and the anemia associated with increased and decreased serum levels or test results.

Other diseases that cause variations in iron test results include acute hepatitis, cirrhosis of the liver, malnutrition, protein deficiency, cancer of the small intestine, and chronic diseases such as lupus and rheumatoid arthritis.

Interfering Circumstances. Recent blood transfusions or hemolysis of the blood sample affect test results. Drugs that may affect test results include oral contraceptives, estrogens, ACTH, testosterone, and fluorides.

Summary

- Blood chemistry tests in this chapter are categorized as enzyme, hormone, thyroid function, and iron tests.
- Increased blood levels of enzymes usually indicate cell death or destruction and can be linked to specific organs and disease processes.
- Acid phosphatase and prostate-specific antigen tests are used to diagnose diseases of the prostate gland.
- Liver disorders are identified by serum increases of alanine aminotransferase, alkaline phosphatase, and aspartate aminotransferase.

- The cardiac enzyme series tests include aspartate aminotransferase, creatine phosphokinase, and lactic acid dehydrogenase.
- Creatine kinase has three isoenzymes that are organ-specific: CK-BB, brain tissue; CK-MB, cardiac muscle and cells; CK-MM, skeletal muscle.
- Lactic acid dehydrogenase has five isoenzymes that are organ-specific: LDH-1, heart and red blood cells; LDH-2, heart, kidney, and brain; LDH-3, lungs, skeletal muscle, brain, and liver; LDH-4, skeletal muscle, liver, and brain; LDH-5, liver and skeletal muscle.
- Serum lipase levels provide diagnostic information about the pancreas.
- Measuring serum hormone levels provides diagnostic information concerning the glands that secrete hormones and the cells and organs that respond to hormone activity.
- Thyroid hormones affect almost all cells in the body by increasing the metabolic rate, increasing cardiac output, stimulating cellular differentiation, and lowering blood calcium levels.
- Thyroid stimulating hormone stimulates the thyroid to produce and secrete thyroid hormones.
- Iron tests are valuable diagnostic tools that are used to differentiate anemias, identify available iron stores, and diagnose disorders of iron metabolism.

CHAPTER REVIEW

1. Identify the following blood chemistry tests:

   a. Male PAP test   _____

   b. Main enzyme(s) studied in patients with heart disease   _____

   c. Provides information for a delayed diagnosis of myocardial infarction   _____

   d. Identifies ectopic pregnancy and hydatidiform mole of the uterus   _____

e. Normal levels are consistent with routine peptic ulcer disease

_____

f. Confirms over- or underactive pituitary disease

_____

g. Provides specific diagnostic information about the pancreas

_____

h. Identifies and differentiates primary and secondary hypothyroidism

_____

i. Levels provide a good indication of the available iron stores in the body

_____

j. The serum protein that transports iron

_____

2. Organize the listed enzyme tests with the following diagnoses:

a. Prostate cancer

_____

b. Benign prostatic hypertrophy

_____

c. Metastatic liver tumor

_____

d. Osteomalacia

_____

e. Obstructive jaundice

_____

f. Myocardial infarction

_____

g. Acute pancreatitis

_____

h. Muscular dystrophy

_____

i. Cerebral infarction

_____

j. Multiple myeloma

_____

acid phosphatase/PAP

alanine aminotransferase/ALT

alkaline phosphatase

aspartate aminotransferase/AST

creatine phosphokinase/CPK

lactic acid dehydrogenase/LDH

lipase

prostate-specific antigen/PSA

3. Match the isoenzymes in column I with the diagnoses in column II.

Column I	Column II	
a. CK-BB (CK1)	Infectious mononucleosis	_____
b. CK-MB (CK2)	Polymyositis	_____
c. CK-MM (CK3)	Cerebrovascular accident	_____
d. LDH-1	Recent convulsions	_____
e. LDH-2	Myocardial cellular damage	_____
f. LDH-3	Muscular dystrophy	_____
g. LDH-4	Reye's syndrome	_____
h. LDH-5	Intestinal ischemia	_____
	Myocardial infarction	_____
	Pulmonary infarction	_____
	Acute pancreatitis	_____
	Malignant lymphoma	_____
	Myocarditis	_____
	Acute glomerulonephritis	_____
	Skeletal muscle trauma	_____

4. Identify a disease that is related to an increase and decrease of each serum hormone level.

Hormone	Increase	Decrease
a. Antidiuretic hormone	_____	_____
b. Gastrin	_____	_____
c. Growth hormone	_____	_____
d. Human chorionic gonadotropin	_____	_____
e. Cortisol	_____	_____
f. Testosterone	_____	_____

5. Briefly discuss the iron test(s) associated with the specific types of anemias listed. Include whether there is an increase or decrease in blood levels of the substances being measured.

   a. Iron deficiency anemia   _____

   b. Hemolytic anemia   _____

   c. Thalassemia   _____

   d. Aplastic anemia   _____

   e. Microcytic anemia   _____

   f. Pernicious anemia   _____

   g. Sickle cell anemia   _____

Case Studies

1. Frank Carlson, a 69-year-old man, has recently had a prostatectomy due to cancer of the prostate. As part of the diagnostic process prior to determining that Mr. Carlson had prostate cancer, the urologist ordered a PSA test. What does this test measure? What PSA levels might be found before and after surgery? In addition, Mr. Carlson's physician may also utilize the PAP test. What enzyme does this test measure and when might it be used?

2. Jeff Smith, a 15-year-old boy, has been referred to an orthopedic specialist because he has an elevated ALP. Discuss the implication of an elevated ALP. Review the range of diseases indicated by an elevated ALP. Evaluate Jeff Smith's situation and describe why he is seeing an orthopedic physician.

3. Paula Johnson, a 52-year-old woman, is undergoing a series of thyroid function tests. The physician suspects that Mrs. Johnson may be experiencing hypothyroidism. What hormone tests would the physician order? What results would be expected if Mrs. Johnson did have hypothyroidism?

Challenge Activity

> Construct a laboratory printout that contains blood chemistry test results that support the diagnosis of myocardial infarction.

Chapter 4

Coagulation Studies

Key Terms, Abbreviations, and Acronyms

acquired deficiencies

activated partial thromboplastin time, APTT

bleeding tendencies

bleeding time test

clot retraction test

coagulation factors

common pathway

disseminated intravascular coagulation, DIC

Duke method

extrinsic pathway

factor assay test, coagulant factors test

fibrin

fibrinogen

fibrinogen assay test

fibrinolysis

hemostasis

hypercoagulability state

inherited deficiencies

international normalized ratio, INR

intrinsic pathway

Ivy method

partial thromboplastin time

plasmin

platelet aggregation test

prothrombin

prothrombin time, PT, Pro Time

thrombin

thrombin time, thrombin clotting time, TCT

Learning Objectives

Upon completion of this chapter, the learner should be able to:

1. Describe the hemostatic process.
2. Identify and define commonly performed coagulation tests.
3. Discuss the diagnostic significance of commonly performed tests.
4. Compare two methods used to measure bleeding time.
5. Differentiate between extrinsic, intrinsic, and common coagulation pathways.
6. Evaluate the benefits of tests that measure the fibrinogen levels in the blood.
7. Relate specific coagulation factors to specific disease processes.

Introduction

Hemostasis, stopping or controlling the escape of blood from its vessels, is accomplished by a series of reactions that involve the blood vessel wall, platelet activity, and the complex process of coagulation. The hemostatic process is triggered by any injury that damages vascular endothelium, the inner lining of blood vessels. Once the damage occurs, the blood vessel constricts in order to narrow the vessel opening and restrain the flow of blood.

The vascular injury causes platelets already present in the blood to adhere to tissue at the site of the injury. The platelets begin to change shape and activate platelet aggregation, which is the sticking of platelets to each other. More platelets move to the injured area and, in about one minute, form a platelet plug that is capable of stopping small hemorrhages.

Vascular injury or damage initiates both platelet plug formation and the coagulation process. The coagulation process is dependent on the activation of a series of plasma proteins called coagulation factors. Table 4-1 lists the coagulation factors by name and number in the order in which they were discovered. Note that factor IV is the mineral calcium.

Coagulation is a complex process that involves a series of reactions classified as the extrinsic pathway, intrinsic pathway, and common pathway. The ultimate objective of all reactions is to develop a stable blood clot that results in hemostasis.

Table 4-1. Coagulation Factors

Factor Number	Factor Name
Factor I	Fibrinogen
Factor II	Prothrombin
Factor III	Thromboplastin, tissue factor
Factor IV	Calcium
Factor V	Prothrombin accelerator
Factor VII	Proconvertin
Factor VIII	Antihemophilic factor
Factor IX	Christmas factor
Factor X	Stuart (Prower) factor
Factor XI	Plasma thromboplastin antecedent
Factor XII	Hageman factor
Factor XIII	Fibrin-stabilizing factor

The extrinsic pathway is so named because one of the coagulation factors, Factor III thromboplastin, is not present in circulating blood. Factor IV calcium and Factor VII proconvertin are also part of the extrinsic pathway.

The intrinsic pathway is so named because all of the required coagulation factors are present in circulating blood. Factors of the intrinsic pathway are Factor VIII antihemophilic factor, Factor IX Christmas factor, Factor XI plasma thromboplastin antecedent, and Factor XII Hageman factor.

Factors involved in the extrinsic and intrinsic pathways respond to a series of chemical reactions that lead to the common pathway. Common pathway factors are Factor I fibrinogen, Factor II prothrombin, Factor V prothrombin accelerator, Factor X Stuart (Prower) factor, and Factor XIII fibrin-stabilizing factor. The common pathway ultimately results in the formation of a stable clot. Figure 4-1 is a simplified schematic of the coagulation process.

Near the beginning of the common pathway, coagulation factors undergo chemical reactions that lead to the release of an active enzyme called **thrombin**. Thrombin acts on the plasma protein **fibrinogen**, a soluble plasma protein, and converts it to **fibrin**. Fibrin is an insoluble, stringy plasma protein that is deposited on the initial platelet plug in

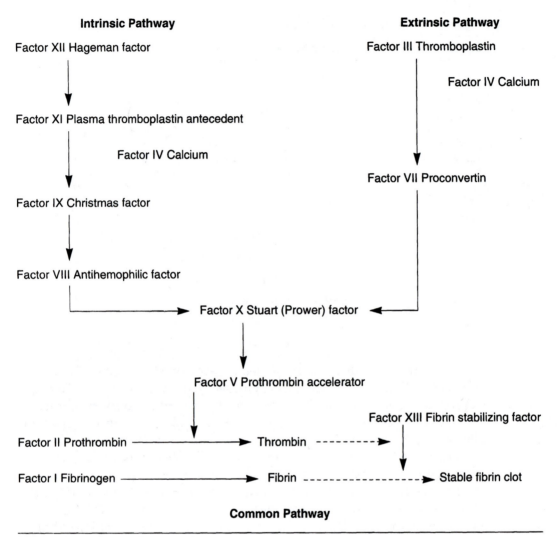

Figure 4-1.   Coagulation pathways

order to stabilize the plug. This stabilized plug or clot is capable of stopping the escape of blood.

Once the clot has served its purpose of hemostasis, it must be dissolved or destroyed. **Fibrinolysis**, destruction of blood clots, must be accomplished in a timely manner. Early clot destruction compromises the hemostatic process. Fibrinolysis is achieved by the action of the enzyme **plasmin.** Plasmin is also called fibrinolysin.

The hemostatic process is dependent on a functioning coagulation process. Coagulation tests of blood provide the health practitioner with diagnostic information about a patient's hemostatic abilities. Coagulation disorders can be categorized as **bleeding tendencies**, caused by delayed clot formation or premature clot destruction, and **hypercoagulability states,** caused by an abnormal tendency toward thrombosis, or clot formation.

Hemostasis and Coagulation Tests

There are a variety of tests that evaluate the nature and extent of hemostatic and coagulation disorders. These tests can include the analysis of platelets and platelet function; and the presence, absence, and clotting ability of plasma coagulation factors.

Platelet and Platelet Function Tests

Platelets are necessary for hemostasis and coagulation. Laboratory tests that measure the number of platelets in the blood include the platelet count and the mean platelet volume. These tests and the effects of an increase or decrease in the number of platelets have been discussed in Chapter 1. Laboratory tests that measure platelet function are covered in this chapter and include the **bleeding time test,** which measures platelet quality and vascular abnormalities; the **platelet aggregation test**, which identifies the platelets' ability to aggregate or form a platelet plug; and the **clot retraction test**, which provides information about platelet quality and fibrinolysis.

Bleeding time

Bleeding time measures how long it takes platelets to interact with the blood vessel wall in order to form a platelet plug. Bleeding time is dependent on the quantity and quality of platelets, and the constriction ability of the blood vessel wall. The bleeding time test is very helpful in identifying vascular abnormalities, and somewhat helpful in detecting platelet problems.

There are two methods for measuring bleeding time: the **Ivy method** and the **Duke method**. The Ivy method is performed by making an incision on the forearm of the patient and measuring the time it takes for the bleeding to stop. This method is preferred because the results can be standardized. The Duke method is performed by making a 2–3 mm deep puncture in the earlobe and measuring the time it takes for bleeding to stop. Results of the Duke method are not standardized.

Normal Range

Ivy method: 2–9 minutes
Duke method: 1–3 minutes

Variations from Normal. Bleeding time is increased when platelet quantity or quality is compromised, as in thrombocytopenia, leukemia, anemia and in problems wherein platelets are unable to function. Platelet size can influence platelet function, as in Bernard-Soulier syndrome, a disorder in which the platelets are large and platelet count is low. It is believed that the ability of platelets to adhere to the vascular wall is compromised in this syndrome. As a result of this adhesion problem, bleeding time would be increased.

In thrombasthenia, a rare hemorrhagic disease characterized by an abnormality in the membrane surface of thrombocytes, the platelets are not able to aggregate and therefore a clot does not form. Bleeding time is definitely increased in thrombasthenia, also called Glanzmann's thrombasthenia.

Vascular defects and abnormalities in the walls of small blood vessels also cause a prolonged bleeding time. Other diseases associated with an increased bleeding time include severe liver disease, leukemia, aplastic anemia, disseminated intravascular coagulation (DIC) disease, and von Willebrand's disease.

Platelet Aggregation Test

One of the early stages of hemostasis is the formation of a platelet plug that involves platelet adhesion and platelet aggregation. Without a properly functioning platelet aggregation process the body would be subject to literally hundreds of small hemorrhages per day. The platelet aggregation test is used to identify platelet aggregation abnormalities.

In order to measure platelet aggregation, platelet-rich plasma and chemical agents that cause platelet aggregation are combined in a test tube.

The platelet-rich plasma is derived from a sample of the patient's blood. Normal platelet aggregation is evidenced as the platelet aggregates settle to the bottom of the test tube and the platelet-rich plasma becomes clear. Platelet aggregates should be visible in less than five minutes.

Normal Ranges. Normal ranges depend on the testing method used and the patient's medical history.

Variations from Normal. Abnormal platelet aggregation results can be seen in both congenital and acquired diseases. Congenital disorders that display a reduced ability of the platelets to aggregate include von Willebrand's disease, Bernard-Soulier syndrome, and Glanzmann's thrombasthenia.

Acquired diseases that result in abnormal platelet aggregation are uremia, acute leukemia, and infectious mononucleosis. Certain drugs such as aspirin and antibiotics interfere with the ability of platelets to aggregate.

Clot Retraction Test

The clot retraction test is used primarily as a screening test to evaluate platelet function and fibrinolysis. Fibrinolysis is the process of fibrin destruction and is necessary for the dissolution of fibrin clots. If fibrinolysis is very active, clots may be dissolved as quickly as they are formed. The clot retraction test also measures the quality of a therapeutic blood clot.

For this test, the blood sample is left in a test tube without an anticoagulant additive. Whole blood should clot and retract or pull away from the sides of the tube. The clot retraction test is considered to be normal when the clot begins to retract within one hour and retraction is complete by four hours. When the clot is removed from the tube, the remaining serum should represent approximately 44–64% of the total blood volume.

The quality of a therapeutic blood clot is directly related to the number and quality of the platelets that participate in the formation of the clot, and the degree of fibrinolytic activity. A defective clot is soft and soggy and does not retain its shape once it is removed from the testing container. Heightened fibrinolysis causes a premature dissolution of the therapeutic blood clot.

Normal Range

Clot retraction	Begins within 1 hour
Complete clot retraction	Completed within 24 hours

Variations from Normal. Abnormal clot retraction results are noted in diseases such as thrombocytopenia, von Willebrand's disease, increased red blood cell mass, severe anemia, and hypofibrinogenemia, a decrease in the amount of fibrinogen in the blood.

Interfering Circumstances. An increased hematocrit due to polycythemia interferes with the results of a clot retraction test.

Plasma Coagulation Factor Tests

As stated previously, coagulation factors are plasma proteins, with the exception of Factor IV calcium. These plasma proteins circulate in the blood in an inactive form and are activated when tissue or blood vessel damage occurs. Refer to Table 4-1 to review the name and number of each of the coagulation factors.

In order for the coagulation process to be effective, there must not only be an adequate supply of each of the plasma coagulation factors but each factor must also be functional. Disorders of coagulation factors are divided into inherited deficiencies, a lack of certain factors passed from parent to child, and acquired deficiencies, a lack or decrease in the amount of any given factor due to diseases that influence the production of the coagulation factors.

The liver plays a major role in the production of several coagulation factors. For example, if the liver cannot obtain an adequate amount of vitamin K, the manufacture of Factors II, VII, IX, and X is compromised. Therefore, disorders that affect the ability of the liver to function, or the ability of the liver to utilize or obtain vitamin K, also affect the coagulation process.

Tests that measure the quantity and quality of plasma coagulation factors include the prothrombin time, a test that measures plasma levels of several coagulation factors; the activated partial thromboplastin time and the partial thromboplastin time, tests that measure coagulation and anticoagulation activities in the blood; thrombin time (thrombin clotting time), a test that measures blood levels of fibrinogen; the fibrinogen assay test, which measures the serum concentration of fibrinogen; and the factor assay test, which measures the plasma coagulation factors as they relate to inherited and acquired bleeding disorders.

Prothrombin time (Pro Time; PT)

Prothrombin time, also known as Pro Time, is one of the most important blood tests used to diagnose coagulation problems. Prothrombin, coagulation Factor II, is a protein that circulates in the blood. It is produced in the liver, and is vitamin K dependent. Although the test is called the prothrombin time, it actually measures deficiencies of Factors I, V, VII, and X, as well as deficiencies of prothrombin itself. The prothrombin time is also performed when the patient is undergoing anticoagulant therapy with medications such as Coumadin or as a component in liver function assessment.

There are three ways to report Pro Time results: (1) as time in seconds; (2) as a percentage of normal activity; and, in warfarin therapy, (3) as an **international normalized ratio (INR).** Time in seconds indicates how long it takes the blood sample to clot. The percentage measurement expresses how long it takes the blood to clot when compared to normal clotting activity.

The INR is considered to be the most accurate reporting method of Pro Time test results when such results are used to monitor and adjust drug levels in anticoagulant therapy. Simply stated, the INR is the result of a mathematical calculation that uses Pro Time results and other standard laboratory measurements that are expressed as a ratio. This text uses the time in seconds for the normal ranges of Pro Time results, and the desirable or therapeutic INR ranges for anticoagulation therapy.

Normal Range

Non-anticoagulant therapy	10–12.5 seconds
Therapeutic range for anticoagulant therapy:	2.0–3.0 INR

Variations from Normal. An increase in the patient's prothrombin time can indicate a deficiency in any one of the five coagulation factors measured by the prothrombin time test. Anticoagulant therapy can cause an elevated Pro Time.

During anticoagulant therapy, oral drugs work in the liver and interfere with the action of coagulation Factors II, VII, IX, and X. Anticoagulant therapy is commonly ordered for cardiac patients and in the treatment of blood clots.

Conditions that exhibit an increased prothrombin time include prothrombin deficiency, vitamin K deficiency, toxic levels of vitamin A, and disseminated intravascular coagulation (DIC) syndrome. This syndrome is an acquired hemorrhagic disease in which the coagulation factors of the blood are depleted. Many coagulation test irregularities are associated with DIC.

An increase in the Pro Time is also seen in hemorrhagic disease of the newborn, liver diseases such as alcoholic hepatitis, biliary obstruction, and salicylate poisoning. Salicylate poisoning is most often caused by excess ingestion of aspirin or oil of wintergreen.

Interfering Circumstances. A high-fat diet may cause decreased prothrombin levels, whereas alcohol consumption may increase prothrombin levels. Many drugs can interfere with blood prothrombin levels. Medications that result in an increased level include chlorpromazine, methyldopa salicylates, barbiturates, and sulfonamides. Decreased levels are associated with anabolic steroids, digitalis, estrogens, and vitamin K.

Activated Partial Thromboplastin Time (APTT); Partial Thromboplastin Time (PTT)

The activated partial thromboplastin time is a modification of the partial thromboplastin time. The APTT is slightly more sensitive than the PTT. Both tests measure deficiencies in coagulation Factors I, II, V, VIII, IX, X, XI, and XII. These factors represent both the intrinsic and common coagulation pathways.

The activated partial thromboplastin time is also used to detect circulating anticoagulants, substances that interfere with the clotting process, and to monitor heparin therapy. The APTT is often used in conjunction with the prothrombin time in order to differentiate between defects in the intrinsic and extrinsic pathways.

Normal Range

No anticoagulant therapy	30–40 seconds
Anticoagulant therapy (heparin)	1.5 to 2.0 times the APPT of the normal plasma control

Variations from Normal. A prolonged or increased activated partial thromboplastin time is expected when the patient is undergoing heparin therapy. Both the APTT and the prothrombin time can be used to measure the effects of anticoagulant therapy. The Pro Time is used more often to monitor warfarin therapy and the APPT to monitor heparin therapy.

In the absence of heparin therapy, an increased APTT indicates a bleeding disorder. Since this test screens for more than one coagulation factor deficiency, an increased APTT may result in additional tests to identify specific factor problems. Diseases that can cause a prolonged APTT include hemophilia, vitamin K deficiency, liver disease, the presence of circulating anticoagulants, and disseminated intravascular coagulation (DIC) disease.

A decreased APTT time can be present in extensive malignancies, excluding those involving the liver; immediately after an acute hemorrhage; and in the early stages of DIC. A decreased APTT may also indicate hypercoagulability.

Interfering Circumstances. A variety of medications can interfere with the results of the activated partial thromboplastin time. An increased or prolonged APTT time is associated with salicylates such as aspirin. A decreased or shortened APTT time is associated with the use of digitalis, tetracyclines, antihistamines, and nicotine.

Thrombin Time; Thrombin Clotting Time

Although this test is called thrombin time, it is actually used to measure the blood plasma levels of fibrinogen, coagulation Factor I. Fibrinogen is the precursor to fibrin, the stringy substance that traps platelets at the site of vessel injury.

Thrombin time is a nonspecific test in that it does not identify any particular disease. It does detect fibrinogen deficiencies. When thrombin is added to the blood sample, the presence of fibrinogen causes a clot to form almost instantly. This test is also used for monitoring heparin therapy.

Normal Range. Normal ranges may vary: Check your laboratory standards.

14–16 seconds or within 5 seconds of control

Variations from Normal. The total absence of fibrinogen results in the absence of clot formation. A decreased amount of fibrinogen produces a small but visible clot. Fibrinogen deficiencies or abnormalities result in a prolonged thrombin time. Levels of fibrinogen are affected by diseases such as multiple myeloma and congenital abnormalities of fibrinogen.

Anticoagulant therapy, such as heparin therapy, also results in a prolonged thrombin time. It is important to review the patient's record to determine whether or not the patient is receiving anticoagulant therapy.

Interfering Circumstances. Inappropriate handling of the blood sample may alter test results.

Table 4-2 identifies coagulation factors measured by the prothrombin time, the activated partial thromboplastin time, and the thrombin time tests.

Table 4-2. Coagulation Factors Measured by Prothrombin Time, Activated Partial Thromboplastin Time, and Thrombin Time

Test	Coagulation Factors
Prothrombin time Pro Time (PT)	Factor I, Factor II, Factor V, Factor VII, Factor X
Activated partial thromboplastin time (APTT)	Factor VIII, Factor IX, Factor X, Factor XI, Factor XII
Thrombin time	Factor I

Fibrinogen Assay Test

Although the thrombin time measures the presence or absence of fibrinogen (Factor I), the actual concentration of fibrinogen in the blood is identified via the fibrinogen assay test. Fibrinogen is manufactured by the liver, it does not need vitamin K for its production, and it is essential for the formation of fibrin.

Normal Range

200–400 mg/dl

Variations from Normal. An increase in fibrinogen is associated with diseases such as hepatitis, multiple myeloma, cancer, nephrosis, rheumatic fever, tuberculosis, and septicemia. Given the serious nature of each of these diseases, it seems that the increased fibrinogen levels do not trigger any specific or unique medical intervention. Decreased fibrinogen levels present an entirely different picture.

Low fibrinogen concentrations can be caused by genetic disorders or severe liver disease. These cases are rare and are usually identified by the activated partial thromboplastin time or the partial thromboplastin time test. In most cases, a decreased fibrinogen level is attributed to **disseminated intravascular coagulation (DIC) syndrome**. This syndrome causes a depletion or decrease of fibrinogen and other clotting factors by overstimulating the coagulation process. Many small thrombi are formed and coagulation factors are thus depleted. DIC is the result of various clinical conditions and is not a primary condition in and of itself.

DIC has been linked to obstetrical problems such as amniotic fluid emboli, toxemia, and abruptio placentae. Other causes of DIC include lysis of red blood cells, incompatible blood transfusions, malaria, infections that promote platelet aggregation, severe trauma, burns, and heat stroke.

Interfering Circumstances. Fibrinogen levels can be increased by estrogen and oral contraceptive therapy. Decreased levels can be associated with anabolic steroids, androgens, and streptokinase.

Factor Assay Test; Coagulant Factors Test

The factor assay test measures the plasma concentration of specific coagulation factors. Coagulant factor deficiencies are classified as inherited, familial, or acquired and usually result in bleeding tendencies. Inherited and familial deficiencies, as the name suggests, are passed from parent to child and are sometimes called congenital factor deficiencies. Acquired factor deficiencies occur as a result of diseases, disorders, or drugs that lead to clotting factor deficiencies.

An abnormal prothrombin time or activated partial thromboplastin time may trigger a factor assay test. The factor assay is quite specialized and may not be performed in many laboratories. However, when the clinician needs to know the precise nature of the coagulation factor deficiency, the factor assay test provides that information.

In the rare event that a factor assay would be performed, Factor XIII and Factor I (fibrinogen) are measured in a different manner than the remaining factors. The fibrinogen assay test has already been presented. Factor XIII, fibrin-stabilizing factor, is analyzed by observing a blood clot for twenty-four hours. If the clot dissolves within that time, a severe Factor XIII deficiency exists.

Normal Range. The level of coagulation factor in the patient's blood must fall within the percentages of the level found in the control sample.

Factor VII	Proconvertin	65–135% of normal
Factor VIII	Antihemophilic factor	55–145% of normal
Factor IX	Christmas factor	60–140% of normal
Factor X	Stuart factor (Stuart-Prower factor)	45–155% of normal
Factor XI	Plasma thromboplastin antecedent	65–135% of normal
Factor XII	Hageman factor	50–150% of normal
Factor XIII	Fibrin-stabilizing factor	Fibrin clot remains normal for 24 hours

Variations from Normal. For purposes of clarity, the variations from normal for this test are presented in Table 4-3. This table lists the coagulation

Table 4-3. Coagulation Factors Associated with Inherited Disorders/Diseases or Acquired Bleeding Disorders

Factor	*Disorder/Disease(s)*
Inherited	
Factor VII	Hypoproconvertinemia
Factor VIII	Classic hemophilia, von Willebrand's disease
Factor IX	Hemophilia B, also known as Christmas disease
Factor XI	Hemophilia C
Acquired	
Factor VII	Hepatic diseases, vitamin K deficiency
Factor IX	Cirrhosis of the liver, severe kidney syndromes, vitamin K deficiency
Factor X	Liver disease, vitamin K deficiency, hemorrhagic disease of newborns
Factor XI	Liver disease, vitamin K deficiency, congenital heart disease
Factor XII	Nephrotic syndrome
Factor VIII	Coronary artery disease, myeloma, hypoglycemia

factors measured in a factor assay test and diseases associated with a deficiency of each factor. Inherited factor deficiency diseases as well as acquired factor deficiency diseases are included in Table 4-3. Liver disease, vitamin K deficiency, and disseminated intravascular coagulation can lead to acquired coagulation factor deficiencies.

Increases in coagulation factors rarely occur. Elevated Factor VIII (antihemophilic factor) plasma levels are associated with coronary artery disease, hyperthyroidism, hypoglycemia, and Cushing's syndrome. In addition to these disease processes, an increase in Factor VIII is seen in normal pregnancies and postoperative period. In all of these situations, there is a tendency toward clot formation.

Several of the blood coagulation factors have been discussed in the context of the factor assay test and diseases that cause an increase or decrease in the blood levels of those factors. Note that the diseases identified here do not always lead to an increase or decrease of coagulation factors. If the patient presents with the identified diseases and evidence of a bleeding disorder, then the clinician may be prompted to investigate the possibility of a coagulation factor problem.

Summary

- Hemostasis is accomplished by constriction of vessel walls, platelet aggregation, and the complex process of coagulation.
- The coagulation process is triggered by platelet response to damaged vascular endothelium.
- The coagulation process is dependent on the presence of specific coagulation factors.
- Coagulation Factors are plasma proteins, with the exception of Factor IV, which is calcium.
- Coagulation disorders are categorized as bleeding tendencies and hypercoagulable states.
- Bleeding time, platelet aggregation, and clot retraction tests measure the coagulation function of platelets and vascular walls.
- Prothrombin time measures deficiencies of five plasma coagulation factors and is performed to monitor anticoagulant therapy.

- Activated partial thromboplastin time measures deficiencies of the co-agulation Factors VIII, IX, X, XI, and XII.
- Thrombin time and the fibrinogen assay test are performed to measure the presence and concentration of fibrinogen.
- The factor assay test measures plasma levels of Factors VII through XIII and is able to identify congenital and acquired coagulation deficiencies.

CHAPTER REVIEW

1. Identify the following coagulation tests:

    a. Measures length of time for platelet plug formation   _____

    b. Measures deficiencies of five coagulation factors   _____

    c. Detects circulating anticoagulants and deficiencies in several coagulation factors   _____

    d. Nonspecific test to detect fibrinogen deficiencies   _____

    e. Measures the concentration of serum fibrinogen   _____

    f. Test of specific coagulation factors   _____

2. Identify a disease or disorder associated with a *deficiency* in the following coagulation factors:

Factor	Disease/Disorder
a. Factor I fibrinogen	_____
b. Factor VII proconvertin	_____
c. Factor VIII antihemophilic factor	_____

    d. Factor IX Christmas factor _____

    e. Factor X Stuart factor _____

    f. Factor XI plasma thromboplastin antecedent _____

    g. Factor XII Hageman factor _____

    h. Factor XIII fibrin–stabilizing factor _____

3. Briefly describe the hemostatic process from vascular injury to fibrinolysis.

4. What is the difference between the Duke and Ivy Methods? What is the purpose of these techniques?

5. Briefly discuss the role of platelets in the coagulation process. Describe the three platelet-related coagulation tests. Include the name of the test, a brief description, and diseases or disorders associated with each test.

6. Coagulation disorders are categorized as *inherited deficiencies* or *acquired deficiencies*. Define each type of deficiency and provide examples of diseases or disorders associated with the deficiency. Examples should include the name of the disease or disorder and the coagulation factor involved.

7. Both the thrombin time and the fibrinogen assay test provide information about fibrinogen, coagulation Factor I. What is the difference between these tests? What is gained by performing both tests? Are there specific diseases associated with each test? What are those diseases?

Case Studies

1. Reba Alexander, a 45-year-old female, has recently been hospitalized because she has a blood clot in her left iliac artery. Dr. Jason, a vascular surgeon, has written a progress note indicating he suspects that Mrs. Alexander has a clotting disorder. Based on this conclusion the physician has placed her on the medication warfarin for anticoagulation therapy. This therapy requires frequent blood tests to measure the INR. What blood tests are performed in order to measure the INR? If Mrs. Alexander has an INR value of 2.5, is she within the therapeutic range for anticoagulation therapy? How could anticoagulant therapy, such as warfarin, affect other tests such as the APTT or the PTT?

2. You are reviewing the record of Randy Robertson, a child seen by Dr. Carson, a pediatrician. The physician has just determined that the child has hemophilia. In order to reach this decision, the physician ordered a factor assay test. Which blood coagulation factors are found to be deficient in hemophilia? How might the test results in this patient vary from the normal results?

Challenge Activity

> Define the *extrinsic, intrinsic,* and *common coagulation pathways*. Note the point at which each coagulation factor enters the coagulation process. In your own words, or using illustrations, prepare a description of the coagulation process.

Chapter 5

Infectious Disease and Immunodiagnostic Blood Tests

Key Terms, Abbreviations, and Acronyms

agglutination test

anti-DNase B, ABD

antinuclear antibody (ANA) test

antistreptolysin O titer, ASO

complement fixation (CF) test

Coombs' test

C-reactive protein (CRP) test

direct (forward) ABO blood grouping

direct fluorescent antibody, DFA

enzyme immunoassay, EIA

enzyme-linked immunosorbent assay, ELISA

fluorescent treponemal antibody absorption (FTA-ABS) test

hemagglutination inhibition (HAI) test

herpes simplex virus type 1 (HSV-1)

herpes simplex virus type 2 (HSV-2)

human immunodeficiency virus type 1 (HIV-1)

human immunodeficiency virus type 2 (HIV-2)

hyaluronidase

indirect (reverse) ABO blood grouping

indirect fluorescent antibody, IFA

infectious mononucleosis, IM

latex agglutination

microhemagglutination, MHA

microhemagglutination for Treponema pallidum antibody (MHA-TP) test polymerase chain reaction (PCR) test

precipitation

radioimmunoassay, RIA

rapid plasma reagin (RPR) test

rapid slide test

rheumatoid factor, RF

reagin

Rh typing

Western blot assay test

Additional Abbreviations

ABO	human blood grouping system
AIDS	acquired immunodeficiency syndrome
anti-HBc	antibody to hepatitis B core antigen
anti-HBe	antibody to hepatitis B envelope antigen
anti-HBs	antibody to hepatitis B surface antigen
anti-HCV	antibody to hepatitis C virus
anti-VCA	antibody to the viral capsid antigen
BFP	biological false-positive
CMV	cytomegalovirus
EBNA	antibodies to Epstein-Barr virus nuclear antigen
EBV	Epstein-Barr virus
ECM, EM	erythema chronicum migrans
HAV	hepatitis A virus
HBcAg	hepatitis B core antigen
HBeAg	hepatitis B envelope antigen
HBsAg	hepatitis B surface antigen
HBV	hepatitis B virus
HCV	hepatitis C virus
HIV-1	human immunodeficiency virus type 1

HIV-2	human immunodeficiency virus type 2
HSV-1	herpes simplex virus type 1
HSV-2	herpes simplex virus type 2
IgG anti-HAV	IgG antibodies against hepatitis A virus
IgM anti-HAV	IgM antibodies against hepatitis A virus
IM	infectious mononucleosis
SLE	systemic lupus erythematosus
total anti-HAV	total antibody against hepatitis A virus
TORCH	toxoplasmosis, rubella, cytomegalovirus, and herpes virus.
VDRL	venereal disease research laboratory

Learning Objectives

Upon completion of this chapter, the learner should be able to:

1. Explain the antigen-antibody reaction as it relates to infectious disease blood tests.
2. List and define tests used to identify the presence of antibodies in the blood.
3. Relate various antibody tests to specific diseases or diagnoses.
4. Differentiate between diseases of bacterial, viral, and fungal origin.
5. Discuss ABO blood groups and the serologic tests used to identify the groups.
6. Compare the direct and indirect Coombs' tests and the diagnostic significance of each test.

Introduction

Previous chapters have covered blood tests that measure increases and decreases of cells and substances that are normally found in the blood. This chapter presents information about blood tests that identify a variety of substances that may or may not normally be present in the blood. Infectious diseases are caused by various organisms that invade or "infect" the body and subsequently trigger the immune system to defend the body from the invader. This process is called the antigen-antibody reaction. The tests discussed in this chapter describe how blood is tested in order to identify the antibodies that have been produced in response to a specific antigen, or to identify the antigen itself.

In order to lay the foundation for the discussion of these tests, there is a brief review of the antigen-antibody reaction. Frequently performed blood tests that rely on the antibody-antigen reaction to identify disease are defined and related to disease processes. Selected diseases of bacterial, viral, and fungal origin and the tests used to diagnose them are presented. Tests that are unique to a specific disease are reviewed with that disease.

The blood grouping tests included in this chapter measure those substances that are normally present in the blood and identify the various blood types. Blood grouping tests identify the antigens present on red blood cells and the antibodies present in circulating blood. Antigen-antibody reactions are used to identify blood types as well as diseases. Therefore, information related to the antigen-antibody reaction or response is useful in understanding both disease and ABO blood type tests.

Antigen-Antibody Reaction

The antigen-antibody reaction is part of the body's natural defense mechanism. An antigen, also called an immunogen, is any substance that stimulates the formation of specific antibodies and reacts with those specific antibodies. Antigens may enter the body by way of the bloodstream, through breaks in the integrity of the skin, and by infiltrating the respiratory and gastrointestinal tract.

An antibody, also called an immunoglobulin, is a substance that appears as the result of the introduction of an antigen and reacts specifically with that antigen. The antibody reacts with specific sites on the antigen to form an antigen-antibody complex (Ag-Ab complex). Antibodies do not actually destroy the antigen; rather they can set off a series of reactions that allow phagocytes and T-cells to destroy the foreign organism. Antibodies also bind to the antigens to prevent the antigens from binding to their target cells. In order to reach a specific diagnosis or to identify a specific disease, blood serum can be tested for the presence of the antibody, the antigen, the antigen-antibody complex, or any part or combination of the three.

Serology Tests for Antigen-Antibody Reactions

The most common specimen used for testing the antigen-antibody reaction is serum derived from a clotted blood sample. Fasting specimens are preferred but not required. Once the blood has clotted, it is centrifuged to separate cells from the serum. The serum is transferred to a clean test tube and can be refrigerated for seventy-two hours. Frequently performed serology tests include the agglutination test, precipitation test, complement fixation, and several categories of labeled immunoassays. These serology tests are described below and are used to identify a variety of disease processes.

Agglutination Test

Agglutination is the visible clumping or aggregation of cells or particles due to their reaction with an antibody. The cells or particles must have antigens on their surface in order for the agglutination to occur. The presence of agglutination usually indicates a positive test result.

Types of agglutination tests include **microhemagglutination (MHA)**, a test in which the clumping of red blood cells is observed via a microscope; **latex agglutination**, which uses a latex component that allows the agglutination reaction to be visible; and the **hemagglutination inhibition test (HAI)**, a variation of the agglutination test in which the red blood cells (RBCs) are prevented or inhibited from clumping. A positive HAI result is indicated by the absence of agglutination. Agglutination tests are often used in blood typing, in slide tests for rheumatoid factor and infectious mononucleosis, and in bacterial identification.

Precipitation Test

The precipitation test is carried out in a semisolid medium such as agar. Precipitation occurs when a specific antibody reagent reacts with an antigen and an insoluble complex is formed. This insoluble complex then settles out and is visible as a white precipitate, which indicates a positive test result. This test is used to detect and classify the streptococcus bacteria.

Complement Fixation (CF) Test

The complement fixation (CF) test is used primarily to identify viral antibodies, but can be used to detect some fungal antibodies as well. Complement fixation is a complex test that relies on the ability of complement, an enzymatic serum protein, to interact with antibody and specific antigen to cause cell lysis. A negative result indicates an absence of the antibody being tested for, as evidenced by cell lysis. A positive result indicates that the antibody being tested for is present, as evidenced by the absence of cell lysis.

Labeled Immunoassays

Antigen-antibody reactions are for the most part invisible both microscopically and to the naked eye. When the antigen is not large enough to be visualized, the antigen must be bound to a larger particle so that the antigen-antibody reaction can be visualized. Agglutination or precipitation are good examples of visible antigen-antibody reactions.

Labeled immunoassays are laboratory tests to detect an antigen-antibody reaction by using "labels" attached either to the antigen or the antibody. The label provides a means to visualize whether an antigen-antibody reaction has occurred and to measure the amount of antigen or antibody present. Labels can be a fluorescent compound, an enzyme, or a radioactive isotope.

Fluorescent Immunoassay (FIA)

There are two main types of fluorescent immunoassay tests: the direct fluorescent antibody (DFA) and the indirect fluorescent antibody (IFA). Both of these methods use a fluorescent compound as the label and are fairly complex. Either the direct or indirect method can be used to detect an antigen, whereas antibody detection requires the use of the indirect fluorescent immunoassay. Whichever method is used, the presence of the antigen or antibody is evidenced by the simple fact that if an antigen-antibody reaction occurs, the fluorescent compound is visible.

Enzyme Immunoassay

Enzyme immunoassay tests use enzymes as the label. The enzymes are targeted to a specific antigen or antibody and react with the target. The two main types of enzyme tests are the **enzyme immunoassay (EIA)** and the **enzyme-linked immunosorbent assay (ELISA)**. The ELISA is a variation of the EIA and both are used for detecting antibodies or antigens in viral or parasitic diseases.

Radioimmunoassay

Radioimmunoassay (RIA), performed to identify viral diseases, use a radioactive isotope as the label. The label is bound to an antibody that is specific to a particular virus. If the virus is present in the patient's serum, it reacts with the labeled antibody and measurable radiation is present. RIA procedures are being replaced by EIA procedures.

Diseases of Bacterial Origin

Bacteria are defined as small unicellular microorganisms that exhibit metabolic activity and are therefore classified as living organisms. A single organism is a bacterium and the multiplication or growth from a bacterium results in a colony. Bacteria are identified by their morphology or shape as coccus (round), bacillus (rod), spirochete (spiral), and vibrios (comma shaped). Cocci can occur in pairs called diplococci as well as in clusters. Most bacteria do not cause disease and exist as independent cells in soil, water, and as part of the normal flora of the human body. Figure 5-1 displays the morphological types of bacteria.

Bacteria that are capable of causing disease are called pathogens. Bacterial growth or bacterial toxins are responsible for tissue damage. While most bacterial infections can be successfully diagnosed by culture, testing for antibodies is done to screen for past, recent, or existing infections when

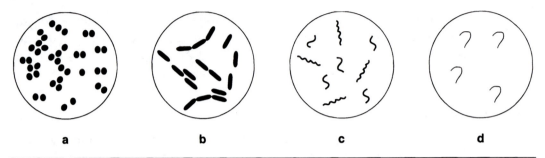

Figure 5-1.   Morphological types of bacteria: **(a)** cocci and diplococci, **(b)** bacilli, **(c)** spirochetes, **(d)** vibrios

culture results are negative and the patient continues to exhibit symptoms of disease. Antibody screening is a useful diagnostic tool for those individuals who have been treated with antibiotics, which may have destroyed or inhibited the growth of the bacteria. Syphilis, Lyme disease, Legionnaires' disease, chlamydia, and streptococcal diseases are often identified via antibody tests. Each of these disease processes is discussed individually.

Syphilis Detection Tests

Syphilis is a sexually transmitted disease caused by the spirochete *Treponema pallidum*. The spirochete is able to pass through the placenta, which results in congenital syphilis for the fetus. Syphilis progresses through three distinct stages and left untreated can lead to mental and physical disability and premature death. There are four serum tests for syphilis that are used to detect antibodies to *Treponema pallidum*. Two types of antibodies are associated with *Treponema pallidum*. The first is a nontreponemal antibody known as **reagin,** an antibody-like substance found in the serum of individuals with syphilis. The nontreponemal antibody tests include the Wassermann test or the **Venereal Disease Research Laboratory (VDRL) test** and the **rapid plasma reagin (RPR) test**.

The second type of antibody is directed against the treponema bacteria. The treponemal-specific antibody tests include the **fluorescent treponemal antibody absorption (FTA-ABS) test** and the **microhemagglutination Treponema pallidum antibody (MHA-TP) test**. Each test is discussed below and Table 5-1 provides a summary of these tests.

Table 5-1. Syphilis Detection Tests

Test/Description	Results
Nontreponemal Antibody Tests: Reagin Antibody	
Rapid plasma reagin agglutination test	Detects reagin
VDRL	Detects reagin
Treponemal Antibody Tests: Treponemal Antibodies	
FTA-ABS labeled antibody	Specific for treponemal antibodies sensitive for primary syphilis, confirms positive RPR or VDRL
MHA-TP hemagglutination	Detects presence of treponemal antibodies, more specific than the FTA-ABS

Rapid Plasma Reagin Test (RPR)

The rapid plasma reagin test is an agglutination test designed to detect the antibody-like substance reagin. The RPR test is a nonspecific syphilis screening test similar to the VDRL test. Results are reported as reactive (positive), slight to large clumping agglutination; or nonreactive (negative), no agglutination. A reactive result does not mean that the patient definitely has syphilis; it only indicates the presence of reagin. Several nonsyphilitic diseases can cause biological false-positive (BFP) results as listed in Table 5-2. The RPR may also give negative or nonreactive test results in some cases of late-stage syphilis.

Venereal Disease Research Laboratory (VDRL) Test

The Venereal Disease Research Laboratory test is one of the most widely recognized screening tests used to detect syphilis. It is a nonspecific test that identifies the presence of reagin. Test results are reported as nonreactive when no clumping or only slight roughness appears in the sample, weakly reactive when small clumps are present, and reactive when medium to large clumps are present. As with the RPR, the VDRL test can fail to show positive or reactive results in late-stage syphilis. False-positive results are caused by the factors listed in Table 5-2.

Table 5-2. Diseases and Conditions That Cause Biological False-Positive Results in VDRL and RPR Tests

Chickenpox
Infectious hepatitis
Infectious mononucleosis
*Leprosy
Lupus erythematosis
*Malaria
Measles
Pneumonia, pneumococcal
Rheumatoid arthritis
Rheumatic fever
Tuberculosis
Scarlet fever

*These diseases cause BFP more than 50% of the time.

Fluorescent Treponemal Antibody Absorption (FTA-ABS) Test

The fluorescent treponemal antibody absorption test is a direct method of detecting treponemal antibodies. It is the most sensitive serologic test for the identification and diagnosis of primary syphilis. The FTA-ABS is usually done in order to confirm a reactive RPR or VDRL test result and to identify syphilis when other tests are negative but clinical signs of syphilis are present.

Microhemagglutination Treponemal Pallidum Antibody (MHA-TP) Test

The microhemagglutination assay for *Treponema pallidum* antibodies test is a hemagglutination test that identifies the presence of treponemal antibodies. It is even more specific than the FTA-ABS test. The MHA-TP is used to confirm a positive VDRL or RPR test result.

Interfering Circumstances. Excess chyle, the liquid products of digestion, and alcohol interfere with syphilis test results. Patients should avoid alcohol consumption for at least twenty-four hours before blood is drawn and the blood sample should not be taken immediately after a meal.

Lyme Disease Tests

Lyme disease is an inflammatory disease caused by the spirochete *Borrelia burgdorferi*, which is transmitted to humans by deer ticks. Lyme disease is characterized by a distinctive skin lesion called erythema migrans (EM), also known as erythema chronicum migrans (ECM), which may appear within three to thirty-two days after the tick bite. Whether EM is present or not, this disease can exhibit early systemic manifestations such as malaise, fatigue, migratory arthralgia, fever, headache, and related symptoms that may last for weeks.

Lyme disease can cause multisystem problems for months and even years. Neurologic disorders such as aseptic meningitis, facial palsy, and encephalitis can develop within weeks to months after the onset of the ECM lesion. Symptoms of these problems may last for months and may become chronic. Cardiac abnormalities include atrioventricular block and myocarditis, which may occur within a few weeks of the ECM lesion. Swelling and pain in the large joints, especially the knees, may develop and recur for several years. Chronic arthritis is an occasional result of Lyme disease. Serum tests used to diagnose Lyme disease include IFA, ELISA, Western blot assay, and the polymerase chain reaction (PCR) test.

Serologic tests must be interpreted with caution since they may be insensitive during the first several weeks of infection. Test sensitivity increases as the patient progresses to later stages of the disease, but some individuals continue to have negative results throughout the course of the disease. The ELISA is considered to be highly diagnostic during the early stages of Lyme disease, especially if the ELISA is used to identify IgM, one of the five classes of antibodies produced by the immune system. IgM can be found in the serum within three to four weeks after Lyme disease onset.

Western Blot Assay Test

The **Western blot assay test** is used to detect the presence of a specific antigen or antibody. In order to conduct a Western blot test, serum is subjected to electrophoresis, which separates the serum proteins in a gel-like medium. A membrane is then "blotted" onto the electrophoretic gel and the membrane becomes a duplicate of the electrophoretic pattern. A specific antibody is applied to the membrane to detect the specific corresponding antigen. Results of the Western blot test as related to Lyme disease must be cautiously interpreted. The Western blot test may not identify the disease during the first several weeks of infection and may remain negative for individuals who have been treated with antibiotics.

Polymerase Chain Reaction (PCR) Test

The **polymerase chain reaction** test utilizes blood, urine, synovial fluid, or other body tissue to identify the presence of the genetic material of *Borrelia burgdorferi*. The appearance of this genetic material may be helpful in confirming the diagnosis of Lyme disease.

Interfering Circumstances. The presence of other spirochete infections and high levels of rheumatoid factor may cause false-positive test results. Patients with infectious mononucleosis, HIV infection, syphilis, lupus, and Rocky Mountain spotted fever may also have false-positive reactions to Lyme disease tests.

Legionnaires' Disease Tests

Legionnaires' disease, also known as legionellosis and Legionnaires' pneumonia, is an acute bacterial disease that attacks the respiratory system. The causative bacteria are *Legionella pneumonophila*. Hot-water systems, cooling towers, humidifiers, whirlpool spas, and respiratory therapy devices have been identified as containing or "housing" these bacteria. The mode of transmission is airborne. Legionnaires' disease can be diagnosed by blood, sputum, or pleural fluid cultures. However, the most common methods of identification involve the IFA or ELISA serum tests, with the IFA being the test of choice. These tests detect the presence of *Legionella pneumonophila* antibodies during the acute and convalescent phases of the disease.

Interfering Circumstances. Legionnaires' disease may be mistaken for Pontiac fever, another manifestation of legionellosis. Both diseases initially present with anorexia, malaise, muscle pain, and headache. Legionnaires' disease is more serious than Pontiac fever since Pontiac fever is not associated with pneumonia or death. Patients with Pontiac fever tend to recover spontaneously within two to five days without treatment. Because both manifestations present with similar initial symptoms, health care practitioners must carefully assess any patient who exhibits legionellosis symptoms.

Chlamydia Antibody Tests

Chlamydia is a bacterium that requires living cells for growth. There are three recognized species of chlamydia, all of which are pathogenic to humans. Chlamydia infections are considered to be the most frequently occurring sexually transmitted disease in North America, particularly the United States. These infections occur primarily in the genitalia, and are also found in the conjunctiva, pharynx, urethra, and rectum.

Chlamydia trachomatis is the species of chlamydia that causes trachoma, lymphogranuloma venereum, pelvic inflammatory disease, and inclusion conjunctivitis. In addition to these diseases, chlamydia is a frequent cause of sterility. Infections caused by *Chlamydia trachomatis* produce an immune response. Antibodies can be measured using complement fixation, IFA, and PCR techniques.

Interfering Circumstances. Routine menstrual flow and antibiotic therapy can interfere with antibody testing.

Streptococcal Antibody Tests

Group A beta-hemolytic streptococci are nonmotile bacteria that can occur in pairs or chains. These bacteria are responsible for a variety of diseases ranging from streptococcal sore throat to scarlet fever. Impetigo, pyoderma, otitis media, wound infections, and rheumatic fever are also associated with group A beta-hemolytic streptococci. Acute infections are best diagnosed by direct streptococcal cultures.

Group A beta-hemolytic streptococci produce several enzymes—streptolysin O, hyaluronidase, and DNase B—that act as antigens in the human body. Since these enzymes are antigens, they trigger the formation of antibodies specific to each enzyme. Serologic tests that measure the presence or level of the enzyme-specific antibodies are valuable diagnostic tools in the identification of conditions or diseases associated with previous streptococcal infections. The streptococcal antibody tests include **antistreptolysin O titer (ASO)**, which detects antibodies to streptolysin O; streptozyme, a test that identifies antibodies to several enzymes; and **anti-DNase B (ADB)**, which detects antibodies to DNase B. The antistreptolysin O titer and the anti-DNase B test are discussed individually.

Antistreptolysin O Titer (ASO)

The ASO titer aids in the diagnosis of several conditions associated with streptococcal infections such as rheumatic fever, glomerulonephritis, endocarditis, and scarlet fever. ASO production is especially high in rheumatic fever and glomerulonephritis. Clinicians should not rely on a single test result, but should monitor titer levels over several weeks.

Anti-DNase B Test (ABD)

The anti-DNase B test is more sensitive for diagnosing streptococcal pyoderma and ABD titers are high in the presence of that disease. Some evidence suggests that the ABD antibodies may appear earlier than ASO in streptococcal pharyngitis. Using the ASO and ABD tests concurrently can identify up to 95% of streptococcal infections.

Interfering Circumstances. Healthy individuals who are carriers of streptococci exhibit high antibody titers. False-positive or elevated ASO titers can be associated with high beta-lipoproteins. Decreased titer levels are associated with antibiotics and adrenal corticosteroid medications.

Diseases of Viral Origin

Viruses are defined as minute microorganisms that can only replicate by invading a living cell. Figure 5-2 demonstrates the relative size of different viruses. All viruses consist of a nucleic acid core, either deoxyribonucleic acid (DNA) or ribonucleic acid (RNA), and an antigenic protein coat. Some viruses have an additional layer called an envelope, which is a lipoprotein. The virus provides the genetic code for replication and the cell provides the needed energy and raw materials.

As the virus continues to multiply, it will eventually cause the cell membrane to rupture, thereby releasing multitudes of viruses into the bloodstream. Each virus has the potential to invade another cell and promote the disease process. Since the virus has an antigenic protein coat, the body responds by producing antibodies to the virus.

The standard method for virus identification has been cell culture. Other approaches to detect viruses include identification of the viral antigen in a clinical specimen and several antibody screening tests. Frequently ordered

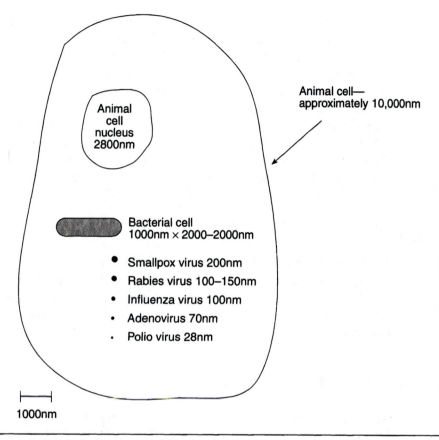

Figure 5-2. Relative size of different viruses

antibody screening tests include complement fixation, agglutination, IFA, and ELISA. These tests have already been described and defined. Specific tests that may relate to specific viral diseases are presented with the disease process discussions.

Infectious Mononucleosis Tests

Infectious mononucleosis (IM) is an acute viral infection characterized by fever, sore throat, swollen lymph glands, splenomegaly, abnormal liver function, and bruising. Infectious mononucleosis is spread from person to person by way of saliva. In childhood, the disease is mild and usually unnoticed.

Infectious mononucleosis is often associated with young adults, particularly college-age individuals. Older adults present with more severe symptoms. The causative agent for IM is the Epstein-Barr virus (EBV).

The Epstein-Barr virus causes an increase in heterophil antibody formation. The presence of heterophil antibodies is highly diagnostic for infectious mononucleosis. Other specific EBV antibodies include antibodies to the viral capsid antigen (anti-VCA) and antibodies to EBV nuclear antigen (EBNA). Several serological tests are used to identify the presence of EBV antibodies. These tests include the IFA and ELISA tests for the anti-VCA antibodies and the EBNA antibodies, and the rapid slide test for heterophil antibodies. The rapid slide test is the most common test for EBV.

Rapid Slide Test

The rapid slide test for heterophil antibodies is a hemagglutination test that quickly identifies the presence of heterophil antibodies in serum. The rapid slide test is usually positive after the first week of illness. If the results are negative and symptoms persist, the test should be repeated after a week.

Rubella Antibody Tests

Rubella, also known as German measles, is a contagious disease characterized by fever and rash caused by the rubella virus. Children and adults who contract rubella are usually able to survive the disease course with few complications. In fact, rubella must often be differentiated from measles and scarlet fever.

Rubella, however, does present a significant risk to the developing fetus. Congenital rubella syndrome (CRS) occurs in 90% of women who acquire confirmed rubella during the first trimester of pregnancy. Congenital malformation of major organ systems, fetal death, and miscarriage are associated with first-trimester rubella infections.

Since clinical diagnosis of rubella is often inaccurate, laboratory confirmation is usually indicated. Antibody tests include complement fixation, ELISA, hemagglutination inhibition (HAI), and latex agglutination. The hemagglutination inhibition test is an agglutination test in which the RBCs are prevented or inhibited from "clumping" when the antibody is present. While antibody tests are helpful in differentiating rubella from measles and scarlet fever, the tests are often done in order to identify the individual's immune status to the rubella virus. The presence of specific levels of rubella antibodies can indicate that the individual is not susceptible to rubella. This information is especially significant for pregnant women.

Hepatitis Tests

Hepatitis can be caused by bacteria, drugs, toxins, alcohol ingestion, and viruses. Five types of viral hepatitis have been identified: A, B, C, D, and E. Although each type of hepatitis has similar clinical manifestations, they differ in etiology and outcome. Hepatitis A, B, and C are discussed in this chapter.

Hepatitis A

Hepatitis A, also known as infectious hepatitis, is caused by the hepatitis A virus (HAV). Hepatitis A is transmitted from person to person by the fecal-oral route. In developed countries, the disease is often present in day care centers that accept diapered children. It is worthy to note that most young children can remain asymptomatic, while adults will most frequently exhibit the usual symptoms including jaundice.

Acute hepatitis A is diagnosed by identifying the presence of two specific antibodies directed against the hepatitis A virus. The first type of antibody is the **IgM antibodies against hepatitis A virus (IgM anti-HAV)**. This antibody appears three to four weeks after exposure and can be detected for up to six months after onset. The second type of antibody is the **total antibody against hepatitis A virus (total anti-HAV)**. The presence of these two antibodies in the patient's serum is diagnostic for acute hepatitis.

The chronic or convalescent stage of hepatitis A is identified by the presence of the **IgG antibodies against the hepatitis A virus (IgG anti-HAV)**. This antibody appears after the increase in IgM anti-HAV and can be detected in serum for more than ten years after the infection. Tests that identify these antibodies include the radioimmunoassay (RIA) and the ELISA.

Hepatitis B

Hepatitis B, also known as serum hepatitis, is caused by the hepatitis B virus (HBV). The hepatitis B virus is transmitted to humans by way of infected saliva, blood and serum-derived fluids, semen, and vaginal fluids. The highest risk of contracting hepatitis B is associated with activities or occupations that involve frequent contact with blood and blood products.

Since only a small portion of acute hepatitis B infections may be clinically recognized, diagnosis is confirmed by identifying specific antigens or antibodies in the serum. The hepatitis B virus has three distinct antigen-antibody substances: (1) hepatitis B surface antigen (HBsAg), and the antibody to HBsAg (anti-HBs); (2) hepatitis B core antigen (HBcAg), and the antibody to HBcAg (anti-HBc); and (3) hepatitis B envelope antigen (HBeAg), and the antibody to HBeAg (anti-HBe). Detection of the presence of either the HBV antigens or the corresponding antibodies provides valuable information about the chronic or acute stage of hepatitis B and the infectious potential of the individual who has the disease. Table 5-3 summarizes the diagnostic and clinical significance of the HBV antigens and antibodies. With the exception of hepatitis B surface antigen, all other hepatitis B antigens and antibodies are detected by using radioimmunoassay and ELISA.

Hepatitis C

Hepatitis C, also called non-A, non-B hepatitis, is transmitted by percutaneous exposure to contaminated blood and plasma derivatives, and is caused by the hepatitis C virus (HCV). Prior to blood donor screening for the antibody to hepatitis C virus (anti-HCV), 90% of all cases of posttransfusion hepatitis in the United States were caused by the hepatitis C virus. Hepatitis C is difficult to diagnose since the clinical manifestations closely resemble or parallel hepatitis B. The enzyme immunoassay (EIA) test, which has been established as a screening test for blood donors, detects anti-HCV. This antibody is generally not detectable in patients with initial signs or symptoms of hepatitis C. The presence of anti-HCV seems to indicate that this is a chronic disease process.

Human Immunodeficiency Virus (HIV-1, HIV-2); Acquired Immunodeficiency Syndrome (AIDS) Test

AIDS is a severe, life-threatening condition that represents the late clinical stage of human immunodeficiency virus infection. There are two types of

Table 5-3. Diagnostic and Clinical Significance of the Presence of Hepatitis B Antigens and Antibodies in the Serum

Antigen/Antibody	Significance
Hepatitis B surface antigen (HBsAg)	Antigen level first to rise Indicates active infection Abnormal test results appear before symptoms Sustained serum levels identify carrier status
Hepatitis B surface antibody (anti-HBs)	Signifies end of acute phase Immunity to subsequent infections Immunity after receiving hepatitis B vaccination
Hepatitis B core antigen (HBcAg)	No tests currently available to detect this antigen
Hepatitis B core antibody (anti-HBc)	Present in chronic hepatitis
Hepatitis A envelope antigen (HBeAg)	Present in early and active disease Signifies high infectivity
Hepatitis B envelope antibody (anti-HBe)	Indicates acute phase of HBV is nearly over Infectivity is greatly reduced Suggests recovery

HIV: **type 1** and **type 2**. Infection with HIV-1 is most common in the United States and HIV-2 is predominantly reported in West Africa. An individual is diagnosed as having AIDS if he or she has contracted the human immunodeficiency virus and exhibits one or more of the specific signs or symptoms associated with AIDS. Some of these signs include various types of pneumonia, cancer, and fungal and parasitic infections. Specific diseases associated with AIDS are Kaposi's sarcoma, chronic cryptosporidiosis, wasting syndrome, extrapulmonary tuberculosis, and pulmonary cytomegalovirus infection.

The World Heath Organization and the Centers for Disease Control recognize that HIV antibody testing is diagnostically significant in the identification of AIDS. Serologic tests for HIV antibodies have been available since

1985 and are used to screen blood and blood products that will be used for transfusion, as well as to confirm the AIDS diagnosis. The most commonly used screening test to determine the presence of HIV-1 antibodies is the ELISA or EIA test. If the ELISA is reactive (positive), the Western blot (WB) test should be done. A positive result with Western blot confirms HIV infection. The observed range for AIDS development is from one to ten years.

Interfering Circumstances. HIV antibodies must be sufficiently developed in order to be detected. The acute or early stages of HIV infection may not be identified by any of the serologic tests.

Herpes Simplex

Herpes simplex is a viral infection characterized by localized primary lesions, latency, and recurrence in the localized areas. There are two types of herpes simplex virus: **herpes simplex type 1 (HSV-1)** and **herpes simplex virus type 2 (HSV-2)**. HSV-1 is the causative agent for fever blisters and cold sores, as well as more serious diseases such as meningoencephalitis.

HSV-2 is the causative agent for herpes genitalis, a sexually transmitted disease of the urogenital tract. Primary and recurrent infections may occur with or without symptoms. Painful, vesicular eruptions can occur on the skin and mucous membranes of the genitalia, anus, rectum, and mouth depending on sexual practices. Serologic identification of the specific HSV relies on tests that identify the type-specific antibody. Enzyme immunoassay and IFA are two tests that identify the presence of HSV antibodies in the blood. In addition to providing diagnostic information concerning HSV infections, HSV antibody testing is used for bone marrow donors and recipients.

Cytomegalovirus (CMV) Antibody Test

Cytomegalovirus is a human viral pathogen that belongs to the herpes virus family. This virus causes serious illness in people with AIDS, in newborns, and in individuals being treated with immunosuppression therapy. CMV is the most common cause of posttransplant infection. The most severe form of CMV infection is seen in congenital infections. Infected newborns can exhibit permanent damage such as microcephaly, hydrocephaly, and chronic liver disease. Newborn diagnosis of CMV infection can be accomplished by isolating the virus from urine. Diagnosis of CMV infection in adults is more difficult.

Serologic tests that detect the CMV-specific IgM antibody include IFA, ELISA, and latex agglutination. These tests are performed on individuals who are candidates for CMV infection. Sexually active persons who present with mononucleosis-like symptoms but do not exhibit the heterophil antibodies associated with the Epstein-Barr virus should be tested for CMV antibodies. Blood banks routinely screen for CMV antibodies.

Diseases of Fungal Origin

Fungi are defined as thallus-forming organisms, with defined nuclei, which require an external carbon source. Fungus may invade living as well as nonliving organisms. Most fungi are found in the soil and on decaying plant matter. Of the 250,000 known fungal species, less that 200 are considered capable of causing disease. Deep-seated and opportunistic fungal diseases are more common in individuals who are immunosuppressed. Most pathogenic fungi stimulate antibody formation. Serologic tests for fungal antibodies are used to diagnose recent or current infections. These tests include agglutination, complement fixation, and immunodiffusion, which is a type of precipitation test. Several diseases of fungal origin are discussed next.

Histoplasmosis

Histoplasmosis, a systemic infection caused by inhaling the spores of the fungus *Histoplasma capsulatum*, is characterized by fever, malaise, cough, and lymphadenopathy. The lungs and respiratory structures are the usual sites of primary lesions. Diagnosis can be confirmed by culture or actual visualization of the fungus.

Serologic antibody tests used to diagnose histoplasmosis include complement fixation, latex agglutination, and immunodiffusion. The immunodiffusion test has been identified as the most specific and reliable.

Interfering Circumstances. Recent fungal skin tests may alter antibody test results. Also, fungal antibodies may be found in seemingly healthy individuals.

Coccidioidomycosis

Coccidioidomycosis, also known as valley fever, San Joaquin fever, and desert fever, is an infectious disease caused by inhaling the spores of the fungus *Coccidioides immitis.* The primary infection may be entirely asymptomatic, or may resemble an acute influenza illness or a common cold. Diagnosis is made by microscopic examination or culture of sputum, pus, urine, or cerebrospinal fluid.

Serologic tests for coccidioides antibodies include complement fixation and immunodiffusion. These tests are usually positive within the first three months of clinical disease.

Interfering Circumstances. Individuals who are immunocompromised may have negative serologic test results. As stated previously, antibodies against fungi may be found in blood samples from apparently healthy individuals.

Candidiasis

Candidiasis, an infection caused by *Candida albicans,* is usually confined to the superficial layers of the skin or mucous membranes. Thrush, diaper rash, intertrigo, and vaginitis are common manifestations of candidiasis. Debilitated patients can present with endocarditis, and infection of the kidney, spleen, liver, bones, eyes, and lungs. Microscopic identification of the yeast cells in infected tissue or body fluids is highly diagnostic.

Serologic identification of candidal antibodies is necessary when culture or tissue sample tests are inconclusive for systemic candidiasis. Immunodiffusion is the test of choice for this purpose.

Interfering Circumstances. Individuals with tuberculosis may test positive for candida antibodies.

Miscellaneous Serological Blood Tests

There are several serological blood tests that fall into the immunodiagnostic studies but do not fit into the bacterial, viral, or fungal categories. Some of the tests are diagnostic for specific diseases, whereas others are associated with several disease processes. Blood group and related tests are also included in this section.

TORCH Test

The **TORCH** test is a diagnostic kit that is often used as a screening test panel during pregnancy to identify viruses that may be harmful to the fetus. This kit can test for the presence of **toxoplasmosis, rubella, cytomegalovirus, and herpes virus**.

C-Reactive Protein (CRP) Test

C-reactive protein (CRP), an antibody-like protein, is not normally found in the serum. It is produced by the liver during an acute inflammatory process. C-reactive protein is functionally similar to immunoglobulin G, except that CRP is not antigen specific.

The C-reactive protein test is a nonspecific test used for evaluating inflammatory diseases and conditions that involve tissue necrosis. Although the erythrocyte sedimentation rate (ESR) is also used to detect inflammatory disease, the CRP is more sensitive and responds more rapidly than the ESR. A positive test result indicates the presence, but not the cause, of an acute inflammatory response.

Normal Range

<0.8 mg/dl

Variations from Normal. A positive C-reactive protein test is associated with rheumatic fever, rheumatoid arthritis, acute myocardial infarction, postoperative wound infection, Crohn's disease, and other inflammatory diseases.

Interfering Circumstances. A positive test result may be caused by an intrauterine device. Oral contraceptives may cause increased CRP levels, whereas nonsteroidal anti-inflammatory medications, salicylates, and steroids can cause levels to decrease.

Rheumatoid Factor (RF) Test

Rheumatoid factor is an autoantibody often found in the serum of individuals with rheumatoid arthritis. An autoantibody is an antibody that is directed against the person producing it. It is still unclear whether or not rheumatoid factor causes or perpetuates the rheumatoid arthritis process. Approximately 80% of patients with rheumatoid arthritis test positive for rheumatoid factor.

The sheep cell agglutination or the latex fixation test is usually performed to detect rheumatoid factor. Both of these tests are agglutination tests and a positive result is evidenced by visual agglutination if RF is present.

Normal Range

Negative

Variations from Normal. Positive test results are usually associated with rheumatoid arthritis. However, patients with other diseases such as lupus, hepatitis, scleroderma, subacute bacterial endocarditis, and tuberculosis may also show the presence of rheumatoid factor.

Interfering Circumstances. Elderly individuals may have false-positive results. Individuals who have received multiple vaccinations and transfusions may also show positive results.

Antinuclear Antibody (ANA) Test

The antinuclear antibody (ANA) is an autoantibody that reacts against cellular nuclear material. The presence of antinuclear antibodies is highly indicative of systemic lupus erythematosus (SLE) because 95% of individuals with SLE will test positive for ANA. It must be noted that antinuclear antibodies can occur in other rheumatic diseases, and therefore it is not a specific test for SLE. Antinuclear antibodies are identified via IFA.

Normal Range

Negative

Variations from Normal. False-positive results may be caused by many drugs including tetracyclines, penicillin, procainamide, streptomycin, and sulfonamides. False-negative results may be caused by steroids.

Blood Groups; ABO Red Cell Groups

Human blood is grouped according to the presence or absence of specific antigens that are found on the surface of red blood cells. The ABO system is the major human blood group system that is used to type or group blood according to the antigens present on the red blood cell. Group A blood has A antigens, group B blood has B antigens, group AB blood has both antigens, and group O blood has neither antigen. In addition to the blood group antigens, blood group antibodies are present in human blood, specifically in the serum. Type A blood has anti-B antibodies, type B blood has anti-A antibodies, type AB blood has neither antibody, and type O blood has both anti-A and anti-B antibodies. Table 5-4 summarizes the ABO blood groups and the corresponding antigens and antibodies.

ABO grouping is performed so that blood may be matched if a transfusion is necessary. An individual should be transfused with blood of the same ABO group in order to avoid introducing a different antigen into the individual receiving the transfusion. Since type O blood has neither A nor B antigens, it can be transfused into nearly all individuals, although this practice is limited. Two agglutination tests are used to identify ABO blood groups: the slide test method and the tube method.

Table 5-4.   ABO Blood Groups with Corresponding Antigens and Antibodies

ABO Group	Antigen on Red Blood Cells	Antibody in Serum
A	A	Anti-B
B	B	Anti-A
AB	A and B	Neither anti-A nor anti-B
O	Neither A nor B	Both anti-A and anti-B

Slide Test Method

The slide test method is quick, easy, and requires no special equipment. It is also called **direct** or **forward grouping** because it is used to group or type blood by directly identifying the antigen present on the surface of the red blood cell. A drop of blood is placed on the right and left side of a microscopic slide. Anti-A serum is mixed with one drop of blood and anti-B serum is mixed with the other. Blood type A agglutinates with anti-A serum and blood type B agglutinates with anti-B serum.

Tube Test Method

The tube test method is more sensitive and reliable than the slide method and is widely used in blood banks and clinical laboratories. The tube test method can type the individual's blood using two procedures: (1) direct grouping, which identifies the antigens present on red blood cells; and (2) **indirect,** or **reverse grouping,** which identifies the blood group antibodies in the *serum.* The direct grouping method is similar to the slide test method with the reaction carried out in test tubes.

The indirect or reverse grouping procedure uses the patient's serum, samples of which are placed in three test tubes. Commercially prepared suspensions of group A cells and group B cells are added to two of the tubes. The patient's own blood cells are added to the third test tube. The contents of the tubes are mixed, centrifuged, and observed for agglutination. A positive test result indicates the presence of serum antibody. Serum that reacts to group A cells contains the anti-A antibody, which is indicative of blood type B. The results of direct and indirect grouping should lead to the same blood group type for the patient. Table 5-5 summarizes the direct and indirect ABO blood grouping results.

Rh Typing

The presence or absence of the Rh antigen on the red blood cell membrane identifies human blood as Rh negative or Rh positive. Next to the A and B antigen blood grouping, the Rh antigen is the most important antigen in transfusion practice. There are many antigens in the Rh system, but the D antigen is the major one. Red blood cells that possess the D antigen are classified as Rh positive and cells that lack the D antigen are classified as Rh negative.

Table 5-5.   ABO Direct and Indirect Grouping Results

ABO Group	Direct Grouping Reactions of Cells with:		Indirect Grouping Reactions of Serum with:		
	Anti-A	*Anti-B*	*A Cells*	*B Cells*	*O Cells*
O	0	0	+	+	0
A	+	0	0	+	0
B	0	+	+	0	0
AB	+	+	0	0	0

0 = no agglutination

+ = agglutination

The Rh system does not have naturally occurring antibodies. If an individual with Rh-negative blood is transfused with Rh-positive blood, then the Rh-negative individual can produce an antibody to the D antigen called anti-D. Subsequent transfusions with Rh-positive blood can cause a severe transfusion reaction when the anti-D antibody reacts with the D-positive transfused cells.

Production of the anti-D antigen can also occur during pregnancy. When an Rh-negative mother gives birth to an Rh-positive infant, the infant's Rh-positive blood can stimulate the production of the anti-D antibody by the mother. In subsequent pregnancies an Rh-positive fetus may be at risk for a condition called hemolytic disease of the newborn. In this condition, the anti-D antigens in the mother's blood enter the fetal bloodstream and "attack" or hemolyze the infant's red blood cells.

Rh typing, the identification of the presence or absence of the D antigen, can be accomplished by the slide typing technique and the tube typing technique.

Rh Slide Typing Technique

Slide typing uses two slides: one as the test slide and one as a control. A drop of the patient's blood is placed on each slide. One drop of anti-D is added to one slide and a control solution is added to the other slide. The slides are placed on a heated, lighted view box and are rocked gently for a specified period of time. If the red blood cells contain the D antigen (Rh positive), agglutination is observed on the anti-D slide only.

Rh Tube Typing Technique

The tube method for identification of the Rh factor is preferred by blood banks. Two test tubes are used: one containing serum with the anti-D antibody and one containing a control substance (usually albumin). A specified amount of the patient's red blood cells, in suspension, are added to each tube. The contents are mixed well and centrifuged. As with the slide test, agglutination in the tube containing the anti-D antibody indicates that the patient's blood cells contain the D antigen and the patient's blood is Rh positive.

Coombs' Test

The **Coombs' test** is an antiglobulin test used to detect the presence of antibodies that coat and damage red blood cells. This test can detect Rh antibodies in maternal blood, can be used to diagnose and screen for autoimmune hemolytic anemias, and can determine the compatibility of blood types. There are two types of Coombs' tests: direct and indirect.

Direct Coombs' Test

The direct Coombs' test is used to detect autoantibodies against red blood cells. These antibodies can attack red blood cells, can cause cellular damage, and may result in hemolytic anemia. The direct Coombs' test is performed when the patient's red blood cells are suspected of being covered with autoantibodies against red blood cells. The test is conducted by mixing the patient's red blood cells with Coombs' serum, a solution containing antibodies against human blood serum. The presence of red blood cell autoantibodies causes an agglutination reaction between the red blood cell autoantibodies and the Coombs' antibodies. Agglutination indicates a positive test result, which means the patient's red blood cells are coated with autoantibodies. When the red blood cells are not coated with autoantibodies, agglutination does not occur and a negative test result is noted.

Indirect Coombs' Test

The indirect Coombs' test is used to identify circulating or serum antibodies against red blood cells and is used as the crossmatching portion of blood testing prior to transfusion. For crossmatching, a small amount of recipient serum is added to the donor's red blood cells. When Coombs' serum is added to the mixture, agglutination indicates that the recipient's serum has antibodies to the donor's red blood cells and the blood is incompatible. The absence of agglutination indicates that the blood is compatible and the transfusion may proceed.

Circulating antibodies against red blood cells may also occur in Rh-negative women who carry Rh-positive babies. In this situation, the women may develop antibodies to Rh-positive blood groups. The indirect Coombs' test may be used to identify the presence of anti-D in the mother's blood.

Normal Range. The absence of agglutination for both the direct and indirect Coombs' test is a normal result and is reported as negative.

Variations from Normal. Positive or abnormal direct Coombs' test results are seen in autoimmune hemolytic anemia, transfusion reaction, and hemolytic disease of the newborn. Other diseases that can cause a positive direct Coombs' test are lupus erythematosus, infectious mononucleosis, and some types of lymphomas.

Abnormal indirect Coombs' results are found in incompatible cross-matched blood, anti-Rh antibodies, acquired hemolytic anemia, and hemolytic disease of newborns.

Interfering Circumstances. False-positive results may be caused by antiarrhythmics, chlorpromazine, methyldopa, penicillins, phenytoin, and tetracyclines.

Summary

- The antigen-antibody reaction occurs when disease-causing substances enter the body.
- Identification of specific antibodies, antigens, the antigen-antibody complex, or any part or combination of the three can aid in diagnosing disease.
- Serology tests for antigen-antibody reactions include agglutination, precipitation, complement fixation, and labeled antibody.
- Microhemagglutination, latex agglutination, and hemagglutination inhibition are categorized as agglutination tests.

- Fluorescent antibody, indirect fluorescent antibody, enzyme immunoassay, enzyme-linked immunosorbent assay, and radioimmunoassay are examples of labeled antibody tests.
- Bacteria are unicellular, living organisms; viruses have genetic material, but rely on a living host to replicate; fungi have a defined nucleus and need an external carbon source to replicate.
- The ABO blood grouping system utilizes the direct method to identify the type of antigen present on the surface of red blood cells and the indirect method to identify the antibodies present in serum.
- ABO blood grouping can be accomplished via the slide test method (direct) and the tube test method (indirect).
- The direct Coombs' test identifies autoantibodies that are present on red blood cells and the indirect Coombs' test detects serum antibodies against red blood cells.

CHAPTER REVIEW

1. Identify the following serology tests:

   a. Clumping of cells or particles indicates a positive result _____

   b. Visible insoluble complex settles out _____

   c. Microscopic visualization of red blood cell clumping _____

   d. Red blood cell clumping is prevented _____

   e. Absence or presence of cell lysis indicates positive or negative results _____

   f. Enzymes, radioisotopes, or fluorescent compounds are used in immunoassays _____

   g. Detects the antibody-like substance called reagin _____

   h. Membrane is a duplicate of the
      electrophoretic enzyme pattern   _____

   i. Detects inflammatory disease   _____

   j. Diagnostic kit used as a screening panel
      during pregnancy; viral identification   _____

2. Describe the following tests. Include the full name of the test and the type of label used.

   a. FIA   _____

   b. IFA   _____

   c. EIA   _____

   d. ELISA   _____

   e. RIA   _____

3. Organize the listed tests according to these categories:

   a. Bacterial   _____

   b. Viral   _____

   c. Fungal   _____

FTA-ABS   IFA   MHA   MHA-TP   CF

RIA   RPR   EIA   PCR   HAI

4. Organize the listed tests according to the following diseases:

   a. Candidiasis   _____

   b. Histoplasmosis   _____

   c. Infectious mononucleosis   _____

   d. Lyme disease   _____

   e. Rheumatic fever   _____

   f. Rubella   _____

g. Streptococcal pyoderma   _____

h. Syphilis   _____

anti-DNase B (ADB)   MHA-TP

antistreptolysin O titer (ASO)   polymerase chain reaction (PCR)

FTA-ABS   rapid plasma reagin

hemagglutination inhibition (HAI)   rapid slide test

immunodiffusion   VDRL

latex agglutination   Western blot

5. Briefly discuss the differences between bacterial, viral, and fungal diseases. Include a general description of the characteristics of each type of organism and how it may cause disease.

6. Briefly describe what is meant by a "labeled antibody test." Include the types of molecules used as labels and the purpose of "labeling."

7. Discuss the three types of viral hepatitis presented in this chapter. Include the causative agent, route of transmission, antibodies that are diagnostic of the disease, and serologic tests used to identify the antibodies.

8. How is direct ABO blood grouping accomplished? What specific information about blood groups does this method produce?

9. How is indirect ABO blood grouping accomplished? What specific information about blood groups does this method produce?

10. Which antigen in the Rh system is most commonly tested for? How is the absence or presence of this antigen expressed in the Rh system? Why is Rh typing necessary?

11. Compare the direct and indirect Coombs' tests. Include the substances tested for, the indications for the tests, and the implications of positive or negative results.

Case Studies

1. Robert Sanders is a 26-year-old sexually active single male. Although he does not feel he has syphilis, his physician is concerned and has ordered a VDRL. Would a positive VDRL prompt the physician to order other tests? Is so, what are the tests and what do they measure or identify? Under what conditions might there be a biological false-positive result?

2. Dr. Samson is seeing a patient who she suspects has a streptococcal infection. The physician has ordered ASO and ABD tests. What are these tests? Identify the diseases these tests are able to detect. How effective are the tests for identifying streptococcal infections?

3. Maria Rodriguez, a 20-year-old college student, has entered the health center because she has swollen lymph glands, a sore throat, fever, and other symptoms that may be indicative of infectious mononucleosis. Identify the causative agent for mononucleosis. What is the standard method of testing for this disease? Describe the antibody tests used to diagnose mono.

Challenge Activity

Prepare an in-service education presentation using HIV and AIDS as your topic. Assume the in-service will be presented at a department orientation for transcriptionists and record processors (health information clerks). Include information about the difference between HIV infection and AIDS. Explain the types of tests used to identify HIV infection and the implications of positive test results.

Chapter 6

Urine and Fecal Studies

Key Terms, Abbreviations, and Acronyms

Acetest

Bence-Jones protein test

broad casts

casts

catheterized specimen

cellophane tape test

cellular casts

clean-catch midstream

Clinitest

confirmatory tests

cystine

cystinuria

fasting specimen

fatty casts

first morning specimen

granular casts

hyaline casts

Ictotest

leukocyte esterase urine test

maple syrup urine disease

mucoprotein

nitrite urine test

phenylketonuria, PKU

postprandial specimen

random urine specimen

reagent strips

special-purpose specimen

specific gravity

steatorrhea

straight catheter method

sulfonamide

supernatant

timed specimen

trophoblastic disease

tyrosine

urinary tract infection (UTI)

urine sediment

urobilinogen

waxy casts

Learning Objectives

Upon completion of this chapter, the learner will be able to:

1. Describe the importance of urine and feces in diagnosing human disease.
2. Discuss how urine and feces tests are performed.
3. Categorize urine and feces tests according to physical, chemical, and microscopic examination.
4. Identify and discuss abnormalities that can be detected through urine and feces testing.
5. Review circumstances that may interfere with successful urine and feces testing.

Introduction

Urine and fecal studies cover a variety of diagnostic tests. Analysis of the urine or feces provides information about the physiologic functions the body. Identification of abnormalities in the composition of urine and feces is an important diagnostic tool.

The chapter is divided into sections on urine testing and fecal testing. Each section begins with an overview of the purpose and nature of the tests and proceeds with a discussion of specific tests. Information for each test includes a brief description of the test, indications for the test, abnormalities associated with the test, and factors that may interfere with test results.

Overview of Urine Studies

The formation and excretion of urine by the kidneys is an essential body function. The kidneys excrete about 1500 milliliters of urine per day. Urine is about 95% water and 5% other constituents such as urea, electrolytes, amino acids, uric acid, creatinine, carbohydrates, bile pigments, and peptides. All substances found in the urine are also contained in the blood, but at different concentrations.

The purpose of urine studies is to identify variations in substances normally found in the urine and to detect substances that should not be present in the urine. Diseases of several organs and systems can alter the composition of urine. Urinary output, color, appearance, odor, and the constituents of urine can be affected by a variety of abnormal conditions. Diseases that affect urine and urine properties are presented with the individual test.

Collecting the urine specimen is dependent on the type and purpose of the urine test itself. Since characteristics of the urine are affected by collection techniques and time of day, collection methods address those issues. Three familiar urine collection methods include **first morning specimen**, meaning the specimen is collected when the individual first awakens; **random urine specimen**, which can be collected at any time; and **clean-catch midstream**, which is used when specimen contamination is a serious concern. The midstream technique is accomplished by voiding a small amount of urine into the toilet, stopping midstream, and continuing to void into the collection container.

The first morning specimen is preferred for routine urinalysis because it is more concentrated than urine produced at other times of the day. The most common specimen collection method is the random urine specimen. There are no special preparation procedures or dietary restrictions for the first morning and random urine specimen collection methods.

When a urine specimen must be free from contamination, the midstream or clean-catch collection procedure is necessary. After thorough handwashing, the patient is instructed to cleanse the genital area with an antiseptic wipe, to void a small amount of urine into the toilet, to stop voiding midstream, and to collect a urine sample by voiding into the collection container. The specimen container must be free of feces, mucus, or vaginal discharge.

Other urine specimen collection methods include **timed specimens**, **catheterized specimens**, and **special-purpose specimens**. Timed specimens are collected when it is necessary to analyze urine that is excreted over a certain number of hours. Timed specimen collection can cover between two and twenty-four hours. The twenty-four-hour timed collection method is fairly common. The patient is given written instructions that describe the procedure. The first specimen of the twenty-four-hour period is discarded and the time is noted on a labeled specimen container. All urine produced during the subsequent twenty-four-hour period must be stored in the same container. The container must be capped and refrigerated unless a preservative is added.

Catheterized specimens are collected if there is concern for specimen contamination or when voiding is difficult as with obstruction and severe urinary tract infection. The **straight catheter method** is accomplished by inserting a sterile, lubricated catheter into the urinary bladder and collecting the urine. For patients who have an indwelling catheter, commonly called a Foley catheter, the urine specimen must not be collected from the urinary drainage bag. The indwelling catheter is equipped with a specimen collection port that allows urine to be collected with a syringe before it reaches the drainage bag.

Special-purpose specimens include **fasting specimens** and **postprandial specimens**. For fasting specimens the patient voids and discards the first urine specimen at least four hours after food ingestion. The next voided urine is the fasting specimen. The postprandial specimen is urine voided two to three hours after a meal.

Urine Tests

Urine tests involve the analysis of the physical, chemical, and microscopic properties of urine. The physical analysis of urine includes examination of the odor, color, clarity, and specific gravity. Chemical analysis includes the assessment of bilirubin, blood (whole blood and hemoglobin), glucose, ketones, leukocyte esterase, nitrites, pH, protein, and urobilinogen levels. Microscopic analysis of the urine includes an examination of urine sediment for the presence of cells, crystals, casts, and microorganisms. Other urine tests are the urine pregnancy test and the urine test for drugs.

Physical Analysis of Urine

Routine urinalysis examines the physical properties of urine such as clarity, color, odor, and specific gravity. Variations in these physical characteristics may be indicative of renal or metabolic disorders. However, many things can impact the urine's physical characteristics, such as diet and the manner in which the specimen is handled and stored. In order to assure accuracy, the sample should be analyzed immediately. Urine samples that cannot be analyzed within one hour of collection must be refrigerated.

Clarity

Urine clarity, also called transparency, can indicate the presence of disease. Fresh urine is normally clear or slightly cloudy immediately after voiding. The terminology used to describe the clarity of urine includes clear, hazy, cloudy, turbid, or opalescent (milky). Each clinical laboratory has a standard system of nomenclature for describing the clarity of urine.

Alterations in the clarity of urine may occur in a variety of ways. Urine can become cloudy if it sits at room temperature or is refrigerated. However, cloudiness in a fresh urine specimen is usually indicative of an abnormal condition. Elements that alter urine clarity and may be associated with disease are blood cells, renal epithelial cells, mucus, casts, abnormal crystals, amorphous urates, and bacteria, yeast, fungus, or parasites.

Color

Normally urine is yellow in color, but the concentration of urine affects its color. Highly concentrated urine is a darker yellow or amber and diluted urine is a lighter yellow. The color of urine may be affected by diet, hydration, medications, and disease. Urine colors are useful in providing clues that may lead to the diagnosis of abnormal conditions. Table 6-1 presents the variations in urine color and possible causes.

Odor

Fresh urine has a characteristic aromatic odor. Diet, drugs, disease, and microorganisms may alter the odor of urine and alert the practitioner to potential problems or abnormalities. Although odor itself is not diagnostic, the presence of specific types of odors may be associated with certain diagnoses.

The urine of an uncontrolled diabetic may have a fruity odor because of the presence of ketones. Infants with **phenylketonuria (PKU)**, a metabolic disorder involving the amino acid phenylalanine, have a mousy or musty odor to their urine. **Maple syrup urine disease**, a metabolic disorder that can be diagnosed in infants, is characterized by urine that smells like maple syrup. Urine containing bacteria may present an ammonia odor, particularly if the urine is left unrefrigerated. A fresh urine specimen that has a foul order usually indicates a urinary tract infection.

Table 6-1.   Urine Colors and Their Causes

Color	Cause
Color Caused by Food or Medication	
Red	Beets, rhubarb (in alkaline urine)
Yellow-orange	Carrots, some antibiotics
Green, blue-green	Drugs such as amitriptyline, Clorets
Brown-black	Methyldopa, metronidazole
Color Caused by Disease States	
Red, red-brown	Red blood cells, hemoglobin, myoglobin
Wine-red	Porphyrin
Brown-black	Melanin, homogentisic acid, hemoglobin or myoglobin (in acid urine)
Yellow-brown or green-brown, foamy when shaken	Bilirubin
Pale to pale greenish	Diabetes insipidus, Diabetes mellitus
Pale, foamy when shaken	Nephrotic syndrome
Dark yellow, brown-red	Fever

Specific Gravity

The **specific gravity** of urine is the ratio of the weight of a given volume of urine to the weight of an equal volume of water at a given temperature. Specific gravity provides information about the ability of the kidney to reabsorb water and essential chemicals before they are excreted in the urine. Urinary specific gravity is an indication of the concentration of substances dissolved in urine. These substances can include phosphates, chlorides, urea, proteins, and sugars. Specific gravity may be measured using a urinometer, a refractometer, or a reagent strip.

Normal Range

Clarity	Clear, not cloudy
Color	Yellow, straw to amber
Odor	Characteristic aromatic odor
Specific Gravity	1.005–1.035

Variations from Normal. Abnormalities in the physical characteristics of urine may indicate renal or metabolic disease, infections, or obstructions.

Interfering Circumstances. Food, fluids, and medications can alter the physical characteristics of urine. Improper storage and handling of the urine sample may negatively affect the physical analysis of urine.

Chemical Analysis of Urine

Chemical urinalysis is performed to identify or evaluate the bilirubin, blood (whole blood and hemoglobin), glucose, ketones, leukocyte esterase, nitrate, pH level, protein, and urobilinogen in the urine. Chemical analysis of the urine provides health practitioners with information about the patient's kidney and liver function, carbohydrate metabolism, and acid-base balance.

Chemical tests use **reagent strips**, also called dipsticks, to identify the presence and concentration of the labeled substances. Reagent strip testing can be performed manually by dipping the strip into urine and comparing the color changes on the strip to the appropriate color chart. Reagent strips can also be inserted into an automated strip reader that analyzes the strip, displays the results, and creates a printed document. The findings of reagent testing are often confirmed by additional chemical tests called **confirmatory tests**. Chemical testing should be done within an hour of sample collection; if not, the urine should be stored in a refrigerator.

Bilirubin

A reagent strip is used to detect the presence of bilirubin in the urine. Bilirubin is formed in the liver, spleen, and bone marrow when hemoglobin is broken down. It is then transported to the liver and is normally excreted in the stool. Bilirubin in the urine is an indication of abnormal conditions of the liver or bile ducts. If the bilirubin reagent test indicates the presence of bilirubin, a confirmatory test called the **Ictotest** is performed. The Ictotest is a specific bilirubin test.

Normal Findings. Normal urine does not contain detectable bilirubin.

Variations from Normal. Bilirubin in the urine is seen in diseases such as hepatitis, obstructed biliary tract, or other liver disorders. The presence of bilirubin can also indicate liver damage caused by exposure to toxins or drugs.

Interfering Circumstances. Since direct light causes decomposition of the bilirubin, the urine specimen should be protected from exposure to light. Certain drugs, vitamin C, nitrites, and the age of the sample may alter the reliability of the test.

Blood

Urine is routinely evaluated for the presence of blood, red blood cells, and hemoglobin. Blood that is visible in the urine is a nonspecific symptom and necessitates additional analysis. The presence of red blood cells is called hematuria and the presence of hemoglobin is known as hemoglobinuria. The reagent strip is used to detect the presence of red blood cells and hemoglobin in the urine. A positive result may indicate the need for microscopic analysis of a fresh urine specimen.

Normal Findings. Negative for blood, red blood cells, and hemoglobin.

Variations from Normal. Blood in the urine is a nonspecific abnormal finding that may indicate infection or trauma of the urinary tract, or bleeding in the kidneys. Red blood cells in the urine can be an indication of bleeding somewhere along the urinary tract, which may be caused by urinary tract infection, trauma, neoplasms, or other urinary system abnormalities.

Hemoglobin is an indication of an abnormal condition outside of the urinary system. Conditions that demonstrate hemoglobin in the urine are burns or injuries, hemolytic anemias, severe infections, smallpox, malaria, mushroom poisoning, renal infarction, and reactions to blood transfusions.

Interfering Circumstances. Myoglobin, an oxygen-carrying substance similar in structure to hemoglobin but formed in muscles, reacts with the blood reagent strip. Various substances can cause a false-negative or false-positive result.

Glucose

The presence of glucose in urine is an abnormal condition known as glucosuria or glycosuria. The reagent strip test and the **Clinitest** are used to detect glucose in urine. Both tests rely on color change to identify the presence of glucose. The most common cause of glycosuria is diabetes mellitus.

Normal Findings. Negative for glucose.

Variations from Normal. Positive glucose tests may indicate diabetes mellitus, or Cushing's syndrome, a pituitary gland disorder. Glucosuria may also signify the malfunction of glucose reabsorption by the kidneys.

Interfering Circumstances. Time of the testing, particularly after a heavy meal, and a vitamin C excess may cause a false-positive glucose test. In addition, stress, certain fruits and other foods, and drugs may cause a positive urine glucose test.

Ketone

Ketone urine testing is done to detect the presence of ketones, also called acetone or ketone bodies, in the urine. This condition, known as ketonuria, is a manifestation of abnormalities that limit the metabolism of carbohydrates. When carbohydrates cannot be metabolized, fats are metabolized to meet the body's energy needs and excessive amounts of ketones are produced and excreted into the urine. Ketonuria is detected by the reagent strip test and confirmed by the **Acetest**.

Normal Findings. Negative, that is, ketones are not detected.

Variations from Normal. Ketonuria is seen in a variety of conditions such as uncontrolled diabetes, anorexia, diets low in carbohydrates and high in fats, starvation, fasting, or excessive vomiting. Pregnancy and fever may cause ketonuria.

Interfering Circumstances. Certain drugs can produce false-positive ketone tests. Urine must be capped and refrigerated since ketones evaporate at room temperature.

Leukocyte Esterase

The purpose of the **leukocyte esterase urine test** is to identify the presence of granulocytic leukocytes, primarily neutrophils, in the urine. The primary granules found in neutrophils contain esterase, an enzyme that breaks down fats. Esterase reacts with the reagent strip when it is present in the urine. A positive reagent test is cause for a microscopic examination to confirm the presence of neutrophils or bacteria. The leukocyte esterase is not performed in all laboratories.

Normal Findings. Negative for leukocyte esterase and white blood cells.

Variations from Normal. The presence of white blood cells in the urine indicates urinary tract infection or inflammatory disorder.

Interfering Circumstances. Contamination of the urine specimen with vaginal bleeding, mucus, or other substances can produce unreliable results. Vitamin C, protein, and some drugs may yield a false-negative result.

Nitrites

The **nitrite urine test** is a screening test that may indicate a **urinary tract infection (UTI)**. This test may not be included in the routine urinalysis in all laboratories. Nitrites are found in the urine when nitrate, a substance normally present in urine, is converted to nitrites by the action of enzymes produced by gram-negative bacteria. Nitrites produce a chemical reaction in the reagent strip. A positive reagent test result should be verified by microscopic examination, or urine culture and sensitivity tests. The best urine specimen for nitrite testing is the morning specimen that has been in the bladder overnight. The clean-catch method should be used to prevent contamination of the specimen. A negative nitrite urine test may not indicate the absence of a UTI since some bacteria do not convert nitrates to nitrites.

Normal Findings. Negative for the presence of nitrites.

Variations from Normal. A positive nitrite urine test may indicate the present of a UTI caused by microorganisms such as *Escherichia coli*, proteus, pseudomonas, or klebsiella.

Interfering Circumstances. Bacterial contamination of the urine specimen alters test results.

pH

The pH of urine is measured to determine its acidity or alkalinity. A reagent strip color change indicates the pH value of the sample. Acidic urine has a pH below 7 and alkaline urine has a pH above 7. Urine pH is a useful screening tool for diagnosing metabolic disorders, renal disease, and respiratory disease.

Normal Range

Urinary pH   4.6–8.0
Average pH   6.0

Variations from Normal. Urine pH that exceeds the upper limit of the normal range may be indicative of UTIs, chronic renal failure, and respiratory disease with hyperventilation. Urine pH that does not meet the lower limit of the normal range can be associated with uncontrolled diabetes, emphysema, starvation, diarrhea, and certain respiratory diseases. The pH results are not disease specific and should be evaluated with other diagnostic studies.

Interfering Circumstances. Improper handling and storage of the urine specimen can affect pH levels. Diet and medications can alter pH results. Diets high in animal fat may result in acidic urine and those high in citrus may produce alkaline urine.

Protein

The urine of a normal person is usually free of protein, although a trace of protein in the urine specimen may not be unusual. The reagent strip is used to detect the presence or absence of protein, indicated by the color of the strip. Presence of increased amounts of protein in the urine is called proteinuria and is an indication of renal or systemic diseases.

The **Bence-Jones protein test** is performed to identify the presence of Bence-Jones protein in the urine. This specific protein is named for Henry Bence-Jones, an English physician. The protein is found almost exclusively in the urine of individuals who have multiple myeloma.

Since the reagent strip test does not identify the Bence-Jones protein, a precipitation test is necessary. Under appropriate test conditions, the Bence-Jones protein settles out of the urine sample. A positive Bence-Jones protein test is cause for additional tests to confirm the neoplastic diagnosis.

Normal Findings. Absence of all protein, including the Bence-Jones protein.

Variations from Normal. Positive urine protein tests can be attributed to diseases such as nephrosis, glomerulonephritis, pyelonephritis, and polycystic kidney disease. Urinary tract infection, diabetes, systemic lupus erythematosus (SLE), as well as poisoning from various chemicals and drugs, can result in proteinuria. The Bence-Jones protein is associated with neoplastic disorders such as multiple myeloma, lymphoma, and lymphocytic leukemia.

Interfering Circumstances. Certain medications, foods, exercise, emotional stress, pregnancy, and other circumstances can cause protein to be temporarily present in the urine. False-positive Bence-Jones protein findings can occur when the patient is receiving high doses of aspirin or penicillin. Connective tissue disease and chronic renal insufficiency also generate a false-positive Bence-Jones protein level.

Urobilinogen

The urobilinogen test is performed to determine the amount of **urobilinogen** in the urine. Urobilinogen is a compound created by the action of bacterial enzymes on bilirubin. Bilirubin enters the intestine in the bile and is converted to urobilinogen by bacterial enzymes. In a healthy individual, urobilinogen is excreted in feces. Urobilinogen that is not excreted is absorbed into the blood and returned to the liver where it is recycled via the bile.

A small amount of urobilinogen is normally present in most urine and is determined by the reagent strip. Urobilinogen levels can assist in the diagnosis of liver and bile duct diseases and disorders. The reagent strip test does not detect the absence of urobilinogen.

Normal Range

Urobilinogen   0.0–1.0 Ehrlich U/dl (Ehrlich units)

Variations from Normal. An increase in urobilinogen levels can be seen in cirrhosis of the liver, acute hepatitis, pernicious and hemolytic anemias, and hemorrhage. The absence of urobilinogen may indicate an obstructive disorder of the biliary duct system.

Interfering Circumstances. Urobilinogen decomposes when exposed to light or when stored at room temperature. Since urobilinogen is formed by intestinal bacteria, patients who are on antibiotic therapy may have lower urobilinogen levels. In addition, certain medications may increase or decrease urobilinogen and therefore negatively affect the reliability of this urine test.

Microscopic Analysis of Urine

Microscopic urinalysis uses a microscope to examine urine sediment that contains cells, casts, crystals, and microorganisms. In some laboratories, microscopic analysis may not be part of the routine urinalysis, but may be performed only when physical and chemical screening tests yield positive results. Microscopic urinalysis provides information that may be diagnostically significant. An early morning, clean-catch specimen is the most accurate urine specimen for microscopic examination. The specimen should be examined as soon after collection as possible to prevent the deterioration of cells contained in the urine.

Sediment is obtained by placing 10 to 12 milliliters of urine in a test tube, which is subsequently centrifuged. The clear portion of the urine, called **supernatant**, is the liquid that rises to the top of the test tube. The supernatant is poured off and the remaining substance is the **urine sediment**. The urine sediment is placed on a slide and examined microscopically. Each urine sediment constituent is discussed individually.

Microscopic Examination of Urine Sediment Cells

The microscopic examination of urine sediment cells is performed to determine the presence of squamous epithelial cells, transitional epithelial cells of the bladder and renal pelvis, renal tubular epithelial cells, red blood cells, and white blood cells. The presence of renal tubular epithelial cells indicates serious pathologic conditions. The other cell types may be detected in small amounts, with greater numbers of these cells indicating a disease state.

Squamous Epithelial Cells

Squamous epithelial cells are continuously sloughed off from the lining of the lower urinary tract and vagina and thus are normally found in urine. If many squamous epithelial cells are present, specimen contamination with vaginal secretions during the collection procedure is suspected.

Transitional Epithelial Cells

Transitional epithelial cells line the kidney pelvis, bladder, and (in males) the proximal urethra. These epithelial cells are smaller, rounder, and thicker than squamous epithelial cells.

Normal Findings. A few transitional epithelial cells are present in urine samples from healthy individuals.

Variations from Normal. Increased numbers of transitional epithelial cells are seen in bladder infections. Clusters or sheets of these cells indicate a urinary tract lesion.

Renal Tubular Epithelial Cells

Renal tubular epithelial cells line the tubules of the nephrons and also the collecting ducts of the kidney. These cells can be round or cuboidal and have a distinct nucleus. Cuboidal-shaped cells have one flat side and originate in the collecting ducts.

Normal Findings. Absence of renal tubular epithelial cells.

Variations from Normal. The presence of renal tubular epithelial cells indicates renal damage, acute tubular necrosis, glomerulonephritis, or pyelonephritis. Figure 6-1 compares the appearance of squamous epithelial cells, transitional epithelial cells of the bladder and kidney pelvis, and renal tubular epithelial cells.

Erythrocytes and Leukocytes

Although small numbers of erythrocytes and leukocytes are occasionally present in urine, an increased presence raises concern. Larger than expected numbers of red blood cells can be associated with renal and genitourinary disorders as well as urinary tract tumors or lesions. Medications and strenuous exercise may also cause hematuria.

A few white blood cells, primarily neutrophils, are normally found in urine. A large number of leukocytes in the urine is called pyuria and is usually a sign of bacterial infection. Increased leukocytes are also seen in urinary tract inflammatory diseases and urinary calculi. Contamination of the urine specimen may also present an increased number of white blood cells.

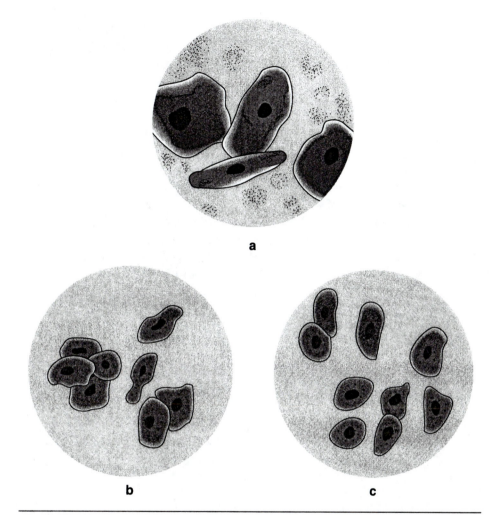

Figure 6-1. Urine sediment epithelial cells: **(a)** squamous epithelial cells, **(b)** transitional epithelial cells of the bladder and kidney pelvis, **(c)** renal tubular epithelial cells

Normal Findings. Only a few white or red blood cells are normally present in urine.

Variations from Normal. Increased numbers of red blood cells can be seen in urinary tract and kidney diseases. Urinary tract infections or specimen contamination demonstrate an increase in white blood cells.

Interfering Circumstances. Contaminated urine specimens may negatively affect the reliability of the urine test. Exercise, drugs, and smoking may cause red blood cells to be present in the urine.

Microscopic Examination of Urine Sediment Casts

The types of casts in urine sediment can be identified under a microscope. **Casts** are formed when protein accumulates and precipitates in the lumen of the renal tubules and assumes the shape of the tubule. Anything that is present in the renal tubules is entrapped within the cast as it is formed. Casts are a means to examine the contents of the renal tubule. Very few casts are found in normal urine and large numbers of casts can indicate renal disease.

Casts are classified according to the substances trapped in them. Three generic types of casts are **hyaline casts**, which are made up of **mucoprotein**, the substance found in all connective and supportive tissue; **granular casts**, which are made up of cell remnants; and **cellular casts**, which contain epithelial cells, erythrocytes, and leukocytes. Miscellaneous types of casts include **broad casts**, **fatty casts**, and **waxy casts**. These casts are named for their appearance and composition.

Hyaline Casts

An occasional hyaline cast is normally present in urine sediment and is composed of clear, glasslike proteins. Hyaline casts can be caused by vigorous exercise and must be differentiated from other sediment casts. Figure 6-2 shows the difference between hyaline, granular, and cellular casts.

Granular Casts

Granular casts contain fragments of disintegrated cells that appear as fine or coarse granules embedded in the protein of the cast. Granular casts are not disease specific, but their presence in urine indicates renal tubular damage.

Cellular Casts

Cellular casts may contain red blood cells, white blood cells, and epithelial cells. The presence of red blood cell casts in urine is always a sign of disease, primarily of the glomerulus. Glomerular inflammation and bleeding is associated with red blood cell casts. White blood cell casts indicate inter-

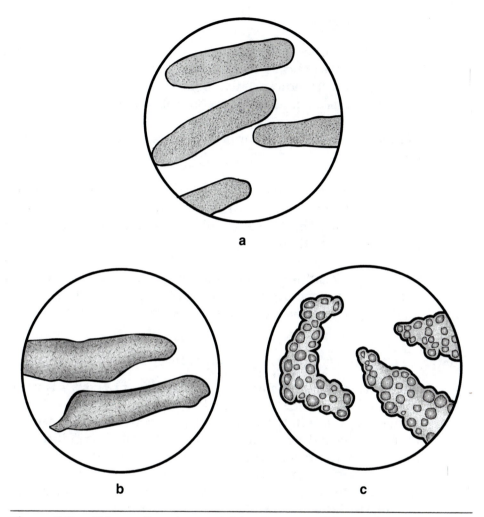

Figure 6-2.   Urine sediment casts: **(a)** hyaline casts, **(b)** granular casts, **(c)** cellular casts

stitial inflammation or infection and can distinguish an upper urinary tract infection from a lower urinary tract infection.

Epithelial cell casts result from the destruction of the cells lining the renal tubules. The presence of these casts represents serious nephrotic disease or damage.

Miscellaneous Casts

Other types of casts include broad casts, fatty casts, and waxy casts. Their presence always indicates renal disease. Broad casts are found only in renal failure, fatty casts indicate fatty degeneration of renal tubular epithelium, and waxy casts are present in several renal diseases.

Normal Findings. Normal urine is free of casts except for occasional hyaline casts.

Variations from Normal. The presence of any cellular, granular, waxy, broad, or fatty casts in urine sediment indicates the need for additional diagnostic testing. These casts are all associated with serious renal diseases, disorders, or infections.

Interfering Circumstances. Casts are difficult to see and can be confused with other substances in urine sediment such as mucus, hairs, molds, and marks or scratches on the microscopic slide.

Microscopic Examination of Urine Sediment Crystals

The microscopic examination of urine sediment crystals is performed to confirm the presence and type of crystals in the sediment. Crystals are formed from salts in the urine. A wide variety of crystals can be found in normal urine and for the most part are clinically insignificant. However, there are some rare forms of crystals that indicate metabolic disorders. Abnormal urine sediment crystals are made up of **cystine**, a nonessential amino acid found in protein; **tyrosine**, an amino acid synthesized from the essential amino acid phenylalanine; and **sulfonamide**, a synthetic medication that is used in treating bacterial infections.

Normal Findings. Presence of normal crystals. Absence of abnormal crystals.

Variations from Normal. Medications and metabolic disorders can cause the formation of crystals that represent abnormal urine sediment. Cystine crystals are associated with **cystinuria**, an amino acid disorder that can lead to renal tubule damage. Tyrosine crystals indicate liver disease or an inherited amino acid disorder. Sulfonamide crystals, though rarely seen in urine sediment, can be present in sulfonamide therapy.

Interfering Circumstances. Improper collection of the urine specimen may negatively affect identification of urine sediment crystals.

Microscopic Examination of Urine Sediment Microorganisms

The microscopic examination of urine sediment microorganisms involves the examination of the sediment to determine the presence of bacteria, yeast, and protozoa. Microorganisms should not be present in properly collected, fresh, normal urine. The presence of a moderate or large number of microorganisms is indicative of disease.

Normal Findings. Microorganism are not present in normal urine.

Variations from Normal. The presence of bacteria in urine sediment may indicate infection or inflammation. The most common form of yeast found in urine sediment is *Candida albicans*, which is associated with yeast infection. *Trichomonas vaginalis*, shown in Figure 6-3, is a protozoan identified in urine sediment. It causes trichomoniasis, a sexually transmitted disease characterized by a copious, foul-smelling vaginal discharge.

Interfering Circumstances. Urine specimens may be contaminated by external sources such as improper handling of the specimen, vaginal secretions, or fecal materials.

Urine Drug Testing

Although blood testing for drugs is available, urine drug testing is an efficient and effective method for drug screening. Some drugs that cannot be detected in the blood are easily discovered in the urine. In addition, some

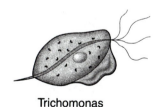

Trichomonas

Figure 6-3.   *Trichomonas vaginalis*

drugs may be present in the urine for several days after ingestion. Many companies use urine drug tests to screen potential and current employees. A wide range of urine drug tests can be performed. Table 6-2 identifies the most common tests.

The urine specimen is obtained and handled following a very strict procedure. Since drug testing results have many legal and personal ramifications, the procedure must assure, beyond all doubt, that the specimen has been collected from an identified individual, tagged properly so that no confusion of specimens can occur, protected against tampering, and kept refrigerated until testing can be done. In addition, special documentation requirements must be followed from the point of obtaining the sample until all testing has been completed.

Normal Findings. Negative for the tested drugs.

Variations from Normal. A positive urine test identifies the drugs present in the sample.

Interfering Circumstances. Variations in urinary pH levels, the presence of other substances, and improper storage of the urine prior to testing alters

Table 6-2.   Common Drug Tests Performed on Urine

Amphetamines
Alcohol
Barbiturates
Benzodiazepine
Cocaine
Cyanide
Opiates
Phencyclidine
LSD
Analgesics
Sedatives
Tranquilizers
Stimulants

test results. Individuals who take major tranquilizers or who eat poppy-seed rolls may also test positive.

Urine Pregnancy Testing

Urine pregnancy testing is used in both clinical laboratories and home pregnancy test kits. Urine pregnancy tests, as is true of all pregnancy tests, are designed to detect the presence of human chorionic gonadotropin (HCG). HCG is produced by a living placenta and excreted in the urine. It is detectable in the urine of a pregnant women twenty-six to thirty-six days after the first day of the last menstrual period, or about eight to ten days after conception. Although any urine specimen can be used for pregnancy testing, it is desirable to have the first voided specimen of the morning since HCG levels are usually more concentrated in that specimen. The reagent strip test or an agglutination inhibition test can be used to detect the presence of HCG in the urine.

Normal Findings. A positive test result indicates the presence of human chorionic gonadotropin, which signifies pregnancy. A negative test result indicates the absence of human chorionic gonadotropin, which signifies either a nonpregnant condition or a clinically undetectable level of HCG because the test was done too early in the pregnancy.

Variations from Normal. The presence of human chorionic gonadotropin can be detected in conditions other than pregnancy. **Trophoblastic disease**, a malignant, neoplastic disease of the uterus, and breast or ovarian cancer may demonstrate the presence of HCG. Urine pregnancy tests are only 65% successful in identifying ectopic pregnancies.

Interfering Circumstances. Tests that are performed too early in the pregnancy may give a false-negative result. Testing kits and supplies that have passed the expiration date should not be used.

Phenylketonuria (PKU) Urine Test

The phenylketonuria (PKU) urine test is a routine screening test performed on newborns to detect the genetic metabolic disorder known as phenylketonuria. Left untreated, PKU can cause brain damage and mental retardation. PKU is characterized by a lack of an enzyme that converts phenylalanine, an amino acid, to tyrosine, which is required for normal metabolism. PKU urine testing is usually performed during the infant's one-month checkup if earlier blood testing has not been completed. A reagent strip is either dipped into a fresh urine specimen or pressed against a wet diaper. The color of the reagent strip indicates the results.

Normal Findings. Absence of any change in the reagent strip.

Variations from Normal. A reagent strip that demonstrates any change indicates that the infant has PKU.

Interfering Circumstances. Due to an immaturely developed liver, urine PKU testing of premature infants may produce inaccurate results.

Overview of Fecal Studies

Feces or stool is the waste product of digestion and is excreted by the gastrointestinal tract. Fecal studies are useful for identifying gastrointestinal conditions and disorders such as colorectal cancer, gastrointestinal bleeding, obstruction, inflammatory bowel disease; malabsorption, parasitic disease, pancreatitis, and bacterial infections.

Normal feces consists of water, indigestible residue, intestinal secretions, large numbers of bacteria, bile, epithelial cells, white blood cells, small amounts of undigested foods, gastric secretions, pancreatic juices, and inorganic products such as calcium and phosphates. As much as 70% of fecal matter can be water, with bacteria contributing up to 35% of the solid matter. The composition of feces is dependent upon the complex process of digestion that involves absorption, secretion, and fermentation. An adult can excrete between 100 and 300 grams of feces per day.

Fecal specimens are usually collected in clean plastic jars with screwtop lids. Parasite testing may require the use of special containers with preservatives. Special kits are used for collecting specimens at home when feces is to be tested for the presence of occult blood. In addition, stool cultures utilize swabs inserted into the rectum for specimen collection. Stool specimens are usually collected at random times; however, some tests may require that stool specimens be collected over a period of several days.

The specific procedure for collecting specimens may vary with the type of testing being performed and whether the patient is hospitalized or at home. In the hospital setting, specimens may be collected in a bedpan or specialized "hat" container that is placed under the toilet seat. When stool collection is done at home, the patient is given very specific written instructions. In all cases, the fecal specimen must not be contaminated with urine, menstrual blood, other bodily discharges, or strong cleaners or oxidizing agents that may be left in a bedpan after cleaning. The fecal specimen must be carefully collected and stored. Since feces can be a source of many disease-producing organisms, proper handling techniques are important to prevent disease transmission.

Fecal Tests

Fecal tests involve the analysis of the physical, chemical, microscopic, and microbiologic properties of feces. Physical examination of feces includes an analysis of the amount, color, consistency, odor, and shape. Chemical testing of feces includes chemical analysis to identify occult blood, carbohydrates, fats, bile, and trypsin. Microscopic testing of feces includes a microscopic examination to determine the presence of leukocytes, fats, and parasites. Microbiologic testing is presented in Chapter 7.

Physical Examination of Feces

Physical examination of feces includes an analysis of the amount, color, consistency, odor, and shape of stool. In addition, some parasites may be identified. Physical observation of feces is not a routine laboratory test but is usually accomplished by a nurse in the hospital or home health setting. The patient may also be asked to describe the physical characteristics of his or her feces. Observations of changes in physical characteristics of feces may identify the need for further diagnostic studies, leading to the discovery of gastrointestinal disorders.

Normal Range

Amount	100–300 g/day (adult)
Color	Brown
Consistency	Soft, formed, plastic
High-fiber diet	Soft, bulky
High-protein diet	Small, dry
Odor	Pungent
Shape	Conforms to the shape of the distal colon

Variations from Normal. Changes in the physical characteristics of feces are seen in gastrointestinal bleeds, ulcerative colitis, and diverticulitis. Table 6-3 summarizes the conditions associated with variations in the physical characteristics of stool.

Interfering Circumstances. Diet and medications can affect the physical characteristics of feces.

Chemical Testing of Feces

Chemical testing of feces is performed to detect the presence of occult blood, carbohydrates, bile, and trypsin. Screening for occult blood is the most common chemical test of feces and has been successfully used as an early detection test for colorectal cancer. However, there are may other abnormal conditions of the colon and rectum associated with occult fecal blood.

Occult Blood Analysis

Specimens for occult blood are usually collected by the patient at home, using a test kit obtained from the health practitioner. The patient is placed on a special diet and must avoid red meat, raw vegetables, aspirin, and medications that may cause blood in the stool. The fecal specimen is collected at each bowel movement over several days. Once the bowel movement is completed, the individual retrieves a stool sample with the stick provided in the test kit. The stool is then placed on the treated paper in the test kit. Once three different stool specimens have been collected, the test kit is brought to the lab for analysis. Stool specimens may also be taken during a rectal examination.

Table 6-3. Conditions Associated with Variations in the Physical Characteristic of Stool

Characteristic	Variation	Conditions
Color	Black	Upper GI tract bleeding, licorice ingestion, iron ingestion, coal ingestion
	Dark brown	Hemolytic anemia, high meat diet
	Gray, silvery	Steatorrhea, pancreatic disease, cystic fibrosis
	Pasty, gray-white	Bile duct obstruction
	Red	Hemorrhoids, lower GI bleed
Consistency	Mucoid, watery, no blood	Irritable bowel syndrome
	Mucoid, bloody	Inflammatory bowel disease, ulcerative colitis
	Loose, purulent with necrotic tissues	Diverticulitis, parasitic infection, ulcerative colitis, bacillary dysentery

Normal Findings. Absence of occult blood.

Variations from Normal. Colorectal cancer is the chief cause of occult blood in the stool.

Other Fecal Blood Tests

The presence of other types of fecal blood can be diagnostically significant. Stool that presents with obvious or frank blood must be analyzed for the cause of the bleed. Any visual observations of blood must be confirmed by additional diagnostic tests.

Normal Findings. Absence of any type of observable blood.

Variations from Normal. Black, tarry stool is associated with upper gastrointestinal bleeding consistent with ulcers and varices. Bright red stool is indicative of lower gastrointestinal tract bleeding as seen in hemorrhoids, ulcerative colitis, and cancer.

Carbohydrate Tests

A fecal carbohydrate test is performed to determine the carbohydrate content of feces. The test involves a Clinitest tablet on a sample of stool that has been emulsified with water. Excessive carbohydrates in feces indicate disorders related to absorption problems caused by metabolic or intestinal abnormalities.

Bile and Trypsin Tests

Bile is normally absent in the feces of adults. Its presence is related to the rapid movement of feces through the gastrointestinal tract and to hemolytic anemias. Trypsin is a pancreatic enzyme that is necessary for the metabolism of carbohydrates, protein, and fats. Trypsin should not be detected in the stool of individuals over 2 years old. The absence of trypsin in the stool of children under the age 2 can signal a pancreatic deficiency.

Normal Findings

Carbohydrates	Negative
Bile	Negative
Trypsin	Negative, adults
	Negative, children over age 2
	Positive, children under age 2

Variations from Normal. Tests that demonstrate an excessive amount of carbohydrates or any amount of bile in adult stool are not diagnostically specific. Additional diagnostic investigations should be completed. Children under age 2 who do not have trypsin present in their stool should be evaluated for pancreatic disorders.

Interfering Circumstances. Failure to follow the proper testing procedures may negatively affect the results of chemical fecal tests. Certain drugs and foods may alter the results of the tests.

Microscopic Testing of Feces

Microscopic testing of feces is performed to identify the presence of leukocytes, fats, and parasites. It may be used as a screening test or to support the findings of other diagnostic interventions.

Leukocyte Tests

A microscopic stool test for leukocytes, especially neutrophils and monocytes, is performed as an initial evaluation for diarrhea of unknown etiology. Although the presence of leukocytes can help determine the cause of diarrhea, there are many types of diarrhea that do not exhibit an increase in fecal leukocytes.

Normal Findings. Leukocytes are not present in stool.

Variations from Normal. Leukocytes in stool, coupled with the presence of diarrhea, is diagnostic for bacterial diarrhea that involves the intestinal wall. Ulcerative colitis also exhibits leukocytes in the stool.

Fat Tests

Microscopic testing for fats is performed to identify the amount of fat present in feces. Using a microscopic exam, the laboratory professional is able to determine the number and size of fat droplets present in feces, as well as the type of fats present. The types of fats in feces include triglycerides, fatty acids, and fatty acid salts. The presence of fat in the stool is called **steatorrhea**, a possible sign or symptom of serious malabsorption syndromes and diseases such as celiac sprue and cystic fibrosis.

Microscopic identification of fats in feces is limited since it only detects the presence of excessive fat and the nature of the fat. In order to adequately assess steatorrhea, the patient must be placed on a fat-controlled diet and collect stool samples over a seventy-two-hour period. After the collection is completed, the feces is analyzed to determine what percentage of the total solid fecal material is fat.

Normal Range

Fat	<60 normal-sized droplets
Triglycerides	1–5%
Fatty acids	5–15%

Variations from Normal. Excessive triglyceride levels in feces are associated with pancreatic enzyme deficiency. Increased fatty acids with normal triglyceride levels are seen in malabsorption syndromes.

Parasite Tests

Microscopic examination for parasites is performed when there is a suspicion of parasitic infestation that may be causing gastrointestinal disorder or distress. Fecal specimens collected for parasite testing should be transported to the lab immediately. Parasites frequently found in feces are tapeworms, hookworms, pinworms, amoebae, and protozoa. In some circumstances multiple fecal specimens are collected over a period of time to determine the presence of parasites. Other methods of obtaining fecal specimens include the use of a rectal swab or the **cellophane tape test**.

The cellophane tape test is used to collect a specimen from the rectal area of the patient. The specimen is then examined for pinworms. This test should be done early in the morning or overnight before the patient has bathed or defecated. A strip of clear cellophane tape is applied to the perineal region; the tape is removed and attached to a slide for microscopic evaluation.

Normal Findings. Absence of parasites in the stool.

Variations from Normal. Parasitic infestation is associated with a wide variety of diseases. Protozoa infestations can cause dysentery, which may lead to perforation and peritonitis. Hookworms attach themselves to the duodenal lining and nourish themselves on the blood of the host, often resulting in anemic conditions. Pinworms cause marked irritation and itching of the skin around the anus, and tapeworms can cause diarrhea, epigastric pain, and weight loss.

Interfering Circumstances. Failure to follow proper specimen collection procedures alters the outcome of fecal tests.

Summary

- Urine, which is excreted by the kidneys, is the product of an essential body function that filters substances from the blood.
- Abnormalities of the renal system or other parts of the body can be detected through urinalysis.
- Urine specimen collection procedures vary with the type of urinalysis being performed.

- Urine testing includes analyzing the physical, chemical, and microscopic properties of urine.
- Physical analysis includes the examination of the odor, color, appearance, and specific gravity of urine.
- Chemical analysis includes the examination of urine, using a reagent strip, to determine the pH value, the amount of protein, bilirubin, blood, nitrate, ketones, urobilinogen, glucose, leukocyte esterase, and leukocytes in urine.
- Microscopic analysis of the sediment of urine examines cells, crystals, casts, and microorganisms that may be present.
- Urine testing is done to screen for drugs, to confirm pregnancy, and to identify PKU in infants.
- Feces, a waste product of digestion, is excreted by the gastrointestinal tract.
- Fecal studies are useful in the diagnosis of gastrointestinal abnormalities such as colorectal cancer, malabsorption syndromes, and gastrointestinal bleeds.
- Physical examination of feces includes an analysis of the amount, odor, shape, color, and consistency of feces.
- Chemical examination of feces includes an analysis to determine the presence of occult blood, carbohydrates, and fats.
- Microscopic examination of feces includes an analysis to determine the presence of leukocytes, fats, and parasites.

CHAPTER REVIEW

1. Organize the listed urine tests according to these test categories:

   a. Physical tests _____

   b. Chemical tests _____

   c. Microscopic tests _____

appearance	cells	glucose	nitrites	protein
bilirubin	color	ketones	odor	specific gravity
blood	crystals	microorganisms	pH level	urobilinogen
casts				

2. Identify the substances found in urine that can be associated with the listed diseases:

a. Anorexia   _____

b. Diabetes mellitus   _____

c. Upper urinary tract infection   _____

d. Glomerulonephritis   _____

e. Hepatitis   _____

f. Multiple myeloma   _____

g. Polycystic kidney disease   _____

h. Uncontrolled diabetes   _____

3. Describe the urine specimen collection methods presented in this chapter. What is the reason for using each of the methods?

4. Compare the differences between chemical, physical, and microscopic analysis of urine. Which type of analysis is more valuable?

5. Explain how urine can be used for drug testing. Why are urine tests used to identify the presence of drugs? Are urine tests accurate? Why or why not?

6. Organize the listed fecal tests according to these test categories:

a. Physical tests   _____

b. Chemical tests   _____

c. Microscopic tests   _____

amount	color	leukocytes	parasites
bile	consistency	occult blood	shape
blood	fats	odor	trypsin
carbohydrates			

7. Identify the substances found in feces that can be associated with the listed diseases:

a. Colorectal cancer _____

b. Diarrhea _____

c. Dysentery _____

d. Irritable bowel syndrome _____

e. Lower GI bleed _____

f. Pancreatic enzyme deficiency _____

g. Ulcerative colitis _____

h. Upper GI bleed _____

8. Describe the diagnostic significance of fecal analysis.

9. Discuss the analysis of fat in feces. Include the types of fats identified, the diagnostic significance of each type of fat, and the implications for steatorrhea.

10. What is the purpose of the cellophane tape test? How is it performed?

Case Studies

1. In reviewing the record of Rochester Mathews, a 63-year-old man whose physician suspects renal problems, you discover that a microscopic urinalysis was ordered. Describe what must be done to carry out microscopic urine testing. How are these urine tests performed and what substances are analyzed? What abnormalities can be detected using these tests?

2. Mary Jo Kline, a 29-year-old married woman, called the Women's and Children's Clinic where you are employed requesting an appointment to see her physician because her urine test for pregnancy was positive. Discuss how a urine pregnancy test works and why. Describe the conditions under which the test may be inaccurate.

3. Dr. Willow has ordered that Annabelle Halverson, a 45-year-old woman undergoing a routine physical, have a screening test for occult blood in the feces. Identify and discuss conditions that might cause occult blood to appear in feces. Describe the special preparation necessary for this test. What circumstances might influence the results?

Challenge Activity

Choose any three to five chemicals or microscopic substances (i.e., blood, glucose, proteins, etc.) that are measured or analyzed in blood, urine, and feces and compare how each substance is collected and analyzed. Are the same or related diseases or disorders identified by the presence, absence, increase, or decrease of these substances?

Chapter 7

Culture and Sensitivity Tests

Key Terms, Abbreviations, and Acronyms

agar

agar diffusion

cerebrospinal fluid, CSF

chocolate agar

cisternal puncture

culture

culture and sensitivity tests, C & S

culture medium

intermediate, I

paramyxovirus

resistant, R

sensitive, S

sensitivity testing

septicemia

sputum

stool culture

suprapubic aspiration

transtracheal aspiration

ventricular punctures

wound cultures

zone of inhibition

Learning Objectives

Upon completion of this chapter, the learner should be able to:

1. Describe the clinical value of culture and sensitivity testing.
2. Define culture and sensitivity as they apply to laboratory tests.

3. Identify the microorganisms associated with specific culture substances.
4. Select the correct indications for each type of culture test.
5. Differentiate between sensitive, resistant, and intermediate organisms in relation to sensitivity testing.

Introduction

Culture and sensitivity testing is a highly effective method for identification of infectious pathogenic microorganisms and the antibiotics will inhibit the growth of those microorganisms. This chapter includes a definition of culture and sensitivity, a brief overview of the process involved in culture and sensitivity tests, and a discussion of the various types of culture specimens collected from the body. Sensitivity testing is covered in the "Overview" section of this chapter and is not included for each type of culture specimen.

Specimens used in culture and sensitivity tests include blood; cerebrospinal fluid; sputum; stool or feces; wound exudates; and secretions or scrapings from the skin, nose, throat, genitalia, and anus. Each specimen is discussed individually with regard to specimen collection methods, organisms that may be found in the specimen, and indications or contraindications for specimen collection. It is important to remember that culture and sensitivity testing is done to identify the organisms that cause disease. Culture and sensitivity testing is usually indicated by the presence of disease, such as a sore throat, wound infection, pyuria, and other suspected diagnoses.

Overview of Culture and Sensitivity (C & S) Tests

Culture is defined as a laboratory test by which samples from body specimens are cultivated in a special growth medium in order to isolate the microorganisms that may be present. Culture is a highly effective laboratory method for identifying the microorganisms that cause infectious disease and for obtaining a definitive diagnosis. For example, a suspected diagnosis of strep throat is confirmed by culturing material taken from the infected throat and observing the growth of a specific type of streptococcal bacteria.

Specimen collection for culture and sensitivity testing must be carried out under standard precautionary techniques in order to avoid contamination of the specimen. Gloves, sterile specimen containers, careful preparation of the culture site, and length of time between collection and actual laboratory preparation or testing can impact the results of culture growth. In addition, each organism's growth requirements, such as oxygen, moisture, temperature, and nutrients, must be considered.

Successful growth of suspected microorganisms is dependent on selecting the appropriate **culture medium**, the substance that provides the nutritional environment for the growth of microorganisms. **Agar**, an extract of seaweed, is used in several types of culture media. A culture medium can be produced as a solid, liquid, or semisolid, and can consist of amino acids, sugars, minerals, salts, and vitamins. Some media can be made of cooked blood, which is known as **chocolate agar**, meat, milk, and other products. Blood is also used as a medium that is simply called blood agar. There are many commercially prepared media kits, which are organism specific, available for purchase. Laboratories, whether they make their own media or purchase prepared kits, must keep the media refrigerated until use. Table 7-1 shows some common bacteria, their preferred growth medium, and an example of a disease associated with the bacteria.

Once the microorganism has been cultured and identified, it is tested for sensitivity to specific antibiotics. **Sensitivity testing** completes the process known as culture and sensitivity. The purpose of sensitivity testing is to identify the antibiotics that may be effective against the microorganism. **Agar diffusion** is the most commonly used sensitivity test and involves the inoculation of a special agar plate with the organism to be tested. Once the plate has been inoculated, antibiotic disks are placed onto the surface of the agar and the plate is turned upside down and incubated overnight.

Table 7-1. Common Bacteria and Growth Medium

Bacteria	*Disease*	*Medium*
Streptococcus	Strep throat	Blood agar
Neisseria gonorrhoeae	Gonorrhea	Chocolate agar
Staphylococcus	Infections, boils	Blood agar
Escherichia coli	Urinary tract infections	Blood agar

The reaction between the antibiotic disks and the organism creates a **zone of inhibition**, an area of no growth, around each antibiotic disk if the antibiotic is effective against that bacterium. The size of this zone is used to classify the organism as **sensitive (S)**, meaning the antibiotic inhibits growth (the organism is sensitive to the antibiotic); **resistant (R)**, meaning the antibiotic does not inhibit growth (the organism is resistant to the antibiotic); and **intermediate (I)**, meaning the antibiotic inhibits growth somewhat, but not enough to be effective. Increasing the dose may increase the organism's sensitivity. Figure 7-1 displays an antibiotic sensitivity test plate showing the zones of inhibition. The size of the zone of inhibition is directly related to the sensitivity of the organism; the larger the size of the zone, the more sensitive the organism to the particular antibiotic.

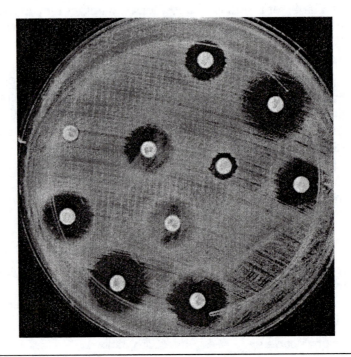

Figure 7-1.   Antibiotic sensitivity plate showing zones of inhibition

Blood Culture

Blood is an important culture specimen since it is used to identify the cause of **septicemia**, a systemic and potentially life-threatening infection in which pathogens are present in circulating blood. Septicemia is also known as blood poisoning. Blood cultures are indicated when there is reason to suspect septicemia, bacteremia, and sepsis in a newborn. Unexplained postoperative shock; an intermittent, persistent, or continuous fever of either unknown origin or associated with a heart murmur; and chills and fever related to infected burns or indwelling venous or arterial catheters, are additional indications for blood culture tests.

Venipuncture is the collection method used for obtaining a blood sample for culture purposes. Care must be taken in order to prevent contamination of the blood sample with the normal flora present on the skin. In addition, standard precautions related to blood-borne pathogens must also be followed.

Normal Findings. No growth of pathogens; negative.

Variations from Normal. Organisms most commonly identified via blood culture are *Escherichia coli (E. coli), Staphylococcus epidermis, Staphylococcus aureus, Listeria monocytogenes, Neisseria meningitidis, Salmonella,* and *Klebsiella*.

Interfering Circumstances. Contamination of the blood sample, especially with skin bacteria, alters blood culture results. Antibiotic or antimicrobial therapy prior to testing may interfere with pathogen growth.

Cerebrospinal Fluid Culture

Cerebrospinal fluid (CSF) flows through and protects the ventricles of the brain, the subarachnoid space, and the spinal canal. Under healthy conditions, CSF is sterile and therefore contains virtually no microorganisms. Suspected diagnoses of meningitis, encephalitis, and brain abscess are indications for CSF culture and sensitivity tests. Central nervous system disorders of unknown cause also indicate the need for CSF culture. Since many organisms can cause meningitis, cerebrospinal fluid is often cultured on several different media. Bacteria, viruses, fungi, protozoa, and tubercle bacilli can be identified by CSF culture.

Cerebrospinal fluid is obtained by way of lumbar puncture, cisternal puncture, and ventricular puncture. Lumbar puncture is the most frequently used technique and involves preparation of the puncture area, usually at the third or fourth lumbar vertebra (L3–L4); infiltration of a local anesthetic into the skin; insertion of a needle with a stylet into the intervertebral space; removal of the stylet; and, if the puncture is accurate, CSF will drip out of the needle and may be collected into sterile test tubes.

Cisternal puncture takes place at the base of the skull, between the first cervical vertebra and the foramen magnum. The procedure for cisternal puncture is the same as for lumbar puncture. During cisternal puncture, the needle is inserted close to the brain stem, which adds to the risk of this procedure.

A **ventricular puncture** is an actual surgical procedure that is rarely performed. It involves a scalp incision, drilling a burr hole into the base of the skull, and inserting the needle into the drilled hole. CSF samples are then drawn directly from one of the ventricles of the brain.

Normal Findings.   Absence of organisms; negative.

Variations from Normal.   Organisms identified in cerebrospinal fluid culture are *E. coli*, commonly found in premature infants and newborns diagnosed with acute bacterial meningitis; streptococci, staphylococci, meningococci, and especially *Haemophilus influenzae*, associated with bacterial meningitis in young children; pneumococcus and meningococcus, which are chiefly responsible for meningitis in adults; and pneumococcus, *S. aureus*, *E. coli*, and *Pseudomonas aeruginosa*, the main organisms that affect the aged.

Interfering Circumstances.   Improper collection techniques, contamination or alteration of the specimen, and a delay in transport to the laboratory interfere with culture results.

Genitalia and Anal Cultures

Cultures taken from the genitalia and anal canal in both men and women are often used to identify sexually transmitted diseases. Indications for these cultures are genital ulcers, signs and symptoms of sexually transmitted diseases, pelvic inflammatory disease, or abnormal discharge and itching. Toxic shock syndrome and infections associated with the herpes simplex virus can also indicate a need for genital and anal cultures.

Specific culture sites include the cervix, vagina, anal canal, and urethra. Culture samples are taken by inserting a sterile, cotton-tipped swab into the specific site, rotating or scraping the swab against the mucosa of the site, placing the swab in an appropriate transport medium, and sending the sample to the laboratory for immediate testing.

The procedure for anal canal samples is the same for men and women. A sterile swab is inserted into the anal canal, carefully avoiding contact with any feces, and moved from side to side. The swab is removed, and if any fecal material is present, the procedure must be repeated.

In order to obtain a vaginal or cervical sample, a vaginal speculum is inserted, the cervix is cleansed of mucus, and a swab is then rotated to collect secretions from the endocervical canal. A separate swab is used to collect vaginal material by moving the swab along the sides of the vaginal mucosa.

Urethral culture, obtained from male patients, utilizes a loop swab that is capable of scraping material from the mucosa of the anterior urethra. Epithelial cells as well as secretions are needed in order to differentiate between gonorrhea and chlamydia organisms. Gonorrhea organisms are found in the secretions or exudate collected from the urethra, whereas chlamydia exists within the epithelial cells.

Normal Findings. No growth of pathogenic organisms; negative.

Variations from Normal. Pathogenic organisms identified by genitalia and anal culture are *Chlamydia, Candida, Mycoplasma, Gardnerella vaginalis, Neisseria gonorrhoeae, Treponema pallidum*, and *Trichomonas vaginalis*. These cultures are also used to distinguish toxin-producing strains of *Staphylococcus aureus* and infectious processes associated with herpes simplex virus.

Interfering Circumstances. Improper collection techniques, contamination of the specimen, and antibiotic treatment may interfere with culture results.

Nose and Throat Cultures

Cultures of the nose and throat are taken to search for specific disease-causing organisms, to diagnose bacterial infections, and to screen for carriers of *Staphylococcus aureus* or *Haemophilus influenzae*. Identification of the pathogenic organisms in the nose and throat can lead to definitive diagnoses such as thrush, diphtheria, pertussis, gonorrhea, and various viral upper respiratory infections. Specific culture sites include the nose, nasopharynx, and throat. Culture samples are taken by inserting a swab into the specific site, rotating the swab against the mucosa or any lesions of the site, placing the swab in an appropriate transport medium, and sending the sample to the laboratory for immediate testing.

Nose or nasal cultures are obtained by inserting a flexible swab into the nares. The swab is rotated against the sides of the nares, making contact with both external nares and the deeper, moist, recesses of the nose. Nasal cultures are useful for the identification of **paramyxovirus**, the organism that causes mumps.

Nasopharyngeal cultures are obtained by inserting a flexible swab along the bottom of the nares. The swab is carefully advanced until it reaches the nasopharynx and then rotated in place to collect secretions from the area. Nasopharyngeal cultures are performed to screen for the organisms that cause pertussis, diphtheria, cerebrospinal meningitis, and influenza. Figure 7-2 exhibits swab placement during nasopharyngeal culture collection.

Throat cultures are obtained by cautiously inserting a swab through the mouth to the pharyngeal and tonsillar area. The swab must not touch any part of the oral cavity. Pharyngeal and tonsillar areas, including lesions, inflammation, or exudates, are rubbed with the swab and specimens are collected. Throat cultures are indicated for children who present with a sore throat and fever.

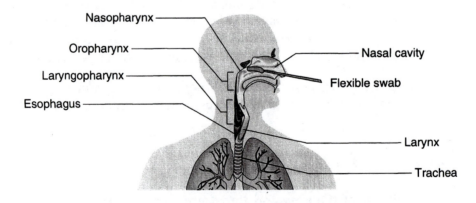

Figure 7-2.   Swab placement for nasopharyngeal culture

The purpose of the culture is to detect the presence of the group A beta-hemolytic *Streptococcus pyogenes* that would provide the diagnosis of beta-hemolytic streptococcal pharyngitis, known as strep throat. This type of streptococcal infection can be followed by rheumatic fever or glomerulonephritis. Since fewer than 5% of adults who present with pharyngitis will have a streptococcal infection, throat cultures are only indicated when the adult patient has severe or recurrent sore throat.

Normal Findings. No growth of pathogenic organisms; negative.

Variations from Normal. Organisms detected by way of nasal and throat cultures are *Staphylococcus aureus*, group A *Streptococcus*, meningococci, gonococci, *Corynebacterium diphtheriae*, *Bordetella pertussis*, and *Haemophilus influenzae*.

Interfering Circumstances. Improper collection techniques, contamination of the specimen, and antibiotic treatment may interfere with culture results.

Skin Culture

Skin cultures include samples taken from the skin, nail, and hair. Although many microorganisms exist in low numbers on the skin of a healthy person, skin cultures are used to identify organisms that cause integumentary infections such as cellulitis, pyoderma, impetigo, folliculitis, furuncles, and carbuncles. Fungal diseases such as athlete's foot, ringworm, rashes with well-defined borders, and tinea cruris (jock itch) are often evaluated via skin culture. Specimen collection methods are dependent on the sample site, but generally include a scraping, swabbing, or actual "clipping" of the specimen and its lesions; placement of the specimen in a growth medium, on a slide, or in an appropriate transport container; and laboratory incubation and examination of the specimen.

Hair culture specimens, such as hair stubs, shaft, and root, as well as scrapings from suspicious areas of the scalp, are clipped or plucked from the affected area and sent to the laboratory in a petri dish. A sterile scalpel or scissors are used to collect nail scrapings or clippings. Skin specimens include scrapings from the skin or several sites from the edge of a lesion, if present; fluid or pus obtained with needle aspiration; and material collected from moist, warm, skin folds that exhibit a rash with well-defined borders.

Normal Findings. Low numbers of microorganisms usually found on the skin; absence of large quantities of pathogenic microorganisms.

Variations from Normal. Boils and furuncles are caused by *Staphylococcus aureus*. Acne and pimples usually contain *Staphyloccus epidermis* or *Propionibacterium acnes*. Impetigo, a contagious skin infection, is caused by *S. pyogenes* or *S. aureus*.

The fungi *Microsporum*, *Trichophyton*, and *Epidermophyton* are associated with ringworm, athlete's foot, and tinea cruris and are cultured from the skin, hair, or nails. *Trichophyton* is a fungal pathogenic microorganism identified by skin, hair, and nail culture. *Candida* is found in skin and hair cultures, and *Epidermophyton* is usually cultured from hair and nails.

Interfering Circumstances. Improper collection techniques, contamination or alteration of the specimen, and a delay in transport to the laboratory interfere with culture results.

Sputum Culture

Sputum is strictly defined as matter ejected from the trachea, bronchi, and lungs through the mouth. Spit and saliva are not synonymous with sputum. Indications for sputum culture are suspected diagnoses of pneumonia; identification of the cause of respiratory infections; a confirmed tuberculosis diagnosis; and monitoring of the effectiveness of treatment for respiratory conditions, particularly tuberculosis. Growth of a pathogen in a sputum culture can provide a definitive diagnosis.

Sputum specimens can be collected by expectoration, **transtracheal aspiration**, and fiberoptic bronchoscopy. The expectoration method is most successful early in the morning. The patient is asked to take two or three deep breaths and to cough deeply. Sputum must be expectorated into a sterile sputum container without touching any part of the container. For patients who are unable to produce sputum via deep coughing and expectoration, transtracheal aspiration or fiberoptic bronchoscopy can be used.

Transtracheal aspiration involves the placement of a suction catheter into the trachea. The catheter can be passed through a nostril or an existing endotracheal or tracheostomy tube. When the catheter enters the trachea, a cough reflex is stimulated, and suction is applied. The specimen is removed, placed in an appropriate container, and immediately sent to the laboratory. Fiberoptic bronchoscopy, an endoscopic procedure described in Chapter 11, utilizes a lighted scope that is passed into the bronchial tree. The scope has a suction port to collect the sputum specimen. The specimen is transported in an appropriate container to the laboratory.

Normal Findings. Presence of normal respiratory flora; absence of large numbers of pathogenic microorganisms.

Variations from Normal. Routine sputum cultures for individuals with bacterial pneumonia can reveal *Streptococcus pneumoniae, Haemophilus influenzae, Klebsiella pneumoniae,* staphylococci, and gram-negative bacilli. *Mycobacterium tuberculosis, Candida, Aspergillus, Corynebacterium diphtheriae,* and *Bordetella pertussis* are also identified with sputum culture.

Interfering Circumstances. Improper collection techniques, contamination or alteration of the specimen, and a delay in transport to the laboratory interfere with culture results.

Stool Culture

Stool culture, also known as fecal culture, is an examination of the waste or excrement expelled from the digestive tract. Stool cultures are done to evaluate diarrhea of unknown etiology, to identify the presence of parasites in the lower gastrointestinal tract, and to identify organisms that cause damage to intestinal tissue. Excessive flatus and abdominal discomfort are additional indications for stool culture. It must be noted that feces of a healthy individual contains a significant number and variety of organisms that are not always pathogenic.

Stool specimens can be collected in a clean bedpan, in a "hat"-type receptacle that is placed under the toilet seat, or by way of a rectal swab. The bedpan or hat must be clean and dry, and urine must not be passed into the fecal sample. Specimen collection via rectal swab calls for the insertion of a clean or sterile swab into the rectum and past the anal sphincter. No lubricant is used, and the swab is carefully rotated in order to obtain an adequate fecal sample. In all cases, the samples must be protected from exposure to the air, must be sent to the laboratory within one hour, and should not be refrigerated.

Normal Findings. Presence of normal intestinal flora; absence of pathogenic microorganisms.

Variations from Normal. Pathogenic bacteria identified by stool culture are *Salmonella, Shigella, Campylobacter, Yersinia, Staphylococcus,* and pathogenic *E. coli.* Parasitic pathogens include *Ascaris,* also known as hookworms; tapeworms; and *Giardia,* also known as protozoas.

Interfering Circumstances. Antibiotic therapy may decrease the amount of bacteria present. In addition, improper collection techniques, contamination or alteration of the specimen, and a delay in transport to the laboratory interfere with culture results.

Urine Culture

Urine is an excellent culture and growth medium for most organisms that infect the urinary tract. Urinary tract infections that do not respond quickly to medication are high indicators for urine culture. Assessment and monitoring of the response to treatment for urinary tract infection is another indication for this culture. For pregnant women, antibiotic therapy for UTI is often instituted only after urine culture and sensitivity tests identify the specific causative organism and the antibiotic to which the organism is most susceptible.

Sample collection techniques for urine culture include the clean-catch midstream procedure; urinary catheterization for individuals who are unable to void; aspiration of urine from an indwelling urinary catheter; and **suprapubic aspiration,** usually performed on infants or neonates, which requires the insertion of a needle into the suprapubic area and withdrawal of urine into the syringe. In all cases, the urine must be placed in a sterile container and transported to the lab within thirty minutes. Urine samples may be refrigerated for up to two hours.

Normal Findings. Absence of pathological organisms; bacterial count less than 10,000 bacteria per milliliter (may indicate contamination of the specimen); negative.

Variations from Normal. E. coli, *Klebsiella*, *Proteus*, *Pseudomonas*, and enterococci are the most common pathogenic organisms identified via urine culture.

Interfering Circumstances. Improper collection techniques, contamination of the specimen, and a delay in transport to the laboratory interfere with culture results. Bacteria multiply quickly in nonrefrigerated urine samples.

Wound Culture

Wound cultures are defined as laboratory tests that attempt to cultivate microorganisms that may be present in an infected wound. Wound infections are often visible even to the untrained eye. The presence of purulent and/or foul-smelling drainage or other exudate is highly suggestive of wound infection and highly indicative for wound culture. Infection in nondraining wounds is evidenced by pain, swelling, and the presence of an abscess. Individuals with surgical wounds, burns, abrasions, decubiti, or other open skin areas are susceptible to wound infections. Wound culture is indicated in order to determine the causative agent, so appropriate treatment can be prescribed.

Wound culture samples are taken from the site of the infection using the swab technique or needle aspiration. Culture specimens from a superficial wound are collected with a sterile, cotton-tipped swab. The swab is placed into the pus or exudate of the wound without touching the wound edges or the intact surrounding skin. The swab is soaked or saturated with exudate and immediately placed into the appropriate transport container.

Needle aspiration is used to collect culture specimens from deep wounds and abscesses. In either situation, a sterile needle is inserted into the deep wound or abscess, material is aspirated from the site, and air is expelled from the syringe. The specimen can be transferred to an appropriate transport tube, or the needle can be capped, and the specimen is then sent to the laboratory.

Normal Findings. No growth of pathogens; negative.

Variations from Normal. Wound infections can be caused by bacteria such as *Staphylococcus aureus*, *Clostridium perfringens* (which can cause gas gangrene in humans), *Klebsiella*, *Proteus*, *Pseudomonas*, *Mycobacterium* species, and group A *Streptococci*. Fungal infectious agents are *Candida albicans* and *Aspergillus* species.

Interfering Circumstances. Antibiotic therapy may delay bacterial growth. In addition, improper collection techniques, contamination or alteration of the specimen, and a delay in transport to the laboratory interfere with culture results.

Summary

- Culture and sensitivity testing is a highly effective method for identifying pathogenic microorganisms and the antibiotics that inhibit their growth.
- Culture medium is the substance that provides the proper nutritional environment for the growth of microorganisms.
- Culture media include blood, cooked blood, agar, meat, and milk, and consist of amino acids, sugars, minerals, salts, and vitamins.
- Microorganisms are classified as sensitive, resistant, or intermediate in their reaction to specific antibiotics.
- Blood cultures are used to identify the cause of septicemia.
- Meningitis, encephalitis, and brain abscesses provide indications for cerebrospinal fluid cultures.
- Genitalia and anal cultures are used to identify the organisms responsible for sexually transmitted diseases.
- Carriers of *Staphylococcus aureus* or *Haemophilus influenzae* can be identified by nose or throat cultures.
- Skin, hair, and nail cultures are performed to identify bacterial and fungal pathogenic microorganisms related to a variety of integumentary infections.
- Tuberculosis can be confirmed via sputum culture.
- Stool cultures are used to evaluate diarrhea of unknown etiology, to identify the presence of parasites in the lower gastrointestinal tract, and to identify organisms that cause damage to intestinal tissue.
- Urine is an excellent culture and growth medium for most organisms that infect the urinary tract.

- Wound cultures are defined as laboratory tests that attempt to cultivate microorganisms that may be present in an infected wound or abscess.

CHAPTER REVIEW

1. Identify the culture tests associated with the listed organisms.

    a. *Bordetella pertussis*   _____

    b. Candida   _____

    c. Chlamydia   _____

    d. Clostridium   _____

    e. *Escherichia coli*   _____

    f. Group A streptococci   _____

    g. *Hemophilus influenzae*   _____

    h. Klebsiella   _____

    i. Microsporum   _____

    j. *Neisseria gonorrhoeae*   _____

    k. Paramyxovirus   _____

    l. Salmonella   _____

    m. *Staphylococcus aureus*   _____

    n. *Streptococcus pyogenes*   _____

2. Organize the listed diseases, problems, or conditions according to the following culture tests:

    a. Blood culture   _____

    b. Cerebrospinal fluid culture   _____

c. Genitalia and anal culture   _____

d. Nose and throat culture   _____

e. Skin culture   _____

f. Sputum culture   _____

g. Stool culture   _____

h. Urine culture   _____

i. Wound culture   _____

diarrhea	meningitis	ringworm	tuberculosis
genital ulcers	pneumonia	septicemia	urinary tract infections
itching	purulent exudate	sore throat	

3. Name the following specimen collection techniques and the culture test associated with the technique.

   a. Catheter placed in the trachea   _____

   b. Deep breathe and cough   _____

   c. First cervical vertebra and foramen magnum   _____

   d. Insertion of a needle, L3–L4   _____

   e. Specimen is drawn from a vein   _____

   f. Sterile needle inserted into wound or abscess   _____

4. Define the listed terms in relation to culture and sensitivity tests:

   a. Culture medium   _____

   b. Agar   _____

   c. Chocolate agar   _____

   d. Agar diffusion   _____

   e. Zone of inhibition   _____

5. Briefly discuss the clinical value of culture and sensitivity tests. Include a definition of culture and sensitivity and a brief overview of the process involved in these tests.

6. Differentiate between the terms "sensitive," "resistant," and "intermediate" as they relate to sensitivity testing.

Case Studies

1. Clinton Barnes, a 69-year-old man with an indwelling catheter, has a high fever. Dr. Newberry has examined him and has ordered blood cultures to find out if there are pathogens in Mr. Barnes's blood. What organisms may be found? Does the indwelling catheter play a role in his problem? If so, what role does it play? List some of the possible illnesses Mr. Barnes may have. What organisms cause the illnesses?

2. Bertha Manning, a 23-year-old female, is being examined at a public heath clinic because she was notified that her sex partner had tested positive for a sexually transmitted disease (STD). Which cultures could the nurse practitioner order? Identify the pathogenic organisms that cause some of the more prevalent STDs. After she was notified to come in for the exam, Ms. Manning took some old antibiotics she had left over from a previous illness. How could her actions affect the culture?

3. Nelson Pickett, a 7-year-old boy, was examined by his pediatrician because he has a severe sore throat. After examining Nelson, Dr. Ling has ordered a throat culture and sensitivity test. What substance will be cultured and what diagnoses can be associated with a severe sore throat? What is the purpose of sensitivity testing?

Challenge Activity

Culture and sensitivity procedures require adherence to standard precautions. What are standard precautions? Why are they applicable and important to culture methods and testing? What are the implications for the patient, lab personnel, and other health care staff, including nonclinical individuals, if standard precautions are ignored?

Chapter 8

Amniotic Fluid and Cerebrospinal Fluid Tests

Key Terms, Abbreviations and Acronyms

acetylcholinesterase, AChE

acid-fast bacillus, AFB

alpha-fetoprotein, AFP

amniocentesis

central nervous system, CNS

cerebrospinal fluid, CSF

cisternal puncture

foam stability test

karyotype

lecithin

lecithin:sphingomyelin ratio, L:S ratio

Limulus assay

lumbar puncture

meconium

neurosyphilis

opalescent

rapid surfactant test

shake test

sphingomyelin

surfactant

ventricular puncture

xanthochromia

Learning Objectives

Upon completion of this chapter, the learner should be able to:

1. Define the body fluids discussed in this chapter.
2. Discuss the diagnostic significance of analyzing each body fluid.
3. Organize body fluid tests according to the diseases or diagnoses identified by the tests.
4. Identify the indications and contraindications for each category of fluid analysis.
5. Compare the risks and benefits of the various sample collection procedures.

Introduction

Many of the substances measured in blood, urine, and feces can also be found in various other body fluids. The diagnostic significance of analyzing these fluids is directly related to the type of fluid analyzed, and the specific diagnosis is associated with changes in the specific body fluid. The presence of glucose, blood, cells, proteins, enzymes, and other substances in body fluids can provide the health practitioner with valuable clinical information.

The body fluids discussed in this chapter include amniotic fluid, the liquid that protects the fetus during pregnancy and is produced by the fetus and fetal membranes; and cerebrospinal fluid, which bathes and protects the brain and spinal cord.

Overview of Amniotic and Cerebrospinal Fluid Tests

Body fluid tests go a step beyond the routine blood, urine, and fecal analysis familiar to many individuals both in and out of the health care industry. Sample collection methods for fluids such as cerebrospinal fluid and amniotic fluid are often highly invasive and can involve substantial risks. Collecting specimens of amniotic fluid and cerebrospinal fluid involves needle punctures or aspiration techniques.

Contamination of body fluid samples is a serious concern for all types of body fluid tests. Caution must be taken so that the specimen is not tainted with skin cells or skin flora from the puncture site. In addition to specimen contamination concerns, collection methods have a potential for introducing bacteria into sensitive areas of the brain and meninges. Strict aseptic techniques must be followed during all collection activities.

While abnormal test results of any type can be traumatic and emotionally devastating, variations from normal in many of the fluids discussed in this chapter often affect some of the most personal aspects of an individual's life. Amniotic fluid tests can reveal irreversible fetal abnormalities and cerebrospinal fluid analysis can identify extremely challenging diseases such as multiple sclerosis.

Amniotic and cerebrospinal fluid tests are discussed individually. The discussions include a description of the fluid being analyzed, specimen collection methods, substances present in the fluid, and the diagnostic significance of the presence of those substances. Interfering circumstances and contraindications are also included.

Amniotic Fluid Tests

Amniotic fluid serves several purposes including protecting the fetus from shock, controlling embryonic and fetal body temperature, and allowing free movement of the developing fetus within the amniotic sac. Analysis of amniotic fluid provides diagnostic information about fetal well-being and fetal maturation.

Indications for amniotic fluid tests are family or parental genetic disorders, mental retardation, chromosome or enzyme anomalies, or inherited blood disorders. Advanced maternal age, at times defined as age 35 and older, may trigger routine chromosomal analysis. The need to determine fetal maturity is another indication for amniotic fluid tests. Contraindications for this type of test include a history of premature labor or incompetent cervix and the presence of abruptio placentae or placentae previa.

Although amniotic fluid tests can identify fetal disorders, the sample collection method, **amniocentesis**, carries inherent risks. Amniocentesis is a needle puncture through the abdomen, uterine wall, and into the amniotic sac in order to withdraw fluid for analysis. Figure 8-1 illustrates this technique.

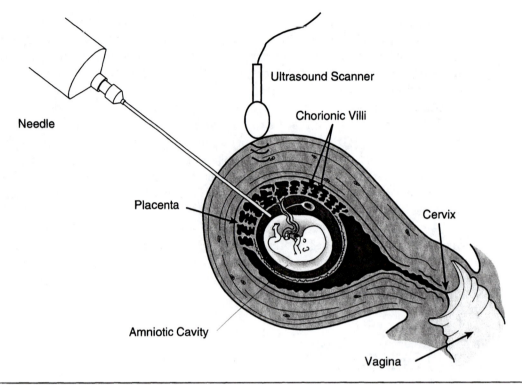

Ultrasound Scanner

Needle

Chorionic Villi

Placenta

Cervix

Amniotic Cavity

Vagina

Figure 8-1. Amniocentesis

Amniocentesis is used to draw samples for both physical and microscopic analysis of amniotic fluid. Risks associated with amniocentesis include miscarriage, fetal injury, introduction of infectious agents from the mother's skin or the external environment in general, abortion, premature labor, and maternal hemorrhage. Since the risks to both fetus and mother can be life-threatening, amniocentesis is carried out utilizing strict aseptic techniques, and only when there is a high probability that a fetal disorder is present or imminent.

Physical, chemical, and microscopic examination of amniotic fluid can assist in the diagnosis of conditions as varied as hypoxia, which is inadequate supply of oxygen at the cellular level, to hemolytic disease of the newborn, a condition in which fetal red blood cells are lysed. Physical analysis of amniotic fluid includes assessment of the color and quantity of the fluid. In early pregnancy, amniotic fluid is usually clear and colorless. As the pregnancy progresses, vernix caseosa, a cheeselike substance covering the skin of the fetus, and fetal urine can alter amniotic color. This color change is normal and expected. Color changes that may indicate pathology include meconium staining (a green-tinged stain) or the actual presence of **meconium**, a material that collects in fetal intestines, in the amniotic fluid. Fetal hypoxia is associated with the presence of meconium or meconium staining. A yellow-brown opaque discoloration can indicate intrauterine death, and a simple yellow appearance may signal blood incompatibility. Port wine staining generally indicates abruptio placentae.

The quantity or volume of amniotic fluid present in the amniotic sac can also indicate various fetal disorders. An excessive accumulation of fluid is associated with both fetal and maternal disorders. Fetal disorders include anencephaly, esophageal atresia, fetal heart failure, and massive fetal edema. Maternal disorders are diabetes and hypertensive disorders of pregnancy. A decreased amount of amniotic fluid can signify chronic fetal illness, placental insufficiency, and urinary tract abnormalities.

Chemical and microscopic analysis of amniotic fluid focuses on identification of proteins, chromosomal makeup, elevated bilirubin levels, and indications of **surfactant** production. Surfactant is a lipoprotein that enables the exchange of gases at the alveolar level and contributes to the elasticity of lung tissue. Tests of amniotic fluid are performed in order to screen for genetic and neural tube abnormalities, to identify hemolytic disease of newborns, and to assess fetal maturity. Each of these categories, and the tests associated with them, are discussed individually. It should be noted that improper handling of specimens and contamination of the sample with blood or meconium may alter test results. Normal ranges for each substance tested are presented in relation to fetal gestational age in weeks.

Genetic and Neural Tube Abnormalities

In order to identify genetic and neural tube abnormalities, amniotic fluid is analyzed to determine the sex of the fetus, to analyze fetal chromosomes, and to measure the presence or level of **alpha-fetoprotein (AFP)**, a glycoprotein found in fetal serum, and **acetylcholinesterase (AChE)**, an enzyme that reduces or prevents neuron activity at neuromuscular junctions.

Amniocentesis for suspected genetic and neural tube defects is usually performed early in the second trimester, between the 16th to 18th week of gestation.

Fetal Sex Determination

Determination of the sex of the fetus is indicated when sex-linked inherited disorders are suspected. Examples of such disorders include hemophilia and Duchenne's muscular dystrophy. In both disorders, the mother carries the abnormal gene, but passes it only to male offspring. Although there are no specific tests to diagnose these conditions in utero, identification of the sex of the fetus, coupled with the carrier status of the mother, can provide parents with information concerning fetal potential for inheriting the disease.

Fetal Chromosome Analysis

Fetal chromosome analysis consists of determining the chromosomal makeup, also called the **karyotype**, in order to detect genetic, chromosomal, and metabolic disorders.

Normal Findings. Normal chromosomal makeup, karyotype.

Variations from Normal. Down's syndrome, hemophilia, and cystic fibrosis are some of the more commonly recognized genetic and chromosomal abnormalities identified with chromosome analysis. Fetal karyotyping can also identify galactosemia and Tay-Sachs disease. Galactosemia is a serious inherited disorder of galactose metabolism that can result in hepatosplenomegaly, cataracts, and mental retardation. Tay-Sachs disease is a neurodegenerative disorder in which mental and physical retardation are progressive and fatal.

Alpha-Fetoprotein (AFP) and Acetylcholinesterase Levels

The presence of alpha-fetoprotein (AFP) and acetylcholinesterase in amniotic fluid can be indicative of neural tube defects. Neural tube defects are defined as a group of congenital malformations involving the skull, spinal cord and column, and brain. The neural tube, which is present during early embryonic development, gives rise to the brain and spinal cord, as well as other neural tissue. Failure of the neural tube to close is the primary cause of neural tube defects. In the presence of neural tube defects, AFP escapes into the amniotic fluid and maternal serum as well.

Normal Range

Alpha-fetoprotein	13–14 μg/mL (13–14 weeks)
	0.2–3.0 μg/mL (at term)
Acetylcholinesterase	None present

Variations from Normal. Elevated AFP levels can signify serious disorders such as anencephaly, spina bifida, and hydrocephalus. Elevated AFP levels suggest a potential neural tube defect, but AFP levels increase in other non–neural tube problems such as congenital nephrosis or Rh immune disease. The presence of acetylcholinesterase in the amniotic fluid, however, is specific to the diagnosis of neural tube defect. Decreased levels of AFP are associated with abnormal conditions such as Down's syndrome and spontaneous abortion.

Hemolytic Disease of Newborns

Hemolytic disease of newborns, also known as erythroblastosis fetalis, is characterized by the hemolysis of fetal red blood cells. The primary cause of this disease is maternal-fetal blood group incompatibility, usually exhibited when an Rh-negative mother is carrying an Rh-positive fetus. Identification of this disease can provide the opportunity for early delivery or blood transfusion in order to increase the possibility of a healthy outcome.

As fetal red blood cells are lysed, bilirubin is released into the fetal bloodstream and amniotic fluid. Amniocentesis is performed during the second half of the pregnancy to assess the level of bilirubin present in amniotic fluid.

Normal Range

Bilirubin   <0.020 mg/dl at term

Variations from Normal. Increased levels of amniotic bilirubin are a direct indication of fetal red blood cell hemolysis and an indirect indicator of fetal anemia.

Fetal Maturity

Tests for fetal maturity are usually performed after the 35th week of gestation. The primary indication for fetal maturity tests is the necessity of preterm or early delivery caused by fetal or maternal problems. Since the lungs are the last fetal organs to mature, amniotic fluid tests that measure lung development are most important. Fetal maturity is determined by analyzing amniotic fluid for the presence of the following substances: (1) **lecithin** and **sphingomyelin**, phospholipids related to lung surfactant; (2) creatinine; and (3) fetal epithelial cells.

Lecithin and Sphingomyelin

The **ratio of lecithin to sphingomyelin (L:S ratio)** is a measure of fetal lung maturity and is determined by analyzing the amniotic fluid for the presence of these phospholipids. When fetal lungs are immature, the sphingomyelin concentration in the amniotic fluid is higher than the lecithin concentration. Since lecithin is a primary component of surfactant, the substance needed for alveolar gas exchange, an increase in amniotic lecithin is an indication of lung maturity. As lecithin increases, sphingomyelin decreases. In fact, an L:S ratio of 2:1 or higher is a reliable indication of fetal lung maturity and therefore fetal maturity.

A direct measure of the amount of surfactant in amniotic fluid can be evaluated by a quick and inexpensive technique called the **shake test**, also known as the **foam stability** or **rapid surfactant test**. For this test a small amount of amniotic fluid is diluted with saline solution, ethyl alcohol is added to the fluid, and the mixture is shaken vigorously. The presence of fine bubbles or foam is a positive result and is highly accurate for fetal lung maturity.

Normal Range

L:S ratio   <1.6:1   35 weeks or less

　　　　　　 >2.0:1   more than 35 weeks

Shake test   Presence of fine bubbles or foam

Variations from Normal. A lack of foam or bubbles in the shake test and an equal or near equal L:S ratio is a direct indication of fetal lung immaturity, which translates into fetal immaturity.

Creatinine

Creatinine is excreted in fetal urine and is thereby present in amniotic fluid. Creatinine levels are used to assess renal function and fetal muscle mass. A creatinine concentration of 2.0 mg/dl or greater places fetal age at 36 weeks or more. Creatinine concentration is less reliable than the L:S ratio, but taken together the accuracy of both tests is greater than the accuracy of either test alone.

Normal Range

Creatinine   >2.0 mg/dl   36 weeks or more

Variations from Normal. Creatinine levels less than 2.0 indicate fetal immaturity.

Fetal Epithelial Cells

During the second and third trimesters, fetal epithelial cells are shed into the amniotic fluid. As the fetus matures, the percentage of cells containing lipids increases. Lipid cells can be identified in the amniotic fluid by adding Nile blue stain to the fluid. Cells containing lipid stain orange. Fetal maturity is proportional to the percentage of orange appearing cells. At 34 weeks' gestation, only 1% of the cells are orange, and a 10% to 50% staining indicates a gestational age greater than 35 weeks.

Cerebrospinal Fluid (CSF) Tests

Cerebrospinal fluid (CSF) is a secretion of the choroid plexus, specialized tangled masses of capillaries located in the lateral, third, and fourth ventricles of the brain. CSF is a clear, colorless fluid that flows through the ventricles of the brain, the subarachnoid space, and the spaces associated with the spinal cord. Cerebrospinal fluid is often defined as the fluid shock absorber for the brain and spinal cord. In addition to cushioning these structures from shock, CSF helps transport nutrients and wastes, and assists in the regulation of intracranial pressure.

Chemical constituents of cerebrospinal fluid are sodium, chloride, magnesium, bicarbonate, glucose, urea, and proteins. The concentration of each of these constituents is carefully controlled by the blood-brain barrier. Comparing the plasma concentrations of these constituents reveals the following: sodium, chloride, and magnesium readily cross the blood-brain barrier and are more concentrated in CSF; bicarbonate, glucose, and urea are less concentrated in CSF; and very small amounts of proteins or cells cross into the cerebrospinal fluid. Analysis of cerebrospinal fluid can identify a variety of diseases from subarachnoid hemorrhage to tuberculosis meningitis. Cerebrospinal fluid can be analyzed for physical, chemical, and microbiological properties.

Obtaining a CSF sample is most often accomplished by **lumbar puncture** (also called a spinal tap), the introduction of a hollow needle into the subarachnoid space of the lumbar portion of the spinal canal. The puncture site selected usually falls between L-3 and L-4 or lower. Figure 8-2 demonstrates the routine puncture site and placement of the puncture needle. Lumbar puncture has the potential for introducing bacteria and other mi-

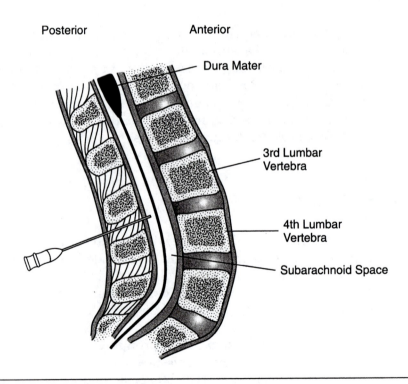

Figure 8-2. Lumbar puncture

croorganisms into the subarachnoid space. Therefore, the procedure must be performed using sterile techniques.

Contraindications for lumbar puncture are an increase in intracranial pressure, anatomic abnormalities in the puncture site that interfere with safe needle placement, and infections near the puncture site. It must be noted, however, that some increases in intracranial pressure necessitate completion of lumbar puncture in order to identify the causative disease. Complications associated with lumbar puncture include persistent CSF leakage, suppurative meningitis, brain-stem herniation, paralysis, and hematoma. Postpuncture spinal headache is the most common aftereffect of a lumbar puncture.

If lumbar puncture is not possible, cerebrospinal fluid may be collected via **cisternal** and/or **ventricular puncture**. The cisternal puncture is accomplished by inserting the needle between the first cervical vertebra and the foramen magnum. This is a hazardous procedure since the needle is placed very near the brain stem. The ventricular puncture is a surgical procedure whereby CSF samples are drawn directly from one of the lateral ventricles of the brain. As with any operative procedure, the patient must be informed of the risks and benefits of the procedure, and appropriate authorization must be obtained. Ventricular puncture is rarely performed. Complications associated with cisternal and ventricular punctures are similar to those discussed with lumbar puncture. Cisternal and ventricular punctures have a greater potential for causing trauma to the brain stem and the brain itself.

Once the cerebrospinal fluid has been collected, CSF tests can be organized into three general categories: (1) physical, chemical, and microscopic analysis; (2) microbiologic analysis; and (3) cytologic analysis. Each of these three general categories is discussed individually. It must be noted that cerebrospinal fluid can be analyzed to identify the diagnosis of **neurosyphilis**, syphilis involving the central nervous system. However, if neurosyphilis is a serious diagnostic consideration, the fluorescent treponemal antibody (FTA) serum (blood) test is the test of choice.

Physical, Chemical, and Microscopic Cerebrospinal Fluid Tests

Cerebrospinal fluid testing includes a physical analysis for color, clarity, viscosity, and pressure; and a chemical or microscopic analysis for the presence of blood, abnormal cells, chloride, glucose, glutamine, lactic acid, and proteins. The presence or absence, increase or decrease, of each of these sub-stances assists the health practitioner with disease identification. Indications for this type of CSF analysis range from suspected multiple sclerosis to di-agnosing various intracranial hemorrhages or neoplastic conditions. Table 8-1 summarizes the normal ranges for the physical, chemical, and micro-scopic CSF tests.

Color

The color of cerebrospinal fluid indicates some type of abnormality. Varia-tions in color may not be disease specific, but can direct the health practi-

Table 8-1. Normal Ranges CSF Tests

Color	Colorless
Clarity	Clear
Viscosity	Watery–fluid
Pressure	less than 200 mm H_2O
Blood	None present
Red blood cells	None present
White blood cells	
Adult	<5 lymphocytes/mm^3
Children	<20 lymphocytes/mm^3
Neonates	<30 lymphocytes/mm^3
Chloride	120–130 mEq/L
Glucose	40–80% blood glucose level
Adults	50–75 mg/dl
Children	35–80 mg/dl
Neonates	20–40 mg/dl
Glutamine	less than 20 mg/dl
Lactic acid	10–25 mg/dl
Proteins	
Adults	15–45 mg/dl
Over 60 and neonates	up to 75 mg/dl
(Normal ranges may vary. Check your laboratory standards.)	

tioner to investigate the cause of color change. It must be noted that blood-tinged CSF may be indicative of a traumatic puncture. This is a transient situation, and should correct itself toward the end of the spinal tap procedure.

Normal Range

Color	Colorless
Clarity	Clear
Viscosity	Waterlike in appearance

Variations from Normal. Cloudy cerebrospinal fluid can indicate the presence of leukocytes, as found with infectious or inflammatory disease processes. Occasionally the CSF is turbid with a low white blood count due to a high concentration of bacteria in an acute untreated bacterial meningitis. A yellowish discoloration, known as **xanthochromia**, may be related to a previous bleed or a protein elevation. Xanthochromia is also suggestive of toxoplasmosis. **Opalescent**, milky and iridescent like an opal, discoloration with a fragile clot is associated with tuberculosis meningitis. An opalescent or purulent appearance with a more substantive clot may identify acute pyogenic meningitis. Brown cerebrospinal fluid generally indicates a chronic subdural hematoma.

Interfering Circumstances. Contamination from the skin disinfectant used at the puncture site can discolor the cerebrospinal specimen. A traumatic spinal tap can allow blood cells and increased fibrinogen into the CSF sample.

Pressure

Cerebrospinal fluid pressure is directly related to intracranial pressure caused by a variety of disease processes. CSF pressure can be affected by patient position and anxiety as exhibited by muscle tenseness and holding of breath. Elevated CSF pressures must be assessed in light of these conditions.

Normal Range

Adults	75–200 mm H_2O
Children	50–100 mm H_2O

Variations from Normal. Significant increases in cerebrospinal fluid pressure (over 500 mm of water) are associated with intracranial tumors, and purulent or tuberculosis meningitis. Other elevations of CSF pressure are present in acute obstruction of the superior vena cava; subarachnoid, subdural, and cerebral hemorrhage; congestive heart failure; and uremia. Decreased pressure, although rare, may occur with circulatory collapse, leakage of spinal fluid, and severe dehydration.

Interfering Circumstances. As stated previously, patient position and anxiety can interfere with accurate recording of CSF pressure.

Blood

The presence of blood in CSF can indicate a subarachnoid or intracerebral hemorrhage, or may be the result of a traumatic lumbar tap. Health practitioners must carefully evaluate bloody cerebrospinal fluid in order to determine the cause. Blood caused by a traumatic lumbar puncture often clears by the end of the procedure and is accompanied by a normal to low CSF pressure.

Normal Findings. No blood present.

Variations from Normal. The presence of blood in cerebrospinal fluid, not attributable to traumatic puncture, is a sign of subarachnoid hemorrhage.

Interfering Circumstances. A traumatic puncture can cause a transient presence of blood in cerebrospinal fluid.

Cells

Cerebrospinal fluid is analyzed for all types of blood cells. Since both the red and white blood cells are counted and identified by type, this test is often called the cell count and differential. CSF cell counts are usually done manually.

Normal Range

Red blood cells	None	
White blood cells	Adult	<5 lymphocytes/mm^3
	Children	<20 lymphocytes/mm^3
	Newborns	<30 lymphocytes/mm^3

Variations from Normal. Except for a few lymphocytes, the presence of white blood cells in cerebrospinal fluid is abnormal. Generally, inflammatory disease, hemorrhage, neoplasms, and trauma cause an overall elevated white blood cell count. An elevated lymphocyte count consisting mainly of blast cells is an indication of lymphocytic leukemia. Bacterial meningitis and cerebral abscess are associated with the presence of neutrophils. Mononuclear leukocytes can be related to viral or tubercular meningitis, viral encephalitis, or syphilis.

Elevated lymphocyte cell levels can help identify multiple sclerosis, syphilis of the central nervous system, and many varieties of meningitis. Viral, aseptic, fungal, parasitic, and atypical meningitis cause an increase in lymphocytes. Partially treated bacterial meningitis or the recuperatory phase also shows increased lymphocytes.

Interfering Circumstances. A delay in transporting the specimen can result in disintegration of the neutrophils that may be present. Blood in the sample due to a traumatic tap can add additional white cells and some protein to the CSF sample.

Chloride

Electrolyte levels found in cerebrospinal fluid are somewhat similar to those found in plasma. Sodium and chloride are higher in cerebrospinal fluid, and potassium and calcium are lower. There is no clear consensus on the value of measuring all electrolytes present in cerebrospinal fluid. However, there does appear to be some diagnostic significance associated with chloride levels. These levels are not routinely evaluated, unless specifically requested.

Normal Range

Adult	120–130 mEq/L
Children	111–130 mEq/L

Variations from Normal. Decreased levels of cerebrospinal fluid chloride can be associated with meningeal infections and tubercular meningitis.

Interfering Circumstances. Intravenous administration of chloride can alter test results. Blood, caused by a traumatic puncture, can also alter chloride test results.

Glucose

The glucose level present in cerebrospinal fluid is affected by the number of cells and microorganisms in the CSF that utilize glucose. Since all types of organisms and cells use glucose, an increase in the number of cells and microorganisms is accompanied by a decrease in CSF glucose levels. Cerebrospinal fluid glucose levels are also affected by blood glucose levels. The amount of glucose present in CSF assists in the assessment of impaired glucose transfer from plasma to cerebrospinal fluid. A blood sample for determining glucose levels should be drawn before the spinal tap is performed.

Normal Range

Adults   40–80 mg/dL
Children   35–75 mg/dL
Infants   20–40 mg/dL
40–80% of blood glucose levels

Variations from Normal. Glucose in cerebrospinal fluid is decreased in the presence of bacteria, fungi, protozoa, or tubercle bacilli. Specific diseases associated with the presence of these microorganisms are acute bacterial meningitis and tuberculous, fungal, and amebic meningitis. Other diseases found with decreased CSF glucose levels are neoplasms, hypoglycemia, and meningeal metastasis of lymphomas, and leukemias. Spinal cord tumors and insulin shock are also associated with decreased cerebrospinal fluid glucose. Glucose levels are elevated in diabetic coma.

Interfering Circumstances. Delay in cerebrospinal fluid analysis causes a false decrease of glucose. An increase in CSF glucose is consistent with diabetes and diabetic coma.

Glutamine

Glutamine is a nontoxic transport mechanism for removing ammonia from the central nervous system, and the body as a whole. When blood ammonia levels are high, as seen in cirrhosis of the liver with altered hepatic blood flow, CSF glutamine levels also increase.

Normal Range

6–15 mg/dl

Variations from Normal. Elevated cerebrospinal glutamine levels are indicative of hepatic encephalopathy. Reye's syndrome also displays increased CSF glutamine levels.

Lactic Acid

Lactic acid is present in cerebrospinal fluid as a result of glucose metabolism. Measuring the level of lactic acid in CSF provides diagnostic information concerning meningitis and the effectiveness of antibiotic therapy for meningitis, and may aid in differentiating bacterial and viral meningitis. Information about lactic acid levels adds to diagnostic information when other test results are inconclusive.

Normal Range

10–25 mg/dl

Variations from Normal. A cerebrospinal fluid lactic acid level greater than 35 mg/dl is diagnostic for bacterial or fungal meningitis. Inadequate antibiotic therapy for meningitis results in a persistent elevation of lactic acid levels. Other diseases associated with increased lactic acid are hydrocephalus, seizures, cerebral ischemia, cerebrovascular accidents, intracranial hemorrhage, epilepsy, and brain abscess or tumor. Any situation that results in a decreased oxygen flow to the brain demonstrates an increased lactic acid level.

Protein

Very little protein is present in cerebrospinal fluid since most protein molecules are too large to pass the blood-brain barrier. Diseases that alter the permeability of the blood-brain barrier result in an elevated CSF protein level.

Normal Ranges

Total protein   15–45 mg/dl
                   up to 70 mg/dl for elderly adults and children

Variations from Normal. Increased cerebrospinal fluid protein levels are consistent with infectious or inflammatory disease processes. Specific diseases are meningitis, encephalitis, or myelitis. Multiple sclerosis, neurosyphilis, and degenerative cord or brain disease can be diagnosed by the presence of an elevated globulin fraction, the total protein present in CSF.

Diagnoses of spinal cord tumors and Guillain-Barré syndrome can be supported by significantly elevated protein levels. Decreased protein levels are associated with intracranial hypertension and hyperthyroidism.

Interfering Circumstances. Drugs or medications may alter test results. A traumatic lumbar puncture may contaminate the specimen.

Microbiologic Tests of Cerebrospinal Fluid

Cerebrospinal fluid is normally sterile. In order to minimize contamination of CSF samples, specimen collection and handling must be carried out under strict aseptic techniques. Identification of microorganisms is accomplished by culture and sensitivity testing, gram stain tests, **acid-fast bacillus (AFB)** smear and culture, and the **Limulus assay** for gram-negative bacteria. The Limulus assay test utilizes the fluid of a horseshoe crab in order to identify gram-negative pathogens.

Cerebrospinal fluid is cultured in order to detect the presence of bacteria, fungi, protozoa, and tubercle bacilli. In addition to culture and sensitivity testing, the CSF samples are subjected to a variety of stained smear evaluations. Amoebae, cryptococcus, *Escherichia coli,* and *Haemophilus influenzae* can be identified via stained smear laboratory evaluation.

Indications for microbiologic examination of cerebrospinal fluid include identification of the cause of infections of the brain, meninges, and spinal cord. Through microbiologic testing the pathogen itself can be detected, and the appropriate antimicrobial agent can also be determined.

Normal Findings. Absence of any microorganisms.

Variations from Normal. Microbiologic testing of cerebrospinal fluid reveals the causative pathogens for meningitis, encephalitis, or brain abscess.

Interfering Circumstances. Delay in transporting the cerebrospinal fluid sample to the laboratory may lead to the disintegration of suspected organisms. Improper collection and handling of the specimen may cause contamination from the normal bacteria found on skin.

Cytologic Analysis

Cerebrospinal fluid can be analyzed for specific cells and substances that assist in the diagnosis of malignancies involving the **central nervous system (CNS)**. Cytologic evaluation focuses on identification of cellular changes due to primary central nervous system malignancies and metastatic CNS malignancies. Primary CNS tumors often originate in the brain, whereas metastatic disease is associated with breast and lung cancer. Another indication for CSF cytologic analysis is suspected acute leukemia involving the central nervous system.

Normal Findings. Absence of abnormal cells.

Variations from Normal. The presence of abnormal cells in cerebrospinal fluid can be diagnostic for primary malignancies of the central nervous system, metastatic disease of the central nervous system, and central nervous system involvement in acute leukemia.

Interfering Circumstances. Delay in specimen transport can result in cell disintegration. Contamination of the sample with skin cells alters test results.

Summary

- Amniotic fluid is the liquid that protects the fetus during pregnancy and is produced by the fetus and fetal membranes.
- Analysis of amniotic fluid is used to identify fetal sex, fetal abnormalities, and fetal maturity.
- Physical analysis of amniotic fluid includes assessment of fluid color and quantity.
- Microscopic examination of amniotic fluid focuses on identification of proteins, chromosomal makeup, elevated bilirubin levels, and indications of surfactant production.
- Amniocentesis is performed to withdraw amniotic fluid from the amniotic sac.

- Cerebrospinal fluid bathes, protects, and helps nourish the brain and spinal cord.
- Cerebrospinal fluid tests include an analysis of CSF color, clarity, viscosity, and pressure.
- The presence of blood, cells, chloride, glucose, glutamine, lactic acid, and proteins can be measured in CSF.
- Culture and sensitivity, gram stain, AFB smear and culture, and the Limulus assay for gram-negative bacteria are some of the microbiological tests run on cerebrospinal fluid.
- Lumbar puncture, cisternal puncture, and ventricular puncture are sample collection methods for CSF analysis.
- Toxoplasmosis, all types of meningitis, multiple sclerosis, neurosyphilis, and tumors can be identified by cerebrospinal fluid tests.

CHAPTER REVIEW

1. Identify the amniotic fluid test(s) associated with the listed diagnoses:

   a. Hypoxia   _____

   b. Abruptio placentae   _____

   c. Fetal lung maturity   _____

   d. Tay-Sachs disease   _____

   e. Neural tube defects   _____

2. Organize the listed amniotic fluid tests according to these categories:

   a. Genetic and neural tube abnormalities   _____

   b. Hemolytic disease of newborns   _____

   c. Fetal maturity   _____

acetylcholinesterase   creatinine   shake test

alpha-fetoprotein   fetal epithelial cells

bilirubin   fetal sex determination

chromosome analysis   L:S ratio

3. Identify the cerebrospinal fluid test(s) associated with the listed diagnoses:

   a. Subarachnoid hemorrhage   _____

   b. Bacterial meningitis   _____

   c. Multiple sclerosis   _____

4. Give an example of a disease associated with a variation from normal for each of the substances tested in a routine cerebrospinal fluid analysis.

   a. Blood   _____

   b. Cells   _____

   c. Chloride   _____

   d. Glucose   _____

   e. Glutamine   _____

   f. Lactic acid _____

   g. Protein   _____

5. Briefly describe sample collection techniques listed below. Include the type of fluid collected, the risks and benefits, and the contraindications associated with each technique.

   a. Amniocentesis   _____

   b. Lumbar puncture   _____

   c. Cisternal puncture   _____

   d. Ventricular puncture _____

6. What are some the pathological color changes associated with amniotic fluid What substances or circumstances cause the color change? What is a normal amniotic fluid color change? What causes the normal color change?

Case Studies

1. In reviewing the record of Lydia St. Arnold, a 30-year-old pregnant woman, you discover that she has had an amniocentesis for amniotic fluid analysis because her husband has a genetic disorder. Describe amniocentesis and how it is performed. Identify the amniotic fluid analysis test(s) that would be performed. What disorders can be detected?

2. Dr. Hill has ordered amniotic fluid testing on Mary Walsh, a 25-year-old pregnant woman, in order to determine fetal maturity. What are the primary indications for fetal maturity testing? Identify and describe fetal maturity test(s), the substances tested, and how the substances help determine fetal age.

3. Lester Lancour is a 2-year-old male patient who has had a high fever for more than seventy-two hours. Dr. Adams is certain that the child has meningitis. He has ordered a spinal tap in order to differentiate if the problem is viral or bacterial. Dr. Adam's order indicates that he wants an identification of the white blood cells that may be present in the CSF. What is a spinal tap and how is it performed? Discuss the diagnostic significance of elevated white blood cells in CSF. List the diseases that can be identified by an elevated white cell count.

Challenge Activity

Create a patient teaching brochure that describes amniocentesis. Include a graphic of the procedure as well as the risks, benefits, indications, and contraindications for amniocentesis.

Chapter 9

Other Body Fluid Tests

Key Terms, Abbreviations, and Acronyms

antinuclear antibody, ANA

arthrocentesis

carcinoembryonic antigen, CEA

chyle

Dressler's syndrome

effusions

exudates

gastric secretions

inclusion bodies

lactate dehydrogenase, LDH

LE cells

paracentesis

pericardiocentesis

RA cells

rheumatoid factor, RF

rice bodies

sperm morphology

sperm motility

thoracentesis

transudates

Zollinger-Ellison syndrome

Learning Objectives

Upon completion of this chapter, the learner should be able to:

1. Define the body fluids discussed in this chapter.
2. Discuss the diagnostic significance of analyzing each body fluid.

3. Organize body fluid tests according to the diseases or diagnoses identified by the tests.

4. Identify the indications and contraindications for each category of fluid analysis.

5. Compare the risks and benefits of the various sample collection procedures.

Introduction

Many of the substances measured in blood, urine, and feces can also be found in various other body fluids. The diagnostic significance of analyzing these fluids is directly related to the type of fluid analyzed and the specific diagnosis associated with changes in the specific body fluid. The presence of glucose, blood, cells, proteins, enzymes, and other substances in body fluids can provide the health practitioner with valuable clinical information.

The body fluids discussed in this chapter include **effusions**, excessive accumulations of fluid in various body cavities; **gastric secretions**, a variety of enzymes, hormones, and other fluids secreted by the stomach; and semen, male ejaculatory fluid that includes sperm and secretions from various glands.

Overview of Body Fluid Tests

Body fluid tests go a step beyond the routine blood, urine, and fecal analysis familiar to many individuals both in and out of the health care industry. A variety of diseases can be identified or confirmed by fluid analysis. Sample collection methods for effusions, gastric secretions, and semen are quite varied. Collecting effusion specimens involves needle punctures or aspiration techniques; gastric secretions can be collected by suction or endoscopic interventions; and semen samples are collected via masturbatory techniques for fertility tests, or by analyzing vaginal fluids and clothing in cases of suspected rape.

Contamination of the body fluid samples is a serious concern for all types of body fluid tests. Caution must be taken so that the effusion specimens are not tainted with skin cells or skin flora from the puncture site. In addition to specimen contamination concerns, puncture collection methods have a potential for introducing bacteria into the body. Strict aseptic techniques must be followed during all collection activities.

Effusions, gastric secretion, and semen tests are discussed individually. The discussions include a description of the fluid being analyzed, specimen collection methods, substances present in the fluid, and the diagnostic significance of the presence of those substances. Interfering circumstances and contraindications are also included.

Effusion Tests

Effusions are defined as excessive accumulations of fluid in body cavities lined with serous or synovial membranes. In health, both serous and synovial fluids are clear to pale yellow in color. Effusions are named for their associated cavities. Therefore, the pericardial cavity produces pericardial effusions, the peritoneal cavity has peritoneal effusions, pleural effusions are found in the pleural cavity, and synovial effusions are related to the cavities of various synovial joints.

Serous cavity effusions, fluids contained within the closed cavities of the body, can be differentiated as **transudates** or **exudates**. Transudates are fluids that are pressed through a membrane or tissue into the space between the cells of the tissue. Transudates are usually characterized as low-protein, cell-free fluids occurring due to a systemic disease. Exudates are effusions resulting from damage to cells or cell membranes. Exudates are usually seen in malignancies, infection, and inflammations and contain cells, cell debris, and proteins.

Both the physical properties and microscopic characteristics of effusions can be analyzed for diagnostic purposes. Physical properties include color, clarity, volume, and clotting ability. Color and clarity changes can indicate a range of disease processes from perforated ulcers to metastatic cancer. The ability for a serious fluid to clot indicates the presence of an inflammatory reaction. Most cavities contain only a small amount of fluid or effusions. An increase or buildup of effusions can indicate mechanical abnormalities related to capillary permeability and/or serous or synovial membrane damage. Microscopic examination of effusions is performed to identify and measure the presence of cells and microorganisms. Chemical testing for a wide variety of effusion constituents such as glucose, protein, enzymes, and tumor markers can be performed on request.

Effusion samples are obtained via needle aspiration. *Centesis* is the suffix that denotes "puncture and aspiration of." The name of each sample collection technique is taken from the structure or cavity involved. Therefore, pericardial effusions are collected via **pericardiocentesis**; since the lungs are located in the thoracic cavity, **thoracentesis** is performed to withdraw pleural effusions; aspiration of peritoneal fluid is accomplished via **paracentesis**; and synovial effusions, usually withdrawn from joint spaces, are taken by **arthrocentesis**. The diagnostic significance of each type of effusion is discussed individually.

Pericardial Effusion Tests

Pericardial effusions are withdrawn from the pericardial sac via pericardiocentesis. The chief indication for pericardiocentesis and pericardial effusion analysis is an abnormal accumulation of fluid in the pericardial space. Contraindications for this test include bleeding disorders and an uncooperative patient. Risks attendant to this procedure are laceration of the coronary artery, needle-induced ventricular dysrhythmias, pneumothorax, and introduction of infective agents from the skin.

Pericardial effusions are routinely analyzed in relation to gross appearance, red blood cell count, and a white blood cell count and differential, glucose levels, and blood. These analyses provide valuable diagnostic information related to all types of pericarditis. Cytologic examination of pericardial effusions is performed to detect malignant cells.

Normal Range

Red blood cells	None
White blood cells	<1000/mm^3
Cytology	No abnormal cells

Variations from Normal. Bloody pericardial effusion, not associated with pericardiocentesis trauma, is seen in hemorrhagic pericarditis, metastatic cancer, aneurysms, and tuberculosis. The presence of red blood cells, an elevation in specific types of white cells, and variations in glucose levels provide diagnostically significant information. Bacterial, tubercular, or fungal pericarditis is evidenced by an elevated white count, predominantly neutrophils; the presence of red blood cells; and a decrease in glucose levels. The presence of red cells and an elevated white count, with lymphocytes dominant, points to a viral pericarditis.

Other diseases that can cause pericardial effusion include **Dressler's syndrome**, a postmyocardial infarction syndrome characterized by fever, pericarditis, pleurisy, and joint pain; hemorrhagic problems due to trauma or anticoagulant therapy; and leukemia or lymphoma as indicated by the presence of abnormal cells, kidney failure, or rheumatic disease. Table 9-1 summarizes the diseases associated with variations of substances present in pericardial effusions.

Interfering Circumstances. Contamination of the effusion sample with skin cells or pathogens, and blood in the sample due to a traumatic needle puncture, alter test results. Hyperglycemia and hypoglycemia also interfere with effusion analysis.

Table 9-1.   Pericardial Effusions

Disease	*Increased/Presence*	*Decreased*
Dressler's syndrome	Red cells White cells, neutrophils	
Bacterial pericarditis	Red cells White cells, neutrophils	Glucose
Fungal, tuberculous pericarditis	Red cells White cells, lymphocytes	
Malignancy	Red cells, abnormal cells	Glucose
Rheumatoid disease; systemic lupus erythematosus	Red cells White cells	Glucose
Viral pericarditis	Red cells White cells, neutrophils	
Kidney failure, uremia	Red cells, white cells	

Peritoneal Effusion Tests

Peritoneal effusions are withdrawn from the peritoneal cavity via paracentesis. The chief indication for paracentesis is the abnormal accumulation of fluid in the peritoneal cavity. The fluid, know as peritoneal effusion or ascitic fluid, is analyzed to determine the cause of the effusion. Contraindications for this test include coagulation abnormalities or bleeding tendencies. Risks attendant to this procedure are vascular collapse if a large volume of peritoneal fluid is removed, hepatic coma in the presence of chronic liver disease, and peritonitis.

Peritoneal effusions are routinely evaluated for color, clarity, red blood cell count, and white blood cell count with differential. Levels of alkaline phosphatase, ammonia, amylase, **carcinoembryonic antigen (CEA)**, glucose, and protein can also be measured on request. Cytologic exams are used to detect malignancies. Suspected ruptured or punctured bladder calls for urea and creatinine measurement. Variations in each of the tested substances are related to specific diagnoses.

Normal Range

Clarity and color	Clear and light yellow, serous <50 mL
Red blood cells	None
White blood cells	<300 wbc/ μ/L with <25% PMNs
Alkaline phosphatase	
Adult male	90–240 U/L
Female <45 yr	76–196 U/L
Female >45 yr	87–250 U/L
Ammonia	<50 μg/dl
Amylase	138–404 U/L
CEA	Negative
Glucose	70–100 mg/dl

Variations from Normal. The mere presence of abnormal amounts of peritoneal fluid is pathological. The color of the effusion supports a variety of diagnoses. Milk-colored (chylous) effusion is associated with blocked thoracic lymph ducts, trauma, cirrhosis, pancreatitis, or tuberculous peritonitis. The two most common causes of chylous peritoneal effusions are malignant lymphoma and carcinoma. Cloudy fluid indicates an inflammatory condition such as pancreatitis, bacterial peritonitis, or neoplasm. Effusion tinged green or stained with bile is consistent with a ruptured gallbladder or perforated intestines. Patients with cirrhosis of the liver present with a light yellow effusion.

The presence of red blood cells in the peritoneal effusion is consistent with neoplasms, tuberculosis, or intraabdominal trauma such as gunshot or stab wounds. Increased white blood cells can indicate cirrhosis of the liver and bacterial peritonitis. Table 9-2 summarizes diseases related to increases and decreases of alkaline phosphatase, ammonia, amylase, carcinoembryonic antigen, creatinine, glucose, and urea in peritoneal effusions.

Interfering Circumstances. Contamination of the effusion sample with skin cells or pathogens, and blood in the sample due to a traumatic needle puncture, alter test results. Hyperglycemia and hypoglycemia also interfere with effusion analysis.

Table 9-2.   Peritoneal Effusions

Disease	*Increased*	*Decreased*
Abdominal malignancy	Red cell count, carcinoembryonic antigen	Glucose
Gastrointestinal necrosis, perforation, or strangulation	Amylase, ammonia, alkaline phosphatase	
Pancreatitis, pancreatic trauma, pancreatic pseudocyst	Amylase	
Tuberculous peritonitis	Lymphocyte count, positive acid-fast bacillus smear and culture	Glucose
Urinary bladder rupture or perforation	Ammonia, creatinine, urea	

Pleural Effusion Tests

Pleural effusions are withdrawn from the pleural space via thoracentesis. The chief indication for thoracentesis and pleural effusion analysis is an abnormal accumulation of fluid in the pleural space. Removing this fluid has both diagnostic and therapeutic benefits. Therapeutic thoracentesis is accomplished to relieve pain and dyspnea. Diagnostic thoracentesis allows for identification of diseases that may cause pleural effusion, as well as better radiographic visualization of the lung. Contraindications for this test include bleeding disorders and an uncooperative patient. Risks attendant to this procedure are pneumothorax, interpleural bleeding, pulmonary edema, and reflex hypertension.

Pleural effusions can be classified as transudates or exudates. It is important to analyze effusions in light of the difference between these two classifications. Congestive heart failure, cirrhosis of the liver, and nephrotic syndromes usually present with pleural transudates. Pleural exudates are associated with pneumonia, empyema, tuberculosis, pulmonary infarction, and malignancies.

Pleural effusions are routinely evaluated for gross color, clarity, clotting, red blood cell count, and white blood cell count with differential. Levels of amylase, CEA, glucose, **lactate dehydrogenase (LDH)**, and protein are also measured. The pH of pleural effusions is also identified. Variations in each of the tested substances are related to specific diagnoses. Gram stain and culture and sensitivity tests are performed in order to identify the pathogens responsible for infections. Cytologic exams are used to detect malignancies.

Normal Range

Red blood cells	Few
White blood cells	0–<1000/mm^3 (mainly lymphocytes)
CEA	<2 ng/mL
Glucose	
Adults	70–115 mg/dl
Children	60–100 mg/dl
Newborns	30–80 mg/dl
Lactate dehydrogenase	70–207 IU/L
pH	7.4 or greater
Protein	3.0 g/dl

Variations from Normal. The mere presence of abnormal amounts of pleural fluid is pathological. The color and gross appearance of the effusion can indicate empyema or the presence of **chyle**, the product of digestion, in the pleural cavity. Thick, foul-smelling, puslike fluid is related to empyema. Chylothorax is evidenced by an opalescent, pearly pleural effusion.

The presence of red blood cells and white blood cells in the pleural effusion is consistent with pneumonia, pulmonary tuberculosis, pancreatitis, tuberculous empyema, pulmonary infarction, carcinoma, or thoracic trauma. Lymphocytes are usually seen in pulmonary tuberculosis and carcinoma. Effusions caused by pneumonia, pancreatitis, and bacterial or tuberculous empyema are rich in neutrophils. Table 9-3 summarizes diseases related to variations in amylase, CEA, glucose, lactate dehydrogenase, pH, and protein levels in pleural effusions. Note that several diagnoses exhibit the same increases and decreases. Other laboratory results such as cell count, AFB smear and culture, and cytological examinations provide additional information needed for a definitive diagnosis.

Interfering Circumstances. Contamination of the effusion sample with skin cells or pathogens, and blood in the sample due to a traumatic needle puncture, alter test results. Variations in blood glucose levels also interfere with effusion analysis.

Table 9-3.   Pleural Effusions

Disease	*Increased*	*Decreased*
Carcinoma	Protein, lactate dehydrogenase (LDH), carcinoembryonic antigen	pH, glucose
Empyema, tuberculous	Protein, LDH	pH, glucose
Esophageal rupture	Amylase	pH
Pancreatitis	Protein, LDH, amylase	pH
Pulmonary infarction	Protein, LDH	pH
Tuberculosis	Protein, LDH	pH, glucose

Synovial Effusion Tests

Synovial effusions are withdrawn from joint cavities by way of arthrocentesis. The most frequently aspirated joint is the knee, but samples may be obtained from other synovial joints if needed. The chief indication for arthrocentesis and synovial effusion analysis is to determine the type or cause of joint disorders. Contraindications for this test include skin and/or wound infections in the area of the needle puncture. Risks attendant to this procedure are joint infection and/or joint hemorrhage.

Synovial effusions are routinely evaluated visually and microscopically for gross appearance, cellular content, crystals, and granulocytes that contain **inclusion bodies**. Inclusion bodies associated with specific diseases are substances that are present in the cytoplasm of granulocytes. Examples of white cells with inclusion bodies are (1) **LE cells**, neutrophils containing an inclusion substance called a "round body," which is the nucleus of another WBC; (2) **RA cells**, neutrophils with dark granules in the cytoplasm that consist of immune complexes; and (3) **rice bodies**, inclusion bodies that resemble polished rice.

Other synovial effusion studies are microbial studies, gram stain, culture and sensitivity, and immunologic tests to identify the presence of **rheumatoid factor (RF)** or **antinuclear antibodies (ANAs)**. Levels of glucose, lactate, protein, and uric acid are also measured. Variations in each of the tested substances are related to specific diagnoses.

Normal Range

Red blood cells	<2000/mm³
White blood cells	<200/mm³
	No abnormal white cells or inclusions
Neutrophils	<25%
Antinuclear antibodies	Negative
Crystals	None present
Glucose	Within 10 gm/dl of serum glucose value
Lactate	5–20 mg/dl
Protein	<3 g/dl
Rheumatoid factor	Negative

Uric acid
Men	2.1–8.5 mg/dl
Women	2.0–6.6 mg/dl
Children	2.5–5.5 mg/dl

Variations from Normal. The presence of specific types of white blood cells in the synovial effusion can be diagnoses specific. An overall elevation of white cells, with a normal differential count, is consistent with osteoarthritis and degenerative joint disease. A high percentage of neutrophils indicates acute bacterial infectious arthritis. An elevated red blood cell count coupled with increased protein levels are diagnostic for hemophilic arthritis, joint trauma, and joint tumor. Effusions are examined for various types of crystals. Crystals are seen in diseases such as gout, chronic joint effusions, and synovitis. Table 9-4 summarizes variations in synovial effusion constituents for gout, rheumatoid arthritis, systemic lupus erythematosus involving the joint, and tuberculous arthritis.

Table 9-4. Synovial Effusions

Disease	*Increased/Present*	*Decreased*
Gout	White cell count, neutrophils, uric acid	Glucose
Rheumatoid arthritis	White cell count, neutrophils, lactate, protein rheumatoid factor (present), rice cells RA cells	Glucose
Systemic lupus erythematosus	White cell count, neutrophils, protein antinuclear antibody (present) LE cells	Glucose
Tuberculous arthritis	White cell count, neutrophils, lactate, rice cells (present)	Glucose

Interfering Factors. Contamination of the effusion sample with skin cells or pathogens, or blood in the sample due to a traumatic needle puncture, alter test results. Hyper- and hypoglycemia also interfere with effusion analysis. Improper handling of the sample in relation to temperature and room air exposure adversely affect test results.

Gastric Secretion Tests

Secretions of the stomach are often referred to as "gastric juices." Gastric secretions prepare food for absorption, initiate the digestion of protein, and assist in vitamin B_{12} absorption. Gastric secretions consist of pepsinogen, pepsin, hydrochloric acid, an alkaline substance that protects the lining of the stomach from damage, electrolytes, and enzymes such as gastric lipase.

Specimen collection for gastric content analysis is accomplished by inserting a nasogastric tube (NG) into the stomach and aspirating gastric secretions. Although risks associated with this procedure are minimal, some individuals may experience extreme anxiety prior to and during tube placement.

The gastric secretion analysis test is covered in this chapter. Analyzing the quantity, quality, and characteristics of gastric secretions can provide diagnostic information concerning ulcers, obstruction diseases, pernicious anemia, and cancer of the stomach.

Gastric Secretion Analysis Tests

Gastric secretions are analyzed for blood, color, mucus, and pH levels. Microscopic analysis involves evaluating the specimen for red blood cells, white blood cells, epithelial cells, bacteria, yeast, and parasites.

Normal Range

Blood	Absence of blood
Color	Pale gray, translucent
Mucus	Normally present
pH	<2.0 (should never be >6.0)
Abnormal cells	Absent

Epithelial cells	Few to none present
Parasites	Absent
Red blood cells	Few to none present
White blood cells	Few to none present
Yeasts	Few to none present

Variations from Normal. A change in the color of gastric secretions must be evaluated in conjunction with other test results. A yellow to green color can indicate bile reflux or an obstruction in the small intestine. The presence of large amounts of blood, or blood that has the appearance of coffee grounds, is consistent with ulcers, gastritis, or cancer. Variations in the pH of gastric secretions is seen in aplastic, hyperchromic, and pernicious anemia, and in **Zollinger-Ellison syndrome**. This syndrome is characterized by severe peptic ulceration, gastric hypersecretion, elevated serum gastrin, and gastrinoma of the pancreas or duodenum.

The presence of red blood cells in gastric secretions usually requires additional diagnostic follow-up. Elevated white blood cells can point to inflammation of the gastric mucosa. Gastritis is associated with large numbers of epithelial cells that cannot be attributed to normal sloughing of mucosal surfaces. Increased numbers of yeast are associated with gastric blockage. The presence of parasitic ova or larvae supports the diagnosis of parasitic infestation of the gastrointestinal tract.

Interfering Circumstances. The presence of food particles and medications or drugs may alter gastric secretions. Specimen contamination and delays in sample analysis interfere with test results. Swallowed saliva or respiratory secretions are the most common specimen contaminants.

Semen Tests

Semen is a thick, whitish secretion of the male reproductive organs. It consists of sperm and fluids from the prostate gland, seminal vesicle, and bulbourethral gland. Semen is analyzed to identify male infertility, to investigate suspected rape, and to evaluate results of vasectomy. Postvasectomy semen tests involve analyzing the ejaculatory fluid for the presence of sperm. This analysis is usually completed twice, at specified postvasectomy intervals.

Semen tests for fertility and suspected rape are discussed in detail. There are no apparent contraindications for any of the semen tests.

Specimen collection is best accomplished by masturbatory methods during which the ejaculatory fluid is deposited into a clean glass or plastic container. Obtaining a semen sample through condom use can be problematic in that many condoms contain spermicides. If used, the condom must be thoroughly washed and dried to remove the spermicide.

Semen Fertility Tests

Initial semen fertility tests are performed to evaluate sperm quantity and quality. Quantity is analyzed in relation to the volume of semen and the number of sperm, called the "sperm count." Quality analysis looks at **sperm motility**, the ability of sperm to move forward with good activity and tail movements; and **sperm morphology**, the shape and form of the sperm. Figure 9-1 shows normal versus abnormal sperm morphology. Variations in

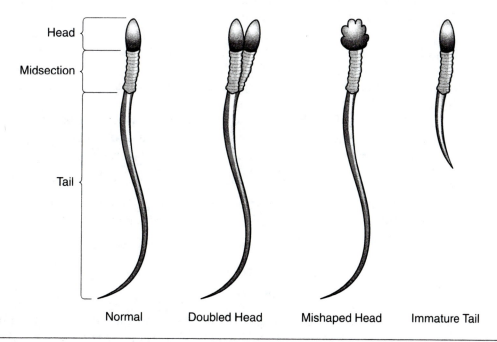

Figure 9-1.   Sperm morphology

sperm quantity or quality trigger tests that measure sperm viability; semen fructose level, fructose being a major sperm nutrient; and the presence of sperm antibodies.

Normal Range

Semen volume	2–5 mL (ejaculatory fluid)
Sperm count	50–200 million/mL
Sperm motility	60–80% actively motile
Sperm morphology	70% and more, normal shape
Fructose	>150 mg/dl
Sperm antibodies	None present

Variations from Normal. A lower than normal sperm count indicates male infertility, although counts of 20–40 million/mL are sometimes called "borderline normal." Sperm counts of less than 20 million/mL can be called oligospermia or aspermia, and often lead to endocrine, pituitary, adrenal, thyroid, or testicular evaluations. Decreased levels of fructose deprive the sperm of necessary nutrients.

Decreased sperm motility is the key indicator of infertility. Even if there are adequate numbers of sperm, the sperm must be able to penetrate the cervical mucus and travel the fallopian tubes in order for fertilization to occur. Abnormal head and tail development interferes with the sperm's ability to reach and fertilize the ovum.

The presence of antibodies produced by the male is evidenced as decreased sperm motility and clumping of sperm. As previously stated, decreased motility is the key indicator of infertility. Radioimmunoassay techniques can be used to further analyze sperm antibodies.

Interfering Circumstances. Improper specimen collection, transport, and handling interfere with test results. Semen must be kept at body temperature for at least 20 minutes.

Tests for the Presence of Semen

Alleged or suspected rape can lead to analysis of vaginal samples and clothing stains for the presence of semen, sperm, and acid phosphatase. Sperm and semen on the body or clothing can be identified by using ultraviolet light scanning. Vaginal secretions can be subjected to various staining and microscopic examinations to observe the presence of sperm. Testing for acid phosphatase is a very sensitive screen for the presence of semen. Semen is the only body fluid that contains high concentrations of acid phosphatase.

Sample collection can be traumatic for an alleged rape victim. The traditional pelvic examination procedure, complete with speculum, lithotomy position, and smears or swabs is used to obtain vaginal specimens. Samples from skin and clothing can be soaked or sponged with saline. The solution is then ready for semen analysis.

Normal Findings. Absence of semen, sperm, or acid phosphatase.

Variations from Normal. The presence of semen, sperm, or acid phosphatase can indicate that sexual intercourse was attempted or completed.

Interfering Circumstances. Individuals who bathe or shower after an alleged rape may destroy all evidence of semen. Clothing should not be washed, since acid phosphatase may be detected in semen stains that are several days old. Improper sampling methods can affect test results.

Summary

- Effusions are excessive accumulations of fluid in various body cavities that are classified as transudates and exudates.
- Pericardial effusions, pleural effusions, peritoneal effusions, and synovial effusions are withdrawn by way of pericardiocentesis, thoracentesis, paracentesis, and arthrocentesis, respectively.
- Pericardial effusion analysis assists in diagnosing pericarditis, aneurysms, tuberculosis, Dressler's syndrome, and malignancies.
- Peritonitis, pancreatitis, ruptured gallbladder, and cirrhosis of the liver can be identified with peritoneal effusion tests.
- Pleural effusions are associated with congestive heart failure, nephrotic syndromes, pneumonia, empyema, and pulmonary infarction.
- Osteoarthritis, degenerative joint disease, gout, and rheumatoid arthritis can be diagnosed by synovial fluid analysis.

- Gastric secretions can be tested to identify diseases such as ulcers, gastritis, cancer, anemias, and Zollinger-Ellison syndrome.
- Semen analysis provides information concerning sperm quality and quantity, which can affect male fertility.
- Tests for the presence of semen are often conducted in cases of alleged or suspected rape.

CHAPTER REVIEW

1. Identify the effusion test(s) associated with the listed diagnoses:

   a. Bacterial pericarditis _____

   b. Cirrhosis of the liver _____

   c. Dressler's syndrome _____

   d. Empyema _____

   e. Gout _____

   f. Hemorrhagic pericarditis _____

   g. Osteoarthritis _____

   h. Pulmonary tuberculosis _____

   i. Rheumatoid disease _____

   j. Systemic lupus erythematosus _____

2. Identify the following body fluids:

   a. Excessive accumulation of fluid in body cavities _____

   b. A variety of enzymes, hormones, and other fluids secreted by the stomach _____

    c. Fluids pressed through a membrane or
tissue into the space between cells   _____

    d. Fluid, cells, and other substances that have
been forced from cells or blood vessels
through breaks in cell membranes   _____

    e. Fluids withdrawn from joint spaces   _____

    f. Effusions that can be classified as
transudates or exudates   _____

    g. Thick, whitish secretion of the male
reproductive organs   _____

    h. Also known as ascitic fluid   _____

3. Briefly describe sample collection techniques listed below. Include the type of fluid collected, the risks and benefits, and the contraindications associated with each technique.

    a. Thoracentesis   _____

    b. Paracentesis   _____

    c. Pericardiocentesis   _____

    d. Arthrocentesis   _____

4. Describe the gastric secretion analysis test. Include information regarding the substances or characteristics analyzed, the purpose of the analysis, and the diseases identified.

Case Studies

1. Jon Rivera, a 53-year-old male patient of Dr. Milltown, has been identified as having a pleural effusion. Describe how the fluid is withdrawn from the pleural space. If Mr. Rivera were diagnosed with pneumonia, what may be detected via pleural effusion analysis?

2. Victoria Schaski, a 68-year-old female patient of Dr. Chabetzi, was diagnosed with Zollinger-Ellison syndrome. Discuss the role of gastric secretion tests in identifying this syndrome. How would the gastric secretion specimen(s) be obtained?

3. Eva and Walter Gilmore, a married couple in their early 30s, have been unable to have children. They are at the fertility clinic for evaluation of their situation. Dr. Cosky ordered semen fertility tests. What do semen fertility tests measure or evaluate? Describe the findings that would indicate Mr. Gilmore has a fertility problem.

Challenge Activity

Create a study guide that describes male fertility tests. Include the relationship between sperm motility, morphology, and sperm count in determining fertility.

S E C T I O N

II

Diagnostic Tests

Chapter 10

Radiology Studies

Key Terms, Abbreviations, and Acronyms

angiography

arteriography of the lower
    extremities

arthrography

barium enema, BE

barium swallow

chest x-ray

cholecystography

computerized (axial) tomography,
    CT, CAT

computerized tomography of the
    body

computerized tomography of the
    brain

coronary angiography

cystography

digital subtraction angiography,
    DSA

hysterosalpingography

intravenous urography, IVU

kidneys, ureters, and bladder
    (KUB) radiography

long-bone radiography

lymphangiography

magnetic resonance imaging, MRI

magnetic resonance imaging of
    the head and brain

mammography

musculoskeletal MRI

myelography

obstruction series

percutaneous transhepatic
    cholangiography, PTC, PTHC

retrograde pyelography, RP

skull radiography

small-bowel follow-through, SBF

spinal radiography

T-tube cholangiography

upper gastrointestinal series, UGI

venography of the lower
    extremities

Learning Objectives

Upon completion of this chapter, the learner should be able to:

1. Briefly describe the purpose and structures examined for each radiography study.
2. Discuss the indications and contraindications for each radiography study.
3. Properly sequence radiography examinations.
4. Relate specific diagnoses to specific radiographic studies.
5. Organize radiography studies in relation to whether or not contrast media are necessary.
6. Compare the benefits and risks of computerized axial tomography, magnetic resonance imaging, and traditional radiographic techniques.

Introduction

Radiography studies cover a broad range of diagnostic and screening tests from a routine chest x-ray to the cross-sectional images of computerized tomography (CT). Information for each examination includes the body structures studied, indications and contraindications for the study, normal findings, variations from normal, and factors that interfere with the study.

Overview of Radiography Studies

Radiography is often the first diagnostic tool or screening device used to identify abnormalities in the structure of soft and bony tissue of the body. Radiographic images rely on the differences in density between various body structures. Dense structures appear white; less dense and air-filled structures are black. Structures that permit little or no x-ray transmission are radiopaque, and structures that permit x-ray transmission are radiolucent. Natural contrasts such as air, water, fat, and bone often provide the varying densities necessary for radiographic studies. When natural contrasts are insufficient, contrast substances must be introduced to allow better visualization of the details needed to diagnose pathologic conditions.

Contrast media are discussed in the section of this chapter that addresses radiography studies that require contrast media.

Proper sequencing of radiologic procedures provides for efficient use of staff time, lessens inconvenience to the patient, and can prevent costly delays, both financial and clinical, in the diagnosis of the patient's condition. When several radiographic examinations are ordered, those that *do not* require contrast media should be scheduled first. Examinations that utilize iodine contrast should be completed before those that require barium contrast. Iodine contrast exams must also precede nuclear medicine examinations that require radioactive iodine administration. There are some examinations that require no preparation and can be scheduled or performed at any time. Chest x-rays and mammograms are examples of no-preparation examinations.

Radiologic examinations are not risk-free. Recent practices have focused on limiting the patient's exposure to the radiation that accompanies any radiographic procedure. Reproductive organs and developing fetuses, especially during the first trimester, are at particular risk for untoward results of radiation exposure. The dangers of radiation exposure can be the result of the absorption of a large amount of radiation over a short period of time, or from the cumulative effects of small amounts over a long period of time. Proper safety precautions can minimize the risks associated with radiation exposure.

Safety precautions include protecting staff and patients. Staff wear lead aprons, gloves, and other protective dress when not within a shielded booth. Patients should be shielded from radiation exposure to the extent possible. Gonads in both males and females should be covered, unless the examination involves the abdomen or gonad area. The size of the x-ray field must be carefully adjusted so that only the necessary tissue is exposed to radiation. Finally, the x-ray equipment itself must be maintained so as to prevent radiation leakage.

In the past, pregnancy was considered a contraindication for nearly all radiographic examinations. Current practice provides many safeguards so that the pregnant client is able to take advantage of this diagnostic tool. Proper shielding and minimizing the length of time of the exposure and the amount of radiation used greatly reduces the potential risks of these examinations. *Although this text does not list pregnancy as a contraindication for radiographic studies, it is universally understood that radiographic studies on the pregnant client are undertaken only when absolutely necessary, and with all safeguards in place.*

Radiography Studies without Contrast Media

Radiography studies that do not require contrast media rely on the inherent contrast quality of various organs or tissue in order to visualize the structures being examined. Precautions for radiation exposure apply to these studies. Preparation considerations are included with the discussion of each examination.

Chest Radiography (Chest X-ray)

The **chest x-ray** is the most frequently performed radiography study. This examination allows for the visualization of the position and appearance of the chest, bony thorax, lungs, pleura, mediastinum, heart, and aortic arch. The chest x-ray is used to diagnose a variety of diseases, to follow the progress or development of a disease, and to confirm the placement of chest tubes, subclavian catheters, and enteric feeding tubes. The chest x-ray is one of the least invasive diagnostic tools, having few if any contraindications. As with any radiographic procedure, pregnant clients must be carefully shielded.

Normal Findings. Normal-appearing lungs and surrounding structures.

Variations from Normal. Diseases such as pneumonia, emphysema, pleuritis, pericarditis, pleural effusion, pneumothorax, and tuberculosis can be identified using chest radiography. Fractures, diaphragmatic hernia, and scoliosis can also be diagnosed with this examination. Chest x-ray can provide visualization of soft-tissue sarcoma, primary and metastatic tumors of the lung, and osteogenic sarcoma involving the bony thorax.

Interfering Circumstances. Conditions that prevent the patient from taking and holding a deep breath can compromise the quality of the chest x-ray.

Mammography

Mammography is an x-ray examination of the breast and surrounding structures that can detect cancer before the lesions are palpable. Early detection of breast cancer is believed to improve the overall outcome of the course of the disease and patient survival. When interpreted by a skilled radiologist, mammography can be approximately 85% accurate in detecting breast cancer. Mammography does not, however, take the place of breast biopsy.

There are many indications for having a mammography such as the presence of signs and symptoms of breast cancer, pendulous breasts that are difficult to examine, breast pain, individuals who have had cancer in one breast or who are at high risk for breast cancer, and as a follow-up for questionable mammography images. In additions to these clinical indications, the American Cancer Society recommends a baseline mammogram for all women at ages 35 and 45. Women over the age of 50 and women in high-risk categories should have annual mammograms. There have been some studies that encourage mammography yearly after age 40. Figure 10-1 is a mammogram that shows both a normal film and one with a large visible mass.

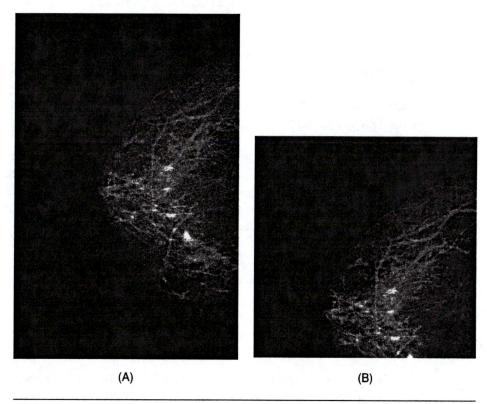

(A) (B)

Figure 10-1. Mammograms: **(a)** a normal film, **(b)** a large mass is visible.

Normal Findings. Negative for tumor and other breast diseases.

Variations from Normal. Mammography is primarily associated with detection of breast cancer. This valuable diagnostic tool is used to identify other diseases of the breast, including fibrocystic breast disease, acute suppurative mastitis, abscess, benign tumors, and breast cysts.

Interfering Circumstances. Breast augmentation, implants, can prevent total visualization of the breast.

Kidneys, Ureters, Bladder (KUB) Radiography

Kidneys, ureters, and bladder (KUB) radiography is an examination of the abdomen. This study is also called a scout film and is often used early in the assessment of abdominal complaints. The KUB is performed to demonstrate the size, shape, and location of the kidneys, ureters, and bladder. Other intra-abdominal diseases can be identified using KUB films. The only contraindication for this study is pregnancy.

Normal Findings. Normal abdominal structures; no evidence of calculi; normal GI gas pattern.

Variations from Normal. Abnormal KUB results can include malformations of the organs studied, calculi, and ascites. Bowel perforation or obstruction, as evidenced by abnormal distribution of gas, can also be diagnosed using KUB. Soft-tissue masses, ruptured viscus, and presence of foreign bodies can be visualized with this radiographic study.

Interfering Circumstances. Retained barium from previous studies can interfere with optimal visualization. The KUB should be completed before any barium studies.

Obstruction Series

The **obstruction series**, also known as an acute abdomen series, is a radiographic examination of the abdomen, bowel, and kidneys. The series consists of at least two x-ray studies. The first film is an erect abdominal film that provides visualization of the diaphragms in order to detect air-fluid levels within the intestine. This film can also be accomplished as a left lateral decubitus film. The second film is very similar to the KUB, which has been previously discussed. Suspected bowel obstruction and ingestion of foreign objects are the primary indications for this exam. The obstruction series can also be used to monitor gastrointestinal diseases such as paralytic ileus.

Normal Findings. Absence of bowel obstruction, no abnormal calcifications, and no free air in the intestine.

Variations from Normal. An abnormal obstruction series can be diagnostic for bowel obstruction, perforated viscus, paralytic ileus, abdominal aortic aneurysm, kidney stones, and abdominal abscesses. It should be noted that the presence of air-fluid levels is consistent with bowel obstruction or paralytic ileus. Free air under either diaphragm is diagnostic for a perforated viscus.

Interfering Circumstances. Previous gastrointestinal barium contrast can interfere with the identification of kidney stones.

Long-Bone Radiography

Long bone radiography is an examination of the bones of the arms and legs. Long bone x-rays are indicated when the patient has complaints that involve the long bones, after trauma when a fracture may be suspected, or to follow the progress of a healing fracture. While there are no identified contraindications, other than precautions taken with a pregnant patient, reproductive organs should be properly shielded. The x-ray itself does not trigger discomfort, but positioning of fractured limbs may exacerbate the patient's pain.

Normal Findings. Absence of fracture, tumor, infection, or congenital abnormalities.

Variations from Normal. Abnormal findings include fractures, and bone spurring or joint destruction often associated with arthritis. Osteomyelitis, arthritis, congenital abnormalities, and abnormal growth patterns can be identified by long-bone radiography.

Interfering Circumstances. Very young patients or individuals with diminished mental capacity may not be able to maintain the position necessary for quality results.

Skull Radiography

Skull radiography is an examination of the bones of the skull, nasal sinuses, and surrounding structures. Skull x-ray also provides visualization of any cerebral calcifications, particularly of the pineal gland. A calcified pineal gland is a useful marker for locating the midline of the brain. Displacement of this calcification can help identify unilateral hematomas or tumors.

Normal Findings. Skull and surrounding structures are normal.

Variations from Normal. Skull fractures, metastatic bone tumors, and congenital anomalies can be identified with this test. Other abnormal results include cerebral tumors, hemorrhages, and hematomas. Skull x-ray can also be used to diagnose sinusitis.

Spinal Radiography

Spinal radiography is an examination of the entire spine or any section of the spine. The x-rays are used to identify a variety of spinal abnormalities as well as to assess back pain. Several views, such as anteroposterior, lateral, and oblique, are often taken and the patient must be able to cooperate in the positioning aspects of this examination. Pregnancy is a contraindication for this test.

Normal Findings. Normal spine and vertebrae.

Variations from Normal. Spinal x-rays are able to identify fractures, degenerative arthritic changes in the spine, metastatic tumor invasion, spondylosis, and spondylolisthesis. Displacement and misalignment of vertebra can also be identified or confirmed by spinal x-rays.

Radiography Studies with Contrast Media

There are many circumstances in which the normal contrast provided by body structures is not adequate for radiographic examinations. In order to enhance visualization, increase film acuity and quality, and provide the best possible diagnostic results, many radiographic studies use additional contrast media. Contrast media can be administered orally, rectally, or by way of injection. The ideal contrast medium does not interfere with the function of the structure being studied. There are four major types of contrast media: (1) barium sulfate, used for gastrointestinal studies; (2) organic iodides, used for kidney, liver, blood vessels, urinary bladder, and urethra; (3) iodized oils, used in myelography, bronchography, and lymphangiograms; and (4) air and gas contrast media, used for visualization of body spaces such as joints, subarachnoid space, pleural space, and pericardial space. Air and barium can be used in combination as a contrast medium.

Although great care is taken to ensure the safety of contrast media, the potential for adverse or allergic reactions always exists. Allergic reactions range from a mild rash to anaphylactic shock. Side effects of contrast media can include nausea and vomiting. Iodine contrast media carry the greatest risk for adverse reactions. Table 10-1 summarizes several adverse reactions associated with iodinated contrast media. In most instances, the patient should be NPO (nothing by mouth) the night before the contrasted study is completed.

Barium contrast media may also pose risks to the patient, or may interfere with completion of other radiographic studies. Ultrasound, radioisotope studies, CT scans, and studies using iodine contrasts must be scheduled before barium studies. Risks to the patient include aggravation of ulcerative colitis, bowel obstruction, impaction in the elderly, and constipation. Proper bowel preparation prior to barium use and bowel evacuation with or without enema following barium use can reduce the risk of several side effects. Barium should not be used when a bowel perforation is suspected. In these situations, an organic iodide can be used as the contrast medium.

In the past, contrast media were problematic for individuals who were pregnant or who had allergies related to shellfish. With the contrast media currently available the contraindication for individuals who have shellfish allergies no longer applies. In the event that a pregnant patient *must* have a specific exam, the physician, patient, and appropriate radiology practitioners use all precautions at their disposal.

Table 10-1. Adverse Reactions Associated with Iodinated Contrast Medium

Cardiovascular	*Cutaneous*	*Gastrointestinal*
Arrhythmia	Erythema	Abdominal cramps
Bradycardia	Feeling of warmth	Diarrhea
Diaphoresis	Pruritus	Metallic taste
Palpitations	Urticaria	Nausea
Tachycardia		Vomiting
Neurological	*Respiratory*	*Urinary*
Coma	Bronchospasm	Albuminuria
Convulsion	Cyanosis	Flank pain
Dizziness	Dyspnea	Hematuria
Headache	Laryngeal edema	Oliguria
Vertigo	Wheezing	WBCs in blood

Selected radiographic studies with contrast media are discussed. The tests are organized into related categories, such as angiography, biliary system radiography, gastrointestinal radiography, urinary system radiography, and miscellaneous studies.

Angiography

Angiography is a generic term used to describe x-ray examinations of the vascular system. Blood and lymph vessels are studied by injecting a contrast medium, usually iodine, into the femoral artery, the brachial artery, or other veins and arteries. A catheter is placed into the artery or vein, the contrast medium is injected, and the x-rays are taken. When satisfactory films have been obtained, the catheter is removed, pressure is applied to the puncture site, and the patient must remain at complete flat bed rest for several hours to prevent bleeding from the puncture site.

Specific angiography studies are named for the structures examined or by the route used to inject the contrast medium. Arteriography of the lower extremities, coronary (cardiac) angiography, digital subtraction angiography, lymphangiography, and venography of the lower extremities are included in this section.

Arteriography of the Lower Extremities

Arteriography of the lower extremities is a contrast x-ray examination of the femoral artery and its branches. A catheter is placed in the femoral artery, iodine contrast media are injected, and a series of x-ray films are taken. Indications for this study include symptoms and signs of peripheral vascular disease, sudden cessation of blood flow to an extremity, and suspected trauma to the femoral artery or its branches. The primary contraindication is an allergy to the contrast media, although current practice allows for the patient to be prepped for suspected allergic responses. Figure 10-2 is an angiogram showing the femoral arteries.

Normal Findings. Normal vascular anatomy with no evidence of disease.

Variations from Normal. Arteriography identifies arteriosclerotic occlusion, thrombi, emboli, arterial aneurysm, and abnormal arterial anatomy. Primary arterial diseases such as thromboangiitis obliterans, also known as Buerger's disease, can be diagnosed via arteriography.

Interfering Circumstances. Inability of the patient to cooperate during the exam can interfere with the quality of the x-ray films.

Coronary Angiography

Coronary angiography, sometimes called cardiac angiography or angiocardiography, is the examination of the heart, great vessels, and coronary arteries. Coronary angiography is accomplished through the invasive procedure known as cardiac catheterization. A catheter is passed through a peripheral vein or artery, is threaded into the heart, and a contrast material is injected so that the vasculature of the heart can be visualized.

This procedure is highly invasive but presents fewer risks than open-heart surgery. Coronary angiography is both a diagnostic and therapeutic modality. As a diagnostic tool it can be used to diagnose a variety of cardiac problems, including occlusive coronary disease, and can assess the extent of heart disease. Coronary angiography identifies different diseases depending on which side of the heart is evaluated. Right-heart coronary an-

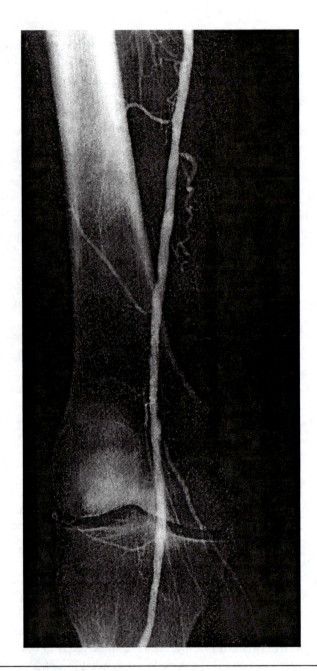

Figure 10-2. An angiogram showing the femoral arteries. The use of a contrast medium makes the arteries visible.

giography provides information about pulmonary artery abnormalities, and left-heart examinations reveal information about the coronary artery and the thoracic aorta.

Coronary angiography is indicated when other tests point to coronary disease, to evaluate angina of sustained and recurrent severity, to assess or monitor cardiac revascularization procedures, and to evaluate the extent or severity of congenital heart abnormalities. This study is contraindicated in the face of severe cardiomegaly, and for patients who are unable to cooperate during the test.

Coronary angiography has risks associated with both the angiography itself and with the catheterization that allows the angiography to take place. Perforation of the heart muscle, catheter-induced emboli or thrombi, cardiac arrhythmias, infection at the catheter site, and possible pneumothorax can result from this examination.

Normal Findings. Normal coronary arteries and great vessels. No evidence of cardiac abnormalities.

Variations from Normal. Cardiac abnormalities ranging from congenital heart and great vessel problems to identification of myocardial infarction sites can be revealed with coronary angiography. Arteriosclerosis, aneurysms, and coronary artery occlusive disease are often diagnosed with this study. Heart conditions identified via coronary angiography are septal defects, ventricular aneurysm, aortic arch disease, and heart tissue tumors.

Interfering Circumstances. Inability of the patient to cooperate compromises visualization of coronary vessels.

Digital Subtraction Angiography (DSA)

Digital subtraction angiography (DSA) is a sophisticated radiographic study that uses computerized fluoroscopy in order to visualize arteries. DSA is a valuable diagnostic tool for the assessment of the carotid and cerebral arteries. Preoperative and postoperative occlusive vascular disease and central nervous system tumors are optimally evaluated using DSA. Visualization of blood vessels that may be obstructed by bone or other tissue is enhanced with DSA.

Digital subtraction angiography is a two-step procedure. An image or "mask" of the areas of the body to be studied is taken and stored in the computer. Contrast media are then injected into an artery or vein, and additional images of the area are taken and stored in the computer. The preinjection images are subtracted, by computer, from the postinjection images, leaving a high-quality arterial image. Essentially, the computer subtracts or removes images of all tissue with the exception of the arterial images.

Indications for digital subtraction angiography include a wide range of suspected vascular abnormalities, and preoperative and postoperative evaluation for vascular and tumor surgery. Contraindications are patient allergies to iodinated contrast media.

Normal Findings. Normal arterial anatomy and absence of disease.

Variations from Normal. Abnormal DSA results include arterial stenosis, large aneurysms, tumors and other masses, occlusion of arteries, and meningiomas. Thrombi and emboli are also identified by DSA.

Interfering Circumstances. Physical movement by the patient can produce poor images.

Lymphangiography

Lymphangiography is a radiographic examination of lymph vessels, ducts, and nodes. Iodinated oil is the contrast medium and is usually injected into the small lymphatic vessels of the hand or foot. The test is used to evaluate the lymph system for cancers and unexplained edema of the extremities. Lymphangiography is also utilized to stage lymphomas and evaluate results of chemotherapy or radiation therapy. Lymphangiography is contraindicated for patients with allergies to iodine or shellfish. Severe lung, cardiac, renal, and hepatic diseases also present contraindications for this test.

Normal Findings. Normal lymphatic structures.

Variations from Normal. Abnormal test results include metastatic tumor involving lymph structures, and retroperitoneal lymphomas associated with Hodgkin's disease.

Venography of Lower Extremities

Venography of the lower extremities is an x-ray examination of the venous system of the legs and feet that is enhanced by the use of a contrast medium. Both legs may be studied even if only one presents with suspected pathology because the normal extremity is used for comparison with the affected extremity. Indications for venography include suspicion of deep-vein thrombosis or other venous defects. Contraindications are allergies to iodinated contrast media.

Normal Findings. Normal venous anatomy and absence of pathology.

Variations from Normal. Abnormal results are tumor, thrombosis, or inflammation, which may cause obstruction of the venous system. Deep-vein thrombosis is also identified via venography.

Gallbladder and Biliary System Radiography

The gallbladder and biliary system consists of the gallbladder and cystic duct; right and left hepatic ducts, which come together as the common hepatic duct; and the common bile duct, which is formed when the cystic duct and the common hepatic duct join. The common bile duct empties into the duodenum. Figure 10-3 reviews the anatomy of the bile duct system.

Several radiography studies, all using contrast media, are available for the examination of the gallbladder and biliary tree. Cholecystography, percutaneous transhepatic cholangiography, and T-tube cholangiography are presented in this section.

Cholecystography

Cholecystography, also known as a gallbladder (GB) series, is the radiographic visualization of the gallbladder using a radiopaque, iodinated contrast medium. The contrast medium can be ingested in the form of pills, oral cholecystography, or it can be administered via intravenous injection.

Indications for the test include suspected gallstones, gallbladder inflammation, and cystic duct obstruction. Contraindications are allergies to iodine contrast media and diseases of the digestive tract that may interfere with the absorption of orally ingested contrast media.

Normal Findings. Normal gallbladder anatomy and absence of pathology.

Variations from Normal. Various gallbladder disorders can be diagnosed via cholecystography. These include gallstones, polyps, and chronic

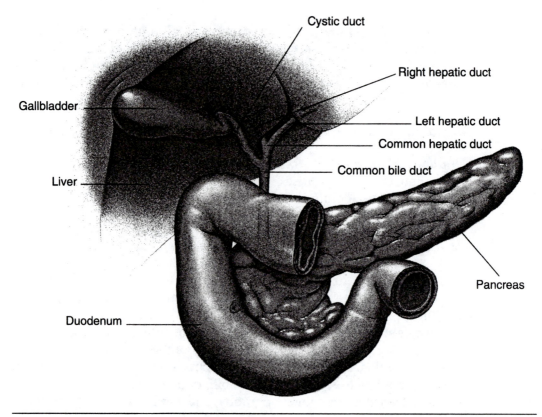

Figure 10-3. Structures of the biliary system

cholecystitis. This examination can identify cystic duct obstruction and gall-bladder cancer. Biopsy is necessary to confirm any cancer diagnosis.

Interfering Circumstances. Vomiting and diarrhea affect the absorption of orally ingested contrast media. Residual barium, usually the result of an upper GI series or barium enema, and an incomplete bowel prep interfere with gallbladder visualization. Any tests that require barium should be scheduled after the cholecystography exam.

Percutaneous Transhepatic Cholangiography (PTC, PTHC)

Percutaneous transhepatic cholangiography (PTC, PTHC), a radiographic examination of the biliary system and sometimes the gallbladder, uses an iodinated contrast medium that is injected through the liver into an intrahepatic bile duct. Visualization of the intra- and extrahepatic bile ducts, and occasionally the gallbladder, is then accomplished. Suspected duct obstruction and unexplained jaundice are the major indications for this procedure. Contraindications include allergies to the contrast media.

Normal Findings. Normal biliary duct anatomy and absence of pathology. If the gallbladder is visualized, normal gallbladder anatomy and absence of pathology.

Variations from Normal. Abnormal results include a variety of bile duct disorders such as tumors, strictures, or presence of gallstones. Sclerosis of the biliary tree and cysts of the common bile duct may also be identified.

T-Tube Cholangiography

T-tube cholangiography, a postoperative examination of the hepatic and common bile ducts, is accomplished by injecting an iodine contrast medium into the common bile duct via a T-tube. This test is usually done within ten days after cholecystectomy. During gallbladder surgery a self-retaining T-tube is often placed in the common bile duct. The tube is left in position until the patency of the hepatic and common bile ducts can be confirmed postoperatively. Indications for this examination include detection of postoperative common bile duct stones and evaluation of bile flow into the duodenum. Figure 10-4 shows the placement of the T-tube during this examination.

Normal Findings. Normal hepatic and common bile duct anatomy and absence of hepatic and common bile duct pathology.

Variations from Normal. T-tube cholangiography is able to identify common bile duct stones, stricture or tumors causing obstruction, bile duct cysts, and anatomic variations.

Interfering Circumstances. Residual barium interferes with bile duct visualization. Any tests that require barium should be scheduled after the T-tube cholangiography.

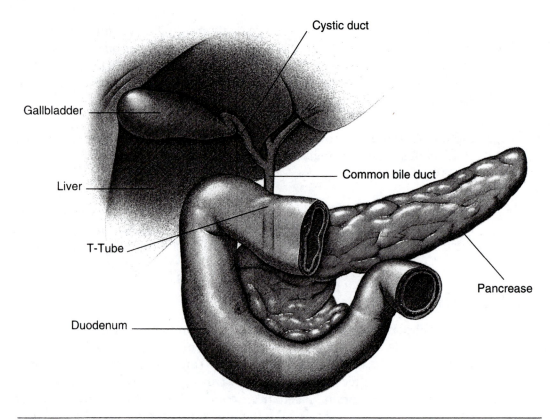

Figure 10-4. Placement of a T-tube for T-tube cholangiography

Gastrointestinal Radiography

Gastrointestinal radiography includes the examination of the GI tract from the esophagus to the rectum. These studies use barium or an iodinated contrast medium. Since barium interferes with iodinated tests, GI studies that use barium as the contrast are usually scheduled after procedures that use iodine. The gastrointestinal radiography studies are presented according to the anatomical location of the structures being studied. Examinations of the upper gastrointestinal tract and small intestine are discussed first, followed by tests related to the large intestine.

Radiographic exams included in this section are barium swallow or esophageal radiography, upper gastrointestinal series, small-bowel follow-through, and barium enema.

Barium Swallow; Esophageal Radiography

Barium swallow, also known as esophageal radiography, is a thorough x-ray examination of all aspects of the esophagus. Size, contour, filling, patency, and position of the esophagus can be evaluated in greater detail than that provided by upper gastrointestinal series.

Barium swallow is indicated when the clinician desires a highly accurate visualization of the esophagus. Contraindications include bowel obstruction, perforated viscus, and unstable vital signs.

Normal Findings. Normal esophagus anatomy and absence of pathology.

Variations from Normal. Esophageal radiography is used to identify hiatal hernia, varices, strictures, esophageal reflux, and peptic ulcer of the esophagus. Diverticula, chalasia, achalasia, and congenital abnormalities can be diagnosed using barium swallow. This examination can also help in the diagnosis of tumors that put pressure on the esophagus, causing esophageal narrowing and filling defects.

Interfering Circumstances. Food in the esophagus prevents accurate visualization of the structure.

Upper Gastrointestinal Radiography; Upper GI Series (UGI)

Upper GI series (UGI) is a radiographic study of the lower esophagus, stomach, duodenum, and upper portion of the jejunum. This examination is done as a series of x-rays and uses barium sulfate as the contrast medium. If barium is contraindicated due to suspected perforation of the gastrointestinal tract, a water-soluble medium can be used.

Once the patient has ingested the contrast medium, the patient is placed in a variety of positions that facilitate movement of the contrast throughout the entire upper GI tract and that enhance x-ray quality. Films are taken at the discretion of the radiologist. Visualization of the lower esophagus, stomach, duodenum, and jejunum allows the clinician to identify anatomic abnormalities and pathologies specific to each structure.

The upper GI series is performed as a first-line diagnostic study, when clinical gastrointestinal symptoms fail to produce a diagnosis. Contraindications for this examination include bowel obstructions and upper GI perforation, which preclude the use of barium.

Normal Findings. Normal anatomy of the structures being studied and the absence of pathology.

Variations from Normal. The upper GI series provides valuable diagnostic information about esophageal strictures, diverticula, varices, and hiatal hernia. Gastric ulcers, inflammatory diseases, tumors, and gastritis can also be diagnosed with this examination. Duodenal ulcers and cancer are identified using UGI. Congenital anomalies and perforation of any visualized structure may be revealed.

Interfering Circumstances. Food, fluid, and retained barium may decrease visualization and film clarity.

Small-Bowel Follow-Through (SBF); Small-Bowel Enema

The **small-bowel follow-through (SBF)** is a radiographic examination of the small intestine from the duodenum to the ileocecal valve. The small-bowel follow-through is sometimes performed in conjunction with an upper GI series. Both tests use barium as the contrast medium. Patients can drink the barium; if this is not possible, the barium is instilled through a nasogastric tube.

Once the contrast medium is in place, x-rays are taken at specified intervals to follow the flow of barium through the small intestine. When barium is seen entering the large intestine, films are no longer taken. The length of the procedure depends on how rapidly the contrast moves through the small intestine.

The SBF is used to diagnose a wide variety of small-intestine disorders such as abnormal positioning and Crohn's disease. Contraindications for this test include small-bowel obstruction and suspected perforations.

Normal Findings. Normal small-intestine anatomy and an absence of pathology.

Variations from Normal. The small-bowel follow-through identifies tumors, obstructions, volvulus, intussusception, and perforations of the small intestine. Crohn's disease, hernias, Meckel's diverticulum, and various anomalies of the small intestine can be diagnosed using this examination.

Interfering Circumstances. Delayed small intestine motility can prolong the test and may decrease the quality of the results. Food or fluid and retained barium from previous studies may interfere with visualization of the small intestine.

Barium Enema (BE); Lower GI Series

Barium enema (BE) is a radiographic examination of the entire large intestine or colon, and is accomplished by taking a series of x-ray films. Barium is the contrast medium of choice and is introduced into the colon by way of a rectal tube. If a colostomy is present, an irrigation cone is used and the barium is instilled directly into the stoma. If small polyps of the colon are suspected, air is included as part of the contrast. The examination may then be called an air-contrast barium enema.

Identification of anatomical defects as well as diagnostic assistance for a variety of colon diseases indicate the need for a barium enema. Contraindications include suspected colon perforation, and the inability of the patient to hold the contrast medium in the rectum and colon.

Normal Findings. Normal colon anatomy and the absence of pathology.

Variations from Normal. Barium enema can identify colon tumors, obstructions, and perforation. Diverticula, polyps, and hernias can be diagnosed with this examination. Other diseases and conditions revealed by barium enema include chronic ulcerative colitis, fistulas, and megacolon.

Interfering Circumstances. Inadequate or poor bowel cleansing is the most common interfering factor for accurate and complete visualization of the colon.

Urinary System Radiography

Radiographic examinations of the urinary system provide diagnostic information about the internal structure and function of the kidneys, ureters, and bladder. Studies included in this chapter are cystography, intravenous urography, commonly called intravenous pyelography (IVP), and retrograde pyelography, all of which use an iodinated contrast medium.

Cystography

Cystography, a radiographic examination of the urinary bladder, is the best tool for examining primary bladder diseases and conditions. The bladder is filled with a radiopaque contrast medium, which allows for visualization of the bladder as it fills and empties. Fluoroscopy can be used to observe bladder function. Suspected primary bladder disorders indicate the need for cystography, while contraindications are urethral or bladder infection or injury.

Normal Findings. Normal bladder anatomy and function, and an absence of pathology.

Variations from Normal. Primary bladder tumors are identified as shadows within the bladder as it fills. Pelvic tumors externally compress or distort the bladder. Bladder rupture and perforation are diagnosed by the presence of contrast medium outside of the bladder.

Intravenous Urography (IVU); Intravenous Pyelography (IVP); Excretory Urography

Intravenous urography (IVU) is a radiographic examination of the structure and function of the entire urinary tract. This examination is commonly known as intravenous pyelography. Some clinicians prefer the term "intravenous urography" because it implies visualization of the entire urinary tract, whereas IVP may be interpreted as visualization of only the kidneys.

The contrast medium, iodinated water, is injected intravenously. It then passes through the arterial system, is filtered in the kidney through the glomeruli, passes through the renal tubes, and eventually reaches the urinary bladder. A series of x-rays is taken in order to follow the progress of the iodinated contrast medium. The contrast medium material should pass through the kidneys and ureters and reach the bladder in approximately thirty minutes.

Intravenous urography is one of the most frequently performed tests in cases of suspected kidney disease or urinary tract dysfunction. Conditions that require special attention before and during the performance of this exam are dehydration, renal insufficiency, and multiple myeloma. Contraindications include allergies to the contrast medium.

Normal Findings. Normal urinary tract anatomy, position and absence of pathology. Normal kidney excretory function.

Variations from Normal. The intravenous urography provides a wealth of diagnostic information that includes identification of pyelonephritis, glomerulonephritis, renal insufficiency, and hydronephrosis. Other diseases identified by IVU are urinary tract calculi, tumors, and renal hematomas.

Structural defects identified via IVU cover congenital as well as acquired defects. Conditions such as an unusual number of kidneys, polycystic kidney disease, horseshoe kidneys, malpositioned kidneys, and altered size, form, and position of the ureter and bladder are categorized as structural defects.

Interfering Circumstances. Feces, gas, or retained barium in the gastrointestinal tract can interfere with the visualization of the urinary system, especially the kidneys.

Retrograde Pyelography (RP)

Retrograde pyelography (RP) is a radiological examination of the urinary tract, particularly the ureters and kidney, and uses an iodinated contrast medium. This exam is often carried out in conjunction with cystoscopy so that ureteral catheters may be introduced up to the level of the renal pelvis. Sedation, analgesia, and even general anesthesia may be required prior to catheter insertion. Once the catheters are in place, the contrast medium is injected directly into renal structures and films are taken. Renal function does not influence the visualization of these structures.

Retrograde pyelography, which often confirms the findings of intravenous urography, is indicated when IVU/IVP yields insufficient results. Patient allergy to the intravenous contrast medium also provides an indication for retrograde pyelography. The contrast medium for RP is not absorbed into the bloodstream.

Normal Findings. Normal size and contour of the ureter and kidney.

Variations from Normal. Retrograde pyelography can identify congenital anomalies of the ureters and kidney pelvis. Tumors, stones, strictures, and ureteral obstruction can be diagnosed by retrograde pyelography.

Interfering Circumstances. Retained barium from previous studies can interfere with visualization of urinary structures.

Miscellaneous Contrast Radiography Studies

Three radiographic studies are discussed in this section. Arthrography, hysterosalpingography, and myelography were selected because they represent different areas of the body. These examinations use an iodinated contrast medium and should be scheduled prior to barium studies.

Arthrography

Arthrography, also known as joint radiography, is the radiographic examination of an encapsulated joint and its related structures. This study is accomplished by taking multiple x-rays of the affected area following the injection of a contrast medium into the joint capsular space. One of several contrast agents can be used, including gas, water, or soluble iodine. Soft-tissue structures of the joint such as the bursa, meniscus, cartilage, and ligaments are clearly visualized with this examination.

Indications for arthrography include persistent and unexplained joint pain or discomfort. Arthrography is usually performed on the knee and shoulder joints, but can be done on other joints as well. Contraindications include pregnancy, active arthritis, and joint infection.

Normal Findings. Normal anatomy of the joint and its structures and the absence of pathology.

Variations from Normal. Arthrography is valuable in the diagnosis of joint derangement, rotator cuff rupture, joint dislocation, and arthritis. Synovial abnormalities, ligament tears, and cartilage diseases such as chondromalacia can be identified with arthrography.

Hysterosalpingography

Hysterosalpingography is a radiographic examination of the uterine cavity and fallopian tubes (oviducts) that uses an iodinated contrast medium. The contrast medium is usually inserted into the uterus by way of the cervix. This examination is used to identify abnormalities that may cause infertility, and other diseases of the uterus and oviducts. Contraindications for hysterosalpingography include infections of reproductive structures, uterine bleeding, and suspected pregnancy.

Normal Findings. Normal anatomy of the uterus and fallopian tubes and an absence of pathology.

Variations from Normal. Abnormal conditions identified by hysterosalpingography include bicornate uterus, tubal tortuosity, and obstruction or occlusion of the oviducts. Uterine fistulas, tumors, and adhesions can be diagnosed with this study.

Myelography

Myelography is the radiographic examination of the spinal canal. The examination is accomplished by injecting an iodine contrast medium into the spinal subarachnoid space. A water-soluble iodine medium is used most frequently because it is absorbed by the blood and excreted by the kidneys. Air contrast is used on rare occasions and iodized oils are no longer part of this examination.

The spinal cord and nerve roots are outlined, and dura mater distortions are visualized. Myelography is usually performed by lumbar puncture. The risks and complications for that procedure exist for myelography as well. Spinal computerized tomography scans and myelography are often performed in conjunction with each other.

Indications for myelography include unrelieved back pain, preoperative assessment of ruptured vertebral disk, and localized neurologic symptoms that indicate spinal canal injury. Contraindications could include multiple sclerosis, increased intracranial pressure, and infection near the puncture site.

Normal Findings. Normal spinal canal anatomy and an absence of pathology.

Variations from Normal. Myelography can be used to diagnose ruptured or herniated intravertebral disks, spinal cord tumors, metastatic spinal tumors, and spinal canal obstruction.

Computerized (Axial) Tomography (CT, CAT) Scans

Computerized tomography (CT, CAT) is a radiographic technique that produces a film representing a detailed cross section of tissue structure. Very narrow x-ray beams rotate in a continuous 360-degree motion around the individual to produce cross-sectional images of the body and its structures. Figure 10-5 is an abdominal CT scan.

Computerized tomography has been an invaluable addition to the diagnostic "tool chest." This technique is able to detect minor differences in the density and composition of tumors versus soft tissue, air spaces versus cerebrospinal fluid, and normal blood versus clotted blood. CT scans can be conducted with or without contrast material. Two examples of computerized tomography scanning are included in this chapter.

The procedure is painless, noninvasive, and usually requires no special preparation. However, depending on the organ or system being studied, an enema prep may be in order. Patients who are claustrophobic or exhibit heightened anxiety about the examination may be given a sedative.

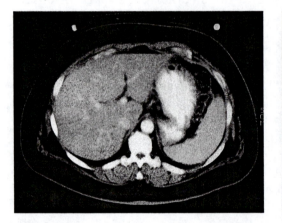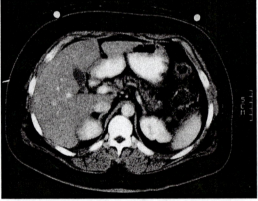

Figure 10-5. Abdominal CT scans: **(a)** The liver is predominant (upper left) and the stomach can be seen (upper right). **(b)** Less of the liver and stomach are visible; however, the pancreas can be seen in the middle of the film.

Computerized Tomography of the Brain

Computerized tomography of the brain is a radiographic technique that provides a three-dimensional view of the cranium and its contents. Once the CT scan is completed, the clinician has a series of anatomic pictures of cross sections of the brain. These pictures are produced so that the head is viewed from the top of the skull to the base of the brain. Symptoms of cerebral pathology that cannot be clinically diagnosed are indications for CT scans of the brain.

Normal Findings. Normal size, shape, position, and anatomy of the brain and an absence of pathology.

Variations from Normal. Diagnoses identified by CT scanning include cerebral infarction, neoplasms, hematomas, and aneurysms. Intracranial hemorrhage and hydrocephalus can be assessed with this radiographic technique. A CT brain scan allows the visualization of changes in the size, shape, position, and symmetry of intracranial structures.

Interfering Circumstances. Patient movement has a negative effect on the accuracy and quality of the image.

Computerized Tomography of the Body; Body Scan

Computerized tomography of the body is a radiologic technique that gives detailed cross-sectional images of the chest, abdomen, spine, and extremities. This technique can be used to evaluate blood flow and vascularity of tissue masses. Some areas of the body may need a contrast medium in order to provide clarification of the image. Body CT scans that include the pelvic area may involve the use of a barium contrast or water-soluble enema. Individuals who present with multiple symptoms, and for whom clinical diagnosis is not forthcoming, may benefit from a CT body scan. Contraindications include extreme obesity or pregnancy. Either condition may inhibit the ability of the patient to move through the confines of the scanning equipment.

Normal Findings. Normal anatomic structure and the absence of pathology.

Variations from Normal. CT scans can identify a host of diseases ranging from tumors, nodules, and cysts to specific diagnoses such as cirrhosis of the liver and lymphoma. Pleural effusion, skeletal bone metastasis, and soft-tissue damage can be seen with CT scans. Abdominal aortic aneurysm, often called the silent killer, is revealed by this diagnostic technique.

Interfering Circumstances. Retained barium from previous tests can obscure abdominal organs. Patient movement can compromise the quality and accuracy of the images.

Magnetic Resonance Imaging

Magnetic resonance imaging (MRI) is a noninvasive procedure that uses a magnetic field and radio waves to measure the activity of the body's hydrogen atoms. This activity is interpreted by computer and the information is converted into high-quality images that provide valuable diagnostic information. Magnetic resonance imaging is able to produce excellent detailed images of body organs and blood flow. MRI provides better contrast between normal and pathological tissue; is able to produce images through bone tissue and fluid-filled soft tissue; and is able to scan or image the transverse, sagittal, and coronal planes of the body.

Although MRI is effective with any organ or system, this technology is most often used in association with the nervous system and the musculoskeletal system. Magnetic resonance imaging is often used to diagnose multiple sclerosis, and to evaluate pathology involving the brain and liver.

The biggest advantage of MRI is the fact that many studies can be accomplished without using any contrast media and there is no exposure to radiation. Patient preparation for MRI is limited to restricting alcohol, caffeine beverages, and smoking for up to two hours before the study, and food for at least one hour. Most medications can be taken as scheduled.

The actual examination takes place in a scanner that can stimulate claustrophobic reactions in the patient. There is a series of clicking noises associated with the procedure. The patient can be given sedation to minimize the claustrophobic feeling and earplugs can be used to block out the clicking noise. Patients may also have the option of listening to piped-in music during the exam. All metallic objects must be removed so that the quality of the image is not compromised.

The major disadvantage of MRI is quite simply the cost. Any use of magnetic resonance imaging must be carefully considered in the face of cost-benefit analysis. There is no doubt, however, that as the cost of the technology decreases, and as the age of the population increases, use of this diagnostic tool will increase.

Since the nervous and musculoskeletal systems are most commonly associated with magnetic resonance imaging, MRI studies of those systems are discussed. **Magnetic resonance imaging of the head and brain**, a study performed to assess conditions of the face and brain, and **musculoskeletal magnetic resonance imaging**, a scan performed to identify abnormalities of bones, joints, cartilage, and other soft tissue of the system, are outlined next.

Head and Brain Magnetic Resonance Imaging

Magnetic resonance imaging of the head and brain provides information about the blood flow to the face, head, and brain. Structure and tissue abnormalities of the nasopharynx, neck, and tongue are also identified. Figure 10-6 is a an example of an MRI of the head and brain.

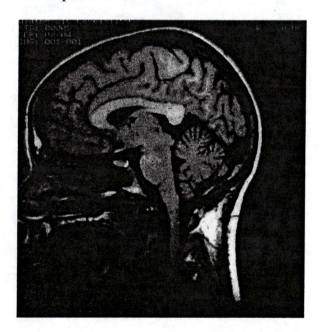

Figure 10-6.   MRI of the brain and head

Normal Findings. Normal structure of the head and brain. Absence of pathology.

Variations from Normal. Head and brain magnetic resonance imaging reveals brain tumors, both primary and metastatic, and tumors involving the optic nerve, pituitary gland, and benign meningioma. Multiple sclerosis, causes of cerebrovascular accidents, and localization of the area of cerebral hemorrhage can be identified via MRI. Figure 10-7 shows an MRI of the brain with the area of a "bleed" visible on the lower right.

Many vascular disorders, infections, and cerebral changes associated with dementia can be assessed with this diagnostic tool. In addition to diagnostic applications, MRI can be used to evaluate both radiation and chemotherapy for tumor reduction. Shunt placement, for hydrocephalus, can be monitored with MRI.

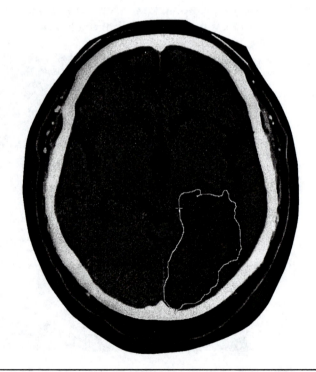

Figure 10-7.   MRI of a brain with the area of a "bleed" visible in the lower right

Interfering Circumstances. Inability of the patient to remain still during the procedure and the presence of metallic objects in the examination area compromise the quality of the image.

Musculoskeletal Magnetic Resonance Imaging

Musculoskeletal MRI provides diagnostic information about bones, joints, and the surrounding tissue. Any part of the musculoskeletal system can be imaged. MRI is particularly useful in identifying herniated disks of the spine and differentiating them from spinal degenerative diseases. Magnetic resonance imaging is a more sensitive diagnostic tool for bone analysis than computerized tomography and x-ray examinations. MRI is also able to assess bone density and is very helpful in distinguishing between stress fractures and bone neoplasms.

Normal Findings. Normal bones, joints, and surrounding tissue. Absence of pathology.

Variations from Normal. Musculoskeletal MRI can identify a wide variety of diseases ranging from a herniated disk to malignant bone marrow disorders such as leukemia or myeloma. Degenerative diseases such as spondylosis and arthritis are readily visible with MRI. Benign and malignant bone tumors such as osteogenic sarcoma, osteochondroma, and osseous hemangioma are a few of the more debilitating diseases that are visualized with MRI. Bone marrow changes associated with aplastic anemia, sickle cell disease, and polycythemia can be evaluated with the information obtained via magnetic resonance imaging. Figure 10-8 is a sample report of an MRI of the right shoulder.

Interfering Circumstances. Inability of the patient to remain still during the procedure and the presence of metallic objects in the examination area compromise the quality of the image.

Summary

- Radiography studies allow for the visualization of the internal structures of the body without surgical intervention.

PATIENT NAME: SHOULDER, SHELLY

MEDICAL RECORD NUMBER: 99-99-99

DATE: April 31, xx

PROCEDURE: MRI of the Right Shoulder.

REPORT: Multiple T1, proton density and T2 weighted paracoronal images of the right shoulder were obtained utilizing spin echo technique, followed by T2 weighted gradient echo axial cartilage sensitive sequences.

There is diffuse enlargement and intermediate signal intensity within the supraspinous and most likely infraspinous tendon on the T1 and proton density sequence. The subscapularis muscle and tendon are normal. No significant glenohumeral joint or bursal effusion is seen. There is right acromioclavicular joint hypertrophy extending superiorly. No intraosseous abnormalities are seen. The glenoid labrum is intact. There is perhaps minimal subacromial fluid. The biceps tendon is normal. Articular cartilage is maintained.

IMPRESSION: Findings as above, most consistent with tendinitis, predominantly involving the supraspinous tendon and most likely also involving the intraspinous. Minimal subacromial fluid. Right acromioclavicular joint hypertrophy, superiorly. No definite "impingement." No definite frank rotator cuff tear.

Figure 10-8.   Report of an MRI of the shoulder

- Radiographic examinations that do not use contrast media have few if any contraindications.
- Four types of contrast media are barium sulfate, organic iodides, iodized oils, and air and gas.
- Radiography studies that use barium as the contrast medium should be scheduled after iodinated contrast media studies.
- A contraindication for iodinated contrast-enhanced radiography is an allergy to iodine.
- Adverse reactions to iodinated contrast media can affect the cutaneous, respiratory, cardiovascular, neurological, gastrointestinal, and urinary systems.

- Angiography includes various studies of blood and lymph vessels.
- Gallbladder and biliary system radiography examines the gallbladder and related ducts.
- Gastrointestinal radiography provides information about all structures of the GI tract, from the esophagus to the large intestine.
- Urinary system radiography provides diagnostic information about the internal structure and function of the kidneys, ureters, and bladder.
- Computerized tomography provides three-dimensional, cross-sectional images of studies organs and tissue.
- Magnetic resonance imaging is a noninvasive procedure that uses a magnetic field and radio waves to measure to create images of body structure.
- Magnetic resonance imaging produces excellent detailed images of blood flow, provides better contrast between normal and pathological tissue, and produces images through bone tissue and fluid-filled soft tissue.

CHAPTER REVIEW

1. Identify the following radiographic studies:

   a. Visualization of the chest, bony thorax, lungs, pleura, and mediastinum   _____

   b. Diagnostic tool for assessment of cerebral and carotid arteries   _____

   c. Also known as a gallbladder series   _____

   d. Examination of the structure and function of the entire urinary tract   _____

   e. Examination from the duodenum to the ileocecal valve   _____

   f. Postoperative evaluation of the hepatic and common bile ducts   _____

    g. Visualization of entire large intestine   _____

    h. Provides three-dimensional, cross-sectional
        images of organs and tissues   _____

    i. Examination of blood and lymph vessels   _____

    j. Heart, great vessels, coronary vessels   _____

2. Identify the radiographic examination(s) that can be used to determine or assess
the listed diagnosis.

    Diagnosis   **Radiographic Examination(s)**

    a. hydrocephalus   _____

    b. Herniated disk   _____

    c. Crohn's disease   _____

    d. Hiatal hernia   _____

    e. Tumor of the bile duct(s)   _____

    f. Gallstones   _____

    g. Deep-vein thrombosis   _____

    h. Chronic cholecystitis   _____

    i. Suppurative mastitis   _____

    j. Abdominal aortic aneurysm   _____

    k. Rotator cuff rupture   _____

    l. Bicornate uterus   _____

    m. Pneumonia   _____

    n. Ureteral calculi   _____

    o. Esophageal varices   _____

3. Briefly describe the structures examined by the listed radiographic studies. Provide examples of the diseases that can be diagnosed by these studies.

Study	Structures	Diseases
a. Arthrography	_____	_____
b. Barium swallow	_____	_____
c. Coronary angiography	_____	_____
d. Cystography	_____	_____
e. Hysterosalpingography	_____	_____
f. Lymphangiography	_____	_____
g. Mammography	_____	_____
h. Obstruction series	_____	_____
i. Retrograde pyelography	_____	_____
j. Skull radiography	_____	_____
k. Upper GI series	_____	_____

4. Organize the listed radiographic examinations according to these categories:

a. Barium contrast   _____

b. Iodinated contrast   _____

c. No contrast   _____

angiography	cystography	mammography
arthrography	hysterosalpingography	obstruction series
barium swallow	intravenous urography	retrograde pyelography
cholecystography	KUB	spinal radiography
CT of the brain	lymphangiography	

5. Sequence the listed radiography exams, assuming they are to be performed in one day on the same patient: hysterosalpingography, KUB, mammography, percutaneous transhepatic cholangiography, small-bowel follow-through

a. _____

b. _____

c. _____

d. _____

e. _____

6. Compare radiography, computerized tomography, and magnetic resonance imaging. What are the benefits of each? What are the risks of each? Identify the organs, systems, or tissues that are best imaged by each technique.

Case Studies

1. Mary Murphy, a 79-year-old-woman, is suspected of having an intracranial hemorrhage. The physician has ordered a CT scan of the brain. Explain what a CT scan consists of and the types of information it can provide to the physician.

2. Dr. Kim, a urologist, has ordered an IVP/IVU for a newly admitted patient. What does this test involve? Is contrast necessary and, if so, what type? Can this test diagnose tumors? If the IVP/IVU does not provide sufficient information, what other tests can the physician order?

3. Oscar Koski, a 50-year-old man, has been scheduled for a barium enema because of intestinal discomfort. Describe a barium enema, including indications and contraindications. What diseases can be identified by this test? Should Mr. Koski be NPO for this test? Why or why not? What circumstances can interfere with test results?

Challenge Activity

A close friend is scheduled for several radiography studies; one is a digital subtraction angiography of the head and neck. Your friend is having a hard time interpreting the "medicalese" used to explain the test. Describe DSA to the friend. Include how the examination is done, the structures studied, and how it compares to other radiography examinations. Use nonmedical terms.

Chapter 11

Nuclear Medicine Studies

Key Terms, Abbreviations, and Acronyms

bone scan

brain scan

cerebrospinal fluid flow scan

cisternogram

cisternography

cold spots

dipyridamole-thallium stress test

dobutamine-thallium stress test

gallbladder and biliary system scan

gallium-67 scan

gastric emptying scan

gastroesophageal reflux scan

gastrointestinal bleeding scan

gastrointestinal reflux scan

hot spots

iodine-131 scan

kidney scan

liver scan

multigated acquisition scan, MUGA

parathyroid scan

persantine-thallium stress test

positron emission tomography, PET

pulmonary perfusion scan

pulmonary ventilation scan

radioactive iodine uptake (RAIU) test

radionuclides

single-photon emission computed tomography, SPECT

scrotal (testicular) scan

spleen scan

testicular scan

thallium stress test

thyroidal hypothyroidism

thyroid stimulating hormone
    (TSH) test

triple renal scan

uptake

tracers

Learning Objectives

Upon completion of this chapter, the learner should be able to:

1. Describe how radionuclides are used in nuclear testing.
2. Compare the types of scans available and the scanning images each produces.
3. Differentiate between the radionuclide distribution pattern of an organ that is normal and one that is abnormal.
4. Organize the scans according to areas of the body and describe each scan.
5. Identify the abnormalities that can be diagnosed with each of the organ scans.

Introduction

Nuclear medicine studies cover a range of diagnostic procedures that use intravenous or oral radioactive pharmaceuticals, specialized radiation detection equipment, and computers to visualize and discover abnormalities of body organs and tissues. This chapter includes a selection of radionuclide scans that cover the entire body as well as specific organs.

Radionuclide scans are presented in relation to the anatomical area under study. Head and neck scans include studies of the brain, thyroid, and parathyroid glands. Scans of the chest cover heart and lung radionuclide examinations. Abdominal radionuclide scans pertain to studies of the gastrointestinal tract, gallbladder, liver, spleen, and kidneys. Miscellaneous scans include evaluations of the scrotum, bone, and gallium-67 studies.

Information for each study includes a brief description of the study, the organ and body tissue examined, indications or contraindications for the study, diseases that are identified by the study, and factors that inter-fere with the results or prevent the use of a particular nuclear study or scan.

Overview of Nuclear Scanning Studies

Diagnostic nuclear medicine involves the use of **radionuclides**, radioactive isotopes that undergo decay and are administered to the patient either orally or intravenously. Radionuclides are also known as **tracers**. As the radionu-clide decays, it emits radiation that can be detected by specialized equip-ment. The radiation detection equipment is able to locate the concentration of radionuclides, known as **uptake**, in the tissues of the organ being studied. The equipment is able to convert the detection of this concentration or uptake into images that are displayed on a computer screen and can be recorded as photographs. Images produced by nuclear scanning include: gray-shaded outlines of the organ; **hot spots**, which are dark gray (at times nearly black) areas of the organ that have a high concentration of the radionuclide; and **cold spots**, which are lighter gray areas of the organ that have a lower con-centration of the radionuclide.

The particular radionuclide utilized varies with the organ and type of nuclear test being performed. Technetium-99m is used in studies of the brain, heart, gastrointestinal tract, liver, spleen, and bone marrow. Iodine is associated with scans of the thyroid gland, brain, and deep veins. Indium is identified with cerebrospinal fluid, bone marrow, and gastric function nu-clear studies. Tumor scans are performed with gallium, and cardiac func-tion scans often involve the radionuclide thallium.

Depending upon the equipment and the type of scan, images may be produced in two or three dimensions; in color or shades of black, gray, and white; and as static or moving images. Color and motion images are partic-ularly helpful for assessing organ function. Nuclear imaging primarily relies on a gamma camera that creates static, two-dimensional images. There are also three-dimensional images constructed by way of **single-photon emis-sion computed tomography (SPECT)**, and a related but more sensitive scanning technique, **positron emission tomography (PET)**. Both SPECT and PET are capable of producing scans that assist in the evaluation of organ function as well as organ structure.

Positron emission tomography has special imaging capabilities that can be used to study the physiological function of an organ. PET scanning requires the use of radionuclides that produce positrons capable of combining with the body tissues' negative electrons. This combination permits the scanner to produce three-dimensional color images, which can be taken in a timed sequence, and provides the clinician with information as the radionuclide moves through the organ. PET provides information about organ anatomy, physiology, and biochemistry. Although it is most often used to assess the physiological function of the brain and heart, PET can be used to study all organs and tissue of the body.

Positron emission tomography utilizes radionuclides such as oxygen-15, carbon-11, fluorine-18, and nitrogen-13. More than one radionuclide can be used in a particular nuclear test. In addition, a radionuclide can be connected or tagged to other products such as red blood cells, albumin, or pyrophosphate, which can direct the radionuclide to a particular organ.

Nuclear studies are performed in a department that specializes in the use and handling of radioactive materials. The physicians and staff have specialized training in nuclear medicine, and agencies that use radionuclides are licensed and regulated by the state and federal government.

The risks associated with the use of radionuclides are considered low because radioactive energy leaves the patient's body in six to twenty-four hours. However, some radionuclides take as long as eight days to dissipate. The patient is typically exposed to less radiation that than of a regular x-ray procedure. Children can be tested using radionuclides due to the low radiation exposure. Nursing mothers can be imaged when the breast milk is stored in advance, since the half-life of radionuclides is usually quite short. Exceptions to radionuclide diagnostic imaging are usually limited to pregnant women.

Radionuclide Scans of the Head and Neck

Radionuclide scans of the head and neck include brain scans, cerebrospinal fluid flow scans, thyroid scans, and parathyroid scans. Iodine-131 studies, radioactive iodine uptake tests, and thyroid stimulating hormone tests are additional studies involving the thyroid gland. These scans provide information regarding organ structure and function. Indications and contraindications are presented in this chapter, as well as diseases associated with each study.

Brain Scan

A **brain scan** is a radionuclide study of the brain that assesses brain structure, function, and the integrity of the blood-brain barrier. The blood-brain barrier is a protective barrier of brain tissues that prevents the movement of substances from the blood to the brain. The radionuclide is administered intravenously and should not cross the blood-brain barrier. Abnormalities or diseases of the brain may prevent the blood-brain barrier from functioning properly and permit the radionuclide to enter brain tissue. When the brain is scanned, the physician is able to visualize the location, size, and shape of the abnormality because of the presence of the radionuclide.

The patient is placed in a supine position, the radionuclide is administered, and in some cases a sedative is given to help the patient relax. Images can be recorded immediately or up to a few hours after administration of the radionuclide. The scanning camera's position can be changed to accommodate various scanning angles. Brain scans are safe, relatively pain-free examinations, although the patient may experience discomfort related to the intravenous administration of the radionuclide. Pregnancy is a contraindication for this scan.

It must be noted that diagnostic tools such as magnetic resonance imaging and computerized tomography have all but replaced nuclear medicine brain scans.

Normal Findings. Scanning does not reveal the presence of radionuclide uptake by the brain, which demonstrates that the blood-brain barrier is intact. There is no other evidence of brain tumor, rupture, or trauma.

Variations from Normal. Brain scans can be used to diagnose ruptured aneurysms, abscesses, cysts, cerebral tumors and masses, hematomas, cerebral thrombosis, and hemorrhage. Scans are also useful for identifying encephalitis and hydrocephalus in children.

Interfering Circumstances. The patient must be cooperative and maintain the desired position during the brain scan.

Cerebrospinal Fluid Flow Scan

A **cerebrospinal fluid flow scan**, also called **cisternography** or **cisterno-gram**, is a radionuclide study that demonstrates the dynamics of cerebrospinal fluid (CSF) flow and reabsorption. Altered cerebrospinal fluid flow or reabsorption patterns indicate abnormalities of the brain. The cerebrospinal fluid flow scan can be used to determine the placement and patency of a shunt when treating hydrocephalus.

After the radionuclide has been injected into the spinal column via lumbar puncture, the patient is placed in the supine position. Scanning may take place over time and the patient must be able to change position to accommodate a variety of viewing angles. At the conclusion of the procedure, the patient is usually asked to be supine for up to four hours in order to reduce the possibility of headaches. The lumbar puncture site must be checked for leakage. Although the actual CSF flow scan has few risks, the lumbar puncture part of the procedure has its own risks, which must be minimized. The patient must be observed for abnormal neurological symptoms, changes in blood pressure, temperature, or complaints of a headache.

Normal Findings.   Normal flow and reabsorption of the cerebrospinal fluid.

Variations from Normal.   Abnormalities such as hydrocephalus, spinal lesion, subdural hematoma, and cysts can be detected using cerebrospinal fluid scanning.

Interfering Circumstances.   The patient must be cooperative and must be able to maintain the desired position for the examination.

Thyroid Scans

There are several nuclear medicine thyroid studies, four of which are presented in this chapter. These scans are the general thyroid scan, iodine-131 scan, radioactive iodine uptake (RAIU) test, and thyroid stimulating hormone (TSH) study. Each scan is presented individually, although all have the same basic goal: to assess the function and health of the thyroid gland.

Thyroid Scan

A thyroid scan is a radionuclide study of the thyroid gland. It is used to evaluate the size, position, shape, and function of the thyroid gland. The patient must remain in the supine position, with the neck well exposed so that the scanner can be passed over the area of the thyroid. Thyroid scanning assists in the identifications and evaluation of masses in the thyroid gland and other areas of the neck, as well as abnormalities associated with hyperthyroidism or hypothyroidism. Thyroid scans are particularly useful in evaluating thyroid nodules. Pregnant women are not candidates for radionuclide thyroid scans.

For thyroid scans the radionuclide can be administered orally or intravenously. During the scan the uptake of radioactive iodine by the thyroid gland is measured. Functioning nodules appear as hot spots (increased uptake), and nonfunctioning nodules appear as cold spots (decreased uptake). A malignant nodule of the thyroid gland is usually viewed as a cold spot and a benign nodule as a hot spot.

Normal Findings. Normal size, position, shape, and functioning of the thyroid gland. Normal distribution of radionuclide with an absence of hot or cold spots.

Variations from Normal. Abnormalities, such as goiters, cancer of the thyroid, Graves' disease, Plummer's disease, Hashimoto's thyroiditis, as well as hyperthyroidism and hypothyroidism, can be identified using the radionuclide thyroid scan.

Interfering Circumstances. The patient must be cooperative and able to maintain the desired position for the examination. Certain drugs that contain high concentrations of iodine as well as medications that decrease thyroid function, affect the results of the scan. Other recent diagnostic tests that use iodine agents, such as computerized tomography with contrast, alter the reliability of the thyroid scan.

Iodine-131 Scans

The **iodine-131** scan is a radionuclide study that is performed to determine if thyroid tissue is present in abnormal locations of the body, to identify residual thyroid following removal of the gland, and to assess the metastasis of thyroid cancer to other parts of the body.

Prior to the scan, the patient's medications, including thyroid medications, may be changed. Patients routinely receive an oral dose of iodine-

131 between twenty-four and seventy-two hours prior to the scan. At the time of the scan, some patients may be given an intravenous injection of thyroid stimulating hormone (TSH). This hormone increases the uptake of the radionuclide in thyroid tissue and tumors. The examination is accomplished with the patient in the supine position, and the entire body is scanned.

Normal Findings. A normal iodine-131 scan demonstrates an absence of abnormally placed thyroid tissue, an absence of residual thyroid following thyroid removal, and no evidence of metastatic thyroid cancer.

Variations from Normal. Metastatic cancer from a primary thyroid cancer, the presence of thyroid tissue in abnormal locations, and evidence of residual tissue following thyroidectomy are the abnormal results associated with this scan.

Interfering Circumstances. The patient must be cooperative and able to maintain the desired posture for the scan. Other recent tests involving the use of radionuclides may negatively affect the results of the iodine-131 scan.

Radioactive Iodine Uptake (RAIU) Test

The **radioactive iodine uptake (RAIU) test** is a nuclear medicine study that evaluates thyroid gland function. The percentage of the radionuclide (radioactive iodine) absorbed over time provides information about hyperthyroidism and hypothyroidism. Hyperthyroidism is indicated by an increased absorption of the radionuclide, and hypothyroidism results in a decreased absorption rate.

The patient is instructed to fast the evening before the test. At the time of the scan the radionuclide can be administered orally or intravenously. Scans are taken at two-, six-, and twenty-four-hour intervals. The percentage of radioactive iodine uptake is the amount found in the thyroid as a portion of the total amount given to the patient. Normal ranges for RAIU vary according to the health agency because the normal consumption of iodine, which impacts the results of the test, varies in each community. Contraindications for radioactive iodine uptake scans include pregnancy, recent radionuclide exams, thyroid medications, and any x-ray exam using a contrast medium.

Normal Range

1–12% absorption after 2 hours

5–20% absorption after 6 hours

15– 40% absorption after 24 hours

Variations from Normal. Percentages above the normal range for each interval indicate hyperthyroidism, and decreased percentages are related to hypothyroidism.

Interfering Circumstances. The patient must be cooperative and must be able to maintain the desired position for the scan. Certain drugs and food may alter the results of the RAIU.

Thyroid-Stimulating Hormone (TSH) Test

The **thyroid stimulating hormone (TSH) test,** also called the TSH stimulation test, is a radionuclide laboratory test that measures thyroid gland response to the administration of thyroid stimulating hormone. This laboratory test is often done in combination with the radioactive iodine uptake study. Combining these tests allows the clinician to differentiate between primary and secondary hypothyroidism.

The patient is prepared for the scan by receiving an intramuscular injection of thyroid stimulating hormone. After injection, the patient is placed in a supine position with the head hyperextended and a baseline scan is completed. A second injection of TSH is administered along with an oral radionuclide containing iodine. Scanning is performed in the first two to six hours and again at twenty-four hours after the administration of the radionuclide. Thyroid gland absorption of the radioactive nuclide is an indication of the gland's response to TSH stimulation. Contraindications for this thyroid scan are similar to those discussed in previous thyroid scans.

Normal Findings. Demonstration of an appropriate increase in thyroid function after the administration of thyroid stimulating hormone.

Variations from Normal. The TSH test is used to differentiate between primary hypothyroidism and secondary hypothyroidism. In primary hypothyroidism, also called **thyroidal hypothyroidism,** the thyroid gland no longer functions and, therefore, does not respond to the intramuscular TSH as demonstrated by a low uptake of the radioactive iodine. In secondary hypothyroidism, or **hypothalamic-pituitary hypothyroidism,** the thyroid gland response to the TSH injection is demonstrated by an abnormal increase in uptake of radioactive iodine.

Interfering Circumstances. The patient must be cooperative and must be able to maintain the desired posture for the scan. Certain drugs and food may negatively impact the results of the TSH test. Other recent tests involving the use of radionuclides may affect TSH test results.

Parathyroid Scan

A **parathyroid scan** is a radionuclide scan of the parathyroid gland performed to assess the size, position, function, and location of parathyroid glands or tissue. This scan helps identify parathyroid adenomas and locate unusually placed parathyroid glands or tissue prior to surgery. The function of both the parathyroid and thyroid gland can be evaluated by measuring the radionuclide absorption of each of these glands.

The patient is prepared for the parathyroid scan in the same manner as the thyroid scan. The parathyroid scan involves individual intravenous administration of two distinct radionuclides: one that targets the parathyroid gland and another for the thyroid gland. Each injection of a radionuclide is followed by a scan of the neck and mediastinum. If each gland absorbs the appropriate radionuclide, both thyroid and parathyroid gland functioning is normal. Pregnancy is the contraindication for this scan, unless testing is essential to maternal welfare.

Normal Findings. Normal size, position, function, and number of parathyroid glands. Normal radionuclide uptake in both thyroid and parathyroid glands.

Variations from Normal. A parathyroid scan provides a differential diagnosis between hyperplasia and adenoma. Abnormally placed glands are also identified.

Interfering Circumstances. The patient must be cooperative and able to maintain the desired posture for the examination. Thyroid medications may affect the results of the scan. Other recent diagnostic testing using iodine agents may alter the reliability of the parathyroid scan.

Radionuclide Scans of the Chest

Radionuclide scans of the chest include heart and lung scans that provide information regarding the organs' structure and function. The heart (cardiac) scans covered in this section are the thallium stress tests and the multigated acquisition scan. The lung scans include the pulmonary perfusion scan and pulmonary ventilation scan. Indications, contraindications, and diseases associated with each study are also presented.

Heart (Cardiac) Scans

Heart (cardiac) scans included in this section are the **thallium stress tests**, assessments of coronary perfusion; and the **multigated acquisition (MUGA) scan**, a technique used to evaluate heart function and wall motion. Each of these tests provides valuable diagnostic information about heart structure and function without surgical intervention. The advent of cardiac scanning techniques has given clinicians important tools for the identification of heart disease.

Thallium Stress Tests

Thallium stress tests are radionuclide scans of the heart that are useful in the assessment of coronary perfusion, the patency of bypass blood vessels, the presence of coronary artery disease, and the effectiveness of medical interventions such as medications and angioplasty.

The patient is prepared for this exam by having an ECG monitor attached to the chest and a blood pressure cuff placed on the arm. The patient is then placed on a treadmill and exercises until obtaining a maximum heart rate. At that time, the radionuclide thallium is injected intravenously, the patient is placed in a supine position, and the scan is performed. The scan is usually repeated approximately four hours later to assess the redistribution of the radionuclide. The scans are then analyzed by computer and appropriate photographic records are developed. SPECT scanning, which provides a three-dimensional image of the physiology of the heart, may also be performed.

Chemical stress testing is available for individuals with physical limitations that prevent them from doing the treadmill exercises. Medications are administered that stress the heart in the same manner as exercise, and thallium scanning is then performed. Chemical stress tests are know as **persantine-thallium stress tests,** also called **dipyridamole-thallium stress tests,** and **dobutamine-thallium stress tests.**

Although thallium stress testing is a safe procedure, the patient must be carefully monitored for severe dyspnea, changes in blood pressure, exhaustion, ECG changes, or angina. Chemical stress tests present additional concerns because of potential adverse reactions to the drugs given to stress the heart. Patients with ventricular hypertrophy, right and left bundle block, and hypokalemia should not participate in thallium stress testing. Pregnancy is a contraindication for stress testing.

Normal Findings. Normal coronary perfusion.

Variations from Normal. Thallium stress tests can reveal coronary artery disease, ischemic disease, myocardial infarction, and cardiac hypertrophy.

Interfering Circumstances. The patient must be cooperative and must be able to hold the desired posture for the examination. Recent nuclear scans and certain drugs can negatively affect thallium stress test results.

Multigated Acquisition (MUGA) Scan

The multigated acquisition (MUGA) scan is a radionuclide study of heart function. MUGA scans are performed while the heart is in motion so that images of heart contraction and relaxation can be recorded. Heart wall motion, ejection fraction, stroke volumes, ventricular function, and cardiac output can be evaluated with this study. ECG signals, recorded during the MUGA scan, are coordinated with the imager and computer so that images can be taken in timed segments called gates.

The MUGA scan may include the following: two separate intravenous injections of radionuclide agents, administration of sublingual nitroglycerin to analyze its effect on ventricular function, and exercise on a bicycle to include stress testing. During the MUGA scan, the radionuclide is observed as it passes through the cardiac cycle. Results are recorded and analyzed by the computer and photographic recordings are made. MUGA scans are safe procedures but require the same observation of the patient as other radionuclide heart scans. Women who are pregnant or nursing should not be considered candidates for this scan.

Normal Findings. Normal wall motion, ejection fraction, cardiac output, and normal cardiac responses to rest, stress, and nitroglycerin.

Variations from Normal. MUGA scans are useful in diagnosing abnormalities such as congestive heart failure, valvular heart disease, cardiomyopathy, and ventricular aneurysm.

Interfering Circumstances. The patient must be able to cooperate and maintain the desired posture for the examination. Medications that affect blood flow may affect MUGA scan results.

Lung Scans

Lung scans are radionuclide studies of the pulmonary system that are performed to assess pulmonary perfusion and pulmonary ventilation. Pulmonary perfusion is related to the blood flow throughout the lungs, and pulmonary ventilation refers to the patency of pulmonary airways. Ventilation also encompasses the air exchange between alveolar spaces and the atmosphere. The **pulmonary perfusion scan**, which requires the use of an intravenous radionuclide, is used to identify areas of the lung where the blood flow is restricted. The **pulmonary ventilation scan**, which utilizes an inhaled radionuclide, can be used to assess the patency of pulmonary airways, and to detect areas of the lung where there is decreased air or gas exchange at the alveolar level.

The perfusion scan is performed to identify pulmonary embolism. A lung ventilation scan is done at the same time in order to differentiate between pulmonary embolism and other pulmonary diseases. When the perfusion scan identifies restricted blood flow and the ventilation scan is normal, embolus is the diagnosis of choice. On the other hand, when both the perfusion scan and the ventilation scan have abnormal results in the same area of the lung, a parenchymal disease is suspected. Parenchymal diseases are disorders of organ tissue and cells.

The perfusion and ventilation scans can be done together, with the ventilation scan done prior to the perfusion study. The ventilation scan is performed with the patient in a sitting position and the radionuclide is inhaled as a gas via a mask. The patient sits still while the scanner takes images over the posterior lung regions of the back. For the perfusion scan the patient is placed into a supine position and injected with an intravenous radionuclide. The patient must remain still while scanning is done from a number of different positions. Lung scanning is a safe procedure with few risks. Pregnant women, however, may not be suitable candidates for this scan.

Normal Findings. Normal perfusion and ventilation of the lungs.

Variations from Normal. Lung scans are most useful for the identification of pulmonary embolism. Tumors, chronic obstructive pulmonary disease, pneumonia, atelectasis, asthma, bronchitis, emphysema, asthma, and tuberculosis are best visualized with a conventional chest x-ray.

Interfering Circumstances. The patient must be cooperative and maintain the desired posture for the examination. Other nuclear examinations may alter the results of the lung scan. Since several lung abnormalities can produce similar perfusion study results, this test alone has limitations for the diagnosis of specific disease. A conventional chest x-ray helps confirm the presence or absence of underlying pulmonary disease.

Radionuclide Scans of the Abdomen

Radionuclide scans of the abdomen include gallbladder and biliary system scans, gastric emptying scans, gastrointestinal bleeding scans, gastrointestinal reflux scans, kidney scans, liver scans, and spleen scans. Indications and contraindications are presented, as well as diseases associated with each study.

Gallbladder and Biliary System Scan

The **gallbladder** and **biliary system scan** is a radionuclide study of the gallbladder, and the hepatic, cystic, and common bile ducts. The scan is performed to identify diseases of the gallbladder and biliary tree, and to assess the patency of the hepatic, cystic, and biliary ducts. A radionuclide is administered intravenously and excreted by the liver into the biliary tree. As the radionuclide passes through the biliary system, scans are performed and images are recorded.

Fluid and food are restricted several hours before the test. The patient is placed in a supine position and the intravenous radionuclide is administered. Scanning of the upper right quadrant of the abdomen is begun immediately and a series of timed images is taken. Depending upon the purpose of the scan, the patient may be given a fatty meal or medications during the scanning procedure. Although this procedure is considered safe, pregnant and nursing women should not be candidates for gallbladder and biliary system scans.

Normal Findings. Normal gallbladder, size, shape, and function and patency of the hepatic, cystic, and common bile ducts are demonstrated during the scan.

Variations from Normal. The gallbladder and biliary system scan is useful in the diagnosis of acute or chronic cholecystitis and obstruction of the cystic and common bile ducts caused by gallstones or tumors.

Interfering Circumstances. The patient must be able to cooperate and remain in the desired posture for the examination. This scan may produce unreliable results if the patient has not eaten for more than twenty-four hours.

Gastric Emptying Scan

The **gastric emptying scan** is a radionuclide study of the ability of the stomach to empty solids and fluids. This study is useful in diagnosing gastric motility abnormalities that interfere with the ability of the stomach to empty its contents in a timely manner.

The patient is scanned after eating a special test meal that includes the radionuclides used for the scan. Once the meal has been ingested, the abdomen is scanned in both the sitting and supine positions. Gastric emptying time is measured by the computerized scanning system and calculations of the emptying time are analyzed. Slow emptying of stomach contents indicates gastric impairment and rapid emptying indicates gastric hypermotility. Although this procedure is considered safe, women who are pregnant may not be candidates for the gastric emptying scan.

Normal Findings. Gastric emptying of the test meal occurs within the expected time frame. Approximately 50% of the ingested meal should clear in ninety minutes.

Variations from Normal. Gastric emptying scans can identify abnormalities such as gastric obstructions resulting from tumors or peptic ulcers, nonfunctioning anastomosis, and neuropathy or diabetic gastroparesis.

Diseases that cause rapid emptying, such as malabsorption syndrome and Zollinger-Ellison syndrome, can be diagnosed using this scan.

Interfering Circumstances. Patients must be cooperative and able to maintain the desired posture for the examination. Noncompliance with pretest food, fluid, and medication restrictions can alter the results of this test.

Gastrointestinal Bleeding Scan

The **gastrointestinal bleeding scan** is a radionuclide study of the upper and lower gastrointestinal tract performed for the purpose of locating the site of gastrointestinal bleeding. Identification of a hemorrhage site prior to surgery is another indication for this scan. The GI bleeding scan can detect bleeding sites in other abdominal organs and in the lungs. Failure of gastroscopy, colonoscopy, or other endoscopic procedures to identify bleeding sites may indicate the need for a gastrointestinal bleeding scan. Figure 11-1 is an example of a gastrointestinal bleeding scan report.

PATIENT NAME: GERVAIS, ERIK

MEDICAL RECORD NUMBER: 00-00-07

STUDY: Gastrointestinal bleeding scan.

RADIONUCLIDE: Technetium-99m.

INDICATIONS: Suspected lower GI bleed.

REPORT: Dynamic vascular perfusion study and subsequent serial images of the abdominal area show continuous accumulation of radionuclide activity in the rectal region indicative of active bleeding. There are multiple foci of abnormal increased radionuclide activity in the proximal transverse colon, splenic flexure, descending, and sigmoid colon. The finding could be due to different foci of active bleeding probably due to rupture of diverticula. Colonoscopy correlation is recommended.

IMPRESSION: Active bleeding from the colon.

Figure 11-1. Gastrointestinal bleeding scan report

The gastrointestinal bleeding scan is carried out with the patient in the supine position. A sample of the patient's blood is taken, and the radionuclide is added or "tagged" to the blood. The blood, with the attached radionuclide, is readministered intravenously and the scanning process is initiated and executed at regular intervals. Both the upper and lower gastrointestinal tract are scanned depending upon the initial findings. If the bleed is extremely slow, scanning may continue intermittently for a twenty-four-hour period. This procedure is consider safe, but women who are pregnant or nursing should not be candidates for the scan. Patients with gastrointestinal hemorrhage may be unstable due to their medical condition and require close observation.

Normal Findings. No evidence of gastrointestinal bleeding.

Variations from Normal. The gastrointestinal bleeding scan is useful in identifying the site of the hemorrhage. Conditions that cause GI bleeding and that may be identified with this scan include tumors, ulcers, diverticula, polyps, angiodysplasia, and inflammatory bowel disease.

Gastrointestinal Reflux Scan

The **gastrointestinal reflux scan**, also called the **gastroesophageal reflux scan**, is a radionuclide study of the esophagus and stomach. Indications for this scan are symptoms associated with gastric reflux, which may include heartburn, vomiting, aspiration, regurgitation, or dysphagia. The gastrointestinal reflux scan may encompass scanning the lungs when aspiration of gastric contents presents a concern. In cases of suspected aspiration, the radionuclide is administered with the evening meal. The patient remains in the supine position until scanning is performed the following day. A gastric emptying scan may be performed at the same time as the reflux scan.

Prior to the scan, the patient is instructed to eat a full meal. At the beginning of the scan, the patient is given a drink containing the radionuclide. For infants, the radionuclide is added to the formula. Individuals who cannot swallow the radionuclide may have it administered through a gastrointestinal tube. The patient is placed in different positions during the scan in order to discern if the gastric reflux is positional.

During the procedure a compression binder is placed on the abdomen and inflated to increase pressure on the abdomen. The scanning system then records the amount of gastric reflux associated with various levels of pressure on the stomach.

Although the gastrointestinal reflux scan is considered safe, women who are pregnant or breast-feeding are not good candidates for this procedure. In addition, persons who have conditions that prevent the use of the compression binder should not be scanned.

Normal Findings. The test fluids pass through the esophagus and remain in the stomach without reflux into the esophagus or lungs.

Variations from Normal. Gastrointestinal reflux scans can identify disorders such as gastric reflux and pulmonary aspiration. Esophageal spasms and achalasia, the inability of the cardiac sphincter muscle of the stomach to relax, can be detected with this scan.

Interfering Circumstances. The patient must be cooperative and able to maintain the desired posture for the examination.

Kidney Scan

Kidney scans, also called renal scans, are radionuclide studies of the size, shape, and function of the kidney. The kidney scan may be done to evaluate renal structure, function, and blood flow; renal excretory function; and glomerular filtration rates.

The type of information obtained from the scan varies according to the purpose of the scan and the radionuclide used. Specific kidney structures are sensitive to different radionuclides. For example, one radionuclide may be used to scan the structure of the kidney, another to assess the glomerulus and glomerular filtration rate, and a third radionuclide may be necessary to assess tubular secretion.

In addition to assessing glomerular and tubular function, kidney structure, perfusion, and excretion can be evaluated by a **triple renal scan**. The triple renal scan is accomplished by intravenous administration of two radionuclides. Scanned images display kidney structure and perfusion. Kidney excretory function is evaluated by measuring the time it takes for the radionuclide to move through the renal cortex and renal pelvis.

During the scanning procedure the patient may be placed in a supine, prone, or sitting position. A diuretic may be administered intravenously in order to encourage sufficient urinary output during the imaging process. Although the kidney scan is considered safe, pregnant women should not be candidates for this procedure.

Normal Findings. Normal kidney size, shape, and function. Absence of evidence of disease.

Variations from Normal. The kidney scan is useful in diagnosing renal infarction, infection, and inflammatory disease. Glomerulonephritis, pyelonephritis, abscesses, and cysts can be identified by renal scans. Abnormal size, shape, and congenital anomalies such as a horseshoe shaped kidney show up on a kidney scan.

Thrombosis or stenosis of renal blood vessels and nonfunctioning kidneys are other diagnoses identified by radionuclide scans. Kidney scans are valuable for assessing transplanted kidneys for rejection and evaluating kidney will damage after trauma.

Interfering Circumstances. The patient must be cooperative and able to maintain the desired posture for the procedure. Antihypertensive medications affect scan results.

Liver Scan

The **liver scan** is a radionuclide study of the size, shape, and function of the liver. Liver and spleen scans are done together since the same radionuclide is used for each study. Indications for liver scan include differentiating between primary and metastatic liver cancer, identifying various liver diseases, and evaluating liver damage caused by drugs, trauma, or radiation therapy.

Preparation for a liver scan includes intravenous administration of the radionuclide. There are no food or fluid restrictions. The patient is placed in the supine position and the right upper quadrant of the abdomen is scanned. Static images and flow images, which show the distribution of the radionuclide, are made in order to assess the size, shape, and function of the liver. SPECT imaging is also done to provide three-dimensional images. Although liver scans are considered safe, pregnant women should not be considered candidates for this procedure.

Normal Findings. Normal size, shape, position, and function of the liver. Absence of evidence of disease.

Variations from Normal. Diseases such as hepatitis, cirrhosis, ascites, and hepatomegaly are detected via liver scans. Benign tumors, abscesses, and cystic lesions are revealed using a liver scan. Primary and metastatic tumors can be differentiated by assessing radionuclide uptake patterns.

Interfering Circumstances. The patient must be cooperative and maintain the desired posture for the examination. Barium remaining in the gastrointestinal tract may alter the results of the liver scan.

Spleen Scan

The **spleen scan** is a radionuclide study of the size, shape, and function of the spleen. Spleen scans identify abnormalities, tumors, obstructions, and cancer. Spleen trauma, rupture, and the impact on the spleen of lymphoma and leukemia can be assessed via nuclear medicine scans of the spleen.

The procedure for the spleen scan is the same as that described under liver scan. Both static and flow images are produced, and SPECT imaging of the spleen may also be performed. Although considered safe, pregnant women are not candidates for this procedure.

Normal Findings. Normal size, shape, position, and function of the spleen, and an absence of evidence of disease.

Variations from Normal. Diagnoses revealed by spleen scan include splenomegaly, splenic infarction or inflammation, and a ruptured spleen. Tumors, abscesses, hematomas, leukemia, and Hodgkin's disease are identified via spleen scanning.

Interfering Circumstances. The patient must be cooperative and maintain the desired posture for the examination. Barium remaining in the gastrointestinal tract may alter test results.

Miscellaneous Radionuclide Scans

Miscellaneous radionuclide scans cover the following: **scrotal scan**, a study of the testes and other contents of the scrotal sac; **bone scan**, a radionuclide study of the skeleton; and **gallium-67 scan**, a nuclear medicine study of the entire body.

Scrotal Scan

A scrotal scan, also known as a **testicular scan**, is a radionuclide study of the contents of the scrotal sac, including the testes, epididymis, and spermatic cord. Indications for scrotal scans are assessment of acute pain and swelling of the testicles, evaluation of scrotal and testicular damage caused by trauma or injury, and identification of abnormalities of the scrotum and its contents.

The patient is placed in a supine position and the radionuclide is administered intravenously. The penis is secured with tape to the lower abdomen. Both blood flow imaging and organ imaging are done to evaluate the blood flow pattern of the scrotum and the distribution of the radionuclide throughout the scrotal area.

Scrotal scanning is considered to be a safe procedure with no risks to the patient. Children undergoing a scrotal scan are usually accompanied by an adult.

Normal Findings. Normal blood flow and structures of the scrotum and scrotal contents. Absence of evidence of disease.

Variations from Normal. The scrotal scan is used to diagnose epididymitis, orchitis, hydrocele, and varicocele. Testicular and spermatic cord torsion, benign or malignant tumors, and hematomas can be revealed via scrotal scanning.

Interfering Circumstances. The patient must be cooperative and maintain the desired posture for the scan.

Bone Scan

Bone scans are radionuclide studies of the skeleton. In normal skeletal tissue there is a uniform uptake of the radionuclide that indicates the usual pattern of bone metabolism. Areas of the skeleton that show a higher concentration of radionuclide uptake, a hot spot, may be involved in an abnormality or disease of bone tissue. However, some skeletal areas that normally have an increased uptake of the radionuclide include the sternum, clavicle, scapular joints, and sacroiliac. Figure 11-2 is a bone scan that shows an increased uptake of the radionuclide.

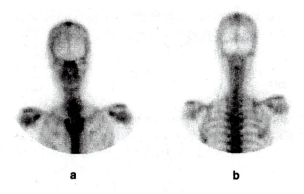

a   b

Figure 11-2.   Bone scan of the head, shoulder, and upper spine: **(a)** anterior view, **(b)** posterior view

Bone scans are usually performed to detect the presence of cancer in the bone, usually metastatic, since cancer in other organs metastasizes to the bone. Bone scans are useful in the diagnosis of abnormalities such as fractures not found by x-ray, arthritis, tumors, osteomyelitis, and degeneration of the bones and joints.

With the patient in the supine position, the radionuclide is administered intravenously. Blood flow imaging is done shortly after the administration of the radionuclide, with static imaging performed after a period of two hours or more. Total skeletal scanning is done when the patient is suspected of having metastatic cancer. SPECT scanning may be used to provide a three-dimensional image. A photographic record is made of the scan. Although bone scanning is considered a safe procedure, women who are pregnant or nursing should not be considered for this procedure.

Normal Findings.   No evidence of abnormality.

Variations from Normal.   Diseases such as osteomyelitis, Paget's disease, fractures, cysts, and arthritis can be identified via bone scans. Metastatic versus primary cancer can be determined. Both Paget's disease of the bone and Perthes' disease are revealed with bone scans.

Interfering Circumstances.   The patient must be cooperative and maintain the desired posture for the scan. The patient should be requested to void, because a full bladder can prevent clear imaging of the pelvis. A bone scan is not a reliable diagnostic study in patients who have multiple myeloma.

Gallium-67 Scan

Gallium-67 scans are radionuclide studies of the entire body that are performed to identify infection, inflammation, tumors, and abscesses. This scan can assist in staging lymphomas, including Hodgkin's disease, and evaluating the effectiveness of cancer treatments. The name of the scan is taken from the radionuclide used during the study. Gallium-67, once injected into the body, distributes itself throughout most of the blood and tissue of the body. A higher than normal uptake of gallium-67 is indicative of some type of abnormality. Some organs, such as the liver, spleen, bone, and colon, normally retain more gallium than other organs or tissue. Gallium uptake in these organs is much less concentrated than the uptake in areas of pathology.

Patient preparation includes a thorough cleansing of the bowel with cathartics and enemas. The presence of stool may lead to an increase in the uptake of the radionuclide by the bowel. Gallium is administered intravenously six or more hours prior to initiating the scan so that the gallium can disperse throughout the body. During the actual scan, the patient is placed in the supine position, the entire body is scanned, and photographic images are recorded. The scan can be repeated at six, twenty-four, forty-eight, and seventy-two hours after injection of the radionuclide. Although gallium-67 scans are considered safe, pregnant women are usually not candidates for the scan.

Normal Findings. Normal or expected distribution of the radionuclide throughout the body. Absence of evidence of pathology.

Variations from Normal. Gallium scanning detects lymphomas and carcinomas of the gastrointestinal tract, kidneys, uterus, stomach, and testicles. Metastatic and primary tumors of the brain, lung, liver, and bone can be diagnosed with gallium scans.

Interfering Circumstances. The patient must be cooperative and maintain the desired posture for the exam. Patients receiving antineoplastic drugs may have unreliable scanning results.

Summary

- Nuclear medicine involves the use of radionuclides that are test and organ specific, and are administered orally or intravenously.
- Scanners are used to take pictures of the uptake of the radionuclide by the body organ or tissue.
- Radionuclide scans identify abnormalities because the radionuclide concentration or uptake in abnormal organs and tissue is different than the uptake exhibited by normal organs and tissue.
- Areas of higher radionuclide concentration appear darker on the scanned image and are called hot spots.
- Areas of lower radionuclide concentration appear lighter on the scanned image and are called cold spots.
- The most common contraindication for radionuclide studies is pregnancy.
- Radionuclide scans of the head and neck include studies of cerebrospinal fluid flow, thyroid, and parathyroid glands.
- Additional thyroid gland studies are the iodine-131 scan, the radioactive iodine uptake test, and the thyroid stimulating hormone test.
- Nuclear scans of the chest include studies of the lungs and heart. Pulmonary perfusion and pulmonary ventilation scans are the lung scans. Heart studies include the thallium stress test and the MUGA scan.
- Scans of the abdomen include studies of the gallbladder, liver, pancreas, spleen, and kidneys. Gastric emptying, gastrointestinal bleeding, and gastrointestinal reflux scans are also associated with abdominal radionuclide tests.
- Miscellaneous radionuclide scans include scrotal scans, a study of the scrotum and contents of the scrotal sac; gallium-67 scans, which are total body scans; and bone scanning, a radionuclide study of the skeletal system.

CHAPTER REVIEW

1. Briefly describe the structures examined by the listed radionuclide studies. Provide examples of the diseases that can be diagnosed by these studies.

   a. Cerebrospinal fluid flow scan _____

   b. Iodine-131 scan _____

   c. Kidney scan _____

   d. Liver scan _____

   e. Parathyroid scan _____

   f. Perfusion scan _____

   g. Radioactive iodine uptake test _____

   h. Spleen scan _____

   i. Thyroid scan _____

   j. Thyroid stimulating hormone test _____

   k. Pulmonary ventilation scan _____

2. Organize the diseases according to the following cardiac radionuclide scan:

   a. Thallium stress test _____

   b. Multigated acquisition (MUGA) scan _____

   cardiac hypertrophy   myocardial infarction
   congestive heart failure   valvular heart disease
   coronary artery disease   ventricular aneurysm
   ischemic heart disease

3. Briefly describe the cardiac scans listed below. Explain the differences between the exams. Include the specific cardiac characteristics identified by each scan.

   a. Thallium stress test   _____

   b. Multigated acquisition (MUGA) scan   _____

4. What are radionuclides? How are they used in nuclear medicine scans?

5. Describe uptake, hot spots, and cold spots as they relate to nuclear medicine studies.

Case Studies

1. Anna Salberg, a 45-year-old woman, is suspected of having hypothyroidism. Dr. Johnston, her physician, has ordered a TSH test. Describe the TSH test. How is it performed? What information concerning the thyroid will this test provide?

2. You are reviewing the record of Russ Walker, a 58-year-old man with a family history of heart disease. He has just been admitted with chest pain. Dr. Ruby Wilbert, a cardiologist, has noted and ordered a thallium stress test for Mr. Walker. Why do you think Dr. Wilbert chose this particular test? What is involved with this study? If Mr. Walker cannot complete the treadmill portion of the test, what impact will that have on the test results?

3. Victoria Andrews, a 67-year-old female who has been on steroid therapy for several months, is complaining about pain in the right hip. Traditional x-rays have failed to identify the problem with the hip. Dr. James Longfellow has decided to order a bone scan. Why could a bone scan be useful in this situation? What abnormal conditions can be detected with this exam?

Challenge Activity

> Write a comparative essay that discusses the advantages and disadvantages of conventional x-ray techniques, with and without contrast medium; magnetic resonance imaging; and nuclear medicine scans.

Chapter 12

Endoscopy Studies

Key Terms, Abbreviations, and Acronyms

amnioscopy

arthroscopy

bronchoscopy

colonoscopy

colposcope

colposcopy

culdoscopy

cystometrogram, CMG

cystoscopy

cystourethrogram

duodenoscopy

endoscopic retrograde
cholangiopancreatography,
ERCP

esophagogastroduodenoscopy,
EGD

esophagoscopy

fetoscopy

gastroscopy

gynecologic laparoscopy

laparoscopy

mediastinoscopy

pelviscopy

peritoneoscopy

proctoscopy

sigmoidoscopy

thoracoscopy

transesophageal
echocardiography, TEE

urethra pressure profile

urodynamic studies

uroflowmetry

Learning Objectives

Upon completion of this chapter, the learner should be able to:

1. Briefly describe the purpose of and the structures involved in each endoscopic study.
2. Discuss the indications and contraindications for each endoscopic study.
3. Identify complications associated with each specific endoscopic procedure.
4. Relate specific diagnoses and treatment interventions to specific endoscopic studies.
5. Organize endoscopic studies according to the organ or system being evaluated.
6. Describe the advantages of endoscopic procedures in relation to surgical interventions.

Introduction

Endoscopic studies cover a range of diagnostic procedures in which an endoscope is inserted into body cavities or organs through a natural body orifice or surgical incision. The endoscopic studies in this chapter include a selection of the more frequently ordered exams such as **colonoscopy**, an endoscopic examination of the colon, as well as unique studies such as **fetoscopy**, an intrauterine endoscopic examination of the fetus. Information for each examination includes a brief description of the procedure, the body cavity and organs studied, indications and/or contraindications for the procedure, diseases that can be identified via the procedure, and factors that interfere with the results or prevent the use of the particular endoscopic procedure.

Overview of Endoscopic Studies

Endoscopic studies, also called endoscopic procedures, are an important tool in the diagnosis and treatment of human pathology and disease. Endoscopic studies allow the physician to examine internal organs and body cavities without subjecting the patient to a surgical intervention. The endoscope itself has been greatly improved, and current scopes provide for the visualization of nearly all internal bodily structures.

Early endoscopes were rigid, inflexible instruments with a simple lighting system. Examinations were limited to those body cavities that were easily accessible. Current advances in science, computers, lasers, and electronics have resulted in the development of highly sophisticated endoscopic instruments that utilize flexible nylon materials and fiberoptic technology. While rigid endoscopes are still in use, most endoscopes consist of flexible fiberoptic scopes that can be inserted into smaller body organs and cavities. The flexible scopes are capable of projecting images around curves, thereby shedding light on previously inaccessible body structures. Figure 12-1 identifies the location of several endoscopic procedures.

Endoscopes are designed for and named after the body cavity or organ being visualized. The cystoscope is designed to visualize the bladder, the laparoscope enters the abdominal wall or pelvic cavity, and the bronchoscope is used to access the bronchial tree and lungs. Endoscopes vary in length, size, and diameter, and are designed to perform a range of functions. In addition to visualizing organs and cavities, the endoscope may be equipped with ports that are used to obtain biopsy specimens; remove foreign bodies; administer medications; suction fluids; perform coagulation to control bleeding; remove tumors, cysts, and stones; and record findings through the use of photography.

Endoscopic studies are invasive procedures and have potential risks to the patient. Endoscopic examinations are usually performed in special endoscopy units, operating rooms, or other comparably equipped environments, by physicians who have specialized in the treatment of diseases related to the organs being studied. Patient preparation for these procedures may include topical, local, or general anesthesia. The patient is often awake for the endoscopic procedure, but is sedated to the point of being relieved of the pain, discomfort, and anxiety that may accompany endoscopy. Children may require general anesthesia more frequently than adults.

Although the risks related to endoscopic procedures are relatively low, there are complications that can occur with any type of endoscopic intervention. The physical condition of the patient, the type of procedure being performed, and the skill of the physician performing the examination are factors that contribute to the potential for complications, which include perforation of a body structure by the endoscope itself, adverse reaction to anesthetic or sedation medications, loss of blood from a biopsy or other

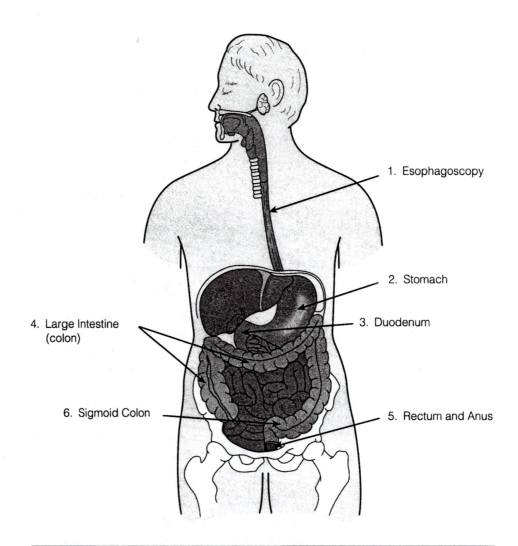

Figure 12-1. Location of several endoscopic procedures: (1) esophagoscopy; (2) stomach; (3) duodenum; (4) large intestine (colon); (5) rectum and anus; (6) sigmoid colon

surgical interventions, and infection. Complication prevention and management is a major concern for all individuals involved with endoscopic procedures.

Endoscopic Studies of the Thoracic Cavity

Endoscopic studies of the thoracic cavity include procedures that examine organs and body tissue located in the thoracic region. These studies are **bronchoscopy**, an endoscopic study of the bronchial tree; **mediastinoscopy**, an endoscopic examination of the mediastinal lymph nodes; **thoracoscopy**, a study of the thoracic cavity; and **transesophageal echocardiography (TEE)**, an endoscopic study of the heart.

Bronchoscopy

The bronchoscopy is a direct visualization of the larynx, trachea, and bronchi. This exam is usually performed with a flexible bronchoscope that allows for the visualization of all structures, including the smaller bronchi. A rigid bronchoscope can be used to visualize the larger bronchi and to suction large amounts of blood or other secretions. Both rigid and flexible bronchoscopes can be used to remove foreign bodies. Foods and fluids are usually withheld for six to eight hours prior to the procedure.

Bronchoscopy is usually performed under local anesthesia, which is sprayed or swabbed onto the back of the throat. The patient may also receive sedation to assist in the toleration of the procedure. The patient is usually placed in a sitting or supine position and the bronchoscope is inserted into the bronchial tree through the nose, mouth, or tracheotomy tube, if necessary.

Upon insertion of the scope, the physician is able to visualize the condition of the larynx, trachea, bronchi, bronchioles, and alveoli. The physician is also able to perform biopsies, aspirate fluids, remove obstructions, stage bronchogenic carcinoma, diagnose diseases, and perform surgical or other therapeutic interventions.

Contraindications for bronchoscopy include severe hypoxemia, severe carbon dioxide retention, bleeding disorders, certain cardiac conditions, and obstruction or stenosis of the trachea. Complications related to bronchoscopy are shock, pneumothorax, bronchospasm, infection, cardiac irregularities, seizures, bleeding from a biopsy, and medication reactions.

Normal Findings. Normal-appearing structure and lining of larynx, trachea, bronchi and alveoli.

Variations from Normal. Abnormal conditions such as abscesses, tumors, carcinoma, blockages, foreign bodies, and inflammation can be discovered through a bronchoscopy exam. Bronchoscopy examination can also be used to identify tuberculosis, bronchitis, *Pneumocystis carinii*, and a variety of fungal infections. Traumatic injury, and injury related to the inhalation of smoke or other harmful substances, can be assessed through the use of the bronchoscope.

Interfering Circumstances. Circumstances that interfere with bronchoscopic examinations are the inability to cooperate when the exam is done under local anesthesia with sedation, and failure to comply with pretest dietary and fluid restrictions.

Mediastinoscopy

Mediastinoscopy is an examination of the mediastinal lymph nodes and body structures located under the sternum and near the lungs. The trachea, esophagus, and heart can also be evaluated with this procedure. The mediastinoscopy is performed under general anesthesia and the mediastinoscope is inserted into a small incision made at the suprasternal notch. From this position the physician is able to visualize, palpate, and biopsy the mediastinal lymph nodes. Since the mediastinal lymph nodes receive drainage from the lungs, the evaluation of these nodes can help identify diseases of the lungs and thoracic region. The mediastinoscopy is also used to stage bronchiogenic carcinoma.

Mediastinoscopy involves a surgical procedure and carries the risks associated with surgery and the use of a general anesthesia. Patients are prepared in the same manner as any other surgical intervention and are carefully monitored during and after the procedure to assure that complications are prevented or minimized. Possible complications from the procedure include pneumothorax, tracheal perforation, puncture of the blood vessels or organs (i.e., esophagus), infection, and laryngeal tear damage. Scarring from previous mediastinoscopy is a contraindication for this examination.

Normal Findings. Normal mediastinal structure, normal lymph glands and gland tissue.

Variations from Normal. Diseases such as tuberculosis, Hodgkin's disease, lymphoma, sarcoidosis, and histoplasmosis can be diagnosed through the use of mediastinoscopy.

Interfering Circumstances. Interfering circumstances specifically related to mediastinoscopy have not been identified.

Thoracoscopy

Thoracoscopy is an endoscopic procedure that is used to examine the thoracic cavity and allows the physician to visualize the thoracic walls, pleura, pleural spaces, pericardium, and mediastinum. This is one of the more complex endoscopic examinations, is a surgical intervention, and requires the administration of local or general anesthesia. The endoscope is passed into the thoracic cavity by way of a small incision made in the chest wall. During the exam the lung at the site of the procedure is collapsed and then reinflated after the thoracoscopy is completed. Severely compromised respiratory function is the chief contraindication for this endoscopic procedure.

Thoracoscopy is performed to biopsy tissue and to evaluate pleural effusion, inflammation, tumor growth, metastasis within the thoracic cavity, emphysema, and other chronic lung diseases. This procedure is also utilized for the resection of small malignancies and for performing laser surgeries. Thorascopic examination can preclude the need for thoracotomy, which involves an even greater surgical intervention. Complications associated with thoracoscopy are atelectasis, aspiration, hemorrhage, empyema, and respiratory distress.

Normal Findings. Normal appearance of organs and tissues examined in the thoracic cavity.

Variations from Normal. Thoracoscopy can be used to identify plural effusion, inflammatory processes, infectious diseases, and tissue damage that can cause bleeding. Specific diagnoses include empyema, tuberculosis, carcinoma, and cancer metastasis.

Transesophageal Echocardiography (TEE)

Transesophageal echocardiography (TEE), a procedure that uses both endoscopic and ultrasonic techniques, is performed in order to evaluate cardiac structure and function. Local anesthetic is applied to the patient's pharyngeal region and a TEE-scope or probe equipped with a transducer is inserted through the esophagus. The scope can be rotated in different directions, which allows ultrasonic images to be taken from behind the heart. Intravenous sedation may be administered to provide comfort to the patient during the procedure.

Transesophageal echocardiography is performed when conventional echocardiography fails to clearly confirm a diagnosis. TEE is especially valuable during surgical procedures that require careful evaluation of cardiac function, and in situations where chest trauma or deformity prohibits other echocardiographic techniques. Contraindications for this procedure include a variety of esophageal pathologies, bleeding disorders, and Zenker's diverticulum. Esophageal bleeding, perforation, and cardiac arrhythmias are potential TEE complications.

Normal Findings. Normal position, size, and function of heart muscle, heart valves, and heart chambers.

Variations from Normal. Abnormalities such as aortic dissection, cardiac tumors, cardiac emboli, cardiomyopathy, myocardial ischemia and infarction, septal defects, valvular heart disease, and other congenital heart problems can be diagnosed using transesophageal echocardiography. This procedure is an excellent detector of ischemia and is most sensitive for detecting air emboli during neurosurgery performed in an upright position.

Interfering Circumstances. The primary interfering circumstance for TEE is the inability to cooperate or remain still during the procedure.

Endoscopic Studies of the Abdominal Cavity

Endoscopic studies of the abdominal cavity include procedures that examine tissues and organs located in the abdominal region of the body. These endoscopic procedures are divided into three categories: (1) abdominal endoscopic examination, (2) upper gastrointestinal (GI) tract endoscopies, and (3) examinations of the lower gastrointestinal tract.

The **laparoscopy**, also known as **peritoneoscopy**, is the overall endoscopic examination of the abdominal organs. It should be noted that the term "laparoscopy" also applies to examinations of pelvic cavity organs. Laparoscopic studies of the pelvic cavity are presented later in this chapter.

Upper GI tract endoscopies include **endoscopic retrograde cholangiopancreatography (ERCP)**, a study of the biliary and pancreatic ducts; and **esophagogastroduodenoscopy (EGD)**, an examination that extends from the esophagus to the small intestine. The EGD is a combination of three distinct endoscopic exams: **esophagoscopy**, a study of the esophagus; **gastroscopy**, a study of the stomach; and **duodenoscopy**, an examination of the duodenum. Studies of the lower GI tract include **proctoscopy**, an endoscopic exam of the anus and rectum; **sigmoidoscopy**, a study of the sigmoid colon; and **colonoscopy**, a study of the large intestine.

Laparoscopy

Laparoscopy, also known as peritoneoscopy, permits direct visual examination of the liver, stomach, gallbladder, and spleen; parietal and visceral peritoneum; and other abdominal organs, tissues, and fluids by way of a rigid laparoscope or peritoneoscope. The scope is introduced into the abdominal cavity through a small surgical incision usually in the umbilical area. The laparoscope often includes a camera system that transmits pictures of the scope's view to a color monitor.

Laparoscopy is a valuable diagnostic and treatment tool that can be used to identify pathology of the listed organs, or to perform a number of surgical procedures. Diagnostic applications of laparoscopy range from evaluating unexplained abdominal pain to diagnosing cirrhosis of the liver. Laparoscopy is often used to obtain a biopsy of liver tissue. Ascites, jaundice, and metastatic cancer can be evaluated via laparoscopy. Laparoscopic examinations can provide useful preoperative information about tumors and abdominal trauma that may cause intra-abdominal bleeding.

Cholecystectomy, appendectomy, tubal ligation, and hernia repair are a few of the surgical procedures that can be accomplished by laparoscopy. Local, spinal, or general anesthetics are used depending on the particular procedure being performed. In addition, the abdominal cavity is inflated with carbon dioxide to permit greater visualization.

Complications associated with laparoscopic procedures include laceration or perforation of organs, tissues, or any part of the bowel; cardiac problems; hemorrhage; and infection. Laparoscopy is contraindicated in the presence of coagulation disorders, unstable cardiovascular and respiratory function, and an acute infection that may result in the introduction of bacteria into the abdominal cavity. Any condition that increases the risk of bowel perforation is also a contraindication for laparoscopic interventions.

Normal Findings. Normal liver, spleen, pancreas, gallbladder, peritoneum, and other visualized organs or tissues.

Variations from Normal. Acute and chronic pancreatitis, cirrhosis of the liver, gallstones, and pancreatic cancer can be diagnosed using laparoscopy. Staging cancers of the liver and lymph system, as well as evaluating metastatic cancers, can also be accomplished with laparoscopic examinations.

Interfering Circumstances. Obesity, adhesions, and an inability to cooperate during the procedure interfere with successful utilization of laparoscopy.

Endoscopic Retrograde Cholangiopancreatography (ERCP)

Endoscopic retrograde cholangiopancreatography (ERCP) provides visualization of the biliary and pancreatic ducts. This study combines endoscopic and radiographic technology, and involves the use of a contrast medium. A side-viewing flexible endoscope is passed through the esophagus, the stomach, and into the duodenum. Using the endoscope, a small catheter is inserted into the ampulla of Vater, the site where bile and pancreatic juices flow into the small intestine. Radiographic dye or contrast media are then injected through the small catheter into the biliary and pancreatic ducts, which are visualized by way of fluoroscopic x-ray. Figure 12-2 shows the structures visualized during an ERCP.

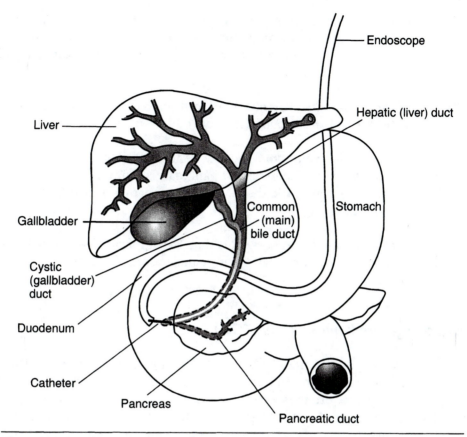

Figure 12-2. Structures visualized during an ERCP

ERCP has both diagnostic and treatment applications. Bile and pancreatic ducts can be assessed for patency, obstruction, and other biliary and pancreatic disorders. Treatment applications include removal of small gallstones from the common bile duct, placement of biliary drains, and dilatation of strictures.

Patients undergoing ERCP usually receive sedation for comfort. A local anesthetic is applied to the pharynx to reduce the gag reflex and the discomfort caused as the scope is passed into the duodenum. Risks and complications associated with ERCP include perforation of the pharynx, esophagus, stomach, or duodenum; respiratory distress; and abnormal cardiac rhythms. In addition, complications related to the contrast media or catheter insertion may occur in the biliary and pancreatic ducts. Contraindications for endoscopic retrograde cholangiopancreatography include coagulation disorders, cardiovascular and respiratory instability, and any condition that increases the risk of perforation.

Normal Findings. Patent biliary and pancreatic ducts, and the absence of gallstones, obstructions, and abnormal tissue.

Variations from Normal. The ERCP can be used to diagnose gallstones, pancreatic stones, cholangitis, and pancreatitis. Tumors, cysts, and strictures of biliary and pancreatic ducts, as well as cirrhosis of the liver, can also be identified.

Interfering Circumstances. Residual barium from previous gastrointestinal studies can interfere with the visualization of the biliary and pancreatic ducts.

Esophagogastroduodenoscopy (EGD)

Esophagogastroduodenoscopy (EGD) involves direct visualization of the esophagus, stomach, and duodenum through the use of a flexible scope. This procedure may be called esophagogastroscopy, esophagoscopy, gastroscopy, or duodenoscopy, depending upon the structures or combination of structures being examined. The EGD allows the physician to examine the mucosa of the upper gastrointestinal tract from the esophagus to the middle of the duodenum. This endoscopic procedure serves many diagnostic and treatment purposes.

Esophagogastroduodenoscopy can be used to identify inflammation of the mucosal lining; to detect tumors, ulcers, and obstructions; and to assess hiatal hernias, varices, or polyps. Surgical interventions include tumor and polyp removal, cauterization in order to control bleeding caused by varices or other problems, and dilatation of strictures. An EGD is particularly useful for the removal of foreign objects from the upper gastrointestinal tract.

Patients undergoing an EGD are given a local anesthetic to the pharynx to minimize gagging, and sedatives to increase the comfort level. Complications of EGD are related to aspiration of gastric content, cardiac and respiratory distress, perforation of the GI tract, and potential bleeding from any surgical intervention.

The diagnostic contraindications for completing an EGD represent serious and even life-threatening risks to the patient. Aortic arch aneurysm or significant esophageal diverticula increase the risk of rupture or perforation as the scope is advanced into the GI tract.

Normal Findings. The interior of the esophagus, stomach, and duodenum are normal.

Variations from Normal. The diseases, pathology, or malformation detected by EGD depend on the particular portion of the upper gastrointestinal tract under study. Examination of the esophagus may find abnormalities as varied as tumors, varices, stenosis, hiatal hernia, or esophagitis. In the stomach, the examination may reveal pathology such as gastritis, gastric ulcers, tumors, or bleeding. Examination of the duodenum may reveal diverticula, ulcers, cancers, and duodenal inflammation or malformation.

Interfering Circumstances. Conditions that prevent the patient from participating in the EGD are the same as those identified in similar endoscopic procedures. Excessive bleeding during the procedure can inhibit the physician's effectiveness in examining the upper GI tract. Patients who have recently undergone a barium swallow may retain barium in sufficient amounts to prevent clear visualization of the GI tract.

Proctoscopy; Sigmoidoscopy; Proctosigmoidoscopy

Proctoscopy is an endoscopic examination of the anus and rectum with an instrument called a proctoscope, and sigmoidoscopy is an endoscopic examination of the sigmoid colon using a sigmoidoscope. When the anus, rectum, and sigmoid colon are examined at the same time, the procedure is known as a proctosigmoidoscopy and the instrument is called a proctosigmoidoscope. The endoscopes, which are inserted through the anal sphincter, can be rigid or flexible. The flexible fiberoptic instruments are the most commonly used endoscopes.

The purpose of these endoscopic procedures is visualization of the mucosa of the anus, rectum, and sigmoid colon. In addition to direct examination of mucosal tissues, endoscopy can also be used to perform biopsy and tissue sampling; to assess blood or mucus in the stool; and to observe ulcers, polyps, and diverticula. These procedures play an important role in the diagnosis of cancer of the anus, rectum, and distal sigmoid colon. Proctoscopy, in any form, may be indicated when there is a significant change in bowel habits, blood present in the stool, or as part of the annual physical examination for individuals after age 50.

Proctoscopic exams usually require no anesthesia or sedation and are usually well tolerated. Patients may experience bloating, cramping, and a strong urge to defecate. Complications of proctoscopy include perforation of the intestinal wall and bleeding caused by biopsy or polyp removal. Coagulation disorders, toxic megacolon, suspected bowel perforation, and some aortic aneurysms are contraindications for this exam.

Normal Findings. Anus, rectum, and sigmoid colon are normal.

Variations from Normal. Proctoscopic examinations are used to diagnose anal hemorrhoids, rectal prolapse, abscesses, fissures, polyps, and malignancies. They can also be used to identify and evaluate inflammatory bowel diseases such as ulcerative and granulomatous colitis. Regional enteritis, intestinal ischemia, and irritable bowel syndrome can be diagnosed and assessed via proctoscopy.

Interfering Circumstances. If the bowel has not been thoroughly cleansed before the examination, clear visualization of the bowel mucosa can be obscured. Patients must be able to cooperate in order for the procedure to be successfully completed.

Colonoscopy

Colonoscopy is an endoscopic examination of the full length of the large intestine from the anus to the ileocecal valve. A flexible fiberoptic colonoscope, which is inserted via the anus, allows the physician to examine the mucosa of the entire colon and the terminal ileum. The patient is sedated with intravenous medication and, once the colonoscope is in place, air is injected to expand the bowel and allow for better visualization of the large intestine. Figure 12-3 is a sample colonoscopy report.

Colonoscopy is used to diagnose cancer, inflammatory bowel diseases, and other abnormal conditions of the lower gastrointestinal tract. It may also be used to remove foreign objects and polyps, and to control bleeding through the use of laser surgery or electrocoagulation. Indications for

PATIENT NAME: Cecum, Carl

OPERATION/PROCEDURE: Colonoscopy to the cecum with polypectomy × 3 of a 1 cm pedunculated polyp in the distal ascending colon, an 8 mm polyp at the hepatic flexure, and a 5 mm polyp in the proximal transverse colon.

PREOPERATIVE DIAGNOSIS: Strong family history of adenomas.

POSTOPERATIVE DIAGNOSIS: 1. Polyps as above.
                          2. Grade 2 internal hemorrhoids.

ANESTHESIA: Demerol and Versed IV.

COMPLICATIONS: None.

INSTRUMENT: Double-channel EC-3801 TL colonoscope.

INDICATION: This is a gentleman who has two sisters and one brother with adenomatous polyps. He has had no symptoms himself. He has a history of BPH and also hypertension. His heart, lungs, and abdomen are normal.

FINDINGS: After historical and physical assessment appropriate for this procedure, the patient was placed on triple monitoring and put in the left lateral decubitus position. He was given IV sedation. A rectal exam revealed a generous prostate. The colonoscope was introduced and advanced through quite a loopy sigmoid to the cecum. Reaching the cecum was facilitated by placing him in the right lateral decubitus position when the scope was at the level of the midtransverse colon. Then advancing it was quite easy. Landmarks were unequivocally identified, including the ileocecal valve, the terminal ileum, which was transiently visualized, and the appendiceal orifice. On slow withdrawal and careful inspection of the mucosa, the above polyps were noted and removed with a minisnare and recovered for pathologic examination. A diminutive polyp at 40 cm was cauterized, and retroflex view of the anal ring showed grade 2 internal hemorrhoids.

The patient will be advised in a high-fiber, low-animal-fat diet, and if these polyps are adenomatous, as I suspect they are, and because of his tortuous colon, we will repeat his study in one year.

Figure 12-3.   Colonoscopy report

colonoscopy are blood in the stool, family history of cancer, changes in bowel function, or other factors that place the patient at high risk for colon disease. Colonoscopy is contraindicated for patients who have had recent bowel surgery or a recent myocardial infarction. Severe bleeding or clotting disorders, pregnancy, and suspected bowel perforation are additional contraindications for this examination.

While colonoscopy is a safe procedure, the patient must be carefully observed during and after the procedure for potential adverse reactions. These include reactions to the medications given for sedation, perforation of the colon during the procedure, or potential bleeding after a biopsy or polypectomy.

Normal Findings. Normal-appearing mucosa of the colon and an absence of pathology.

Variations from Normal. Colonoscopy is used to diagnose and evaluate polyps, colon cancer, diverticulosis, and Crohn's disease. Ulcerative, granulomatous, and infectious colitis can be identified and differentiated via colonoscopy.

Interfering Circumstances. Incomplete cleansing of the colon and severe gastrointestinal bleeding inhibit clear visualization of the tissue.

Endoscopic Studies of the Pelvic Cavity

Endoscopic studies of the pelvic cavity include studies that examine tissue and organs located in the pelvic region of the body. The examinations can be divided into two categories: those related to the urinary tract, and those related to the reproductive system. **Cystoscopy**, an examination of the urethra, urinary bladder, and ureteral orifices; and **urodynamic studies**, which measure the function of the urinary bladder, are included in the discussion of urinary tract endoscopies. **Pelviscopy**, an examination of female reproductive organs; **colposcopy**, an examination of the vagina and cervix; and **culdoscopy**, an examination of the female reproductive organs, rectum, and sigmoid colon, comprise the reproductive system endoscopies.

Cystoscopy

Cystoscopy, an endoscopic examination of the urethra, urinary bladder, ureteral orifices, and the male prostatic urethra, is the most commonly used urological diagnostic procedure. It permits the examination of the lower urinary tract, which often cannot be visualized with other diagnostic tools. Prior to scope insertion, an antiseptic agent is applied to the external genitalia and a local anesthetic jelly is placed into the urethra. There may be circumstances that require general anesthesia. The organs examined via cystoscopy are shown in Figure 12-4.

Cystoscopy is accomplished by inserting a rigid or flexible cystoscope through the urethra into the bladder. The physician is then able to evaluate

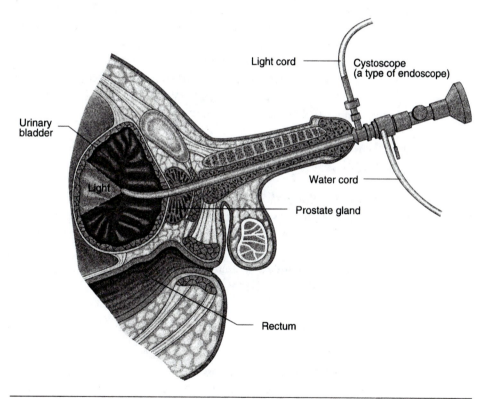

Figure 12-4.   Cystoscopy

the structure and tissue of the urethra, bladder, and prostate. Bladder capacity and function can also be evaluated by using cystoscopy to place ureteral catheters into the ureteral orifices. The catheters drain urine from the renal pelvis, and kidney function can then be evaluated by examining the urine samples.

In addition to diagnostic applications, cytoscopy is an important treatment and therapeutic modality. It can be used to remove stones, resect small tumors, biopsy tissue, and dilate strictures. Transurethral prostatectomy, placement of radioactive seeds into cancerous bladder tumors, and placement of ureteral catheters for retrograde pyelography can be achieved with cystoscopy.

Cystoscopy is indicated when the patient is experiencing chronic urinary tract infection or other urinary tract disturbances such as frequency, urgency, incontinence, retention, and hematuria. Contraindications are bleeding disorders and acute urethritis or cystitis. The presence of infection before or during the procedure is of concern because the instrumentation of the urinary tract can allow bacteria to enter the blood, causing septicemia. Antibiotics may be given before and after the procedure to prevent infections. Urinary retention, hematuria, and perforation of the urinary bladder are potential complications of cystoscopy.

Normal Findings. Normal structure and function of the lower urinary tract including the prostate gland.

Variations from Normal. Cystoscopy is utilized to diagnose cancer of the bladder, tumors, polyps and stones, prostatic hypertrophy and prostatitis, stricture of the urethra, inflammation, and congenital abnormalities.

Interfering Circumstances. Inability to cooperate with the procedure appears to be the only interfering circumstance.

Urodynamic Studies

Urodynamic studies are measurements of the function of the urinary bladder. Although these studies are not endoscopic procedures, they are frequently performed in conjunction with cystoscopy and, therefore, are included in this chapter. Urodynamic studies may include a **cystometro-**

gram **(CMG)**, the measurement of bladder neuromuscular function; **urethra pressure profile**, which measures changes in urethral pressure; **uroflowmetry**, measuring the volume of urine expelled during urination; and **cystourethrogram**, an examination of the bladder and urethra.

These studies are indicated when there is evidence of bladder dysfunction that may be the result of neurological injury, spinal cord injury, major surgery in the pelvic region, or diseases such as spina bifida, tumors, or neuropathies. A cystometrogram measures the neuromuscular function of the bladder. The study is performed by inserting an indwelling catheter into the bladder and using an instrument to measure bladder capacity and pressure. Cystometrograms assist the physician in diagnosing motor and sensory problems, infectious diseases, and obstructions of the urinary tract.

The urethra pressure profile measures changes in pressure in the urethra while the bladder is at rest. It also measures the ability of the urethra to close. The study is performed by inserting a catheter that is equipped with a transducer into the bladder. As the catheter is slowly withdrawn through the urethra, pressure measurements are recorded. The purpose of this procedure is to evaluate abnormalities of the urethral sphincter.

Uroflowmetry measures the volume of urine that is expelled from the bladder during urination. This test is a noninvasive procedure that simply requires the patient to urinate into a flowmeter, which measures the flow. The purpose of uroflowmetry is to evaluate incontinence, urinary tract obstruction, abnormalities of the urethral sphincter, and chronic bladder infection.

A cystourethrogram is an evaluation of the bladder and urethra that utilizes x-ray and a contrast medium. The bladder is filled with medium using a catheter, and x-rays are taken of the full bladder. The catheter is removed, and x-rays are taken as the patient voids the medium. Cystourethrograms are used to evaluate female stress incontinence and abnormalities of the bladder and urethra.

Normal Findings. Normal bladder and urethra functioning. Normal study results vary with each test depending upon the age and sex of the patient.

Variations from Normal. Urodynamic studies may reveal sensory or motor abnormalities that alter normal muscular functioning of the lower urinary tract.

Interfering Circumstances. Ability of the patient to cooperate is essential to successful testing. Urinary tract functions can be altered by drugs such as antihistamines and muscle relaxants.

Pelviscopy; Gynecologic Laparoscopy

Pelviscopy, also known as **gynecologic laparoscopy,** is an endoscopic examination of the pelvic cavity that is used to examine the ovaries, uterus, and fallopian tubes. The pelviscope is inserted into the pelvic cavity through a small incision in the anterior abdominal wall. This procedure is performed in a similar manner as the laparoscopy described earlier in this chapter. Using the pelviscope, the physician is able to visualize the pelvic cavity in order to identify pathological conditions such as tumors, cysts, adhesions, fibroids, inflammation and infections, and malignancies. Tubal ligation, oophorectomy, and other surgical procedures are also performed using the pelviscope. The risks and complications associated with pelviscopy are the same as those associated with laparoscopy.

Normal Findings. Normal uterus, ovaries, and fallopian tubes.

Variations from Normal. Diseases such as endometriosis, pelvic inflammatory disease, ovarian cysts and tumors, uterine fibroid, and cancer can be diagnosed through the use of pelviscopy. The pelviscope can also be used to identify the causes of infertility and pelvic masses.

Interfering Circumstances. Conditions that interfere with successful use of the pelviscopy are the same as those associated with laparoscopy discussed earlier in this chapter.

Colposcopy

Colposcopy is the examination of the vagina and cervix by means of a **colposcope,** a lighted, binocular microscope. Using the colposcope, the physician is able to visualize the cervix and identify abnormal tissue. The colposcope is fitted with a camera, making it possible to photograph the tissue being examined.

Colposcopy makes it possible to detect cancer of the cervix in its early stages, examine tissue from which an abnormal Pap smear has been obtained, and monitor areas of the cervix from which malignant lesions have been removed. Colposcopy is also used to monitor women who are at risk for developing cervical cancer because their mothers were given diethylstilbestrol (DES) during their pregnancy. Colposcopy may also be used to examine male genitalia when sexually transmitted diseases are suspected.

Since the colposcope is not inserted into the vaginal cavity, colposcopy is a relatively safe and painless procedure. Discomfort may occur when the speculum is inserted into the vagina to improve visualization of the tissue. Discomfort and bleeding can occur when tissue is taken for biopsy.

Normal Findings. Normal vaginal and cervical tissues. Absence of abnormal lesions in males.

Variations from Normal. Benign, precancerous, or cancerous lesions may be detected during a colposcopy. Male sexually transmitted diseases that can be identified with this procedure include condylomata or human papillomavirus.

Interfering Circumstances. Improper or inadequate cleansing of the cervix may limit visualization of the tissue or provide unreliable results.

Culdoscopy

Culdoscopy is an endoscopic procedure in which the physician is able to visualize the cul-de-sac of Douglas using an endoscope called a culdoscope. The culdoscope is passed through a small surgical incision made into the posterior vagina. This procedure permits the physician to examine the uterus, ovaries, fallopian tubes, pelvic ligaments, rectum, and sigmoid colon. The pelviscopy, which provides better visualization with fewer risks, has replaced the culdoscopy as the procedure of choice when examining reproductive organs. Culdoscopy continues to be used with women who are extremely obese, especially for tubal ligation. It is useful in assessing ectopic pregnancy, fertility abnormalities, and pelvic pain.

Culdoscopy requires the administration of a local or spinal anesthetic since a small incision is necessary to permit passage of the instrument into the cul-de-sac of Douglas. In addition, the patient is made more comfortable through the use of analgesics and sedatives. Complications or risks of culdoscopy are perforation of the rectum, intestine, or bladder; excessive vaginal bleeding; and infections.

Normal Findings. Normal-appearing uterus, ovaries, fallopian tubes, pelvic ligaments, rectum, and sigmoid colon.

Variations from Normal. Ectopic pregnancy, abnormal fallopian tubes, and pelvic masses can be diagnosed using culdoscopy.

Interfering Circumstances. Palpable pelvic masses, vaginal infection, and adhesions from previous pelvic surgery are conditions that prohibit the use of the culdoscopy.

Miscellaneous Endoscopic Studies

This section includes a discussion of **arthroscopy**, an endoscopic examination of the joint; **fetoscopy**, an endoscopic examination of the fetus; and **amnioscopy**, an examination of the amniotic fluid.

Arthroscopy

Arthroscopy is an endoscopic examination of a joint using a fiber-optic scope called an arthroscope. The physician is able to visualize the internal structure of the joint by introducing the arthroscope through a small surgical incision in the skin. The location of the incision varies with the joint, the type of arthroscopy being performed, and the purpose of the examination. Arthroscopy is also used for surgical intervention. The procedure is most commonly used on the knee, but it can also be used to examine the ankle, hip, wrist, elbow, and shoulder.

Using the arthroscope, the physician is able to evaluate the impact of trauma or disease upon the joint, and perform corrective surgery. Abnormal tissue or fluids can be removed using the arthroscope. Infected wounds or skin are the chief contraindications for arthroscopy.

Patients are given local anesthesia when arthroscopy is used solely for joint examination or evaluation. A general or spinal anesthetic is administered when arthroscopy is the vehicle for a surgical intervention. Patients undergoing arthroscopy must be observed for adverse reactions to the anesthetic; intraoperative damage to the nervous, muscular, or vascular tissue; and postoperative thrombophlebitis or infection.

Normal Findings. Normal cartilage, ligaments, tendons, and membranes appropriate to the joint.

Variations from Normal. Joint injury such as fractures, torn ligaments or cartilage, and diseases such as patellar disease, arthritis, and synovitis can be identified using arthroscopy.

Interfering Circumstances. Severe ankylosis interferes with successful arthroscopy.

Amnioscopy

Amnioscopy is an endoscopic examination that allows visualization of the amniotic fluid. The physician dilates the cervix and then places the amnioscope into the cervical canal until the amniotic fluid can be visualized through the intact amniotic membranes. This procedure is utilized to determine if meconium staining is present in the amniotic fluid. Meconium, which is passed from the rectum of the fetus, may indicate fetal distress or death. The presence of meconium does not always indicate problems as it may be present in normal pregnancies. No amniotic fluid is taken, but fetal blood samples may be obtained from the scalp of the fetus. Blood samples are important in fully assessing fetal distress.

This procedure is done without anesthesia. The patient may experience discomfort related to the dilation of the cervix. Contraindications for amnioscopy include infections, presence of a sexually transmitted disease, active labor, and ruptured membranes. Possible risks or complications are bleeding from the fetal scalp wound, if a fetal blood sample is taken; premature rupture of the membranes; and vaginal discomfort and cramping.

Normal Findings. Amniotic fluid is normal in color and does not contain meconium staining.

Variations from Normal. Amniotic fluid that contains meconium staining may be indicative of fetal hypoxia.

Interfering Circumstances. Patient cooperation is necessary for a successful examination.

Fetoscopy

Fetoscopy is an endoscopic examination of the fetus that uses ultrasonography to guide the placement of the fetoscope. The fetoscope is inserted through a small surgical incision into the uterus. Using this procedure the physician is able to examine the physical structure of the fetus and take fetal blood and skin samples. This procedure permits the diagnosis of congenital malformations, blood disorders, and abnormal skin disorders. Fetoscopy is indicated only if there is a high risk of a severe birth defect. It is usually performed at 18 weeks of gestation.

The patient is given a local anesthetic at the site of the surgical incision. During and after the procedure the patient and fetus must be carefully assessed and monitored since the procedure has the potential to cause spontaneous abortion, amniotic fluid loss, premature delivery, and fetal death. Antibiotics are usually administered before and after the procedure to prevent infection.

Normal Findings. Normal, healthy fetus, and absence of abnormal blood studies and skin conditions.

Variations from Normal. The fetoscopy may reveal abnormal physical defects in the fetus, such as neural tube defects, blood disorders such as sickle cell anemia or hemophilia, and skin disorders.

Summary

- Endoscopic studies allow the direct visualization of internal organs and structures of the body by inserting an endoscope into a body cavity through a natural body orifice or a surgical incision.
- Endoscopic procedures can be used to diagnose and treat a variety of diseases and conditions, and may require local, general, or spinal anesthesia.

- Complications of endoscopic procedures include perforation of a body structure by the endoscope, reaction to anesthetic or sedation medications, blood loss, and infection.
- Bronchoscopy, mediastinoscopy, thoracoscopy, and transesophageal echocardiography are endoscopic studies of thoracic cavity structures and tissues.
- Laparoscopy is the overall endoscopic examination of the abdominal organs.
- Gastrointestinal tract endoscopies include ERCP, EGD, proctoscopy, sigmoidoscopy, and colonoscopy.
- Cystoscopy, pelviscopy, colposcopy, and culdoscopy are the endoscopic studies of the pelvic cavity.
- Fetoscopy and amnioscopy are used to identify birth defects and fetal distress, respectively.
- Arthroscopy is the endoscopic examination of a joint, most commonly the knee.

CHAPTER REVIEW

1. Identify the following endoscopic studies:

a. Visualization of pleura, pleural spaces, pericardium, and mediastinum

_____

b. Diagnostic and treatment tool for organs and tissue of the abdominal cavity

_____

c. Diagnostic tool for assessment of biliary and pancreatic ducts

_____

d. Identifies and evaluates inflammatory bowel disease

_____

e. Assesses amniotic fluid for presence of meconium; fetal blood samples can be obtained

_____

2. Name the endoscopic examination(s) associated with the listed diagnoses.

    a. Ligament and cartilage diseases   _____

    b. Hemorrhoids, polyps, rectal prolapse   _____

    c. Endometriosis, ovarian cysts   _____

    d. Sickle cell anemia, hemophilia   _____

    e. *Pneumocystis carinii*   _____

    f. Gallstones, pancreatitis, cirrhosis of the liver   _____

    g. Hiatal hernia, diverticula, ulcers   _____

3. Which endoscopic examinations are related to the listed treatment interventions?

    a. Oophorectomy, tubal ligation   _____

    b. Transurethral prostatectomy   _____

    c. Polypectomy   _____

    d. Cauterization of varices   _____

    e. Dilation of bile and pancreatic ducts   _____

    f. Cholecystectomy, hernia repair   _____

    g. Resection of smaller tumors or malignancies _____

4. Briefly describe the structures examined by the listed endoscopic studies. Provide examples of the diseases that can be diagnosed by these studies.

    a. Bronchoscopy   _____

    b. Mediastinoscopy   _____

    c. Cystoscopy   _____

    d. Colonoscopy   _____

    e. Transesophageal echocardiography   _____

    f. Colposcopy   _____

5. Discuss the four complications, identified in the chapter, related to endoscopic examinations. Give examples of endoscopies that provide a good example for susceptibility for each complication.

6. Compare the benefits and risks of endoscopic procedures with surgical interventions.

7. Briefly describe the urodynamic studies that are performed in conjunction with cystoscopy.

   a. Cystometrogram   _____

   b. Urethra pressure profile   _____

   c. Uroflowmetry   _____

   d. Cystourethrogram   _____

Case Studies

1. Edgar Raymond, a 46-year-old coal miner with chronic lung congestion, has been scheduled for a bronchoscopy by Dr. Sullivan. Discuss the purpose of a bronchoscopy and how it is performed. What diseases might be found with this endoscopic procedure? Mr. Raymond experienced a pneumothorax during the procedure. Is this normal? If so, why?

2. Sheila Middlebrook, a 56-year-old-woman with a history of alcoholism, has symptoms of abdominal pain and ascites. Dr. Hart has decided that a laparoscopy must be performed to determine the cause of Sheila's problems. Describe how a laparoscopy is performed. Review and discuss the abnormalities that can be diagnosed with this endoscopic procedure. What complications might occur as a result of this examination?

3. Maria Chavez, a 50-year-old-woman, had an annual physical and was told by her physician that she needs a colonoscopy. Describe how the colonoscopy is performed and the organs or tissues visualized? Are there contraindications for this procedure? Is this an invasive or noninvasive procedure? Identify the abnormalities that colonoscopy can detect.

Challenge Activity

Create a table or figure that includes the indications and contraindications for each endoscopic study presented in this chapter. Organize the endoscopies according to related examinations, body cavities, or organs being studied.

Chapter *13*

Ultrasound Procedures

Key Terms, Abbreviations, and Acronyms

abdominal aorta ultrasonography

arterial Doppler studies

bladder ultrasonography

breast ultrasonography

chest ultrasonography

color-flow Doppler imaging

continuous-wave Doppler imaging

coronary artery bypass grafting (CABG)

cross-sectional gray-scale imaging method

Doppler blood vessel studies

Doppler ultrasound method

duplex scanning

echocardiography

fetal ultrasound

gallbladder ultrasonography

hepatobiliary ultrasonography

intravascular ultrasound

kidney ultrasonography

liver ultrasonography

M-mode (echocardiography)

neonate head sonography

obstetric ultrasonography

ocular ultrasonography

pancreas ultrasonography

pelvic ultrasonography

percutaneous transluminal coronary angioplasty (PTCA)

percutaneous ultrasonic lithotripsy, PUL

prostate ultrasonography

pulsed Doppler method

scrotal ultrasonography

spleen ultrasonography

thyroid ultrasonography

transabdominal method

transcranial Doppler studies

transvaginal method

two-dimensional mode
    echocardiogram, 2-D mode

venous Doppler studies

Learning Objectives

Upon completion of this chapter, the learner should be able to:

1. Describe the diagnostic value of ultrasound technology.
2. Discuss how ultrasound images of body organs and tissues are produced.
3. Identify the purpose of and body structures examined by each ultrasound study.
4. Relate specific diagnoses to each ultrasound study.
5. Organize ultrasound studies according to the area of the body and the organs or tissues being studied.
6. Identify the circumstances that interfere with a successful ultrasound study.

Introduction

Ultrasound studies cover a variety of diagnostic techniques that use sound waves to assess the structure and function of organs and tissues. The majority of ultrasound studies are usually categorized as noninvasive procedures, although there are exceptions. Ultrasound procedures are also called ultrasonography or sonogram. The ultrasound procedures presented in this chapter include organ structure studies such as ultrasonography of the kidney, as well as studies of organ function such as **Doppler blood vessel studies**, which provide data on arterial or venous blood flow. Information for each ultrasound procedure includes a brief description of the procedure, the organ structure or function under study, indications for the procedure, abnormalities that can be identified using ultrasound, and factors that interfere with or prevent the use of ultrasound.

Overview of Ultrasound Procedures

Ultrasonography is a safe, noninvasive procedure that uses sound waves to create images of the soft tissues of the human body. A transducer is used to direct sound waves into the body. The skin over the area being studied is coated with conductive gel or lotion, and the transducer is pressed lightly against the skin. Once the sound waves reach the underlying body structures, they bounce back to the transducer that converts the returning sound waves into electrical signals. The electrical signals are processed by computer and ultimately displayed as graphs, scans, or sounds. Ultrasound is performed to evaluate organ size, shape, texture, and position in order to detect abnormalities. Since ultrasound can distinguish the differences in tissue reflectivity and sound-beam absorption, it can detect masses, stones, cysts, and edema. In addition, real-time imaging makes it possible to display organ and tissue movement.

Ultrasound technology is divided into two methods: the **cross-sectional gray-scale imaging method** and the **Doppler method**. The gray-scale image method converts sound-wave echoes into graphs or dots that form pictures of organs and blood vessels. The Doppler method converts the Doppler shifts in the ultrasound signal into audible sounds or colored areas on the gray scale image. The audible sounds are heard as pulsations and can be displayed on a screen as waveforms and recorded. Color-coded Doppler signals, three-dimensional imaging, and contrast enhancement of the ultrasound image provide more accurate images and data related to organ structure and function.

In addition to its diagnostic value, ultrasound technology can also function as a treatment modality. At a frequency higher than that required for diagnostic purposes, ultrasound is used to produce heat in body tissues that treat or relieve back pain. Ultrasound is also used to produce sound waves that are able to pulverize kidney and gallstones in a procedure called **percutaneous ultrasonic lithotripsy (PUL)**.

Administered properly, ultrasound is a very safe procedure because it is carried out using low-intensity sound waves. It does not require the use of x-ray, contrast medium, or invasive instruments. However, ultrasound is not useful in the examination of bone or body organs that contain air or gas, such as the lungs or intestines. Ultrasound results can be inaccurate if the transducer is not properly placed or if body structures, such as ribs, weaken or interfere with sound waves. The procedure must be performed by a technician with special training, and is carried out in outpatient settings, physicians' offices, and, during inpatient hospitalization, in the ultrasound department or at the bedside. The procedure usually does not require the administration of anesthesia or medications. Depending upon the type of procedure, a permanent record can be made of the ultrasound in the form of a graph, picture, or video.

Ultrasonography of the Head and Neck Region

Ultrasonography of the head and neck includes procedures that examine organs and tissues of the brain, eye, and thyroid gland. These studies include **neonate head sonography** (echoencephalography), an ultrasound study of the brain and associated structures of newborns; **ocular ultrasonography**, an ultrasound study of the eye and the eye orbit; and **thyroid ultrasonography**, an ultrasound study of the thyroid gland.

Neonate Head Sonography

Neonate head sonography is an ultrasound study performed to assess midline cerebral structures of the brain. Conductive gel is applied to the appropriate areas of the baby's head. The transducer is then placed lightly over the soft spots (fontanels, occipital and temporal) and the sound waves are directed at the internal structure of the brain. Abnormalities are suspected when the ventricles of the brain are displaced or dilated. Changes in brain tissue texture can also be identified. Tissue texture changes are often associated with bleeding from the fragile brain vessels.

Normal Findings. Normal cerebral structure and texture. Ventricles are not displaced or enlarged.

Variations from Normal. Neonate head sonography can be used to diagnosis and monitor hydrocephalus and cerebral hemorrhages in infants.

Interfering Circumstances. The inability of the patient to remain still during the procedure and closing of the fontanels are the primary interfering circumstance.

Ocular Ultrasonography

Ocular ultrasonography is an ultrasound study of the eye and its orbital structure. This procedure is performed to identify abnormalities in the tissues of the eye and lesions of the orbital area. Ocular sonograms can also be used to locate foreign bodies in the eye. Replacement of the vitreous humor with gas is the primary contraindication for this study.

Ocular ultrasonography is performed having the patient keep the eyes closed and placing conductive gel on the eyelid. The transducer is then placed on the eyelid and the examination is completed. Images are projected on a screen and photographed. Discomfort and blurred vision from the anesthetic may be present after the ultrasound is completed. Rubbing the eye within several hours after the exam can cause injury to the eyeball.

Normal Findings. Normal-appearing eye tissue and ocular structure.

Variations from Normal. Abnormal conditions such as detached retina, changes in the eye related to Graves' disease, abnormalities of the vitreous, intraocular foreign bodies, vascular abnormalities, and hemorrhages can be identified using ocular ultrasonography. In addition, the procedure can be used to assess orbital lesions, and tumors that may indicate glioma, hemangioma, melanoma, meningioma, metastatic lymphoma, and neurofibroma.

Interfering Circumstances. Circumstances that can interfere with the ocular ultrasonography are inability of the patient to cooperate by remaining still during the procedure and air in the eye from trauma.

Thyroid Ultrasonography

Thyroid ultrasonography is an ultrasound examination of the thyroid gland that is performed to evaluate the size, structure, and position of the thyroid gland and to detect thyroid abnormalities. During the thyroid ultrasonography, the individual is placed in a supine position with the neck hyperextended. Once the conductive gel is applied to the neck, the transducer is moved in small increments over the area of the thyroid gland. Images are projected on a screen, recorded, and photographed.

Normal Findings. The thyroid gland is normal in size and structure.

Variations from Normal. Thyroid ultrasonography can reveal abnormalities such as nodules, goiters, tumors, cysts, adenoma, or carcinoma.

Interfering Circumstances. A circumstance that can interfere with thyroid ultrasonography is the inability of the patient to cooperate during the procedure.

Ultrasonography of the Thoracic Region

Ultrasonography of the thoracic region includes procedures that examine the organs and tissues of the breast, heart, and lungs. These studies include **breast ultrasonography**, an ultrasound study of the breasts; **echocardiography**, a noninvasive evaluation of heart structure and function; **intravascular ultrasound**, an invasive procedure that uses ultrasound technology to examine coronary arteries; and **chest ultrasonography**, an ultrasound study of the lungs and surrounding tissue.

Breast Ultrasonography

Breast ultrasonography is an ultrasound examination of the breast that is performed to identify breast lesions, monitor changes in fibrocystic breast disease, and make differential diagnoses of masses. Some women may choose breast ultrasonography in place of the more commonly used x-ray mammography to avoid the exposure to radiation. Despite the usefulness of ultrasound, x-ray mammography has advantages that make it the diagnostic procedure of choice for breast cancer screening. Breast ultrasonography is often used to examine the breasts with silicone implants.

With the individual in a supine position, the chest is exposed and conductive gel is applied to the breasts. The transducer is moved over the breast and images are projected on a screen, recorded, and photographed. Breast ultrasonography is safe for pregnant women.

Normal Findings. Absence of abnormalities in breast tissues.

Variations from Normal. Abnormal conditions such as malignant tumors, cysts, masses, cancer metastasis, and other lesions can be identified using breast ultrasonography.

Interfering Circumstances. The patient must be cooperative during the procedure and maintain the desired posture for the examination. Incorrect use of the ultrasound equipment invalidates the results.

Echocardiography

Echocardiography is an ultrasound examination that is performed to assess the structure and function of the heart. This study is sometimes called "cardiac echo." Visualization of the heart chambers and valves can be accomplished with echocardiography. The shape, size, position, function, and blood flow through the heart can also be evaluated. In addition to providing information for diagnostic purposes, the procedure is performed to assess the condition of prosthetic heart valves.

There are different echocardiographic modes that are identified as the M-mode, 2-D or two-dimensional mode, pulsed Doppler, continuous-wave Doppler, and the color-flow Doppler mode. The **M-mode** provides a linear tracing of the heart that enables the practitioner to assess the structures of the heart while in motion. As the name suggests, two-dimensional heart images are produced via the **two-dimensional** or **2-D mode echocardiogram**. With the 2-D mode, cross-sectional gray-scale images of the heart are taken and recorded. The **color-flow, pulsed,** or **continuous-wave Doppler** mode provides information about blood-flow patterns and blood-flow speed through the heart. Another type of echocardiography is the transesophageal echocardiogram, a combined endoscopic and ultrasonic procedure that is discussed in Chapter 12.

Echocardiography and electrocardiogram are performed simultaneously so that both the structure, function, and electrical activity of the heart can be evaluated. Once the conductive gel is applied to the chest, the transducer is passed over the region and images are produced. The results of the study are recorded in a variety of ways including videotapes, pictures, or a linear graph. The patient experiences no discomfort during this ultrasound procedure. Information from this test combined with other noninvasive diagnostic findings may eliminate the need for a more invasive procedure.

Normal Findings. Normal cardiac anatomy, position, and function. Blood-flow patterns are within normal limits.

Variations from Normal. Echocardiography is a useful diagnostic tool for identification of heart valve abnormalities, including stenosis, closure malfunction, prolapse, and regurgitation. It can also detect cardiomyopathy, pericardial effusion, thrombi, and coronary heart disease. Structural and congenital heart abnormalities, including septal defects, patient ductus arteriosus, or tetralogy of Fallot, can be revealed with echocardiography.

Interfering Circumstances. Patients with chronic obstructive pulmonary disease (COPD) are not good candidates for echocardiography since this condition may increase the amount of space and air between the heart and rib cage, which may alter the test results. Abnormalities of the chest, including obesity, deformity, or trauma, may interfere with the quality of the procedure.

Intravascular Ultrasonography (IVUS)

Intravascular ultrasonography (IVUS) is an ultrasound examination that is performed to assess the internal structure and condition of coronary arteries. Coronary artery disease, atherosclerotic lesions, the distribution and composition of arterial plaque, and arterial occlusion can be evaluated by ultrasonic visualization of the interior of the artery. Intravascular ultrasonography can assist in identifying individuals who are candidates for **percutaneous transluminal coronary angioplasty (PTCA)** or **coronary artery bypass grafting (CABG)**.

Intravascular ultrasonography is performed by threading a small flexible catheter through a peripheral blood vessel into the coronary artery. The catheter has a transducer attached to its tip. The transducer is able to transmit sound waves, which provide a picture of the internal characteristics of the blood vessel. IVUS, which is performed in a cardiac catheterization unit, is an invasive procedure and carries some risks and potential complications. Blood vessel spasms, angina, myocardial infarction, and arterial dissection are possible complications associated with intravascular ultrasonography.

Normal Findings. Normal coronary arteries with an absence of lesions or occlusions.

Variations from Normal. Abnormal conditions such as atherosclerotic lesions, thrombi, and arterial dissections can be detected using IVUS.

Interfering Circumstances. Inability of the patient to cooperate and improper placement of the catheter compromise results of this diagnostic procedure.

Chest Ultrasonography

Chest ultrasonography is an ultrasound test that is performed to evaluate the chest cavity, particularly the lungs. Although ultrasound usually is not used to assess air-filled organs, chest ultrasonography is useful for identifying abnormal conditions of the lungs that result in fluid accumulations. Needle placement during an aspiration biopsy of the fluid can be guided by this ultrasonic technique.

With the individual in an upright position, conductive gel is applied to the chest over the area to be examined. The transducer is passed over the chest and images are projected on a screen, recorded, and photographed. The examination presents no risk to the patient.

Normal Findings. Normal lungs and diaphragm.

Variations from Normal. Chest ultrasonography can identify pleural effusions and abscesses.

Interfering Circumstances. The patient must be cooperative during the procedure and maintain the desired posture for the examination.

Ultrasonography of the Abdomen

Ultrasonography of the abdomen includes studies of organs and body tissues that are located in the abdominal cavity. These studies include **abdominal aorta ultrasonography,** an ultrasound study of the abdominal aorta; **gallbladder ultrasonography,** an ultrasound study of the gallbladder and bile ducts; **kidney ultrasonography,** an ultrasound study of the kidney structure and function; **liver ultrasonography,** an ultrasound study of the liver and hepatic ducts; **pancreas ultrasonography,** an ultrasound study of pancreatic structure and texture; and **spleen ultrasonography,** an ultrasound study of the spleen. For purposes of clarity, each study is discussed individually. However, several organs are usually scanned during the same procedure. When more than one organ is included in the study, the name of the ultrasound examination may vary based on the combination of organs.

Abdominal Aortic Ultrasonography

Abdominal aortic ultrasonography is an ultrasound examination that is performed to assess the abdominal aorta from the diaphragm to the bifurcation of the aorta. External landmarks for this procedure begin with the xyphoid process and proceed to the approximate level of the umbilicus. The purpose of aortic ultrasonography is to detect and monitor abnormalities in the structure of the abdominal aorta. This procedure is highly diagnostic for abdominal aortic aneurysm (AAA). In an effort to prevent rupture, abdominal aortic ultrasonography can be used to monitor AAA.

With the individual in a supine position, conductive gel is applied to the exposed abdominal area. The transducer is passed over the entire abdominal aortic area. Sound waves are converted to images, which are in turn projected on a screen, recorded, and photographed. There is no discomfort or risks associated with aortic ultrasonography.

Normal Findings. Normal abdominal aorta.

Variations from Normal. Abdominal aortic ultrasonography can identify the presence, and monitor the expansion of an abdominal aortic aneurysm.

Interfering Circumstances. Inability of the patient to remain still and maintain the desired position adversely affects image quality. Gas or barium in the intestinal tract may interfere with the results of the ultrasound. Ultrasound image quality may be compromised in obese patients.

Gallbladder Ultrasonography

Gallbladder ultrasonography is an ultrasound examination of the gallbladder and the bile ducts that is performed to assess the size, shape, and position of the gallbladder and biliary ducts. Identification of gallstones, abnormalities, and inflammation can be accomplished with this sonogram. If the liver is evaluated at the same time, the examination is called **hepatobiliary ultra-sonography**. Gallbladder ultrasonography may be used to guide the physician in the process of obtaining a biopsy or dissolving stones.

With the patient in the supine position, the abdomen is exposed, conductive gel is applied, and the transducer is moved over the area. Breathing patterns may be altered during the examination. Images are transmitted through the transducer to a screen and recorded on photographs. Gallbladder ultrasonography is a safe, noninvasive procedure and presents no risks to the patient.

Normal Findings. Normal size, shape, structure, and position of the gallbladder and the bile ducts.

Variations from Normal. Gallbladder ultrasonography can detect cholelithiasis, choledocholithiasis, and obstructions or dilation of the bile ducts. Tumors, polyps, cysts, or masses of the gallbladder and biliary ducts can also be identified with this study. Figure 13-1 is a written report of gallbladder and pancreatic ultrasound.

Interfering Circumstances. Inability of the patient to remain still, maintain the desired position, or alter breathing patterns as requested may adversely affect image quality. Gas or barium in the intestinal tract may interfere

---

NAME: Gervais, Marie

CASE NO.:   12-15-48

PROCEDURE: Ultrasound of the upper abdomen.

CLINICAL INFORMATION: Abdominal pain, nausea.

REPORT: Scans of the upper abdomen show the gallbladder to be small and contracted. There are multiple echogenic areas within the confines of the gallbladder consistent with cholelithiasis. The common bile duct measured 5 mm and is within normal limits. The pancreas and liver are unremarkable.

CONCLUSION: Probable cholelithiasis.

Figure 13-1. Gallbladder and pancreas ultrasound report

with the results of gallbladder ultrasound. Image quality may be compromised with obese patients.

Kidney Ultrasonography

Kidney ultrasonography, also called renal ultrasonography, is an ultrasound examination of the kidney that is performed to asses the kidney size, structure, and position; and to diagnose and monitor various renal disorders. Urinary blockage and abnormal fluid or blood accumulation in the kidney is also assessed via kidney ultrasound.

With the patient in the supine or side-lying position, the area over the kidney is exposed, conductive gel is applied, and the transducer is moved across the area. Sound waves are transmitted through the transducer to a screen and recorded as photographic images. Kidney ultrasonography is a safe, noninvasive procedure and presents no risk to the patient.

Normal Findings. Normal size, shape, structure, and position of the kidneys.

Variations from Normal. Abnormal conditions such as renal calculi, cysts, tumors, polycystic kidneys, and other masses can be diagnosed using kidney ultrasonography. Hydronephrosis can be identified with this study.

Interfering Circumstances. Inability of the patient to remain still and maintain the desired position may adversely affect image quality. Gas or barium in the intestinal tract may interfere with the results of kidney ultrasound.

Liver Ultrasonography

Liver ultrasonography is an ultrasound examination of the liver and the hepatic ducts that is performed to assess the size, shape, texture, and position of the liver and hepatic ducts. Hepatic duct patency and diameter can be evaluated via liver ultrasonography.

With the patient in the supine position, the abdomen is exposed, conductive gel is applied, and the transducer is moved over the area. Breathing patterns may be altered during the examination. Images are transmitted through the transducer to a screen and recorded on photographs. Liver ultrasonography is a safe, noninvasive procedure and presents no risks to the patient.

Normal Findings. Normal size, shape, structure, texture, and position of the liver and hepatic ducts.

Variations from Normal. Liver ultrasonography is used to diagnose cirrhosis, masses, tumors, cysts, and abscesses of the liver. It can also be used to identify hepatic duct obstruction and determine the cause of jaundice.

Interfering Circumstances. Inability of the patient to remain still, maintain the desired position, or alter breathing patterns as requested may adversely affect image quality. Gas or barium in the intestinal tract may interfere with the results of gallbladder ultrasound. Image quality may be compromised with obese patients. In addition, the structure of the rib cage may make it difficult to visualize the right lobe of the liver.

Pancreas Ultrasonography

Pancreas ultrasonography is an ultrasound examination of the pancreas that is performed to assess the size, shape, texture, and position of the pancreas. Pancreatic malignancies and anomalies can be diagnosed with this ultrasound study. As with other needle aspiration biopsies, pancreatic ultrasound can be used to monitor needle insertion.

With the patient in the supine position, the abdominal quadrants are exposed, conductive gel is applied to the epigastric area, and the transducer is moved across the area. During pancreatic ultrasonography the patient may be asked to change position, regulate breathing patterns, and distend the stomach by drinking water in order to aid in the visualization of the pancreas. Images are transmitted to a screen through the transducer and a photographic record is made. This is a safe, noninvasive, procedure that presents no risks to the patient.

Normal Findings. Normal size, shape, structure, and position of the pancreas.

Variations from Normal. Abnormal conditions such as pancreatitis, tumors, pseudocyst, and pancreatic cancer can be detected using pancreatic ultrasonography.

Interfering Circumstances. Inability of the patient to remain still, maintain the desired position, or alter breathing patterns as requested may adversely affect image quality. Gas or barium in the intestinal tract may interfere with the results of gallbladder ultrasound. Image quality may be compromised with obese patients.

Spleen Ultrasonography

Spleen ultrasonography is an ultrasound examination of the spleen performed to evaluate the size, shape, texture, and position of the spleen; to diagnose a variety of abnormalities; and to assess spleen trauma caused by accidents. The necessity for splenectomy can be determined via this study.

The patient is prepared for the spleen ultrasonography in the same manner as other abdominal organ ultrasound studies. In the supine or decubitus position the upper left quadrant of the abdomen is exposed, is covered with conductive gel, and the transducer is moved across the upper left quadrant. Images are transmitted to a screen and developed into photographic recordings. This is a safe, noninvasive procedure that presents no risks to the patient.

Patients who have had traumatic injury or some other abnormality of the spleen may have discomfort when the transducer is pressed against the body. Analgesics may be given to relieve the pain.

Normal Findings. Normal size, shape, texture, and position of the spleen.

Variations from Normal. Abnormal conditions such as splenomegaly, traumatic injury causing rupture or enlargement of the spleen, and splenic cysts and tumors can be detected using spleen ultrasonography.

Interfering Circumstances. Circumstances that interfere with successful use of the spleen ultrasonography are the same as those described earlier for other abdominal organ ultrasound studies. In addition, the left ribs and lung near the spleen may interfere with the ability to carry out a successful ultrasound study.

Ultrasonography of the Pelvic Region

Ultrasonography of the pelvic region includes studies of organs and tissues in or near the pelvic cavity. These studies include **bladder ultrasonography**, a study of the urinary bladder; **obstetric ultrasonography**, a study of the fetus and placenta; **pelvic ultrasonography**, a study of female reproductive organs; **prostate ultrasonography**, a study of the prostate gland; and **scrotal ultrasonography**, a study of the scrotum and its contents. Each examination is discussed individually.

Bladder Ultrasonography

In addition to evaluating bladder size, shape, structure, position, and function, bladder ultrasonography is used to identify tumors, masses, and obstruction of the urinary tract. Masses or tumors pressing against the bladder wall can be detected as changes in the shape or position of the bladder. This ultrasound test is also used to measure the amount of residual urine remaining in the bladder after the patient has voided. A large residual urine volume may be indicative of an obstruction of the urinary tract.

Bladder ultrasonography requires a full bladder to assure effective imaging results. The bladder can be kept full by drinking fluid or via intravenous hydration. The patient is placed in a supine position and the skin over the bladder is coated with a conductive gel. The transducer is passed over the bladder and transmits images to a screen, which in turn provides a photographic recording of the ultrasound.

A residual urine volume, measuring the urine left in the bladder after voiding, can be performed during bladder ultrasonography. For this additional test, the patient is asked to empty the bladder after the initial ultrasound image is obtained. Once the bladder is empty, the ultrasound is repeated and the urine that remains in the bladder is measured. Bladder ultrasonography is a safe, noninvasive procedure and presents no risks to the patient.

Normal Findings. Normal bladder anatomy and residual urine volume.

Variations from Normal. Abnormal conditions such as bladder tumors, metastatic cancer, and urinary tract obstruction can be diagnosed using bladder ultrasonography. In addition, masses from other organs in the pelvic cavity can be detected by this ultrasound study.

Interfering Circumstances. Inability to drink and retain enough fluid to maintain a full bladder negatively affects the imaging process. Gas or barium in the gastrointestinal tract may compromise image quality.

Obstetric Ultrasonography

Obstetric ultrasonography, also called **fetal ultrasound,** is an ultrasound examination of the fetus and placenta. It is a safe, accurate, noninvasive, diagnostic study that does not present risks to the patient or fetus. Obstetric ultrasonography assists the physician in determining the normal progression of fetal growth and development, and in diagnosing abnormal conditions related to pregnancy. This study is performed to confirm normal pregnancy; identify multiple pregnancies; evaluate the size, growth, and position of the fetus; determine gestational age through measurement of the uterus and the fetus; and monitor the placenta and amniotic fluid volume. Obstetric ultrasonography can be accomplished by way of the **transabdominal method,** in which the transducer is moved across the skin of the abdomen, or by way of the **transvaginal method,** in which the transducer is inserted into the vagina.

A transabdominal obstetric ultrasonography is conducted with the patient in the supine position. The abdominal area over the uterus is exposed, conductive gel is placed on the skin, and the transducer is moved across the skin over the uterus. This procedure is done with a full bladder and the bladder is used as a reference point for the cervical os. Clear identification of the cervical os is necessary in order to assess the uterus for placenta previa. Sound waves are transmitted through the transducer, images are displayed on a screen, and photographic recordings are made.

A transvaginal obstetric ultrasound is usually performed during the first trimester of pregnancy, although it can be done throughout the pregnancy, if necessary. It is performed for the same reasons as the transabdominal obstetric ultrasound, and the exams can be performed in conjunction with one another. The transducer used for a transvaginal ultrasound is covered with a condom sheath plus a lubricant and is inserted and moved around in the vagina. Images of the uterus and uterine contents are transmitted, displayed on a screen, and a photographic recording is made. An empty bladder is necessary for the transvaginal method. Figure 13-2 shows a uterine image created by transvaginal ultrasound.

Normal Findings. Normal fetus and placenta. Size, shape, and position of the fetus consistent with normal growth and development patterns for the particular trimester of pregnancy.

Variations from Normal. Multiple fetuses can be detected with obstetric ultrasonography. Diagnoses such as tubal pregnancy, hydatidiform mole,

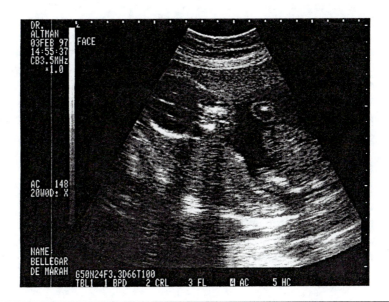

Figure 13-2. Uterine image produced by transvaginal ultrasound

missed abortion, uterine masses, cysts, and neoplasms are identified by this study. Obstetric ultrasound can discover fetal problems such as abnormal fetal position, congenital anomalies, hydrocephaly, and fetal death. In addition, it can be used to detect or confirm placenta previa, abruptio placentae, and other placental abnormalities.

Interfering Circumstances. Circumstances that interfere with successful use of the obstetric ultrasonography are the inability of the patient to cooperate and maintain the desired posture for the examination. Gas or barium in the gastrointestinal tract can interfere with the quality of the ultrasound images.

Pelvic Ultrasonography

Pelvic ultrasonography is an ultrasound study of the vagina, cervix, uterus, ovaries, and fallopian tubes. This procedure can assist the physician in diagnosing abnormalities of the reproductive organs and pelvic cavity. It is also used to monitor the ovarian follicular development of a patient undergoing treatment for infertility and to locate intrauterine devices.

Patient preparation for the pelvic ultrasonography is the same as obstetric ultrasonography. The transabdominal or the transvaginal approach can be used. Pelvic ultrasonography is a safe, noninvasive procedure that does not present risk to the patient.

Normal Findings. Normal structure and location of the reproductive organs. The intrauterine device is in its proper location.

Variations from Normal. Pelvic ultrasonography can be used to diagnose cancer of the uterus, ovaries, and fallopian tubes. It can identify abscesses, ovarian cysts, trauma to the pelvic region, uterine fibroids, and pelvic inflammatory disease.

Interfering Circumstances. Circumstances that interfere are the same as those discussed with obstetric ultrasonography.

Prostate Ultrasonography

Prostate ultrasonography, also called transrectal or rectal ultrasound, is an ultrasound study of the prostate gland. This procedure is used to examine the size, shape, texture, and position of the prostate gland and its tissue, and to diagnose abnormal conditions. Prostate ultrasonography is also used to guide the physician in performing prostate biopsy, and placing radioactive seeds into the prostate gland for cancer treatment.

Prior to prostate ultrasonography, the patient may be placed on antibiotics and given an enema to empty the rectum of stool. The patient is prepared for the procedure by being placed on the left side with the rectal area exposed. Following a rectal exam, a rectal probe equipped with a transducer and covered with a condom sheath is lubricated and inserted into the rectum. The condom sheath is filled with water in order to facilitate the transmission of sound waves between the prostate and the transducer. As the transducer is rotated along the prostate, images are transmitted to a screen and photographic recordings are made.

After reviewing the images, the physician may also perform a needle biopsy through the rectal wall using the probe. During the procedure the patient experiences pressure on the rectum. The patient may show blood in the urine and semen for a few days after a biopsy is performed. Figure 13-3 is a report of a transrectal prostatic ultrasound.

PATIENT NAME: Piper, Peter

MEDICAL RECORD NUMBER: 00-00-08

DATE: March 15, xx

PROCEDURE: TRANSRECTAL PROSTATIC ULTRASOUND

REPORT: Using real-time examination, the prostate gland was examined with ultrasound. The gland measures 5.9 cm in length × 3.1 cm in depth × 4.9 cm in transverse dimension. Prostatic volume is approximately 26 grams.

The gland is generally heterogeneous. In the periphery of the left lobe, there is a nodule measuring 1.7 × 0.9 × 1.4 cm. This nodule is hypoechoic and partly solid. There appears to be a larger hypoechoic solid nodule to the right of midline, measuring approximately 2 cm in diameter. No other focal nodule is identified.

IMPRESSION: 1. Small nodule left lobe peripherally.
                      2. Suspected large nodule right lobe medially.

PLAN: I would advise Mr. Piper to have a biopsy.

Figure 13-3.   Transrectal prostatic ultrasound

Normal Findings. Normal size-prostate, absence of tumors and inflammation.

Variations from Normal. Prostate ultrasonography can be used to help diagnosis benign prostatic hypertrophy (BPH), cancer of the prostate gland, and prostatitis.

Interfering Circumstances. The patient must be cooperative during the procedure and must be able to maintain the desired posture for the examination. Feces in the rectum can interfere with the results of the ultrasound.

Scrotal Ultrasonography

Scrotal ultrasonography is an ultrasound examination of the scrotum and testicles that is performed to assess the size, shape, structure, and texture of the testicles and other intrascrotal tissues. Scrotal ultrasonography is used to diagnose scrotal and testicular abnormalities, and to identify the presence of blood or pus in the scrotal sac.

The patient is prepared for the procedure by being placed in a supine position with the scrotum exposed. A towel is placed over the penis to secure it to the lower abdomen, and another towel is placed under the scrotum. The scrotum is coated with conductive gel and a transducer is moved around the scrotal area. Images are transmitted to a screen and photographic recordings are made. Scrotal ultrasonography is a safe, noninvasive procedure and presents no risks to the patient.

Normal Findings. Normal scrotum and testicles. Intrascrotal tissues are normal in appearance.

Variations from Normal. Scrotal ultrasonography can identify abnormalities, such as testicular cancer, hydrocele, hematocele, pyocele, spermatocele, hematoma, epididymitis, orchitis, scrotal hernia, cryptorchidism, and testicular torsion.

Interfering Circumstances. A circumstance that interferes with successful use of the scrotal ultrasonography is the inability of the patient to cooperate and maintain the desired posture for the examination.

Ultrasonography of the Blood Vessels

Ultrasonography of the blood vessels includes studies that examine the flow of blood through arteries and veins of the extremities, as well as blood vessels located in organs and other locations of the body. These studies are known as **Doppler ultrasound studies**, and include **arterial Doppler studies**, ultrasound studies of the flow of blood through arteries; and **venous Doppler studies**, ultrasound studies of the flow of blood through veins.

Overview of Doppler Ultrasound Studies

Doppler ultrasonography uses a transducer to detect Doppler shift waves, the sound frequency shifts created by moving blood cells. Audible sounds and waveforms are produced by the Doppler ultrasound detector as it recognizes the flow of blood through the blood vessel. These sounds are pulsations or swishing noises and are useful in determining the degree of blood vessel patency. The sounds and waveforms can be recorded on a videotape.

Various Doppler techniques are available, depending on the type and purpose of the study. A continuous-waveform Doppler stethoscope is used to monitor blood flow in patients who have circulatory abnormalities and to monitor fetal heart sounds. Studies known as **duplex scanning** combine pulsed or continuous waveform Doppler ultrasound and real-time ultrasound imaging to study both the organ and the flow of the blood through the organ. This technique is utilized with most Doppler studies. Color-flow Doppler imaging is used to assess blood-flow direction and velocity when doing studies of the heart, fetus, and peripheral blood vessels.

Doppler studies can detect decreased blood flow through the heart, arteries, and veins. Since the ultrasound waves bounce off the blood as it flows, a lower frequency of ultrasound waves indicates decreased blood flow and can identify obstructive disorders. Doppler studies are useful in determining the need for more extensive diagnostic testing. Arterial and venous Doppler studies are discussed individually.

Arterial Doppler Studies

Arterial Doppler studies are ultrasound studies of the arteries. The studies include examination of the peripheral arteries of the extremities; carotid arteries; and cranial arteries, including the basilar artery, vertebral artery, and the circle of Willis. Doppler studies of the cranial arteries are also called **transcranial Doppler studies**.

Patient preparation for an arterial Doppler study is dependent on the area of the body and the artery being examined. For a Doppler study of the carotid artery the patient is in the supine position with the neck exposed. For Doppler studies of the extremities the supine position is also used, and blood pressure cuffs are applied at various points along the leg or arm in order to determine the presence and location of an occlusion. Although both the carotid Doppler and the extremity Doppler are done to identify occlusions, the procedure is tailored to the area of the body being studied.

For all arterial Doppler studies, conductive gel is applied to the appropriate area, the transducer is passed across the skin covering the particular artery, and images are transmitted to a video screen and a photographic record is made. Arterial Doppler studies are safe, noninvasive procedures and present no risk to the patient.

Normal Findings. Normal blood flow through the arteries under study.

Variations from Normal. Arterial Doppler studies are used to diagnose arterial stenosis and occlusions, including thrombosis, arterial occlusive disease, plaque, and occlusions caused by trauma. This diagnostic tool is useful in identifying arterial malformations, aneurysms, basil and vertebral artery insufficiency, and arterial spasms present in Raynaud's disease.

Interfering Circumstances. The inability of the patient to cooperate and maintain the desired posture for the examination may interfere with the successful use of arterial Doppler studies.

Venous Doppler Studies

Venous Doppler studies are ultrasound studies of the veins. These studies include examination of the veins of the lower extremities, the femoral, popliteal, and tibial veins; veins of the upper extremities, the axillary and brachial veins; and the jugular veins located in the neck. Venous Doppler studies are used to evaluate the flow of blood through the veins and to assess veins that are to be used in grafts.

The patient is prepared for the exam by being placed in a supine position with the area under examination exposed. Conductive gel is applied to the site and the transducer is moved over the skin. When examining the extremities, the procedure is performed on both the left and right extremity so that a comparison of the venous flow can be made. The transducer transmits wave images to a video screen and a recording of the findings is created. Venous Doppler studies are safe, noninvasive procedures and present no risk to the patient.

Normal Findings. Normal blood flow through the veins.

Variations from Normal. Venous Doppler studies are used to diagnose superficial and deep venous thrombosis (DVT), and venous obstruction or insufficiency.

Interfering Circumstances. Circumstances that interfere with successful use of arterial Doppler studies include the inability of the patient to cooperate and maintain the desired posture for the examination.

Summary

- Ultrasound studies allow the visualization of an organ or blood vessel by using sound waves emitted and returned to a transducer.
- Ultrasound images are displayed on a video screen in the form of a picture or waveform and are permanently recorded.
- Ultrasonography can be used to diagnose a variety of abnormal conditions of body organs and blood vessels.
- Ultrasonography is usually a noninvasive procedure that does not require anesthetics and presents no risk to the patient.
- Ultrasound studies of the head and neck region include neonate head sonography, ocular ultrasonography, and thyroid ultrasonography.
- Echocardiography, intravascular ultrasound, and transesophageal echocardiography are ultrasound studies of the heart.
- Ultrasound studies of the abdomen include examination of the aorta, gallbladder, liver, pancreas, and spleen.
- Obstetric ultrasonography involves the study of the fetus and the placenta and can be used to evaluate the growth and development patterns of the fetus.
- Prostate ultrasonography requires the insertion of a probe into the rectum of the male patient and is useful in the diagnosis of prostate cancer.
- Ultrasonography of the pelvis is used to study the female reproductive organs.
- Ultrasounds can be used to study the bladder and the scrotum and its contents.
- Doppler studies evaluate the movement of blood through the heart, arteries, and veins.

CHAPTER REVIEW

1. Identify the following ultrasound studies:

   a. Studies that examine the flow of blood
   through arteries and veins   _____

   b. Sound waves are used to pulverize kidneys
   and gallstones   _____

   c. Utilizes M-mode, 2-D mode, and color-flow
   mode   _____

   d. Also known as fetal ultrasound in pregnancy _____

   e. Doppler studies of the basilar and vertebral
   arteries and the circle of Willis   _____

2. Name the ultrasound study or studies associated with the listed diagnoses.

   a. Abdominal aortic aneurysm   _____

   b. Arterial occlusive disease   _____

   c. Atherosclerotic lesions   _____

   d. Cholelithiasis, choledocholithiasis _____

   e. Deep vein thrombosis   _____

   f. Detached retina   _____

   g. Hydrocephalus   _____

   h. Hydronephrosis   _____

   i. Nodules, goiters   _____

   j. Ovarian cancer   _____

   k. Patent ductus arteriosus, septal defects _____

    l. Spermatocele, cryptorchidism   _____

    m. Tubal pregnancy, hydatidiform mole   _____

    n. Urinary tract obstruction   _____

3. Briefly describe the structures examined by the listed ultrasound. Provide examples of the diseases that can be diagnosed by these studies.

    a. Abdominal aortic ultrasonography   _____

    b. Echocardiography   _____

    c. Neonate head sonography   _____

    d. Gallbladder ultrasonography   _____

    e. Thyroid ultrasonography   _____

    f. Intravascular ultrasound   _____

4. Identify the interfering factors that are associated with nearly all the ultrasound studies discussed in the chapter. Explain why these factors apply to so many studies.

5. Describe ultrasound technology and explain why it is such a valuable diagnostic tool.

Case Studies

1. Carol Jeffers, a 70-year-old female, is suspected of having cardiac abnormalities. Dr. Brown has ordered an echocardiogram. Discuss how this ultrasound examination is performed and why it is done. What abnormalities can be identified with this study? How could Carol Jeffers's age affect the test procedure?

2. Wilfred Rice, a 63-year-old man, has been experiencing difficulty urinating. Dr. Hollister, a urologist, has decided to do a prostate ultrasound on Mr. Rice. Why is the prostatic ultrasound an important diagnostic tool? How is the study carried out? What diagnoses can be identified or ruled out?

3. Moyesha Jabral, a 28-year-old pregnant woman in her first trimester, has been scheduled for an obstetric ultrasound. Explain why her physician would order this exam. What information will this study provide? What are types of ultrasound techniques available for obstetric sonography? Describe the techniques.

Challenge Activity

Create a table or figure that organizes the ultrasound studies according to general body areas or body cavities that house the organs studied. Include graphics as well as text. Use computer graphics or desktop publishing, if available.

Chapter 14

Special Organ Studies

Key Terms, Abbreviations, and Acronyms

airway flow rates

auditory brain stem (evoked) response, ABR, ABER

diffusing capacity of the lung

electrocardiography, ECG, EKG

electrodiagnostic studies

electroencephalography, EEG

electromyography, EMG

electromyoneurography

electroneurography

electrophysiology studies, EP, EPS

evoked response studies

event marker

exercise stress test

gas exchange tests

Holter monitor test

hyperventilation EEG

latency period

lung volumes and capacities

oximetry

photostimulation EEG

pulmonary diffusion

pulmonary perfusion

pulmonary ventilation

pulse oximetry

sensory-evoked brain potentials

signal-averaged electrocardiography

sleep EEG

somatosensory-evoked response, SER

spirometry

sweat test

visual-evoked response, VER

Learning Objectives

Upon completion of this chapter, the learner should be able to:

1. Discuss the diagnostic significance of special organ function studies.
2. Organize organ function studies according to the specific organ or system being assessed.
3. Compare the difference between electroencephalography and evoked brain response studies.
4. Differentiate between the electrocardiography studies presented in this chapter.
5. Relate diagnoses and diseases to the appropriate diagnostic tests.
6. Define lung perfusion, ventilation, and diffusion.
7. Organize pulmonary function studies according to lung perfusion, ventilation, and diffusion.

Introduction

Thus far the laboratory and diagnostic tests presented in this text focus on specific body fluids or diagnostic techniques. The majority of these tests are performed or can be performed in a variety of health care agencies regardless of size. Special organ studies present some of the more complex diagnostic studies. Some of these studies require sophisticated equipment that may only be available in regional medical centers, tertiary care centers, or highly specialized treatment centers. The studies included in this chapter are by no means all inclusive or exhaustive. They were selected on the basis of general recognition and interest.

Overview of Special Organ Studies

Special organ studies involve the use of both invasive and noninvasive diagnostic techniques. The majority of studies presented are performed to assess organ or system function. Organ function can be assessed by analyzing organ or tissue electrical activity, monitoring organ movement or response to stress situations; and recording organ response to test situations.

Special organ studies are presented in relation to the specific organ, tissue, or system under study. Information for each study includes a brief description of the study, the organ or tissue examined, indications or contraindications for the study, diseases that are associated with the study, and factors that interfere with or prevent the satisfactory performance of the study. Organ function tests are organized under brain function studies, heart function tests, pulmonary function tests, and miscellaneous function tests.

Brain Function Studies

Special studies of the brain and nervous system tissue involve careful assessment of the electrical activity of the brain. These tests include the familiar **electroencephalography (EEG)**, measuring and recording the electrical activity of the cerebral cortex; and the sophisticated **evoked response studies**, identifying and recording changes and responses of cerebral cortex activity when sensory pathways are stimulated.

Electroencephalography (EEG)

Electroencephalography (EEG) is a diagnostic test that measures and records the electrical activity of the cerebral cortex. EEG is performed to diagnose diseases and disorders of the brain, to monitor cerebral blood flow during surgical procedures such as carotid endarterectomy, and to determine brain death. There are no contraindications for this test.

Electroencephalography is usually performed in a room that is protected from outside interference. It can, however, be done at the patient's bedside. With the patient in a supine position, electrodes are applied to the scalp. Electrode paste is used, the electrodes are placed in a specified pattern, and all areas of the skull are covered. During the recording the patient must lie still with eyes closed. The study may take as long as two hours to complete. Since movement alters EEG results, a technician observes the patient throughout the entire test. In some instances, recording is interrupted at regular intervals and the patient is allowed to move. Figure 14-1 is an example of an electroencephalography report.

PATIENT NAME: THOMPSON, SARA

MEDICAL RECORD NUMBER: 01-23-45

STUDY: Electroencephalography

DESCRIPTION OF THE STUDY: This 18-channel EEG was obtained on a 32-year-old female with a history of multiple sclerosis and cognitive difficulties. Her medications include Tegretol. She is awake and cooperative.

The biposterior-dominant background rhythm consists of poorly organized and regulated 5 to 6 Hz activity, which is of 30 to 50 in amplitude. Occasional generalized bursts of delta activity are seen. The background is reactive to eye opening and eye closure.

CLINICAL DIAGNOSIS: This EEG is consistent with moderately severe, diffuse disturbance in cortical neuronal function that is of nonspecific etiology. Such changes can be seen in the setting of a toxic metabolic encephalopathy and certainly could be related to the patient's history of severe demyelinating disease. The slight left-sided predominance of the slowing might predict more involvement of multiple sclerosis in the left hemisphere. No epileptiform abnormalities.

EEG DIAGNOSIS: This EEG is abnormal because of the presence of severe diffuse slowing and disorganization of the background rhythm.

Figure 14-1. Electroencephalography report

In addition to the resting EEG described above, electroencephalography can be performed under other diagnostic conditions. **Hyperventilation EEG**, during which the patient is asked to breathe deeply for a specific period of time, can identify abnormalities related to cerebral vasoconstriction. **Photostimulation EEG**, performed by flashing a light over the patient's face, may provoke photostimulated seizure activity. **Sleep EEG** is used to detect sleep disorders and sleep-related epilepsy. During sleep EEG, brain activity is recorded as the patient falls asleep, during the sleep, and while the patient is awakening.

Normal Findings. Normal brain structure and function as evidenced by normal cerebral electrical activity.

Variations from Normal. Intracranial lesions and diseases such as hemorrhage, infarction, glioblastoma, or abscesses are identified via electroencephalography. Seizure disorders, including epilepsy, can be diagnosed and evaluated with EEG. This diagnostic study can identify sleep apnea and narcolepsy.

EEG can help delineate areas of brain tissue abnormality associated with Alzheimer's disease, migraine headaches, and schizophrenia. Brain death can be evaluated and confirmed with information provided by electroencephalography.

Interfering Circumstances. Hypoglycemic conditions caused by fasting, caffeine, and body movements can modify brain wave patterns. Oil, dirt, and hair preparations such as hairspray can interfere with electrode placement and contact, and thereby interfere with the recording process. Sedatives, anticonvulsants, and alcohol affect test results.

Evoked Brain-Response Studies

Evoked brain-response studies, also called **sensory evoked brain potentials**, focus on the changes or responses of cerebral electrical activity that are evoked by the stimulation of a sensory pathway. While electroencephalography measures spontaneous electrical activity, the sensory-evoked brain potential studies measure and record brain wave activity produced in response to a specific stimulus.

Evoked brain potential or response studies include the following: **visual-evoked response (VER)**, stimulation of the optic pathways using a strobe light flash; **auditory brain stem (evoked) response (ABR, ABER)**, stimulation of the auditory pathways of the brain stem using a pattern of clicking sounds; and **somatosensory-evoked response (SER)**, electrical stimulation to a specific body area to identify spinal cord, nerve pathway, or cerebral cortex damage. Each of these specialized evoked-response studies is discussed individually.

Interfering circumstances for all evoked-response studies are fairly consistent. Inability of the patient to cooperate or understand requests made during the study may alter results. Special considerations are necessary when studies are done on infants and young children. Improper placement of electrodes obviously cause inaccurate recording of responses. Since the interfering circumstance are virtually the same, they are presented here and not with each individual evoked-response study.

Visual-Evoked Response (VER)

Visual-evoked response studies are conducted to evaluate optic nerves, optic nerve tracts, and the visual center of the brain. The exam is accomplished by placing electrodes along the vertex and occipital lobes of the skull. The eyes and optic nerves are stimulated by having the patient observe a repeated strobe light flashing or reversible checkerboard pattern. This stimulation causes an electrical response in the occipital area of the brain. The response is recorded and graphed. The time that elapses between stimulation and response is called the **latency period**. A greater degree of latency corresponds to disease severity. The exam is done on each eye individually.

Normal Findings. Normal latency period involving optic pathways and the visual centers of the cerebral cortex.

Variations from Normal. Multiple sclerosis and Parkinson's disease are associated with abnormal latency periods. Lesions of the optic nerve, optic tract, and cerebral cortex visual center(s) can be identified with a visual-evoked response exam. Visual field defects due to retinal damage, macular degeneration, and glaucoma may be detected by VER.

Auditory Brain Stem (Evoked) Responses (ABR, ABER)

Auditory brain stem (evoked) response studies are conducted to evaluate the central auditory pathways of the brain stem. The exam is accomplished by placing electrodes along the top or crown of the scalp and on each earlobe. Earphones are placed in the patient's ears. Stimulation is provided by directing clicking noises or tone bursts into one ear, while delivering a continuous (masking) tone into the opposite ear. This stimulation causes electrical responses in the auditory pathway of the brain stem. The electrical responses are recorded and graphed. As with other evoked responses, measuring the latency period between stimuli and response provides diagnostically significant information.

Normal Findings. Normal latency period and stimulation of the auditory pathways of the brain stem and auditory nerve areas.

Variations from Normal. Auditory disorders of low-birthweight newborns are identified by auditory brain stem–evoked response studies. Abnormal latency responses are associated with brain stem tumors, acoustic neuromas, and lesions of the brain stem or auditory nerves. Brain stem and nerve lesions can be caused by a variety of neurological and/or demyelinating diseases, such as multiple sclerosis.

Somatosensory-Evoked Response (SER)

Somatosensory-evoked response studies are conducted to evaluate the neurological and sensory pathways associated with pain and touch. The exam is accomplished by placing stimulation electrodes at nerve sites of the wrist, knee, and ankle. Electrodes are also placed on the scalp over the sensory cerebral cortex area that is on the opposite side of the body as the stimulation electrodes. Electrical stimuli in sufficient magnitude to produce a thumb or foot twitch are applied to the nerve sites. This stimulation causes electrical responses in the sensory cerebral cortex that are recorded and graphed. As with other evoked responses, measuring the latency period between stimuli and response provides diagnostically significant information.

Normal Findings. Normal latency period and stimulation of the sensory pathways of the brain and spinal cord.

Variations from Normal. Multiple sclerosis, Guillain-Barré syndrome, and spinal cord injuries are identified by somatosensory-evoked response studies. Abnormal latency responses are associated with cerebrovascular accident and cervical myelopathy.

Heart Function Tests

Special heart function tests covered in this chapter can be categorized as **electrodiagnostic studies**, which are procedures that use electrical impulses and electronic devices to identify and assess abnormalities of heart function and structure. The tests presented in this chapter are often performed to support or confirm information obtained with other diagnostic interventions.

Heart function studies are covered individually and include **electrocardiography (ECG, EKG)**, a study that measures the electrical activity of the heart during the cardiac cycle; **electrophysiology studies (EP, EPS)**, an invasive procedure used to identify heart arrhythmias and conduction defects; **exercise stress test**, a noninvasive test that measures cardiac function during physical stress; **Holter monitor test**, a continuous recording of the electrical activity of the heart; and the **signal-averaged electrocardiography (SAE)**, a study performed to identify the risk of ventricular arrhythmias in postmyocardial infarction patients.

Electrocardiography (ECG, EKG)

Electrocardiography is a recording of the electrical impulses that stimulate the heart to contract. It is one of the most frequently performed diagnostic tests. ECG is often ordered as part of a routine physical examination, in preparation for any surgical or procedural intervention, or to identify suspected heart conduction problems. Electrocardiography is also performed to monitor cardiac pacemaker function, and to evaluate the effectiveness of cardiac medications.

The actual graphic report is an electrocardiogram that displays the movement of the electrical impulse from the sinoatrial (SA) node to the atrioventricular (AV) node and through atrial and ventricular contraction. The electrical impulse is recorded as a series of waves and peaks. The shape, height, and time intervals between ECG waves and peaks provide valuable diagnostic information about the heart.

Electrocardiography can be accomplished by placing either ten or twelve special electrodes called leads anywhere on the four extremities and on specific sites on the chest. A lead is placed on the right leg to establish the ground. No electricity is directed toward the patient, but the electrical impulses are directed from the heart to the surface of the skin. This is a noninvasive test with few if any contraindications. It must be noted that an ECG can be normal in the presence of heart disease that does not affect the electrical activity of the heart.

Normal Findings. Normal heart rate, rhythm, and wave patterns.

Variations from Normal. A variety of cardiac disorders are identified by electrocardiography. Arrhythmias and their cause, conduction defects, abnormal position of the heart, and ventricular hypertrophy can be diagnosed by performing an ECG. Abnormal waves and interval times can point to diseases such as Wolff-Parkinson-White syndrome, an atrioventricular conduction defect, and pericarditis. Detection and monitoring of myocardial infarction is accomplished with the ECG. Figure 14-2 displays the difference between a normal ECG and abnormal recordings as seen in atrial fibrillation, atrial flutter, and tachycardia.

Interfering Circumstances. There are a wide variety of interfering circumstances associated with electrocardiography. Inaccurate placement of leads and poor contact between the skin and leads alter ECG results. Movement, twitching, electrolyte imbalances, and drugs such as digitalis can lead to an unreliable tracing.

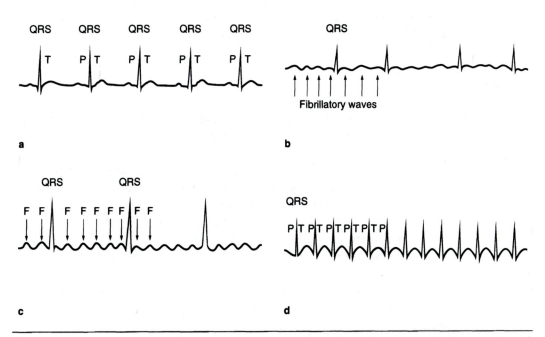

Figure 14-2. An electrocardiogram provides valuable information about the functioning of the patient's heart: **(a)** normal ECG, **(b)** atrial fibrillation, **(c)** atrial flutter, **(d)** tachycardia.

Electrophysiology Study (EP, EPS)

An electrophysiology study is an invasive diagnostic test that is performed to identify heart conduction defects and heart arrhythmias. Electrode catheters are threaded through a peripheral vein and advanced into the right side of the heart. Fluoroscopy is used to ensure proper catheter placement.

Indications for electrophysiology studies are suspected ventricular arrhythmia, identification of the cause of conduction defects, and monitoring the effectiveness of antiarrhythmic medications. Uncooperative patients and the presence of myocardial infarction are the main contraindications for EPS. Since this procedure is invasive, there are rather significant risks such as perforation of the myocardium, hemorrhage, phlebitis at the puncture site, and catheter-induced emboli. The emboli may cause a stroke.

Normal Findings. Normal heart conduction and arrhythmic response to stimuli.

Variations from Normal. Conduction defects and cardiac arrhythmias are the most commonly identified abnormal results. Sinoatrial node, atrioventricular node, and heart block defects can also be diagnosed with EPS.

Exercise Stress Test

Exercise stress test is a noninvasive study that is performed to evaluate cardiac function during physical activity. Electrocardiography is conducted during stress testing and the patient's heart rate and blood pressure are monitored. There are three types of exercise associated with this test: stair climbing, walking a treadmill with the grade of incline gradually increasing, and pedaling a stationary bike with the pedaling tension slowly increasing.

During exercise stress testing, the heart rate is increased to a level that is at or just below the target heart rate. The test is based on the assumption that a heart with compromised vascularity (coronary occlusions) will not be able to meet the heart's increased demand for oxygen. Symptoms such as chest pains, syncope, fatigue, dyspnea, and ECG changes will signal the need to end the test. These same symptoms can indicate a reduction in cardiac efficiency and may be predictive of heart disease.

Exercise stress testing is indicated for patients with chest pain, to evaluate safe exercise limits for cardiac rehabilitation programs, and to evaluate the effectiveness of antianginal or antiarrhythmic medications. There are many contraindications for this evaluation such as unstable angina, severe aortic valve disease, recent myocardial infarction, and impaired lung or motor function. Risks associated with this exam are fatal cardiac arrhythmias, severe angina, myocardial infarction, and fainting.

Normal Findings. Normal heart rate during exercise, based on the patient's age and gender. Normal ECG and an absence of symptoms of cardiac insufficiency.

Variations from Normal. Diseases identified by exercise stress tests are coronary artery occlusive disease, hypertension associated with exercise, and peripheral arterial occlusive disease as evidenced by intermittent claudication.

Holter Monitor Test

Holter monitoring, also called Holter electrocardiography, is a method of continuously recording the electrical activity of the heart over an extended period of time. Recordings are maintained on magnetic tape. The Holter monitor test is used to correlate suspected cardiac rhythm disorders with symptoms such as chest pain, syncope, and palpitations that may occur during the patient's daily activities. Holter monitoring is also used to evaluate pacemaker and defibrillation device efficiency, and to evaluate the effectiveness of cardiac medications.

During the Holter monitoring assessment, the patient wears a portable ECG device that records all cardiac cycles for a specific period of time. A timing device is part of the equipment, and allows accurate monitoring of ECG activity and changes. In addition, the patient is asked to carry a diary and record all activities carried out during the tested hours, as well as any observance of cardiac symptoms. Many Holter units are equipped with an **event marker**, which is a button the patient can push when cardiac symptoms occur. This allows the patient to "mark" the magnetic tape for later evaluation.

There are few if any risks associated with this study. Contraindications are usually related to the patient's inability to keep the Holter monitor lead in place, or to accurately record significant activities and events.

Normal Findings. Normal sinus rhythm. Absence of arrhythmias.

Variations from Normal. Cardiac rhythm disturbances such as bradycardia and tachycardia are identified with Holter monitoring. Premature atrial or ventricular contraction, atrial flutter or fibrillation, and various ischemic changes can be detected with this exam.

Interfering Circumstances. Conditions that interfere with accurate results are improper placement of the electrode(s), the inability to maintain electrode positioning, and incomplete recording of activities and events.

Signal-Averaged Electrocardiography (SAE)

The signal-averaged electrocardiography (SAE) is a noninvasive diagnostic tool that is performed to identify the potential risk for ventricular dysrhythmias in postmyocardial patients. This study is similar to a conventional ECG with the following exceptions: the electrodes are placed at different sites, and signals are processed by computer. The patient is placed in a comfortable position and remains quiet throughout the recording process. There are no apparent contraindications or risks associated with SAE.

Normal Findings. Normal electrocardiogram. Absence of ventricular dysrhythmia or the risk of such dysrhythmia.

Variations from Normal. Ventricular tachycardia can be identified and predicted using signal-averaged electrocardiography. Other diagnoses detected by SAE are ventricular aneurysm, hypertrophic cardiomyopathy, and congenital ventricular defects.

Pulmonary Function Studies

Pulmonary functioning is assessed by measuring **pulmonary perfusion**, blood flow through the pulmonary vessels; **pulmonary diffusion**, the exchange of oxygen and carbon dioxide between the alveoli and capillaries; and **pulmonary ventilation**, the air exchange between the atmosphere and lung tissue. Pulmonary function studies are generally classified into **lung volumes and capacities**, the amount of air inhaled or exhaled from the lungs; **airway flow rates**, the rate at which the air moves or flows through pulmonary airways; and **gas exchange tests** that measure the rate of gas movement between the alveoli and capillaries.

Lung volumes, capacities, and airway flow tests are conducted to assess the ventilation function of lungs. Gas exchange tests are performed to assess the diffusion process associated with lung tissue. Lung perfusion is assessed by evaluating the patency, health, and structure of the lung's blood vessels.

Special organ studies of the lung focus on the ventilation and diffusion aspects of lung function. Therefore, studies related to lung volumes, capacities, and airflow rates, as well as gas exchange tests, are presented in this chapter. It must be noted that pulmonary function tests involve numerous mathematical calculations. There are nearly a hundred formulas and abbreviations related to pulmonary function studies. This chapter covers the general information concerning special pulmonary tests, and should be considered as an overview or introduction to these tests.

The ventilation function of the lungs is measured via **spirometry** and airway flow rates. Spirometry is the evaluation of lung capacity by using an instrument that measures the volume of inhaled and exhaled air. Pulmonary diffusion is assessed by measuring the rate at which oxygen and carbon dioxide are exchanged between alveolar and capillary membranes. This test is called the **diffusing capacity of the lung**. Each test is discussed individually. Pulmonary perfusion is assessed with a nuclear medicine scan of the lungs. The pulmonary perfusion scan is covered in Chapter 11.

Spirometry

Spirometry uses an instrument called a spirometer, and the recording it creates is a spirogram. Lung capacities, volumes, and airflow rates are measured by spirometry. During spirometry the patient breathes into a mouthpiece that is attached to the spirometer. A nasal clamp is placed on the patient's nose so that all breathing is done through the mouth. The patient is asked to inhale as much as possible, briefly hold the breath, and exhale as much as possible. Rests are provided between each breathing cycle. Information gathered via spirometry is used to differentiate between the two major ventilation disorders of the lungs: pulmonary obstructive and pulmonary restrictive disease. Pulmonary obstructive disease is caused by increased airway resistance, and pulmonary restrictive disease is linked to chest wall excursion or movement.

Airway flow rates are also measured by spirometry, but the procedure is modified so that the patient is asked to exhale rapidly and forcefully after maximum deep inhalation. The volume of air exhaled is measured at one-, two-, and three-second intervals. Bronchodilators are then given to the patient and the procedure is repeated. Recordings are evaluated to identify the difference in airway flow rates with and without the aid of bronchodilators. Individuals with pulmonary obstructive disease have decreased airway flow rates.

Normal Findings. Normal respiratory volumes, capacities, and airway flow rates relative to the patient's age, sex, height, and weight.

Variations from Normal. Spirometry is useful for diagnosing diseases such as chronic obstructive pulmonary disease, asthma, bronchitis, and emphysema. These diseases affect the pulmonary airways and are therefore classified as obstructive diseases. The effect of restrictive diseases, such as kyphosis, scoliosis, pneumothorax, and hemothorax, on the ventilation function of the pulmonary system can also be assessed via spirometry.

Interfering Circumstances. Any patient condition that inhibits the ability to participate in the breathing activities negatively affects test results. Improper placement of the nose clamp and mouthpiece alters spirometric recordings.

Diffusing Capacity of the Lung (D_{LCO}, D_L)

The diffusion capacity of the lung test is performed to evaluate the ability of the alveoli and capillaries to exchange gas. D_L is the diffusing capacity of the lung; D_{LCO} indicates that carbon dioxide is the gas used to measure the diffusing capacity of the lung. Since carbon dioxide has a strong affinity for the hemoglobin component of red blood cells, carbon dioxide levels are often used to measure lung diffusion.

During the diffusion test the patient inhales a gas mixture containing carbon dioxide. The breath is held for a few seconds and then exhaled. The amount of carbon dioxide exhaled is compared to the amount inhaled. Variations from the expected values signify pulmonary diseases related to the alveolar-capillary diffusion process.

Normal Findings. Normal gas exchange based on the patient's gender, age, height, and weight.

Variations from Normal. Decreased diffusion rates are associated with pulmonary diseases such as emphysema, pulmonary fibroses, asbestosis, and even pneumonia. Other diseases that cause a decreased diffusion rate are scleroderma, systemic lupus erythematosus, and anemia. Increased diffusion rates are associated with polycythemia, an increase in the number of red blood cells.

Interfering Circumstances. Smoking and exercise can affect the lung diffusion rate. Inability of the patient to complete the breathing cycles also impairs test results.

Miscellaneous Special Organ/System Studies

There are numerous diagnostic tests that could be included in this section. Some tests are related to more than one organ or system and do not neatly fit one category or another. A few of the more interesting studies are included in this chapter. These tests are **electromyography**, a study performed to assess the electrical activity of muscles; **oximetry**, a method of measuring arterial blood oxygen saturation; and the **sweat test**, a noninvasive test performed to assist in the diagnosis of cystic fibrosis.

Electromyography (EMG)

Electromyography (EMG) is an invasive diagnostic test that is used to detect a variety of primary and secondary muscular disorders. Primary muscular diseases are a result of problems with the muscle tissue itself, whereas secondary muscular disorders are associated with other disease processes such as nerve dysfunction. Contraindications for EMG include anticoagulant therapy and infection at or near the sites of electrode placement. EMG is often done in conjunction with **electroneurography**, which is a test that measures nerve conduction potentials. If the two tests are done simultaneously, the term **electromyoneurography** is sometimes used.

Electromyography is often a stressful diagnostic intervention since it requires the placement of fine-needle electrodes directly into muscle tissue. As the needle is slowly inserted, the patient is either asked to keep the muscle at rest, or to contract or move the muscle. The electrical response created by muscle rest or movement is recorded as an electromyogram. Figure 14-3 is a sample of an EMG report.

Normal Findings. Normal muscle electrical activity. No evidence of muscular abnormalities.

Variations from Normal. Primary muscle diseases such as muscular dystrophy, myasthenia gravis, and traumatic muscle injury are diagnosed by electromyography. Muscular disorders associated with diseases such as Guillain-Barré syndrome, diabetic neuropathy, and rabies are detected with EMG.

Interfering Circumstances. Excessive pain can cause false results. Edema, hemorrhage, or thick subcutaneous fat may interfere with test results.

PATIENT NAME: OSTWALD, TINA

MEDICAL RECORD NUMBER: 67-89-00

STUDY: Electromyography

CLINICAL INFORMATION: Suspected carpal tunnel syndrome.

REPORT: An EMG using the model J Teka machine with monopolar needle electrode was done on the following muscles: the left deltoid, biceps, triceps, brachioradialis, pronator teres, first dorsal interosseous, and opponens pollicis.

FINDINGS: There was complete electrical silence in all of the muscles tested. On minimal voluntary effort, the motor unit action potentials appeared of normal amplitude and duration. On maximal voluntary effort, the interference patterns appeared grossly normal.

IMPRESSION: Normal EMG in the muscles tested.

Figure 14-3.   Electromyography report

Oximetry

Oximetry, also called **pulse oximetry**, is a noninvasive method of monitoring the oxygen saturation of arterial blood. Oximetry is often used to monitor the patient's oxygenation status during the operative period. Individuals receiving mechanical ventilation may also have their oxygen saturation levels assessed by oximetry. Sleep laboratories, stress testing, and pulmonary rehabilitation programs provide other clinical applications for oximetry. Since oximetry does not require any type of intervention, there are few, if any, contraindications.

Oximetry is accomplished by placing a specialized sensor clip on the patient's finger or earlobe. The sensor warms and increases the blood flow to the site, and a beam of light passes through the tissue. The amount of light absorbed into the tissue is an indication of the amount of oxygen present in arterial blood.

Normal Findings. Arterial oxygen saturation level of 95% or higher.

Variations from Normal. Decreased oxygen saturation can be associated with impaired cardiopulmonary function or abnormal gas exchange between the alveoli and capillaries. Anemic conditions with a reduction of hemoglobin, and vasoconstriction caused by hypotension and vessel construction may alter oximetry results.

Interfering Circumstances. Moving the finger or ear affects oximetry readings.

Sweat Test

The sweat test is a noninvasive evaluation that is performed to identify a definitive diagnosis of cystic fibrosis. Cystic fibrosis is an inherited disease that exhibits a variety of symptoms and conditions, including abnormal secretion of sweat. The sweat test is not very reliable during the first few weeks of life or after puberty. Indications for the sweat test include a family history of cystic fibrosis, recurrent respiratory tract infections, malabsorption syndromes, and failure to thrive syndrome. There are no contraindications for this test.

The forearm, back, or thigh can be used as sites for the sweat test. A sweat-inducing technique is completed and the sweat is collected and analyzed for sodium, chloride, and, at times, potassium content. Individuals with cystic fibrosis have increased levels of these substances in their sweat.

Normal Range

Sodium content	<70 mEq/L
Chloride content	<50 mEq/L

Variations from Normal. Sodium content in sweat that exceeds 90 mEq/L is abnormal and diagnostic for cystic fibrosis. Values between 70 and 90 mEq/L may indicate the need for a repeat sweat test. Chloride content that exceeds 60 mEq/L is abnormal and diagnostic for cystic fibrosis. Values between 50 and 60 mEq/L may indicate the need for a repeat sweat test.

Summary

- Special organ studies involve the use of both invasive and noninvasive techniques that assess organ function or structure.
- Brain function studies assess cerebral cortex function by passively recording electrical activity of the brain with an electroencephalography.
- Cerebral cortex and related nerve pathways are evaluated by evoked brain response studies.
- Visual-evoked response studies assess the optic pathways and optic centers of the brain.
- Auditory brain stem response studies can identify disorders of the auditory pathways of the brain stem.
- Somatosensory-evoked response studies detect spinal cord, nerve pathway, or cerebral cortex abnormalities.
- A variety of electrocardiography studies are performed to monitor and assess heart function.
- The Holter monitor is a continuous recording of the electrical activity of the heart.
- Signal-averaged electrocardiography is performed to identify the risk of ventricular arrhythmias in post–myocardial infarction individuals.

- Pulmonary function studies analyze the efficiency of lung perfusion, diffusion, and ventilation.
- Lung ventilation is evaluated by assessing lung volume, capacity, and airway flow using spirometry.
- Lung diffusion is evaluated by the gas exchange test.
- Pulmonary obstructive and pulmonary restrictive diseases are the major categories of lung ventilation disorders.
- Electromyography is an invasive test that measures the muscle function.
- Oximetry is performed to detect the oxygen saturation rate of arterial blood.
- The sweat test is an analysis of the sodium, chloride and, at times, potassium levels present in sweat. Values are diagnostic for cystic fibrosis.

CHAPTER REVIEW

1. Identify the following special organ studies:

a. Evaluates the auditory pathways of the brain stem   _____

b. Evaluates the ability of the alveoli and capillaries to exchange gas   _____

c. Measures and records the electrical activity of the brain   _____

d. Invasive diagnostic study of the conduction system of the heart   _____

e. Measures and records brain wave activity produced by stimulation of a pathway   _____

f. Measures arterial blood oxygen saturation   _____

g. Identifies the potential risk for ventricular dysrhythmias in post–myocardial infarction clients   _____

h. Detects sleep disorders and sleep-related epilepsy

_____

i. Measures the volume of inhaled and exhaled air

_____

j. Diagnostic for cystic fibrosis

_____

k. Evaluates the optic nerve, nerve tracts, and visual centers of the brain

_____

2. Organize the listed organ function studies according to the specific organ or system being assessed.

a. Brain

_____

b. Heart

_____

c. Lungs

_____

airway flow rates	gas exchange tests
auditory brain stem response	Holter monitor test
electrophysiology studies	oximetry
evoked response studies	somatosensory-evoked response
exercise stress test	spirometry

3. Identify the organ function test(s) that can be used to detect the listed diseases or disorders.

Disease/Disorder	Organ Function Test(s)
a. Glioblastoma	_____
b. Epilepsy	_____
c. Optic nerve lesions	_____
d. Acoustic neuromas	_____
e. Cardiac conduction defects	_____
f. Coronary artery occlusion disease	_____

    g. Ischemic changes _____

    h. COPD _____

    i. Emphysema _____

    j. Myasthenia gravis _____

4. Describe the electrocardiography studies presented in this chapter. Differentiate between the studies. What is the diagnostic significance of each study?

5. Define lung perfusion, ventilation, and diffusion. What pulmonary function studies evaluate perfusion, ventilation, and diffusion?

6. What is the difference between conventional EEG studies and evoked brain response studies? Describe the evoked brain response studies as well as other variations of electroencephalography.

Case Studies

1. Jess Raybone, a 24-year-old patient of Dr. Westergard, is being evaluated for a seizure disorder. Dr. Westergard has ordered an EEG for Mr. Raybone. What is an EEG and how is it performed? Describe the different techniques that can be used for an EEG. Which techniques are most suited to suspected seizure disorders? What other conditions can EEGs identify?

2. Barbara Parsons, a 50-year-old woman, has been experiencing chest pain. After an evaluation by her physician it was decided that Mrs. Parsons should complete a Holter monitor test. Describe the Holter monitor test, indications for the test, and the diagnostic significance of the test. It should be noted that the Holter monitor Mrs. Parsons will use has an "event marker." What is an event marker? How will this help the physician assess Mrs. Parsons's condition?

3. Dixie Buchanan, a 43-year-old patient, came into the clinic and presents the staff with an order from Dr. Jones for an EMG. Mrs. Buchanan announces she has been having "terrible muscle problems." What is the purpose of an EMG?

Challenge Activity

Create a poster for the "Focus on Cardiology" week at your place of employment. The poster should include a graphic of the conduction system of the heart and a representation of a normal EKG segment. Prepare a nonmedical explanation of the conduction system of the heart.

Alphabetical List of Tests

Abdomen Scan
Abdominal Aortic Ultrasonography
ABO Red Cell Groups
Acetylcholinesterase
Acid Phosphatase
Acquired Immunodeficiency Syndrome
Activated Partial Thromboplastin Time
Agglutination Test
Alanine Aminotransferase
Alkaline Phosphatase
Alpha-Fetoprotein Test
Amnioscopy
Angiography
Anti-DNase B Test
Antidiuretic Hormone
Antinuclear Antibody Test
Antistreptolysin O titer
Arteriography of the Lower Extremities
Arthrography
Arthroscopy
Aspartate Aminotransferase
Auditory Brain Stem (Evoked) Response
Barium Enema
Barium Swallow
Bicarbonate, Blood
Bile, Feces
Biliary System Radiography

Biliary System Scan
Bilirubin, Blood
Bilirubin, Urine
Bladder Ultrasonography
Bleeding Time
Blood, CSF
Blood Culture
Blood, Feces
Blood Groups
Blood Urea Nitrogen
Blood, Urine
Bone Scan
Brain Scan
Breast Ultrasonography
Broad Casts, Urine Sediment
Bronchoscopy
C-Peptide, Blood
C-Reactive Protein Test
Calcitonin
Calcium, Blood
Candidiasis
Carbohydrates, Feces
Cells, CSF
Cells, Urine Sediment
Cellular Casts, Urine
Cerebrospinal Fluid Culture
Cerebrospinal Fluid Flow Scan

Chest Ultrasonography
Chest Radiography
Chest X-ray
Chlamydia Antibody Tests
Chloride, Blood
Chloride, CSF
Cholecystography
Cholesterol
Clarity, Urine
Clot Retraction Test
Coccidioidomycosis
Colonoscopy
Color, CSF
Color, Feces
Color, Urine
Colposcopy
Complement Fixation Test
Complete Blood Count
Computerized (Axial) Tomography
Computerized Tomography, Body
Computerized Tomography, Brain
Consistency, Feces
Coombs' Test
Coronary Angiography
Cortisol
Creatine Kinase
Creatinine, Blood
Creatinine, Urine
Crystals, Urine Sediment
Culdoscopy
Cystography
Cystoscopy
Cytomegalovirus Antibody Test
Differential White Blood Cell Count
Diffusing Capacity of the Lung
Digital Subtraction Angiography
Direct Coombs' Test
Drug Testing, Urine
Echocardiography
Electrocardiography
Electroencephalography
Electromyography

Electrophysiology Study
Endoscopic Retrograde
    Cholangiopancreatography
Enzyme Immunoassay Tests
Enzyme-Linked Immunoassay Test
Erythrocyte Sedimentation Rate
Erythrocytes, Urine
Esophageal Radiography
Esophagogastroduodenoscopy
Evoked Brain Response Studies
Exercise Stress Test
Factor Assay Test
Fasting Blood Sugar
Fat, Feces
Fat Casts, Urine
Ferritin
Fetal Chromosome Analysis
Fetal Epithelial Cells
Fetal Sex Determination
Fetoscopy
Fibrinogen Assay
Fluorescent Immunoassay Tests
Fluorescent *Treponema pallidum* Antibody
    Absorption Test
Gallbladder Radiography
Gallbladder Scan
Gallbladder Ultrasonography
Gallium-67 Scan
Gastric Emptying Scan
Gastric Secretion Analysis
Gastrin
Gastrointestinal Bleeding Scan
Gastrointestinal Radiography
Gastrointestinal Reflux Scan
Genitalia and Anal Cultures
Glucagon
Glucose, CSF
Glucose, Urine
Glucose Tolerance Test
Glutamine, CSF
Granular Casts, Urine
Growth Hormone

Gynecologic Laparoscopy
Head and Brain Magnetic Resonance
    Imaging
Hematocrit
Hemoglobin
Hepatitis A
Hepatitis B
Hepatitis C
Herpes Simplex
High-Density Lipoprotein
Histoplasmosis
Holter Monitor Test
Human Chorionic Gonadotropin
Human Immunodeficiency Virus
Hyaline Casts, Urine
Hysterosalpingography
Indirect Coombs' Test
Insulin
Intravascular Ultrasonography
Intravenous Urography (Intravenous
    Pyelography)
Iodine-131 Scans
Ketones, Urine
Kidney Scan
Kidney Ultrasonography
Kidneys, Ureters, Bladder Radiography
Lactic Acid, CSF
Lactic Acid Dehydrogenase
Laparoscopy
Lecithin and Sphingomyelin Ratio
Leukocyte Esterase, Urine
Leukocytes, Feces
Leukocytes, Urine
Lipase
Liver Scan
Liver Ultrasonography
Long-Bone Radiography
Low-Density Lipoprotein
Lung Scan
Lymphangiography
Magnesium, Blood
Magnetic Resonance Imaging

Mammography
Mean Corpuscular Hemoglobin
Mean Corpuscular Hemoglobin
    Concentration
Mean Corpuscular Volume
Mean Platelet Volume
Mediastinoscopy
Microhemagglutination *Treponema pallidum*
    Test
Microorganisms, Urine
Miscellaneous Radionuclide Scans
Multigated Acquisition Scan
Musculoskeletal Magnetic Resonance
    Imaging
Myelography
Neonate Head Sonography
Nitrites, Urine
Nose and Throat Cultures
Obstetric Ultrasonography
Obstruction Series
Occult Blood, Feces
Ocular Ultrasonography
Odor, Feces
Odor, Urine
Oximetry
Pancreas Ultrasonography
Parasites, Feces
Parathyroid Scan
Pelvic Ultrasonography
Pelviscopy
Percutaneous Transhepatic
    Cholangiography
Pericardial Effusion Tests
Peritoneal Effusion Tests
pH, Urine
Phenylketonuria Test, Urine
Phosphate, Blood
Phosphorus, Blood
Platelet Aggregation Test
Platelet Count
Pleural Effusion Test
Polymerase Chain Reaction Test

Postprandial Blood Sugar
Potassium, Blood
Precipitation Test
Pregnancy Test, Urine
Pressure, CSF
Proctoscopy
Proctosigmoidoscopy
Prostate Ultrasonography
Prostate-Specific Antigen
Prostatic Acid Phosphatase
Protein, CSF
Protein, Urine
Prothrombin Time
Radioactive Iodine Uptake Test
Radioimmunoassay Test
Radionuclide Scan of the Chest
Rapid Slide Test
Rapid Plasma Reagin Test
Red Blood Cell Count
Renal Tubular Epithelial Cells, Urine
Rh Typing
Rheumatoid Factor Test
Rubella Antibody Tests
Scrotal Ultrasonography
Semen Fertility Test
Semen Test
Sigmoidoscopy
Signal-Averaged Electrocardiography
Skin Culture
Skull Radiography
Small-Bowel Follow-Through
Sodium, Blood
Somatosensory-Evoked Response
Specific Gravity, Urine
Spine Radiography
Spirometry
Spleen Scan

Spleen Ultrasonography
Sputum Culture
Squamous Epithelial Cells, Urine
Stool Culture
Sweat Test
Synovial Effusion Test
T-Tube Cholangiography
Testosterone
Thallium Stress Test
Thoracoscopy
Thrombin Time
Thyroid Scan
Thyroid Stimulating Hormone
Thyroid Ultrasonography
Thyroxine
TORCH Test
Total Iron-Binding Capacity
Transesophageal Echocardiography
Transferrin Test
Transitional Epithelial Cells, Urine
Triglyceride
Triiodothyronine
Trypsin, Feces
Upper Gastrointestinal Series
Uric Acid, Blood
Urine Culture
Urobilinogen, Urine
Urodynamic Studies
Venereal Disease Research Laboratory Test
Venography of Lower Extremities
Venous Doppler Studies
Very-Low-Density Lipoprotein
Visual-Evoked Response
Waxy Casts, Urine Sediment
Western Blot Assay
White Blood Cell Count

List of Test by Body System

Blood, Lymph System

ABO Red Cell Groups
Activated Partial Thromboplastin Time
Bleeding Time
Blood Groups
Blood Culture
Clot Retraction Test
Complete Blood Count
Coombs' Test
Differential White Blood Cell Count
Direct Coombs' Test
Erythrocyte Sedimentation Rate
Factor Assay Test
Ferritin
Fibrinogen Assay
Hematocrit
Hemoglobin

Indirect Coombs' Test
Mean Corpuscular Hemoglobin
Mean Corpuscular Hemoglobin
    Concentration
Mean Corpuscular Volume
Mean Platelet Volume
Platelet Aggregation Test
Platelet Count
Prothrombin Time
Red Blood Cell Count
Rh Typing
Thrombin Time
Total Iron-Binding Capacity
Transferrin Test
White Blood Cell Count

Cardiovascular System

Abdominal Aortic Ultrasonography
Angiography
Arteriography of the Lower Extremities
Aspartate Aminotransferase
Chest X-ray

Cholesterol
Coronary Angiography
Creatine Kinase
Digital Subtraction Angiography
Echocardiography

Electrocardiography
Electrophysiology Study
Exercise Stress Test
High-Density Lipoprotein
Holter Monitor Test
Intravascular Ultrasonography
Low-Density Lipoprotein
Multigated Acquisition Scan
Myocardial Infarction Scan

Pericardial Effusion Test
Radionuclide Scan of the Chest
Signal-Averaged Electrocardiography
Thallium Stress Test
Transesophageal Echocardiography
Triglyceride
Venography of Lower Extremities
Venous Doppler Studies
Very-Low-Density Lipoprotein

Digestive System

Abdomen Scan
Alkaline Phosphatase
Alpha-Fetoprotein Test
Aspartate Aminotransferase
Barium Enema
Barium Swallow
Biliary System Radiography
Biliary System Scan
Bilirubin
Blood, Urea, Nitrogen
Cholecystography
Colonoscopy
Endoscopic Retrograde
    Cholangiopancreatography
Esophageal Radiography
Esophagogastroduodenoscopy
Fat, Feces
Gallbladder Radiography
Gallbladder Scan
Gallbladder Ultrasonography
Gastric Emptying Scan

Gastric Secretion Analysis
Gastrin
Gastrointestinal Bleeding Scan
Gastrointestinal Radiography
Gastrointestinal Reflux Scan
Lactic Acid Dehydrogenase
Laparoscopy
Lipase
Liver Scan
Liver Ultrasonography
Obstruction Series
Occult Blood, Feces
Percutaneous Transhepatic
    Cholangiography
Proctoscopy
Proctosigmoidoscopy
Sigmoidoscopy
Small-Bowel Follow-Through
Stool Culture
T-Tube Cholangiography
Upper Gastrointestinal Series

Endocrine System

Antidiuretic Hormone
C-Peptide
Calcitonin

Calcium
Cortisol
Fasting Blood Sugar

Gastrin
Glucagon
Glucose
Glucose Tolerance Test
Growth Hormone
Human Chorionic Gonadotropin
Insulin
Iodine-131 Scan
Ketones, Urine
Pancreas Ultrasonography

Parathyroid Scan
Phosphorus
Postprandial Blood Sugar
Radioactive Iodine Uptake Test
Testosterone
Thyroid Scan
Thyroid-Stimulating Hormone Test
Thyroxine
Triiodothyronine

Nervous System

Auditory Brain Stem (Evoked) Response
Blood, CSF
Brain Scan
Cerebrospinal Fluid Culture
Cerebrospinal Fluid Flow Scan
Chloride, CSF
Color, CSF
Computerized Tomography, Brain
Coronary Angiography
Electroencephalography
Electromyography
Evoked Brain Response Studies

Head and Brain Magnetic Resonance
    Imaging
Lactic Acid, CSF
Myelography
Neonate Head Sonography
Pressure, CSF
Protein, CSF
Signal-Averaged Electrocardiography
Skull Radiography
Somatosensory-Evoked Response
Visual-Evoked Response

Reproductive System

Alpha-Fetoprotein Test
Amnioscopy
Breast Ultrasonography
Colposcopy
Culdoscopy
Fetal Chromosome Analysis
Fetal Sex Determination
Fetal Epithelial Cells
Fetoscopy
Genitalia Cultures
Gynecologic Laparoscopy
Hysterosalpingography

Laparoscopy
Mammography
Obstetric Ultrasonography
Pelvic Ultrasonography
Pelviscopy
Phenylketonuria Test, Urine
Pregnancy Test, Urine
Rubella Antibody Test
Scrotal Ultrasonography
Semen Fertility Test
Semen Test
TORCH Test

Respiratory System

Bronchoscopy
Chest Radiography
Chest Ultrasonography
Chest X-ray
Diffusing Capacity of the Lung
Lung Scan
Mediastinoscopy

Nose and Throat Culture
Pleural Effusion Test
Radionuclide Scan of the Chest
Spirometry
Sputum Culture
Thoracoscopy

Skeletal System

Alkaline Phosphatase
Arthrography
Arthroscopy
Bone Scan
Electromyography

Long-Bone Radiography
Musculoskeletal Magnetic Resonance
    Imaging
Skull Radiography
Spine Radiography

Urinary System

Acid Phosphatase
Bilirubin, Urine
Clarity, Urine
Color, Urine
Creatinine, Blood
Crystals, Urine Sediment
Cystography
Cystoscopy
Drug Testing, Urine
Erythrocytes, Urine
Fat Casts, Urine
Glucose, Urine
Granular Casts, Urine
Hyaline Casts, Urine
Intravenous Urography (Intravenous
    Pyelography)
Ketones, Urine
Kidney Scan
Kidney Ultrasonography

Kidneys, Ureters, Bladder Radiography
Leukocyte Esterase, Urine
Leukocytes, Urine
Microorganisms, Urine
Nitrites, Urine
Odor, Urine
pH, Urine
Pregnancy Tests, Urine
Protein, Urine
Renal Tubular Epithelial Cells, Urine
Specific Gravity, Urine
Squamous Epithelial Cells, Urine
Transitional Epithelial Cells, Urine
Uric Acid, Blood
Urine Culture
Urobilinogen, Urine
Urodynamic Studies
Waxy Casts, Urine Sediment

Abbreviations

AAA	abdominal aortic aneurysm
ABD	anti-DNase B test
ABO	human blood grouping system
ABR, ABER	auditory brain stem (evoked) response
ACTH	adrenocorticotropic hormone
ADH	antidiuretic hormone
AFB	acid-fast bacillus
AFP	alpha-fetoprotein
AIDS	acquired immunodeficiency syndrome
ALP, alk phos	alkaline phosphatase
ALT	alanine aminotransferase
ANA	antinuclear antibody
anti-HBc	antibody to hepatitis B core antigen
anti-HBe	antibody to hepatitis B envelope antigen
anti-HBs	antibody to hepatitis B surface antigen
anti-HCV	antibody to hepatitis C virus
anti-VCA	antibody to the viral capsid antigen
APTT	activated partial thromboplastin time
ASHD	arteriosclerotic heart disease
ASO	antistreptolysin O titer
AST	aspartate aminotransferase
AV	antrioventricular
bands	immature neutrophils
basos	basophils
BE	barium enema
BFP	biological false-positive
BPH	benign prostatic hypertrophy
BUN	blood urea nitrogen

C & S	culture and sensitivity test
Ca^+	calcium
CABG	coronary artery bypass graft
CAT	computerized axial tomography
CBC	complete blood count
CEA	carcinoembryonic antigen
CF	complement fixation
CHEM 12, 24	automated blood testing methods, used to analyze 12 and 24 different chemical components of blood
CK	creatine kinase
Cl^-	chloride
CMG	cystometrogram
CMV	cytomegalovirus
CNS	central nervous system
CO_2	carbon dioxide
CPK	creatine phosphokinase
CRP	C-reactive protein
CSF	cerebrospinal fluid
CT	computerized tomography
DIC	disseminated intravascular coagulation disorder
diff	differential white cell count
DSA	digital subtraction angiography
DVT	deep venous thrombosis
E. coli	*Escherichia coli*
EBNA	antibodies to Epstein-Barr virus nuclear antigen
EBV	Epstein-Barr virus
ECG, EKG	electrocardiography
ECM	erythema chronicum migrans
ECT	emission computed tomography
EEG	electroencephalography
EGD	esophagogastroduodenoscopy
EIA	enzyme immunoassay
ELISA	enzyme-linked immunoabsorbent assay
EM	erythema chronicum
EP, EPS	electrophysiology studies
eosinos	eosinophils
ER	emergency room
ERCP	endoscopic retrograde cholangiopancreatography
ESR	erythrocyte sedimentation rate

FBS	fasting blood sugar
FIA	fluorescent immunoassay test
FTA-ABS	fluorescent treponemal antibody absorption test
GB	gallbladder
GH	growth hormone
GI	gastrointestinal
GTT	glucose tolerance test
HAI	hemagglutination inhibition test
HAV	hepatitis A virus
HbcAg	hepatitis B core antigen
HbeAg	hepatitis B envelope antigen
HbsAg	hepatitis B surface antigen
HBV	hepatitis B virus
HCG	human chorionic gonadotropin
HCO_3	bicarbonate
Hct	hematocrit
HCV	hepatitis C virus
HDL	high-density lipoprotein
Hgb	hemoglobin
HIV-1	human immunodeficiency virus type 1
HIV-2	human immunodeficiency virus type 2
HSV-1	herpes simplex virus type 1
HSV-2	herpes simplex virus type 2
I	intermediate
IDDM	insulin-dependent diabetes mellitus
IFA	indirect fluorescent assay
IgG anti-HAV	IgG antibodies against hepatitis A virus
IgM anti-HAV	IgM antibodies against hepatitis A virus
IM	infectious mononucleosis
INR	international normalized ratio
ITP	idiopathic thrombocytopenic purpura
IV	intravenous
IVC	intravenous cholangiography
IVU	intravenous urography
IVUS	intravascular ultrasound
K^+	potassium
KUB	kidneys, ureters, and bladder

L:S ratio	lecithin:sphingomyelin ratio
LD	lactic acid dehydrogenase
LDH	lactate dehydrogenase
LDL	low-density lipoprotein
lymphs	lymphocytes
MCH	mean corpuscular hemoglobin
MCHC	mean corpuscular hemoglobin concentration
MCV	mean corpuscular volume
Mg^+	magnesium
MHA	microhemagglutination
MHA-TP	microhemagglutination for treponema pallidum
monos	monocytes
MPV	mean platelet volume
MUGA	multigated acquisition scans
Na^+	sodium
NIDDM	noninsulin-dependent diabetes mellitus
NPO	nothing by mouth
P, PO_4	phosphorus
PAP	prostatic acid phosphatase
PCR	polymerase chain reaction test
PCV	packed cell volume
PET	positron emission tomography
PKU	phenylketonuria
PMN	polymorphonuclear leukocyte
PO_4	phosphate
polys	polymorphonuclear leukocytes
PPBS; 2-hour PPBS	postprandial blood sugar
PSA	prostate-specific antigen
PTC, PTHC	percutaneous transhepatic cholangiography
PTCA	percutaneous transluminal coronary angioplasty
PTT	partial thromboplastin time
PUL	percutaneous ultrasonic lithotripsy
R	resistant
RAI	radioimmunoassay
RAIU	radioactive iodine uptake test
RBC	red blood cell (count)
RF	rheumatoid factor

RP	retrograde pyelography
RPR	rapid plasma reagin test
S	sensitive
SA	sinoatrial
SBF	small-bowel follow-through
sed rate	erythrocyte sedimentation rate
segs	segmented neutrophils
SER	somatosensory-evoked response
SGOT	serum glutamic oxaloacetic transaminase
SGPT	serum glutamic pyruvic transaminase
SIADH	syndrome of inappropriate ADH secretion
SLE	systemic lupus erythematosus
SMAC 12	Sequential Multiple Chemical Analyzer by Technicon, an automated method that analyzes 12 different chemical components of blood
SOGTT	standard oral glucose tolerance test
SPECT	single-photon emission computed tomography
stabs	immature neutrophils
STH	somatotropic hormone
T_3	triiodothyronine
T_4	thyroxine
TEE	transesophageal echocardiography
TORCH	toxoplasmosis, rubella, cytomegalovirus, and herpes virus
total anti-HAV	total antibody against hepatitis A virus
TSH	thyroid stimulating hormone
UGI	upper gastrointestinal series
UTI	urinary tract infection
VDRL	Venereal Disease Research Laboratory
VER	visual-evoked response
VLDL	very-low-density lipoprotein
WBC	white blood cell (count)

abdominal aorta ultrasound an ultrasound study of the abdominal aorta from the sternum and bifurcation of the aorta.

Acetest a urine test performed to confirm ketonuria.

acetylcholinesterase (AChE) an enzyme that reduces or prevents neuron activity at neuromuscular junctions.

acid-fast bacillus (AFB) a smear culture test used to identify microorganisms that may be present in cerebrospinal fluid.

acid phosphatase an enzyme present in various tissues, including the bone, liver, kidneys, spleen, and red blood cells.

acquired deficiencies a lack or decrease in the amount of any given coagulation factor due primarily to disease.

activated partial thromboplastin time a blood test that measures coagulation and anticoagulation activities in the blood.

agar an extract of seaweed used in several types of culture media.

agar diffusion a commonly used sensitivity test that involves the inoculation of a special agar plate with the organism to be tested.

agglutination test the visible clumping or aggregation of cells or particles due to their reaction with an antibody.

airway flow rate the rate at which the air moves or flows through pulmonary airways.

alanine aminotransferase (ALT) an enzyme found in liver cells that behaves as a catalyst in various bodily functions; also known as serum glutamic pyruvic transaminase (SGPT).

alkaline phosphatase (ALP) an enzyme found in the liver, bone, and epithelium of all bile ducts.

alpha-fetoprotein (AFP) a glycoprotein found in fetal serum.

amniocentesis a needle puncture through the abdomen, uterine wall, and into the amniotic sac in order to withdraw amniotic fluid.

amnioscopy an endoscopic examination that allows visualization of the amniotic fluid.

angiography x-ray examination of the vascular system.

antidiuretic hormone (ADH) a hormone that controls the amount of water reabsorbed by the kidneys.

anti-DNase B (ADB) a test that detects antibodies to DNase B.

antinuclear antibody (ANA)   a blood test that is used to detect the presence of antinuclear antibodies in serum, which are highly indicative of system lupus erythematosus and other rheumatic diseases.

antistreptolysin O titer (ASO)   a streptococcal antibody test that helps diagnose conditions associated with streptococcal infections such as rheumatic fever, glomerulonephritis, endocarditis, and scarlet fever.

aorta ultrasonography   an ultrasound study of the abdominal aorta.

arterial Doppler studies   ultrasound studies of the flow of blood through arteries.

arteriography of the lower extremities   a contrasted x-ray examination of the femoral artery and its branches.

arthrocentesis   the aspiration of fluid from joint spaces.

arthrography   a radiographic examination of an encapsulated joint and its related structures; also known as joint radiography

arthroscopy   an endoscopic examination of the joint using a fiber-optic scope called an arthroscope.

aspartate aminotransferase (AST)   an enzyme found in tissues and cells where there is high metabolic activity; also known as serum glutamic oxaloacetic transaminase (SGOT).

auditory brain stem (evoked) response (ABR, ABER)   tests that use a pattern of clicking sounds to evaluate the the central auditory pathways of the brain stem.

bands   immature neutrophils.

barium enema (BE)   a radiographic examination of the entire large intestine or colon using barium as the contrast medium.

barium swallow   a radiographic examination of all aspects of the esophagus; also known as esophageal radiography.

basophilia   an increase in basophils.

Bence-Jones protein test   a specific urine protein test that identifies the presence of the Bence-Jones protein; diagnostically significant for multiple myeloma.

bicarbonate   a negatively charged ion that helps maintain the blood buffer system.

biliary system scan   a radionuclide study of the gallbladder, and the cystic and common bile ducts.

bilirubin   a waste product resulting from the lysis of red blood cells and the release of hemoglobin.

bladder ultrasonography   a study of the urinary bladder.

bleeding tendencies   coagulation disorders caused by delayed clot formation or premature clot destruction, and hypercoagulability states.

bleeding time   a blood test that measures how long it takes platelets to interact with the blood vessel wall in order to form a platelet plug.

blood buffer system   a series of chemical reactions that helps maintain the normal blood pH of 7.4.

blood urea nitrogen (BUN)   a test that measures plasma urea.

bone scan   a radionuclide examination of the skeleton.

brain scan   a radionuclide study of the brain.

breast ultrasonography   an ultrasound study of the breasts.

broad casts   a urine sediment cast found in the presence of renal failure.

bronchoscopy   an endoscopic study of the larynx, trachea, and bronchi.

calcitonin   the hormone secreted by the parafollicular cells of the thyroid gland, functions to lower blood calcium levels.

calcium (Ca)   a positively charged ion that is associated with muscle contraction, nerve function, and coagulation.

casts   urine sediment that is formed when protein accumulates and precipitates in the lumen of the renal tubules and assumes the shape of the tubule.

catheterized specimen   a method of collecting urine that involves placement of a straight catheter or drawing urine from the collection port of an indwelling catheter.

cellophane tape test   a technique used to collect a specimen from the rectal area of the patient so that it can be examined for pinworms.

cellular cast   a urine sediment cast that may contain various types of cells.

central nervous system (CNS)   the brain and spinal cord.

cerebrospinal fluid (CSF)   a clear, colorless fluid that flows through the ventricles of the brain.

cerebrospinal fluid flow scan   a radionuclide study of the size and patency of cerebrospinal fluid pathways and reabsorption.

Chem 12   an automated blood testing method that analyzes 12 different chemical components of the blood.

Chem 24   an automated blood testing method that analyzes 24 different chemical components of the blood.

chest ultrasonography   an ultrasound study of the chest.

chest x-ray   a radiographic examination of the chest, bony thorax, lungs, pleura, mediastinum, heart, and aortic arch.

chloride   a negatively charged ion that helps control the distribution of water between the cells and blood plasma.

chocolate agar   a culture medium made of cooked blood.

cholecystography   a radiographic examination of the gallbladder with a contrast medium; also known as a gallbladder (GB) series.

cholesterol   a lipid that plays a role in the manufacture of bile, steroids, and cell membranes.

chyle   the product of digestion.

cisternal puncture   a technique for withdrawing cerebrospinal fluid that is accomplished by inserting a needle between the first cervical vertebra and the foramen magnum.

cisternography, cisternogram   a radionuclide study of the size and patency of cerebrospinal fluid pathways and reabsorption.

clean-catch specimen   a urine collection technique that is used when specimen contamination is a serious concern.

Clinitest   a commercially prepared test that is used to identify the presence of glucose in urine.

clot retraction test   a test used to determine the clotting capability of the blood and to measure the quality of a therapeutic blood clot.

coagulation factors   plasma proteins that are necessary for blood clotting (coagulation).

cold spots   areas of an organ that have a lower concentration of the radionuclide.

colonoscopy   an endoscopic examination of the large intestine from the anus to the ileocecal valve.

color-flow Doppler imaging   an echocardiographic mode that provides a color image of blood-flow patterns and blood-flow speed through the heart.

colposcope   a lighted, binocular microscope used to visualize the vagina and cervix.

colposcopy   an examination of the vagina and cervix.

common pathway   a series of chemical reactions that lead to the formation of a stable clot; one of three identified pathways of the coagulation process.

complement fixation test   a plasma test used to identify viral antibodies.

complete blood count (CBC)   a laboratory test that identifies the number of cells per cubic millimeter of blood.

computerized (axial) tomography (CT, CAT)   a radiographic technique that produces an image that shows a detailed cross section of tissue structure.

computerized tomography of the body   a radiologic technique that gives detailed cross-sectional images of the chest, abdomen, spine, and extremities.

computerized tomography of the brain   a radiographic technique that provides a three-dimensional view of the cranium and its contents.

confirmatory tests   chemical tests that are performed to confirm the findings of reagent strip testing.

Conn's syndrome   the excessive secretion of aldosterone.

continuous-wave Doppler method   an echocardiographic mode that images blood-flow patterns and blood-flow speed through the heart.

Coombs' test   an antiglobulin test used to detect the presence of antibodies that coat and damage red blood cells.

coronary angiography   a radiographic examination of the heart, great vessels, and coronary arteries using a contrast medium.

cortisol   a glucocorticoid hormone secreted by the adrenal cortex.

C-peptide   the residue of insulin formation.

C-reactive protein test   a blood test to detect C-reactive protein, an antibody-like protein that is indicative of an acute inflammatory process.

creatine kinase (CK)   an enzyme found in heart and skeletal muscle; main cardiac enzyme studied in patients with heart disease; also called creatine phosphokinase.

creatinine   a waste product of creatinine phosphate, which is the substance used in skeletal muscle contraction.

cross-sectional gray-scale imaging method   an ultrasonographic imaging method that converts sound wave echoes into graphs or dots that form pictures.

culdoscopy   an endoscopic examination of the cul-de-sac of Douglas.

culture   a laboratory test during which various body specimens are cultivated in a special growth medium in order to identify the presence of microorganisms.

culture and sensitivity test (C & S)   a laboratory test used to identify pathogenic microorganisms and the antibiotics that inhibit the growth of microorganisms.

culture medium   the substance that provides the nutritional environment for the growth of microorganisms.

cystine   a nonessential amino acid found in protein.

cystinuria   an amino acid disorder that may result in damage to the renal tubules.

cystography   a radiographic examination of the urinary bladder.

cystometrogram (CMG)   the measurement and recording of bladder neuromuscular function.

cystoscopy   an endoscopic examination of the urethra, urinary bladder, ureteral orifices, and male prostatic urethra.

cystourethrogram   an examination of the bladder and urethra.

differential white cell count (diff)   part of the complete blood count that identifies the percentage of each type of white cell relative to the total number of leukocytes.

diffusing capacity of the lung   a test that measures the rate at which oxygen and carbon dioxide are exchanged between alveolar and capillary membranes.

diffusion   the exchange of oxygen and carbon dioxide between the alveoli and capillaries.

digital subtraction angiography (DSA)   a radiographic study that uses computerized fluoroscopy in order to visualize arteries.

dipyridamole-thallium stress test   a thallium stress test that uses medications to stimulate heart activity.

direct bilirubin or **conjugated bilirubin**   a product that is converted from indirect bilirubin, direct bilirubin is eventually excreted in the feces and urine.

direct fluorescent immunoassay (DFA)   a labeled immunoassay test that uses a fluorescent compound in order to identify the antigen-antibody reaction.

direct (forward) ABO blood grouping   a test used to group or type blood by directly identifying the antigen present on the surface of the red blood cell.

dobutamine-thallium stress test   a thallium stress test that uses medications to stimulate heart activity.

Doppler blood vessel studies   an ultrasonographic technique that provides data about arterial or venous blood flow.

Doppler method, studies   an ultrasound technique that is used to assess moving blood or fluid.

Dressler's syndrome   a post–myocardial infarction syndrome characterized by fever, pericarditis, pleurisy, and joint pain; hemorrhagic and viral pericarditis; and malignancy as indicated by the presence of abnormal cells.

Duke method   a method for measuring bleeding time that is performed by making a 2–3 mm deep puncture in the earlobe and measuring the time it takes for bleeding to stop.

duodenoscopy   an endoscopic examination of the duodenum.

duplex scanning   ultrasonographic studies that combine Doppler ultrasound and real-time imaging of both the organ and the flow of the blood through the organ.

echocardiography   a noninvasive ultrasonographic evaluation of heart structure and function.

effusions   excessive accumulations of fluid in various body cavities.

electrocardiography (ECG, EKG)   a recording of the electrical impulses that stimulate the heart to contract.

electrodiagnostic studies   procedures that use electrical impulses and electronic devices to identify and assess abnormalities of heart function and structure.

electroencephalography (EEG)   a diagnostic test that measures and records the electrical activity of the cerebral cortex.

electromyography   a diagnostic test that measures and records the electrical activity of muscles.

electromyoneurography   a combined diagnostic test that measures and records the electrical activity of muscles and nerve conduction potentials.

electroneurography   a diagnostic test that measures nerve conduction potentials.

electrophysiology studies (EP, EPS)   an invasive procedure performed to identify heart arrhythmias and conduction defects.

endoscopic retrograde cholangiopancreatography (ERCP)   endoscopic examination of the biliary and pancreatic ducts.

enzyme immunoassay (EIA)   a labeled immunoassay test that uses enzymes as the means to visualize the antigen-antibody reaction.

enzyme-linked immunoabsorbent assay (ELISA)   a variation of the enzyme immunoassay test.

eosinopenia   a decrease in eosinophils

eosinophilia   an increase in eosinophils

erythrocyte sedimentation rate (ESR, sed rate)   the rate at which red blood cells settle out of unclotted blood in an hour.

esophagogastroduodenoscopy (EGD)   an endoscopic examination of the esophagus, stomach, and duodenum.

esophagoscopy   an endoscopic exam of the esophagus.

esterase an enzyme that breaks down fats.

event marker a button on the Holter unit that the patient can push when cardiac symptoms occur.

evoked response studies diagnostic studies that identify and record changes and responses of cerebral cortex activity when sensory pathways are stimulated.

exercise stress test a noninvasive test that measures cardiac function during physical stress.

extrinsic pathway one of three pathways identified in the coagulation process so named because one of the coagulation factors is not present in circulating blood.

exudate effusions containing cells, cell debris, and proteins that result from damage to cells or cell membranes.

factor assay test a blood test performed that measures the presence, absence, increase, or decrease in coagulation factors; also known as the coagulant factors test.

fasting blood sugar (FBS) a blood test that is performed to determine the level of glucose in the blood.

fasting (urine) specimen a urine specimen collected during the seconded voided urine that occurs at least four hours after eating.

fatty cast a type of urine sediment cast for appearance and composition and indicating fatty degeneration of renal tubular epithelium.

ferritin the storage form of iron.

fetal ultrasound another name for obstetric ultrasound.

fetoscopy an intrauterine endoscopic examination of the fetus.

fibrin a stringy plasma protein that traps blood cells in order to form a clot capable of stopping the escape of blood.

fibrinogen a soluble plasma protein that is a precursor to fibrin.

fibrinogen assay test a blood test that measures the serum concentration of fibrinogen.

fibrinolysis the destruction of blood clots by the action of plasmin.

first morning specimen a urine collection method where the specimen is collected when the individual first awakens.

flocculation a variation of an agglutination test.

fluorescent treponemal antibody absorption (FTA-ABS) Test a direct method of detecting treponemal antibodies that are diagnostic for primary syphilis.

foam stability test a test that measures the amount of surfactant in amniotic fluid; also known as the shake test and the rapid surfactant test.

gallbladder and biliary system scan a radionuclide study of the gallbladder, cystic, and common bile ducts.

gallbladder ultrasonography an ultrasound examination of the gallbladder and the bile ducts.

gallium-67 scan   a nuclear medicine study of any part of the body using gallium-67 as the radionuclide.

gas exchange tests   tests that measure the rate of gas movement between the alveoli and capillaries.

gastric emptying scan   a radionuclide study of the stomach that evaluates the ability of the stomach to empty.

gastric secretions analysis test   a laboratory test that analyzes quantity, quality, and characteristics of gastric secretions.

gastrin   a hormone produced and secreted by specialized cells in the stomach that stimulates the secretion of gastric acid.

gastroesophageal reflux scan   a radionuclide study of the esophagus and stomach.

gastrointestinal bleeding scan   a radionuclide study of the upper and lower gastrointestinal tract performed to identify and evaluate gastrointestinal bleeding.

gastrointestinal reflux scan   a radionuclide study of the gastrointestinal tract.

gastroscopy   an endoscopic examination of the stomach.

glucagon   a hormone secreted by pancreatic alpha cells that assists in the maintenance of blood glucose levels.

glucose tolerance test (GTT)   a timed test of the concentration of glucose in both the blood and urine.

granular casts   a urine sediment cast that contains fragments of disintegrated cells that appear as fine or coarse granules embedded in the protein of the cast.

growth hormone (GH)   a hormone released by the anterior lobe of the pituitary that is essential for growth; also known as somatotropin and somatotropic hormone (STH).

gynecologic laparoscopy   an endoscopic examination of the pelvic cavity that includes visualization of the ovaries, uterus, and fallopian tubes.

head and brain MRI   an examination of the structures and blood flow of the face, head, and brain.

hemagglutination inhibition test (HAI)   a variation of the agglutination test in which the RBCs are prevented or inhibited from clumping.

hematocrit   the percentage of red blood cells in a volume of whole blood.

heme   the iron portion of the hemoglobin molecule.

hemoglobin   the protein-iron complex that is the major constituent of a red blood cell.

hemostasis   stopping the escape of blood from its vessels.

hepatobiliary ultrasonography   an ultrasonic examination of the liver and gallbladder.

high-density lipoproteins (HDLs)   cholesterol-rich plasma proteins often called the "good" cholesterol.

Holter monitor test   a continuous recording of the electrical activity of the heart.

hot spots   areas of an organ that have a high concentration of radionuclide uptake.

human chorionic gonadotropin (HCG)   a hormone that appears in the blood and urine of pregnant women as early as ten days after conception.

hyaline cast   a urine sediment cast made up of mucoprotein, the substance found in all connective and supportive tissue.

hypercoagulability state   an abnormal tendency toward thrombosis, or clot formation.

hyperventilation EEG   an electroencephalogram that identifies abnormalities of cerebral vasoconstriction.

hypochromic anemia   a classification anemia characterized by a decreased hemoglobin concentration.

hysterosalpingography   a radiographic examination of the uterine cavity and fallopian tubes (oviducts) that uses a contrast medium.

Ictotest   a specific test for bilirubin.

inclusion bodies   substances that are present in the cytoplasm of granulocytes and are associated with specific diseases.

indirect fluorescent antibody (IFA)   a labeled immunoassay blood test that uses a fluorescent compound to visualize the antigen-antibody reaction.

indirect (reverse) ABO blood grouping   a test used to group or type blood by indirectly identifying the antigen present on the red blood cells.

indirect (unconjugated) bilirubin   a form of bilirubin that must be transported to the liver and is eventually converted to direct bilirubin.

inherited deficiencies   an inherited lack of certain coagulation factors.

insulin   a hormone secreted by the pancreas that plays a role in moving glucose from the plasma into the cells.

insulin-dependent diabetes mellitus (IDDM) (Type I)   a disorder of glucose metabolism that may be characterized by a lack of insulin or the absence of its secretion.

intermediate (I)   a term used in sensitivity testing to denote that an organism is somewhat sensitive to an antibiotic.

intravascular ultrasound   an invasive procedure that uses ultrasound technology to examine internal structures and condition of coronary arteries.

intravenous urography (IVU)   a radiographic examination of the structure and function of the entire urinary tract; also known as intravenous pyelography (IVP) and excretory urography.

intrinsic coagulation pathway   part of the coagulation process that uses the clotting factors found only in the blood.

iodine-131 scan   a radionuclide examination and evaluation of thyroid tissue.

isoenzyme   a chemically distinct form of an enzyme, specifically the enzyme creatine kinase; an isoenzyme is usually associated with specific organs, organ damage, and diagnoses.

Ivy method   a method for measuring bleeding time that is performed by making an incision on the forearm of the patient and measuring the time it takes for the bleeding to stop.

karyotype   the process of determining chromosomal makeup in order to detect genetic, chromosomal, and metabolic disorders.

kidney scan   a radionuclide examination of the size, shape, and function of the kidney.

kidney ultrasonography   an ultrasound examination of the kidney.

kidneys, ureters, and bladder (KUB)   a radiographic examination of the lower abdomen.

lactic acid dehydrogenase (LDH)   an enzyme found in many body tissues such as the heart, liver, kidneys, skeletal muscle, brain, and lungs.

laparoscopy   an endoscopic examination of the abdominal organs.

latency period   time that elapses between stimulation and response.

latex agglutination   an agglutination test that uses a latex component to promote the agglutination reaction.

lecithin   a phospholipid related to lung surfactant.

lecithin:sphingomyelin ratio (L:S ratio)   a measure of fetal lung maturity that is determined by analyzing the amniotic fluid for the presence of lecithin and sphingomyelin.

leukocyte esterase urine test   a urine test that is able to identify the presence of granulocytic leukocytes, primarily neutrophils, in urine.

leukocytopenia, leukopenia   a decrease in the number of leukocytes.

leukocytosis   a slight increase in the number of leukocytes.

Limulus assay   a laboratory test that is able to identify the presence of gram-negative pathogens in cerebrospinal fluid.

lipase   an enzyme produced and secreted by the pancreas, assists in the breakdown of triglycerides.

lipoprotein   a complex molecule consisting of plasma proteins and lipids that transport cholesterol and triglycerides.

liver scan   a radionuclide study of the size, shape, and function of the liver.

liver ultrasonography   an ultrasound examination of the liver and hepatic ducts.

long-bone radiography   a radiographic examination of the bones of the arms and legs.

low-density lipoproteins (LDL)   the cholesterol-rich product of very-low-density lipoprotein breakdown, often called "bad" cholesterol.

lumbar puncture   the introduction of a hollow needle into the subarachnoid space of the lumbar portion of the spinal canal done to collect a cerebrospinal fluid sample; also known as a spinal tap.

lung volume and capacities   the amount of air inhaled or exhaled from the lungs.

lymphangiography   a radiographic examination of lymph vessels, ducts, and nodes using a contrast medium.

lymphocytopenia   a decrease in lymphocytes.

lymphocytosis   an increase in the number of lymphocytes.

lytes   the four plasma ions, sodium, potassium, chloride, and bicarbonate, most commonly measured when electrolytes are ordered as a laboratory test.

magnesium   an electrolyte necessary for muscular contraction and carbohydrate metabolism.

magnetic resonance imaging (MRI)   a noninvasive imaging examination of organs, tissue, or systems that uses a magnetic field and radio waves to produce images.

mammography   an x-ray examination of the breast and surrounding structures.

maple syrup urine disease   a metabolic disorder that is characterized by urine that smells like maple syrup.

mean corpuscular hemoglobin (MCH)   the average weight of the hemoglobin in each red blood cell.

mean corpuscular hemoglobin concentration (MCHC)   the average concentration or percentage of hemoglobin within each red blood cell.

mean corpuscular volume (MCV)   the average volume (size) of an average red blood cell.

mean platelet volume (MPV)   the average volume (size) of an average platelet.

meconium   material that collects in fetal intestines.

mediastinoscopy   an endoscopic examination of the mediastinal lymph nodes and body structures located under the sternum and near the lungs.

microhemagglutination (MHA)   an agglutination test in which the clumping of red blood cells is observed via a microscope.

microhemagglutination Treponema pallidum (MHA-TP) test   a hemagglutination test that identifies the presence of treponemal antibodies associated with syphilis.

M-mode (echocardiography)   an echocardiographic mode that provides a linear tracing of the heart and heart motion.

monocytosis   an increase in the number of monocytes.

mucoprotein   a substance found in connective and supportive tissue.

multigated acquisition (MUGA) scan   a nuclear medicine examination of heart function and wall motion.

musculoskeletal MRI   a magnetic resonance imaging examination of the bones, joints, and surrounding tissue.

myelography   a radiographic examination of the spinal canal using a contrast medium.

neonate head sonography   an ultrasound study of the brain and associated structures of newborns; also called echoencephalography.

neurosyphilis   syphilis involving the central nervous system.

neutropenia a decrease in the number of neutrophils.

neutrophilia an increase in the number of neutrophils.

nitrite urine test a screening test that identifies the presence of nitrites in the urine, which indicates a urinary tract infection.

noninsulin-dependent diabetes mellitus (NIDDM) (Type II) a metabolic disorder that exhibits an elevated plasma glucose level, characterized by a delay in the secretion of insulin or a decreased number of insulin receptor sites.

obstetric ultrasonography a study of the fetus and placenta.

obstruction series a radiographic examination of the abdomen, bowel, and kidneys.

ocular ultrasonography a study of the eye and the eye orbit.

opalescent milky and iridescent like an opal; describes cerebrospinal fluid discoloration associated with tuberculosis meningitis.

oximetry method of measuring arterial blood oxygen saturation.

packed cell volume the percentage of red blood cells in whole blood; hematocrit.

pancreas ultrasonography a study of pancreatic structure and function.

paracentesis the puncture and aspiration of fluid from the peritoneal cavity.

paramyxovirus the organism that causes mumps.

parathyroid scan a radionuclide scan of the parathyroid gland.

partial thromboplastin time a blood test that measures coagulation and anticoagulation activities in the blood.

pelvic ultrasonography a study of female reproductive organs.

pelviscopy an endoscopic examination of the pelvic cavity.

percutaneous transhepatic cholangiography (PTC, PTHC) a radiographic examination of the biliary system and sometimes the gallbladder using a contrast medium.

percutaneous ultrasonic lithotripsy (PUL) an ultrasound technique that produces sound waves that are able to pulverize kidney and gallstones.

pericardiocentesis the puncture and aspiration fluid from the pericardial cavity.

peritoneoscopy an endoscopic examination of the abdominal organs.

persantine-thallium stress test a thallium stress test that uses medications to stimulate heart activity.

phenylketonuria (PKU) a congenital metabolic disorder involving the amino acid phenylalanine.

phosphorus an electrolyte primarily found in bones and teeth, which is necessary for generation of bony tissue and the metabolism of glucose, fats, and proteins.

photostimulation EEG an EEG that is performed by flashing a light over the patient's face, which may provoke photostimulated seizure activity.

plasmin the enzyme used to achieve fibrinolysis; also called fibrinolysin.

platelet aggregation the process of forming a platelet plug as a response to vessel injury.

platelet count   the number of platelets in the blood.

polymerase chain reaction   a laboratory test that utilizes blood, urine, synovial fluid, or other body tissue to identify the presence of the genetic material of *Borrelia burgdorferi.*

positron emission tomography (PET)   a sensitive scanning technique that is used to study the physiological function of an organ.

postprandial blood sugar (PPBS)   a blood test that is performed to confirm the diagnosis of diabetes.

precipitation   the reaction between a specific antibody reagent and an antigen characterized by the visible presence of an insoluble complex.

proctoscopy   an endoscopic exam of the anus and rectum.

prostate-specific antigen (PSA)   a protein found in normal prostate cells of all males.

prostate ultrasonography   a study of the prostrate gland.

prostatic acid phosphatase test   a blood test that measures the level of acid phosphatase in relation to prostate disease.

prothrombin   a coagulation factor that circulates in the blood.

prothrombin time   a test that measures blood levels of several coagulation factors.

pulmonary diffusion   exchange of oxygen and carbon dioxide between the alveoli and capillaries.

pulmonary perfusion   blood flow through the pulmonary vessels.

pulmonary perfusion scan   a nuclear medicine study that is used to assess pulmonary perfusion.

pulmonary ventilation   air exchange between the atmosphere and lung tissue.

pulmonary ventilation scan   a nuclear medicine study that is used to assess pulmonary ventilation.

pulse oximetry   a noninvasive method of monitoring the oxygen saturation of arterial blood.

pulsed Doppler method   an ultrasound method that converts sound wave echoes into graphs or dots that form pictures or anatomical outlines of organs.

RA cells   neutrophils with dark granules in the cytoplasm that contain immune complexes.

radioactive iodine uptake (RAIU)   a nuclear medicine study that evaluates thyroid gland function.

radioimmunoassay (RIA)   a laboratory method that uses radioactive substances to determine the concentration of specific blood constituents.

radionuclides   radioactive isotopes that undergo decay and emit radiation that can be detected by scanning equipment.

random urine specimen   a urine collection method that can be done at any time.

rapid plasma reagin test (RPR)   an agglutination test designed to detect the antibody-like substance reagin.

rapid slide test an agglutination test that quickly identifies the presence of heterophil antibodies in serum.

rapid surfactant test a technique used to measure the amount of surfactant in amniotic fluid; also known as the shake test and the foam stability test.

reagent strips laboratory material that is used to identify the presence and concentration of the labeled substances.

reagin an antibody-like substance found in the serum of individuals with syphilis.

red blood cell indices part of the complete blood count including the mean corpuscular volume, the mean corpuscular hemoglobin, and the mean corpuscular hemoglobin concentration.

red blood cell (RBC) count a laboratory test that identifies the number of red blood cells found in a given volume of blood.

red blood cell tests part of the complete blood count including the red blood cell count, hematocrit and hemoglobin count.

resistant (R) a term used in sensitivity testing to denote that an organism is resistant to the antibiotic.

retrograde pyelography (RP) a radiological examination of the urinary tract, particularly the ureters and kidney, using a contrast medium.

Rh typing a blood test that identifies the presence or absence of the D antigen on the red blood cell.

rice bodies inclusion bodies that resemble polished rice.

scrotal scan a nuclear medicine study of the testes and contents of the scrotal sac.

scrotal ultrasonography a study of the scrotum and testicles.

segmented neutrophils (segs) mature neutrophils.

sensitive (S) a term used in sensitivity testing to denote that an organism is sensitive to the antibiotic.

sensitivity testing a laboratory test that is performed to identify antibiotics that may be effective against microorganisms.

sensory evoked brain potentials changes or responses of cerebral electrical activity that are evoked by the stimulation of a sensory pathway.

septicemia a systemic and potentially life-threatening infection in which pathogens are present in circulating blood.

shake test a technique to measure the amount of surfactant in amniotic fluid; also known as the foam stability test or rapid surfactant test.

sigmoidoscopy an endoscopic examination of the sigmoid colon.

signal-averaged electrocardiography (SAE) a study performed to identify the potential risk for ventricular arrhythmias in post–myocardial infarction patients.

single-photon emission computed tomography (SPECT) a nuclear scanning technique that constructs three-dimensional images.

skull radiography a radiographic examination of the bones of the skull, nasal sinuses, and surrounding structures.

sleep EEG   an electroencephalogram that detects sleep disorders and sleep-related epilepsy.

SMAC 12   Sequential Multiple Analyzer by Technicon, an automated method used to analyze twelve different chemical components of the blood.

small-bowel follow-through (SBF)   a radiographic examination of the small intestine from the duodenum to the ileocecal valve using a contrast medium.

sodium   a positively charged ion that plays an important role in controlling the distribution of water between extracellular and intracellular fluid.

somatosensory evoked response (SER)   study conducted to evaluate the neurological and sensory pathways associated with pain and touch.

special-purpose specimens   urine specimens that are collected as fasting specimens or postprandial specimens.

specific gravity   a component of a routine urinalysis that measures the ratio of the weight of a given volume of urine to the weight of an equal volume of water.

sperm morphology   the shape and form of the sperm.

sperm motility   the ability of sperm to move forward with good activity and tail movements.

spherocytosis   an increase in the number of abnormal, spheric, red blood cells called spherocytes.

sphingomyelin   a phospholipid related to lung surfactant.

spinal radiography   a radiographic examination of the entire spine or any section of the spine.

spirometry   evaluation of lung capacity using an instrument that measures the volume of inhaled and exhaled air.

spleen scan   a radionuclide study of the size, shape, and function of the spleen.

spleen ultrasonography   an ultrasound examination of the spleen.

sputum   strictly defined as matter ejected from the trachea, bronchi, and lungs through the mouth.

stabs   immature neutrophils.

steatorrhea   the presence of fat in feces.

stool culture   a laboratory test performed on feces in order to detect the presence of pathogenic microorganisms.

straight catheter method   a method of collecting urine that is accomplished by inserting a sterile, lubricated catheter into the urethra and urinary bladder.

sulfonamide   a synthetic medication that is used in treating bacterial infections.

supernatant   the clear portion of the urine that rises to the top of a test tube once a urine sample has been centrifuged.

suprapubic aspiration   a urine collection procedure that requires the insertion of a needle into the suprapubic area and withdrawal of urine into a syringe.

surfactant   a lipoprotein that enables the exchange of gases at the alveolar level and contributes to the elasticity of lung tissue.

sweat test a noninvasive test performed on sweat that assists in the diagnosis of cystic fibrosis.

syndrome of inappropriate ADH secretion (SIADH) a condition marked by inappropriately high levels of antidiuretic hormone secretion.

testicular scan a radionuclide study of the contents of the scrotal sac, including the testes, epididymis, and spermatic cord; also called a scrotal scan.

testosterone a male hormone that is responsible for sperm production and development of male secondary sex characteristics.

thallium stress test a nuclear medicine assessment of coronary perfusion during exercise or "stress."

thoracentesis the puncture and aspiration of fluid from the thoracic cavity.

thoracic ultrasonography an ultrasound study of the lungs.

thoracoscopy an endoscopic examination of the thoracic cavity that enables visualization of thoracic walls, pleura, pleural spaces, pericardium, and mediastinum.

thrombin an enzyme that is active in converting fibrinogen into fibrin.

thrombin time a blood test that measures blood levels of fibrinogen.

thrombocythemia an excessive increase in the number of platelets.

thyroidal hypothyroidism below normal thyroid functioning caused by the inability of the thyroid to respond to thyroid stimulating hormone.

thyroid stimulating hormone (TSH) a hormone secreted by the anterior lobe of the pituitary gland that stimulates the thyroid gland to produce and secrete thyroxine (T_4) and triiodothyronine (T_3).

thyroid stimulating hormone (TSH) test a radionuclide and laboratory study of the thyroid glands' ability uptake thyroid stimulating hormone.

thyroid ultrasonography an ultrasound study of the thyroid gland.

thyroxine (T_4) a thyroid hormone secreted by thyroid follicular cells that increases the body's metabolic rate; sensitizes the cardiovascular system in order to increase cardiac output; stimulates cellular differentiation; affects the maturation of the skeletal and central nervous systems; and is involved in other physiological processes.

timed specimen a urine collection method that is characterized by collecting and saving all urine over a specified time period.

total bilirubin the sum of direct and indirect bilirubin.

total iron-binding capacity (TIBC) an indirect measure of serum transferrin.

toxoplasmosis, rubella, cytomegalovirus, and herpes virus (TORCH) test a diagnostic test kit that is used as a screening panel during pregnancy to identify the presence of the named viruses in the maternal blood.

tracer another name for radionuclide.

transabdominal ultrasound a technique used to perform an obstetric ultrasound during which the transducer is moved across the skin of the area over the uterus.

transcranial studies   Doppler ultrasound studies of the cranial arteries.

transesophageal echocardiography (TEE)   a combined endoscopic and ultrasound procedure used to examine and evaluate cardiac structure and function.

transferrin   a trace protein found in the blood that transports iron throughout the body.

transferrin saturation   the percentage of transferrin bound to iron that can be calculated by dividing the serum iron level by the TIBC.

transtracheal aspiration   a sputum collection method that involves the placement of a suction catheter into the trachea.

transudates   fluids that are pressed through a membrane or tissue into the space between the cells of the tissue.

transvaginal ultrasound   an obstetric ultrasound that uses a probed transducer covered with a lubricant and condom sheath which is inserted into and moved around the vagina.

triglyceride   the main form of stored fat in humans.

triiodothyronine (T_3)   a hormone secreted by the follicular cells of the thyroid gland and appearing to have the same functions as thyroxine.

triple renal scan   a nuclear medicine scan that evaluates kidney structure, perfusion, and excretion.

trophoblastic disease   a malignant, neoplastic disease of the uterus.

T-tube cholangiography   a radiographic examination, usually done during the postoperative period, of the hepatic and common bile ducts using a contrast medium.

two-dimensional mode, 2-D mode   an echocardiographic mode that records cross-sectional images of the heart.

tyrosine   an amino acid synthesized from the essential amino acid phenylalanine.

upper gastrointestinal (UGI) series   a radiographic study of the lower esophagus, stomach, duodenum, and upper portion of the jejunum using a contrast medium.

uptake   the concentration of a radionuclide in body tissue.

urea   the nitrogenous waste product of protein metabolism.

urethra pressure profile   measurement of changes in urethral pressure taken during cystoscopy.

uric acid   a waste product of the breakdown of nucleic acids.

urine sediment   that portion of a urine sample that settles to the bottom of a test tube after it has been centrifuged.

urobilinogen   a compound created by the action of bacterial enzymes on bilirubin.

urodynamic studies   a series of measurements that evaluates urinary bladder function.

uroflowmetry   measurement of the volume of urine expelled during urination.

Venereal Disease Research Laboratory (VDRL) test a widely recognized syphillis screening test.

venography of the lower extremities a radiographic examination of the venous system of the legs and feet that is enhanced by the use of a contrast medium.

venous Doppler studies ultrasound studies of the flow of blood through the veins.

ventricular puncture a surgical procedure whereby CSF samples are drawn directly from one of the lateral ventricles of the brain.

very-low-density lipoproteins (VLDL) triglyceride-rich plasma proteins that give rise to low-density lipoproteins.

visual evoked response (VER) stimulation of the optic pathways using a strobe light flash or a checkerboard pattern.

waxy cast a type of cast named for appearance and composition and present in several renal diseases.

Western blot assay a specific type of blood assay test that is used to detect the presence of a specific antigen or antibody.

white blood cell (WBC) count part of the complete blood count that measures the number of white blood cells in a cubic millimeter of blood.

wound culture a laboratory test that attempts to cultivate microorganisms that may be present in an infected wound.

xanthochromia a yellowish discoloration of the cerebrospinal fluid.

Zollinger-Ellison syndrome a condition characterized by severe peptic ulceration, gastric hypersecretion, elevated serum gastrin, and gastrinoma of the pancreas or duodenum.

zone of inhibition a space on the culture medium that is created by the reaction between antibiotic disks and organisms.

References

Benenson, A. S. (Ed.). (1995). *Control of communicable diseases manual* (16th ed.). Washington, DC: American Public Health Association.

Burtis, C. A., and Ashwood, E. R. (1994). *Teizt textbook of clinical chemistry*. Philadelphia: W. B. Saunders Company.

Fischbach, F. T. (1996). *A manual of laboratory and diagnostic tests* (5th ed.). Philadelphia: Lippincott.

Goldberg, S. (1995). *Clinical physiology made ridiculously simple*. Miami: MedMaster.

Harmening, D. (1997). *Clinical hematology and fundamentals of hemostasis* (3rd ed.). Philadelphia: F. A. Davis Company.

LeFever Kee, J. (1995). *Laboratory and diagnostic tests with nursing implications* (4th ed.). Norwalk: Appleton & Lange.

LeFever Kee, J., and Paulanka, B. J. (1994). *Fluids and electrolytes with clinical applications* (5th ed.). Albany: Delmar.

Linne, J., and Ringsrud, K. (1992). *Basic techniques in clinical laboratory science* (3rd ed.). Chicago: Mosby Year Book.

Marshall, J. R. (1993). *Fundamental skills for the clinical laboratory professional*. Albany: Delmar.

Mosby's medical, nursing, and allied health dictionary. (1994). (4th ed.). St. Louis: Mosby.

Pagana, K. D., and Pagana, T. J. (1995). *Mosby's diagnostic and laboratory test references* (2nd ed.). St. Louis: Mosby.

Palko, T., and Palko, H. (1996). *Laboratory procedures for the medical office*. New York: Glencoe/McGraw-Hill.

Sormunen, C., and Moisio, M. (1995). *Terminology for allied health professionals* (3rd ed.). Cincinnati: South-Western.

Tilkian, S. M., Conover Boudreau, M., and Tilkian, A. G. (1995). *Clinical and nursing implications of laboratory tests* (5th ed.). St. Louis: Mosby.

Turgeon, M. L. (1993). *Clinical hematology and theory and procedures* (2nd ed.). Boston: Little, Brown and Company.

Van Wynsberghe, D., Noback, C. R., and Carola, R. (1995). *Human anatomy and physiology* (3rd ed.). New York: McGraw-Hill.

Walters, N. J., Estridge, B. H., and Reynolds, A. P. (1996). *Basic medical laboratory techniques* (3rd ed.). Albany: Delmar.

Watson, J., and Jaffe, M. S. (1995). *Nurse's manual of laboratory and diagnostic tests* (2nd ed.). Philadelphia: F. A. Davis.

Index